The First Emancipator

of Slaves the property of Robert Carter

№	names of Males	№	№
35	Abram, son of Milly ———	½ XIV	65
36	James, son of Winney ———	⅔ XV	66
37	Harry, son of Ditto ———	⅔ XV	
38	Tom, son of Judith ———	⅙ XVIII	
39	Apollo, son of Kitty ———	2 i.	16th
40	Adderson, son of Sally ———	2 ii.	68
41	James, son of Patt ———	2 iii.	69
42	Timothy, son of Jenny ———	2	70
43	Thadeus, son of Kate ———	2 iv.	71
44	Elijah, son of Rose ———	2 IX.	72
45	Daniel, son of Judith ———	2	
46	Moses, son of Molly ———	2 X.	73
47	Aron, son of Ditto ———	2	74
48	Alexander, son of Mary ———	2 XI.	75
49	George, son of Rachel ———	2 XIII.	76
50	Tom, son of ———	2 XV.	77
51	George, son of Mary ———	2 XVII.	
52	Newman, son Judith ———	2 XVIII.	15th
53	Solomon, son of Sukey ———	3	79

THE FIRST EMANCIPATOR

The Forgotten Story of
ROBERT CARTER
the Founding Father Who Freed His Slaves

Andrew Levy

 RANDOM HOUSE | NEW YORK

Published in the United States by Random House, an imprint of
The Random House Publishing Group, a division of Random
House, Inc., New York.

RANDOM HOUSE and colophon are registered trademarks of Random
House, Inc.

LIBRARY OF CONGRESS CATALOGING-IN-PUBLICATION DATA
Levy, Andrew
    The first emancipator: the forgotten story of Robert Carter, the
founding father who freed his slaves / Andrew Levy.
        p. cm.
    Includes bibliographical references and index.
    ISBN 0-375-50865-1
    1. Carter, Robert, 1728–1804. 2. Plantation owners—
Virginia—Biography. 3. Slaveholders—Virginia—Biography.
4. Gentry—Virginia—Biography. 5. Revolutionaries—United
States—Biography. 6. Slaves—Emancipation—Virginia.
7. Slavery—Virginia—History—18th century. 8. Virginia—
History—Colonial period, ca. 1600–1775. 9. Virginia—History—
Revolution, 1775–1783. 10. Slaves—Emancipation—United
States—Case studies. I. Title.
F229.C34L485 2005
973.3'092—dc22
[B]   2004054054

Printed in the United States of America on acid-free paper

www.atrandom.com

9 8 7 6 5 4 3 2 1

First Edition

Text design by Simon M. Sullivan

To Siobhán and Aedan

Emancipation was the key to a promised land of sweeter beauty than ever stretched before the eyes of wearied Israelites. In song and exhortation swelled one refrain—Liberty; in his tears and curses the God he implored had Freedom in his right hand. At last it came,—suddenly, fearfully, like a dream. . . .

W.E.B. DuBois,
The Souls of Black Folk

CONTENTS

Celebrated

"My plans and advice have never been pleasing to
the world."

—ROBERT CARTER III,
to his daughter Harriot, 1803.

On September 5, 1791, Robert Carter III of Nomony Hall, one of Virginia's wealthiest slaveholders, delivered to the Northumberland District Court a document he called a "Deed of Gift." It was a dry document, lists for the most part, little more than a census, with none of the memorable turns of phrase that marked the writing of other, more famous Virginians of the Revolutionary period. It possessed none of the polished rage of Jefferson's Declaration of Independence, for instance, nor the keen ideologies of Madison's share of the Federalist Papers. And yet, Carter's document was among the most incendiary songs of liberty to emerge from that freedom-loving period, so explosive in its implications that it has remained obscured into our present day: for what that census signaled was Carter's intent to free his slaves, more than four hundred fifty in number, more American slaves than any American slaveholder had ever freed, more American slaves than any American slaveholder would *ever* free.

What made Carter's act even more striking, however, were the circumstances that surrounded it. Carter lived next to the Washingtons and the Lees on the Northern Neck of Virginia; he was friend and peer to Jefferson, George Mason, Patrick Henry, and other members of the

Revolutionary-era elite. And Robert Carter, at least at first, was wealthier than any of these men; owned more land, more slaves, as many books; and was the scion of the most powerful family of the Virginian eighteenth century. But as his friends and peers ascended to the mythic status of founders, Carter disappeared from the national stage: he died almost alone in a modest house on Green Street in Baltimore in 1804, and was buried in a grave that remains unmarked to this day.

Similarly, as the stories of his friends and neighbors were told and re-told, as the American story itself was shaped around their strengths and their sins, Robert Carter's story disappeared. No monuments honor him, nor the Deed of Gift. No published map exists that can direct you to the patchwork ruins of his house and plantation; no stone tells you exactly where his body lies. Sweep through the great bestselling histories of the Revolution and the founders, and you will rarely find even a footnote mentioning Robert Carter. Dig deeper, and go to the library bookshelves full of books and articles on slavery, the founders, and the American Revolution, and you will find an occasional sentence, at best a long paragraph, but usually nothing, and among the best historians, tantalizing patterns of evasion: Philip D. Morgan, in his most recent, most encyclopedic profile of slavery in the Chesapeake, refers to Carter thirty-seven times, not once mentioning that he privately freed more slaves than any individual in American history; Ira Berlin told a newspaper interviewer in 1991 that the Deed of Gift was an "extraordinary, very, very exceptional event," yet the one reference to Carter in his sweeping *Many Thousands Gone* resides more than fifteen pages from the sections of the book describing emancipations. Even the one roadside historical marker commemorating Robert Carter's existence, a rusting, wearied affair nestled on the shoulder of Virginia's rural Route 202, equivocates: it calls him "celebrated," but doesn't say why. One might say Robert Carter and the Deed of Gift have been forgotten, but "forgotten" is a word that implies they were once acknowledged. This is a stranger story: it is as if, metaphorically speaking, the grave is not marked, and never was, and yet people know to step over and around it *anyway.*

In early 1998, I began looking for Robert Carter III, my curiosity inspired by a five-sentence reference to the Deed of Gift in Fox Butterfield's *All God's Children.* Butterfield's citation was so short, so confident, that I felt embarrassed: this was surely the kind of detail about American history that everyone knew, and that I had somehow missed. It turned out, however, that Butterfield's five sentences were almost as good as it got. As I traveled to libraries, as I found Robert Carter and the Deed of Gift almost completely absent from book after book, article after article, my curiosity increased: something buried this deep must be buried for a reason. Soon, I found my way to the best sources about Robert Carter, in their own ways reproducing the same patterns of evasion I had already observed: an ancient article from an 1893 issue of the *Magazine of American Biography* that does not make a single reference to the Deed of Gift, but provides an abundance of information about Carter's clothing purchases; an intelligent but dated "study" of Carter from 1941 that dedicates fewer pages to the Deed of Gift than to Carter's "Agricultural Readjustments"; a diligent Ph.D. dissertation that sits unpublished on a shelf in Duke University's Perkins Library, an authoritative source, if only more than a handful of people knew it existed.

Every source I could find was expressive, but somehow muted. Shomer S. Zwelling published an insightful, very modern article about Carter in the Spring 1986 issue of *American Quarterly;* he devotes fewer than one hundred words to the Deed of Gift. Joy Hakim provides Carter four pages in her *A History of Us,* making her the only author to actually incorporate the Deed of Gift into a textbook. But the audience for her short, photo-laden chapter is nine- to twelve-year-olds: "Emancipated!" she tells her readers. "That means free! Robert Carter freed his slaves!" Meriwether Delano composed a sensitive account of a personal search for the meaning of the Deed of Gift in 1991; at that time, she was a senior at St. Timothy's School outside Washington, writing for the *Alumnae Bulletin.* Her father, Frank Delano of Warsaw, Virginia, organized a gorgeous, even heroic bicentennial celebration for the Deed of Gift on the grounds of Carter's home plantation. The event drew a thousand people, journalists from *USA Today, The New York Times,* and *The Washington Post,* and provided Robert Carter with two days' worth of publicity he had never experienced before, and has not experienced since.

Let us try to quantify forgetting, if that is possible: The longest description of Robert Carter's Deed of Gift ever published is eighteen pages long (and insists on its failure). The total number of published pages devoted to Robert Carter's Deed of Gift—including school newspapers, children's books, newspapers local to the Northern Neck, and history journals also local to the Northern Neck, as well as notices in major American newspapers and glancing references in scholarship published in national venues—is fewer than one hundred. In over two hundred years. Since Louis Morton published *Robert Carter of Nomini Hall* in 1941 (across two centuries, "Nomony" became "Nomini"), the total number of scholarly articles published about Robert Carter as the main subject was roughly one per decade. Berlin, in his groundbreaking *Slaves Without Masters: The Free Negro in the Antebellum South,* provides the best extended discussion of the Deed of Gift available in any major book-length historical scholarship about the antebellum South published before 2004. His extended discussion, however, extends roughly two pages across a four-hundred-page volume.

Let us try to give nuance to forgetting, if that is possible. From late-nineteenth- and early-twentieth-century histories of Virginia and the South, Carter is wiped clean, like one of Stalin's commissars fallen from grace: Philip Alexander Bruce's *Virginia Plutarch* and Matthew Page Andrews's *Virginia: The Old Dominion* combined mention every famous Virginian from Powhatan to George Rogers Clark, mention Robert Carter I and Robert Carter II, mention Robert Carter III's uncles and cousins (the famous ones and the reprobates both), but don't mention Robert Carter III once. Religious historians of early America, when they mention Carter, do so with no small sneer: Bishop William Meade, in his *Old Churches, Ministers, and Families of Virginia,* gives Robert Carter III a relatively gracious half paragraph, but still calls him "unhappy" and "death-dreading" and the best example of the Carter family's reputation for "eccentricity." Otherwise diligent research scholars conflate Carter with his father and grandfather. In some books, Robert Carter I and Robert Carter III are combined into one reference in the index. In others, the two men are combined in the text of the book itself, creating one Robert Carter who was born in the middle of the seventeenth century and died at the beginning of the nineteenth.

Guides for public history, such as that equivocating marker on Route 202, hint at something important: the *Official Guide to Colonial Williamsburg* from 1970 provides a description of Robert Carter III (since the house where he lived from 1761 to 1772 still stands, though is rarely opened to the public), calling him "liberal," but does not mention what made him so, or whether "liberal" means "progressive" or "eccentric." The great biographers of the first American presidents make claims about their subjects that the

Deed of Gift seemingly contradicts: Douglas Southall Freeman, in his landmark *George Washington,* is only one of many biographers of the founders who has written that the general would surely have freed his slaves had a practicable plan existed. Authors for whom the Deed of Gift would make compelling evidence instead work around it: Robert McColley wrote an entire book tearing down the myths of slavery in Jeffersonian Virginia, but does not mention Carter's manumission, even though McColley dedicates a chapter entitled "The True Emancipators" to manumissions that freed fewer slaves and left thinner paper trails; Rhys Isaac, in his Pulitzer Prize–winning *Transformation of Virginia,* does not mention the Deed of Gift once, even though Carter's act was motivated by his religious dissent, and Isaac's claims about the importance of religious transformation of Revolutionary Virginia remain the most provocative aspect of that acclaimed work. Lastly, important historians make clear that they know Robert Carter represented some unusually humane perspective on the social politics of the Revolutionary era, but then decline to cite the one act most likely to inspire interest in that perspective. Eugene D. Genovese, in his classic *Roll, Jordan, Roll,* refers to Carter three times, once as an example of a slaveholder who consulted his slaves on the performance of their overseers, once as an example of a slaveholder who allowed his slaves to practice medicine, and once as a slaveholder who believed that slavery was unprofitable. When Genovese discusses private emancipations, however, he does not mention Carter once.

One can see from many angles why fame has not come easily to Robert Carter III. He could not write like Jefferson or Madison: he left behind volumes of correspondence, diaries, and ledgers, but they are gracelessly composed, filled with errors, and weighed down by the minutiae of rent collections, church service schedules, shipping manifests, and lawsuit after lawsuit. He left no great edifice like Monticello: Nomini Hall burned to the ground in 1850, and was replaced by a smaller frame house that was itself only recently salvaged from disrepair. He did not look the part of a Revolutionary: he was a fourth-generation patriarch, an aloof, ludicrously wealthy man who was unable to adapt to the egalitarian changes that transformed America in the years before and during the Revolution. He didn't savor the rough music of democracy: he described the "new system of politicks in british north america" with distress in his voice, and his few election campaigns were utter disasters.

More to the point, he wanted to be forgotten. He asked for that un-marked grave, after all, requesting "no Stone, nor Inscription," preferring instead "to be laid under a shady Tree where he might be undisturbed, & sleep in peace & obscurity." He understood that he had spent his life making losing bets on history: when he told his youngest daughter, Har-riot, in 1803 that "my plans and advice have never been pleasing to the world," he seemed to be grasping his future as well as his present. His per-sonality, from the moment he could write until the moment that age stilled his pen, was a strange and elusive entity, full of silences, ellipses, and un-expected turns, understandably uncharismatic to historians who like those men and women who seem to be writing to future generations, who pos-sess the visionary gift of gab of a Jefferson or an Adams. "It is hard to know his opinion from any thing he declares," Philip Vickers Fithian, the family tutor in 1773 and 1774, observed.

His Deed of Gift, in turn, was barely a whisper, though an emphatic one. As important documents go, it is almost no document at all: a four-page list of slave names *followed* by a two-page statement from Carter in the public version, and a web of detailed censuses and schedules in the ver-sion Carter kept for himself and his agents. It offered no conversation with the public moment; it offered no conversation with history. It was meant to work, and to be forgotten, which might have been Robert Carter's ge-nius: he might well have understood that the emancipation that would work best would not call attention to itself, would cause, to use his own words, "the least possible disadvantage to my fellow Citizens."

It did work—though nobody until John Randolph Barden, the author of that unpublished dissertation, bothered to check—and it was forgotten, woven into the fabric of a vision of America that we have buried to make room for the one we esteem. From the time we receive our first civic lessons, our first filtered glimpses of national history, Americans are taught one crucial lesson about slavery and the American Revolution: that there was no practical way, public or private, to free the slaves. We are taught, for instance, that the law forbade such emancipations, that economic obstacles prevented it, that many slaveholders wanted to do it, but their debts pre-vented it. We are taught, in particular, that the founders *wanted* to free their slaves, but could not, because they faced insurmountable obstacles, because freed slaves would be unable to care for themselves and would face so much resistance from resentful whites that they would have to be removed, placed west of the Appalachians, or shipped back to Africa. Most important, we are taught that the young nation was too fragile to support large emancipations: the founders knew, and historians have reiterated this point for two centuries, that compromise on slavery was the price of a republic, and every reasonable man and woman wanted a republic. Slavery, Jefferson famously wrote, was like holding a "wolf by the ears": you couldn't hold on, but you didn't dare let go.

There has always been good evidence to support these claims. Historians have well documented how deep ran Revolutionary-era opposition to general emancipation, and how difficult life for free blacks could be. But one need only hear the basic facts of the Deed of Gift to wonder if the whole story has yet emerged. In the summer of 1791, for instance, as Robert Carter composed the Deed of Gift, the private emancipation of slaves in the state of Virginia had been lawful for almost a decade. Such emancipations were difficult financial propositions, but certainly feasible: before Robert Carter freed his slaves, small slaveholders across Virginia had liberated almost ten thousand of their black servants, and entire states with significant slave populations, such as New Jersey, were learning how to finance emancipations on a public scale. Similarly, like many smaller slaveholders before him, Carter provided financial support and sponsorship that eased the transition to freedom, provided for disabled and indigent freed slaves, and laid the primitive groundwork for an interracial republic, challenging in numerous small instances the notion that young America would fall apart if blacks and whites were free at the same time.

This historical moment would pass by the early 1800s, however. Economically, politically, and socially, slavery would be stronger in 1810 than it was in 1790. The cotton gin, invented in 1793, transformed plantation profit margins, and the newfound financial might of the large planters strengthened slaveholding interests in the Southern states and the federal government. New laws restricted voluntary emancipations and threatened free blacks with re-enslavement. Southern religious and political leaders who preached abolition either learned to accommodate themselves to the peculiar institution, moved northward, or, like Robert Carter, fell out of sight. But the fact that subsequent generations of Americans made voluntary emancipations impossible should not have so successfully obscured the fact that they were first possible, that a window of opportunity existed at the time of the founding through which a freer, more coherent republic could be grasped.

If Robert Carter had done nothing with his life, if he was an irrelevancy during a period of remarkable cultural and political transformation, one might understand why we have forgotten him and his achievement. But the fact that he freed more slaves than Washington and Jefferson owned *together* ought to have made some mark on the historical record. No one ever walked away from slaveholding and slavery with as much to lose, simply gave up the plantation and moved on. And no other Virginian of the Revolutionary era, including those who founded a great nation and spoke eloquently of the immorality of slavery, managed to reconcile freedom in theory and freedom in practice with such transparent simplicity.

The mystery of Robert Carter, then, is really two mysteries: why he freed his slaves, and why we couldn't care less.

PART I | REVELATION

CHAPTER I

King of America
[1728-1768]

"But where says some is the King of America?"
—TOM PAINE, *Common Sense*

There is only one known portrait of Robert Carter III. He posed for it in 1749 or
1750 in Thomas Hudson's London studio, and two hundred fifty years
later, it is easy enough to imagine what the painter was thinking. Probably,
Carter was just another colonial gentleman, raw but wealthy, and the por-
traitist knew his type, and knew their vanities. And so Carter was draped
in a billowing gold suit and silver cape, brown hair neatly tied back and
powdered gray, smirking, a mask dangling from the tapered fingers of his
left hand. The suit is a century out of date, as if Carter were a courtier to
Charles I, or masquerading as one. He looks like he is on his way to a ball,
to a lifetime of balls, and has stopped just for a moment before donning
the mask.

It is an extraordinary portrait. It takes two glances before one even notices Carter's head, because brilliant shades of silver and gold cover more
than half the canvas: Carter is dressed like money. And Carter's mask is a
wonder: red-rouged cheeks, dark drawn eyebrows, full red lips, and starkly
pale otherwise, a minstrel mask in reverse, as if the masquerade Carter was
about to attend required him to perform the role of a white man. Finally,
however, Carter's face draws the observer. The smirk is no ordinary smirk:
it has *Mona Lisa* mystery. And the eyes are huge and dark, and imply

something open and unfinished, something that resisted being posed as the young patriarch on the rise.

When Carter stood for this portrait, he was twenty-one and poised for a brilliant, even notorious, career. He had wealth: more than sixty-five thousand acres of New World soil and more than one hundred slaves. He had family: his grandfather was Robert "King" Carter, who, in his own brilliant and notorious career, acquired large swaths of the Virginian frontier and distributed huge parcels of land and slaves to his progeny. He had connections: his uncles and aunts had intermarried with some of Virginia's richest families, the Fitzhughs, Pages, Churchills, and Harrisons; his father's estate resided within twenty miles of both Stratford Hall—the Lee manse—and Pope's Creek, where George Washington was born and reared. And lastly, he had arrogance, or some quality worse than arrogance: his cousin John Page, who would later become one of the first governors of the state of Virginia, called him an "inconceivable illiterate and also corrupted and vicious."

But he also had another quality, something that drew upon the arrogance that wealth and connections provided, but that fought against the destiny that wealth and connections presented. As much as any Virginian of his era, Robert Carter exemplified what it meant to be powerful and wealthy in prewar America: he looked and acted like the kind of aristocrat who needed to fall so that the United States and its new heroes could rise. At the same time, Carter was about to undertake the same education in manners and society that trained other Virginians to become our great, hallowed Revolutionaries. He read the same books and the same newspapers, sold his tobacco on the same markets, negotiated the same land deals. He attended the same political debates, and voted—when he possessed a vote—for the Revolutionary path almost every time. He shared a pastor with George Washington, and teachers with Thomas Jefferson. He even played alongside Jefferson in a musical quartet, the future composer of the Declaration of Independence tuning his fiddle to Carter's harpsichord amid the echoes of the Virginia royal governor's long ballroom.

That Carter chose to transcend the conservative roots of his childhood and young adulthood, then, is no surprise. Many did. The surprise lies elsewhere: why did the same republican influences that moved the founders instead move Carter to become their mirror image, capable of doing what they could not, and unable to do what they did so well?

2

For John Carter, the first Carter to plant himself in Virginian soil, the logic of emigration was irrefutable. On the one hand, he was a stubborn royalist, a member of a family of London vintners who supported the monarchy, and Charles I would soon lose his head to Cromwell's revolution. On the other hand, he was the youngest son in his family, which meant that, according to the ancient law of primogeniture, he would receive little of his father's wealth. Instead, he would be expected to join the clergy, take the bar, or serve under his brothers in the family firm. Under the old system, he had little future; under the new, it seemed, he had even less.

The Virginia Colony, however, was another story. By 1635, the year that twenty-two-year-old John Carter sailed to the New World, almost three decades had elapsed since a few score of merchants, soldiers, and indentured servants had begun settling on the banks of a wide river they named after King James I. Over the course of those three decades, the free English of Virginia, who numbered in the low thousands, kept the Indians at bay, "seasoned" themselves to the mysterious, infectious American climate, and transformed their family names and modest merchant fortunes into large tracts of American soil. They filled the new colony with little wooden homes, one-and-a-half-story frames with steep cat-slide roofs like they remembered from the English West Country, or multichamber log cabins that undulated with the ground beneath them. They built orchards and laid out cornfields, but mostly they seeded tobacco, in thousands upon thousands of tiny hills each no bigger than a small child, each requiring the care of a small child. To tend those fields, they imported so many Irish, convicts, and recalcitrant indentured servants that reformers on both sides of the Atlantic began to regard Virginia as "a sinke to drayen England of her filth and scum."

It was an age of great possibility, and great horror. On July 30, 1619, in a small brick church in Jamestown, the first democratically elected assembly in North America gathered, twenty-two men calling themselves "Burgesses." Three weeks later, perhaps fifty yards down a short embankment to the Jamestown wharf, a Dutch man-of-war delivered the first "twenty and odd" Africans to the continent, men with Spanish names purchased to alleviate the labor shortage. John Carter, possessing a younger brother's hunger for advancement and wealth, acclimated himself quickly. By 1641, he was elected to the House of Burgesses representing Upper Norfolk, frontier land well northwest of Jamestown. By 1652, he had moved to the Northern Neck, the verdant spit of land reaching out into the Chesapeake between the wide Potomac and Rappahannock rivers. There he had purchased 1,300 acres of land on a windblown, pine-covered little peninsula on the Rappahannock: an exposed place, more bay than land almost, defiantly cool in a Virginia summer, and covered with rich, loamy soil that held tobacco plants like nothing he could have possessed in England.

He built a one-room wooden house on the edge of his windblown peninsula, coated it with stucco made of oyster shells, and called the surrounding farm Corotoman, after the local Indian tribe. Three miles inland, he built a church he named after Christ, another one-room wooden affair. By the time he died, in 1669, he had married five times, produced an unrecorded number of children (four of whom survived him), and served in the House of Burgesses and as a member of the powerful, royally appointed Governor's Council. As well, he convinced the crown to allow him to "patent" more than six thousand acres of land, and he led an exploratory force against the Rappahannock Indians. Perhaps most important, for himself and his children, he left behind a significant legacy of "tithables"—still mostly white indentured servants, but now also African-born servants for whom no indenture contract promised freedom.

Upon his death, however, he committed the same error of tradition that had inspired his own restlessness: he left control of most of his property to his oldest surviving son, John, and left his youngest surviving son, Robert, with only a thousand acres of land around Corotoman and six years of education in London in the keep of a merchant family named Bailey. One look at an early portrait of Robert Carter I, and a modern reader can easily grasp how little the obstacle of a small inheritance would have mattered to him: he poses in his older brother's periwig, holding his older brother's sword, both symbols of family leadership, and the sneer on his face implies that he would rather use the latter than surrender the former.

And when his older brother died, in 1690, and Robert Carter I earned the sword and periwig in earnest, he undertook what is arguably one of the most extraordinary careers in the history of American capital and politics. One year later, he was elected to the House of Burgesses, and he made his reputation there by delivering fearless speeches against the power of English land agents and by inspiring the construction of a "family" bloc of voters—Byrds, Churchills, and Fairfaxes, among others—who would govern Virginia for two generations. By 1696, he became Speaker. By 1700, he was appointed to the Governor's Council. By 1703, he was taunting English power with even greater ferocity, denouncing Royal Governor Francis Nicholson with such vehemence that the startled Queen recalled her charge.

Shuttling back and forth between London (where he befriended, among others, the great philosopher John Locke) and Virginia, Carter acquired one lucrative administrative post after another: treasurer, naval officer, receiver of duties in the Rappahannock River, and, in 1702, agent for the proprietary of the Northern Neck, a position he had once denounced, and which gave him the right to survey, lease, and deed all lands between the headwater of the Potomac River and that of the Rappahannock. By 1711, the year he surrendered the agency, he had patented more than three hundred thousand acres of land—sometimes in his own name but usually in the names of close relatives.

By 1726, the year he became acting governor, he was one of the two richest men on the continent, a brilliant, eclectic businessman who frequently stayed awake until three in the morning, drinking red wine or brandy with a sea captain, and rising again at dawn to ride out across his fields. He owned forty-seven plantations (to which he gave names such as Changeling, Old Home, and Hills) and supervised the settlement of small farms across the colony. He collected rents, traded tobacco, maintained a fleet of commercial ships, and operated so many small businesses, ranging from brick kilns to copper mines, that Corotoman grew under his guidance to a complex of eighteen buildings, all surrounding a staggeringly large two-and-a-half-story brick mansion forty yards from the Rappahannock waterfront.

With two wives, he sired fifteen children, ten of whom lived into adulthood—five daughters, and five sons: John, Landon, George, Charles, and Robert II, the second son. Carter invested dynastic dreams in these children, and in the boys in particular. He sent them to school in England and assigned them reading lists filled with classics. He cleared Virginian forests for them and financed the construction of great brick mansions in the clearings. And then he prayed in letters to British merchants that he might be getting "a pennyworth for my penny."

There was nothing he would not do, it was believed, to advance his fortune and that of his family. He used a coat of arms that belonged to an English family of Carters, but not his Carters, to impress British royals with his pedigree. He pled with English merchants for their business, telling Micajah Perry of London, for instance, to "pray allow me to be one of your first favorites. . . . I know 'tis easy for you to do, if you please." He fought for every pound to which he thought himself entitled, no matter how callous it made him appear: when a fellow Virginian committed suicide in July 1725, for instance, Carter sued for the man's possessions, arguing that "the goods of felons they have allowed me to take for several years," and that "self-murder" is the "highest species of murder."

Similarly, when Virginians began importing slaves in earnest around the turn of the eighteenth century, Carter enthusiastically joined the commerce. He became an aggressive and fastidious slave trader, mediating the sale of thousands of Africans, famed for rowing out to slave ships anchored off Corotoman to inspect the cargo. And he became an even more aggressive slaveholder, weeding out seven hundred men and women for his own use. Whenever possible, he saved for himself the "Gambers" from Senegambia—because he believed they possessed the African equivalent of the Protestant work ethic. And he treated them with relentless, businesslike cruelty: in 1723, he convinced the Virginia Council to permit the removal of toes as a punishment for the captured runaway slave, adding that he had "cured many a negro . . . by this means."

Despite the great ambition with which Carter built his empire, however, he also possessed a leveling instinct: Francis Nicholson, the governor he helped drive out of Virginia, observed that some people called Carter "King," and then only "in contempt," but others called him "Robin" to his face. Carter regarded Virginia, not England, as his "country," and felt toward the young colony an emotion not unlike patriotism. Similarly, while he viewed the loss of the affection of English merchants with "terror," he savored the opportunity to harangue the symbolic keepers of English power, and not just land agents and governors. For two decades, he fought the king himself in English courts, arguing for a configuration of the Northern Neck proprietary that would have shifted control of vast reaches of America from the Royal Court in London to the piazza at Corotoman. Across every western horizon, he saw a dynasty, but a more egalitarian one: not only did he make sure that every one of his sons owned a vast estate, in itself a rebellion against the laws of primogeniture that limited his own opportunities to rise, but he made sure that his daughters and even his daughters-in-law were deeded large grants of cash, slaves, and property that would remain theirs no matter whom they married or how long they lived.

In the slave cabins, as well, Carter saw something to which others were blind. While other slaveholders expected their slaves to sleep on the hard dirt floors of their cabins, Carter ordered slave cabins built with shelves eighteen inches off the ground to accommodate beds. In a like manner, he ordered slave cabins with interior lofts to provide private storage spaces for the slaves. In his ledgers, he listed slaves by families, a small mercy that increased the likelihood that parents and children would not be separated from one another.

By the late 1720s, however, it was clear that his ability to sustain the many contradictory impulses that had guided him for decades was faltering with his old age. A lifetime of prodigious eating and drinking had left him plump and gouty, limping on a perpetually swollen right ankle, often restricted to bed and chair, gruel, small beer, and patent pills. Too many hours spent on the decks of slave ships left him susceptible to every pleurisy and fever. He tried crutches, then cupping and blistering. He became a "great smoker": that soothed him. He hated losing his second wife so much that he refused to marry again, treating the loss like a fresh wound in letters for decades afterward.

Then there were his children. Landon, George, and Charles showed him every indication that they would give him his pennyworth, but Robert II, a portly, unfocused young man, was harder to gauge. He married well—a Carter had to marry well—to a young heiress named Priscilla Churchill, whose father was a councillor. But otherwise, he showed no real zeal for empire, preferring to survey the wilderness than run the plantation his father built for him on the Potomac—and named, like Corotoman, after the local Indian tribe, the Nomony—and unwilling to hold the lucrative government position his father secured for him collecting taxes on the Rappahannock. "Thus you see I am no stranger to the story of the Gospel," Carter wrote in 1721, referring to the namesake who was turning out to be more prodigal son than monarch-in-waiting.

More important, however, King Carter was sick about the state of his own soul, acting more and more like a man who didn't savor wealth and empire as much as he thought he would. He built Corotoman, for instance, and filled it with white marble and delft tile imported from Europe, but kept his father's old wooden house intact on the grounds. He wore a diamond ring and a gold watch, but refused to own any silver—a telling refusal, given that most Virginian gentry were infatuated with the metal. He found a coarse word to describe people he thought were "too great lovers of this world": they were "muckworms." He began to fill his business correspondence with "sublunary blessings" for peace, and miss sermons at Christ Church.

Finally, he became convinced that he was going insane: revising his will, he actually described himself as being in "a crazy, disordered condition." Shortly later, he regarded the legal disadvantages of this claim, and rewrote the clause to read "sound mind." But the mind was not satisfied, and it may not have been sound. He began to write of the "madness of the people," a vision of a future conflict born from his own failure, and that of his neighbors, to attain what they came to America to acquire: "It is an old adage that oppressions make a wise man mad," he wrote. "What our madness will produce, I can hardly promise myself to live to see the end of."

When Robert Carter III was born, at Corotoman in February 1728 to Robert Carter II and Priscilla Churchill—their second child, after a daughter named Elizabeth—King Carter was briefly overjoyed. Grandchildren soothed him more than even tobacco: "I have the blessing of seeing my children's children before me," he told one correspondent the winter before. And he made sure that the child entered the world well: when Robert III was three months old, King gave him his first African slave, one of "three Girls for my three Grand Children" he ordered as gifts.

But King Carter's "blessing" was short-lived. In early 1729, when his grandson was just turning one, a fire gutted the mansion at Corotoman, down to the wine cellar. Rather than rebuild, King Carter simply moved his family back into the wooden house his father built. Events only worsened, however. In February 1732, Robert II, his prodigal son, died suddenly. He was twenty-nine and had overdosed on opium, a condition his brother Landon described as "blood so divided and rarified as to finish life with an universal Mortification." The funeral, which took place at Nomony, where Robert II had settled his family, was warm but brief: watch over the "dearly beloved pretty Babes," the minister asked God, as he looked upon Robert III and his older sister, Betty.

King Carter grieved so deeply that he could barely write letters, and six months later, on August 4, he also died. The *American Weekly Mercury* reported that he "died of the Flux, which 'tis supposed he caught on board a Vessel from which he bought several Negroes." Regally, he left the world, leaving few signs of the ambivalence that had marked his last few years. His will ran sixty-five pages. His tomb, rising from the lawn of the stately new version of Christ Church that he had commissioned and financed, was engraved with a lengthy ode to his statesmanship and energy, composed in Latin: *cum regiam dignitatem et publicam libertatem aequali jure asseruit* ("he defended with equal justice the royal authority and the common freedom"). Others felt differently: according to legend, the stone was large enough to bear a second epitaph, scrawled by an anonymous and scarcely reverent mourner:

> Here lies Robin, but not Robin Hood,
> Here lies Robin that never was good,
> Here lies Robin that God has forsaken
> Here lies Robin the Devil has taken.

By his fourth birthday, an age when the typical gentry boy was still wearing a petticoat, a frock, and a rope around the waist tied to something or someone sturdy, Robert Carter III had suddenly inherited one of the largest fortunes in America. As well, he had inherited sole possession of the most respected, and the most reviled, name in Virginia.

3

Robert "King" Carter was protean, a manipulator of systems who was so serpentine that it was easy to think of him as the devil's partner, an acquirer of land who was so high-handed and yet so innocent it was easy to call him King, both because he acted like one and because he dreamed of being one. Eventually, King Carter would get his dynasty, if obliquely: his descendants would include presidents William Henry and Benjamin Harrison, five signers of the Declaration of Independence, and General Robert E. Lee, but all the legendary lines would pass through his daughters, not his sons. Eventually, too, historians would regard him, as did Bishop Meade in the late eighteenth century, as a mythic oddity, the originator (John Carter fading into obscurity) of one of Virginia's most "eccentric" families.

But King Carter's eccentricity was principled, even if it was confused. King could be both a kind and a cruel slaveholder because he saw the financial possibilities in both kind and cruel treatment. He was not driven by the desire to control his slaves, nor to seek their affection. By the same standard, he was not compelled to keep wealth (nor, for that matter, education) away from his daughters simply because they were women, when distributing wealth and breeding to them only made the dynasty stronger. To King Carter, the contradiction between regal fantasies and egalitarian ones was not a weakness but a source of strength: it was easier to have two American dreams than one. He placed no bounds on his wealth and power. And when the time came, he placed no bounds on his criticism of wealth and power, either.

In part, King Carter could be so energetic and so successful in acquiring land, slaves, and a certain wildness of intellect because the Virginia in which he thrived remained such a wild place. Early-eighteenth-century tourists called the colony a "desert," and were depressed by its miles and miles of sandy country road, its monotonous, unmarked forests, and its many ruins, those wooden houses built during the lumber infatuation of the seventeenth century burned by fire in tinderbox Virginian summers, or leveled by "gust."

By the time Robert Carter III was born, however, Virginia had begun to mature. There was a capital now, and even if Williamsburg was a "wretch'd contrived affair," as one London literatus wrote, its streets so soft that a gentleman exiting a tavern could find his foot submerged up to the ankle in leaves, sand, and oyster shells, it nevertheless hosted a maturing political assembly in an imposing brick building on one end of Duke of Gloucester Street, and a new college named William and Mary in an impressive Christopher Wren–influenced "pile" on the other end.

Across the countryside, meanwhile, planters had begun to complete the first generation of great brick mansions, imposing their wealth upon the land in a way that suggested that, after a century, they were here to stay. Within the brick mansions, planters created a rigid, powerful aristocracy, an inbred, watchful group of roughly three dozen families: "They are all Brothers, Sisters, or Cousins," Mary Willing, William Byrd's Philadelphia-born second wife, wrote home in 1760, "so that if you use one person in the Colony ill, you affront all." Within the imposing brick building in Williamsburg, those same aristocrats enacted the legislation that would be known as "slave codes," passed when slave revolts were rumored, or recently suppressed: if a slave practiced medicine, he would "suffer death without benefit of clergy"; if he provided "false testimony," his ears would be "nailed to the pillory, and cut off." Public humiliation, the burgesses believed, would deter disobedience as much as would torture: for small crimes, a slave might be "burnt in the hand, by the goaler in open court," or might receive "thirty nine lashes on your bare back, well laid on, at the common whipping post."

Next door to the mansions, meanwhile, a new breed of colonial freeman was emerging, neither rich nor poor but hungry for status and liberty. For instance, on the same day in February 1732 that Robert Carter II's death was eulogized in the *Maryland Gazette,* George Washington was born in the solid wooden home on his father's ten-thousand-acre farm at Pope's Creek, roughly fifteen miles west of Nomony Hall. One hundred twenty miles farther west, meanwhile, in the forests of Albemarle County, a country gentleman named Peter Jefferson, still more than a decade away from the birth of his first son, Thomas, was sifting through his own younger-brother share of his father's inheritance, which consisted of some lands along the Fine and the Manikin creeks, two slaves, and some livestock and horses.

Robert Carter III joined this stage as Robert Carter I and Robert Carter II left it, as the mansion that represented their family burned and fell to ruin, as if his destiny, to dismantle the empire his grandfather and father built, were foreordained. Even without the mansion, his infancy must have been idyllic, the sensation that a world revolved around him immanent in everything he did and saw: a christening in the marble baptismal font at Christ Church; Sunday morning coach rides down the three-mile road lined with cedars that led straight and unerring from the house at Corotoman to the church; views of the wide, flat, shining Rappahannock, its banks blanketed by pine needles, the river itself "filled" with merchant ships, and pirates—"Spaniards from St. Augustin." Then there were views within Corotoman itself: the sturdy, dependent buildings that housed King Carter's spinners, coachmen, millers, brick-makers, shipbuilders, and army of bookkeepers; the orchards and gardens that were growing apples, peaches, apricots, quinces, strawberries, and gooseberries; the pens housing King Carter's hogs and cattle; thousands of acres of Indian corn and thousands upon thousands of acres of tobacco; and the fields themselves swarmed by "gangs" of slaves all bent over fledgling tobacco plants, fifteen or twenty to a gang, each with a slave foreman to maintain order and rhythm from dawn until dusk.

As well, his material needs, from the moment of his father's death, had been addressed. His uncles—George, Charles, and the tempestuous Landon—expressed love for their nephew in the way that Carters expressed love for one another: in 1734, they authored special legislation ensuring that the six-year-old received his father's entire share of King Carter's fortune, a share equal to theirs. Likewise, his mother shortly provided both surrogate father and surrogate family. In 1735, she remarried, matching her fortune to that of John Lewis of Warner Hall, a stratagem of romance and finance made possible by the Carter dedication to shrewd marriages and strong widows: King Carter, before dying, ensured that his daughter-in-law would retain her right of dower in the event of her widowing, enabling her to marry well the second time.

In practical terms, however, the significance of the loss of Robert Carter's father and grandfather was immense: Virginian men at mid-century rose and fell on their fathers' fortunes and their fathers' influence, and Robert Carter had the former without the latter. Jefferson lost his father at the age of fourteen: he wrote later of the sorrow with which he was "thrown on a wide world . . . without a friend or guardian." But Carter was only four, not fourteen. He quickly slipped through the cracks of family regard, a Cinderella with money: when his stepfather, John Lewis, wrote a letter describing his family during the period, he doted on his own sons, and spoke freely of "Miss Betty Carter," but not Betty Carter's brother. Possessed of a great fortune and a great name but with no true father to sting him with shame when he did wrong, he became unmanageable, and was shuttled around as if his mother and stepfather could find no place for him. They sent him to the grammar school at William and Mary in Williamsburg at the age of nine, which was two years earlier than the college mandated, accompanied by one black servant and a new set of clothes. Then they brought him back two years later, even though the grammar school course of study ran for four years. Upon returning home, he should certainly have been placed under the care of a tutor, the conventional method by which wealthy colonials educated their children. Robert Carter, however, "studied without the assistance of a tutor"—which means, in all likelihood, that he did not study at all.

When Robert Carter III turned twenty-one in February 1749, however, and attained his majority, his education was not relevant. He inherited his one hundred slaves and his sixty-five thousand acres, parceled out across the Northern Neck, areas near Winchester and Alexandria, and several rugged tracts along the Shenandoah River to the west. It did not excite him: four months later, he booked passage on a packet for Liverpool, the *Everton,* and located for himself an amiable traveling companion, Lawrence Washington, George Washington's half brother.

At this time, the provincials of Virginia regarded London with ambivalence. They recognized that London was a better finishing school than Williamsburg and a vastly better arena within which to pursue advantageous business connections. But they also worried, as did Maria Byrd, that their sons might acquire smallpox in the Old World; and, like Landon Carter, who called his own son a "monster" upon the boy's return from London, they lamented the success with which British gamblers, prostitutes, and tailors encouraged the licentious appetites of their children.

Carter pursued some perfunctory version of the former. On December 1, alongside Philip Ludwell Lee, Carter joined the Honorable Society of the Inner Temple, the distinguished law school of the Four Courts of London. Similarly, he made himself the protégé of Edward Athawes, a respected merchant who traded with many of the great Virginia families. But he took no classes, never stood for the bar, and appears to have read little: John Page called him "illiterate." And rather than learning a trade, he learned its opposite: "My gratifications exceeded my yearly income," he would blandly observe a decade later.

By 1751, when Carter returned from London, it was clear that something was wrong. In his wake, he left bad blood: in 1754, Edward Kimber, the editor of London's *Gentleman's Magazine,* published a novel entitled *History of the Life and Adventures of Mr. Anderson: Containing his Strange Varieties of Fortune in Europe and America, Compiled from his Own Papers.* The novel featured as its antagonist a wealthy, corrupt young American slaveholder, "the richest heir" in the colony, but "a lad of bad principles, unlettered, and of coarse manners," who is murdered, in the novel's crowd-pleasing ending, by his own slaves: Kimber named this villain Carter.

In Williamsburg, meanwhile, public opinion was scarcely kinder. John Page's father regarded Carter as yet another example of a young man ruined by London. Page himself described Carter's mind as "confused," in addition to being "vicious." John Blair, who would later become acting governor, wrote in his diary on July 4, 1751, "I hear Mr. R. Carter intends to build and live at Williamsburgh and to persuade all the gentlemen he can to do so too." Two weeks later, Blair became derisive: "Sad news of poor wretched Bob Carter," he wrote. "I hope he won't come to live in Williamsburgh."

Young Robert Carter III was a rogue. Williamsburg, however, had its share of rogues. Robert Carter also returned from London "confused," "wretched," and even "poor": not a man to fear, but to pity. Upon his departure from England, he boldly kissed Edward Athawes farewell, and the kiss—as well as the feeling that inspired it—lingered for him for years afterward: "At that parting the mild part of my composition was predominant!" he recalled, in 1764. "Upon my honor I esteemed him, & loved the family." In contrast, no embrace, intimate or public, awaited him in Virginia. In 1752, Carter ran for the House of Burgesses, the colonial equivalent of a state legislature, and finished last out of three candidates, polling thirty-four votes, less than five percent of the poll, losing to John Bushrod. In 1754, he ran again, after he had spent two years among his neighbors, and had those same two years to learn how to campaign. And he did even worse, getting only seven votes, losing this time to Augustine Washington, not so much beaten as ignored.

It was no great repudiation to lose a House of Burgess election. By the 1750s, in fact, such elections were well recognized as one of the few chances small landholders possessed to tweak the landed gentry. Landon Carter lost his first three elections before winning his fourth, for instance; even George Washington lost his first election. Likewise, one could gain a few dozen votes and lose no standing in the community, or believe one had lost no standing in the community. Robert Wormeley Carter, Robert Carter's cousin, once pronounced himself satisfied after he garnered only forty-five votes: "As for myself I never ask'd but one man to vote for me since the last Election," he argued, "by which means I polled but 45 votes an honorable number."

If losing one House of Burgesses election was no great repudiation, though, not serving in the House of Burgesses at all was a shunning of historical proportions. No one could know it at the time, of course, but election to that rough-hewn political body in the 1750s or 1760s was *the* path to political glory for Virginians of the Revolutionary era. The men who passed through that assembly included the first ten governors of the State of Virginia, all seven Virginia signers of the Declaration of Independence, four of the five Virginia delegates to the Constitutional Convention, every Virginian member of the first and second Congresses of the United States, and every Virginian who served either as president of the United States or as a member of a Virginian-born president's Cabinet.

For Robert Carter, this door to posterity shut early. It was not that he was too young. If anything, he was ripe: James Monroe was elected to the House when he was twenty-four, the same age as Carter during his first election; James Madison and Thomas Jefferson were first elected when they were twenty-five years old; and George Washington, running in his second election, was elected at the age of twenty-six, the same age as was Carter when he was losing *his* second election. Nor was it his family name—which, if anything, was a guarantor of eventual election. Robert Carter's uncles were elected, and several of his cousins were as well. For Robert Carter III to get seven votes, and only seven votes, was a message: despite his name, and perhaps because of it, he was no favorite son.

4

By the 1750s and 1760s, Williamsburg had grown into an alert, confident community, one where Virginians expressed in equal parts their love of sin and their love of liberty. Prostitutes thrived: "When there are so many Purchasers, who can doubt there will be Sellers," one wit wrote regarding the "Ladies of Pleasure" of the town. But sexual license was merely the city's second sin. Everyone gambled: rich and poor, black and white, men and women alike. An unnamed French traveler wrote that "there is not a publick house in Virginia but have their tables all baterd with the boxes." Even slaves crafted dice out of quartz crystals and called them "devil's die." Landon Carter complained that his sons and grandsons dissipated countless nights in card games: "Burn me," he said of their whist losses, "if I pay anything more for such sport." In addition to dice and cards, the planters were also inveterate horsemen, and lotteries were also general, were often used, in fact, to raffle off the estates that had been ruined by the gambling. It troubled the anonymous French traveler: "They are all professed gamesters. . . . In the Day time people hurrying back and forwards from the Capitoll to the taverns, and at night, Carousing and Drinking In One

Chamber and box and Dice in another, which Continues till morning Commonly. . . . I have been here three Days and am heartily sick of it."

In turn, the same taverns that hosted dice and cards and "Carousing" at night often hosted slave markets at noon in the day, the same time that the Council and House of Burgesses convened—a polite hour, one that allowed for sleeping late and for hangovers. In this manner, the ruling class of colonial Virginia maintained an uneasy balance between liberty and libertinism. Their pride was well known, even internationally known: Andrew Burnaby, an English visitor, wrote famously that "they are haughty and jealous of their liberties, impatient of restraint, and can scarcely bear the thought of being controuled by any superior power." Moreover, they were increasingly well educated: Thomas Jefferson was only one of many young Revolutionaries-to-be carrying armfuls of law books along those sandy streets, to be read under a shade tree on the outskirts of town. And some were wildly eloquent: Patrick Henry, schooled at home in Hanover County by his father, came to Williamsburg, passed his law examination in 1760, and by 1763 had already impressed men twice his age with his dexterity in the courtroom.

But their insecurities were also profound. Virginian fortunes depended upon tobacco, an unstable crop subject to soil erosion and the vicissitudes of European markets—and the planters, despite their pride in such matters, knew very little about the European markets. They were commodity rich, but cash poor: even gambling winnings were often reimbursed in tobacco certificates, which were redeemable for hogsheads stored in distant warehouses, hardly a reliable currency. They knew that the British disdained them for all this. They knew that poorer whites also disdained them and savored the biannual festival of bribery and supplication of a Burgess election: George Washington, in order to win his first election, was compelled to offer roughly a quart and a half of beer, rum, or whiskey to every voter in Fairfax County, delivered secondhand by a militia lieutenant and political ally.

Now, in the 1760s, the planters also began to face religious dissent. Almost exclusively, the Virginia gentry were good "churchmen": they were not exactly devout, but they enjoyed the bonds between an official church and their own authority, which showed itself in seating patterns in the pews based on social position, sermons that insisted upon subservience to authority both secular and sacred, and the power that resided in gentry-dominated vestries that dispensed religious patronage in the counties. The Presbyterians, Methodists, and Baptists who now seeped into Virginia, however, were not merely religious dissidents; they were cultural and political rebels, the "negative image," as Rhys Isaac has written, of the gentry. They didn't drink or gamble. They dressed plain. They didn't dance. And when wealthy Virginians mocked and persecuted them, they wore their martyrdom as a badge of honor: William Fristoe, a Presbyterian minister, called it "clearer proof of the genuine quality of religion among us."

If there was one group of men and women that truly disturbed the planters, however, it was their slaves. Wealthy Virginians were aware that there existed powerful arguments against the enslavement of Africans: within their libraries were volumes of antislavery political philosophy such as Montesquieu's *Spirit of the Laws* or Adam Smith's *Theory of Moral Sentiments,* and antislavery polemics such as James Otis's *Rights of the British Colonies,* within which the Massachusetts lawyer claimed that "the Colonists are by the law of nature free born, as indeed all men are, white or black. . . ." They were aware, as well, that the same dissenters who disdained their cultural leadership also frequently held antislavery beliefs: the Quaker Anthony Benezet, for instance, was earning national notoriety for teaching slave children in Philadelphia how to read and write. In isolated cases, the planters themselves were moved to antislavery utterance— especially the younger ones. Arthur Lee, of the Lee family, freshly returned from studying medicine in Scotland, published "Address on Slavery" in the *Virginia Gazette* on March 19, 1767: "Slavery is in violation of justice and religion," he wrote, warning that "on us, or on our posterity, the inevitable blow, must, one day, fall."

In Williamsburg, however, the presence of slaves was a dominant physical fact that overwhelmed all such philosophy: five-sixths of the white families owned at least one servant. On the surface, at least, all was calm. Black men and women were the cooks, waiters, and maidservants at the taverns, trained and coerced into their own forms of politesse: "Negro cooks, women waiters, and chambermaids made their courtesies with a great deal of native grace and simple elegance and were dressed neatly and cleanly," one English visitor wrote. They were jacks-of-all-trades: they were carpenters, blacksmiths, seamstresses. They played violins on request, when the carousing slowed. Some of them were even cosmopolites: an advertisement in the *Virginia Gazette* on July 23, 1767, offered for sale one slave who "shaves, dresses hair, and plays on the French horn. He lately came from London, and has with him two suits of new clothes, and his French horn, which the purchaser may have with him."

Alongside this pervasive spirit of ease and decorum, however, lay a kind of racial chaos that stunned visitors as much as the gambling. Underneath their breeches, many of those refined black waiters were wearing leg irons. Slave children walked around town naked, startling nobody but newcomers to Williamsburg, such as Ebenezer Hazard, who wrote in 1777, "This is so common a sight that even the Ladies do not appear to be shocked at it." Their parents, in turn, hid in closets, basements, and barns all over town, some of them housed in the crannies of civilization by masters hesitant to clutter their small city backyards with slave quarters, others constituting a vast network of runaways not escaping anything. For the planters, it was ominous: Arthur Lee was not the only slaveholder who feared insurrection. And yet the presence of slaves only inspired them to covet their own freedom even more: on May 30, 1765, the day that Patrick Henry delivered a galvanizing call in the House of Burgesses for rebellion against the conglomeration of taxes known as the Stamp Act—"Caesar had his Brutus, Charles the first, his Cromwell, and George the third," he was reputed to have said, before cries of "Treason!" compelled him to calmer attitudes—three black men hung from the public gallows, convicted of the theft of three hundred pence, playing a silent role in the drama of liberty unfolding in the assembly room.

As Williamsburg evolved into a pre-Revolutionary hothouse, it provided the stage for the public rehabilitation of Robert Carter. The election losses stung him, even if, as likely, he was more curious than interested, and had not "kissed the a— of the people," to borrow his uncle Landon's description of what elections were all about. In the spring of 1754, however, when he was twenty-five, he began a process of self-invention that would curry the public favor of Virginians as much as it would keep them at a wary, aristocratic distance. In general, the sons of Virginia patriarchs married the daughters of Virginia patriarchs: the Carters certainly did. Instead, Carter, in early April 1754, left the colony once more, and courted and married Frances Tasker of Baltimore, the sixteen-year-old daughter of Benjamin Tasker, one of Maryland's most powerful men. The marriage shaped Carter's life in crucial new ways. It was a good, counterintuitive mercantile match. Frances's dowry was substantial, and the connection provided Robert Carter a home outside of Virginia, a permanent bond to a slightly different culture, more industrial, more urban: he shortly acquired a one-fifth share of the Baltimore Iron Works, one of America's largest forges, from his wife's family, for ten thousand pounds. It was the kind of investment that few Virginian planters even contemplated.

As well, the marriage provided Robert Carter with a new family laden with bright, courtly men and women. There was Thomas Bladen, former governor of Maryland. There were three sisters-in-law, Anne Ogle, Rebecca Dulany, and Elizabeth Lowndes, each well-read and alert to matters of commerce. There was Daniel Dulany, Rebecca's husband, a brilliant lawyer who, in 1765, would pen *Considerations on the Propriety of Imposing Taxes,* perhaps the most celebrated intellectual protest against the Stamp Act published in America. And there was Tasker himself, Carter's new father-in-law, as mercurial as King Carter but famously mild-mannered, so popular among Maryland planters that he was elected president of their Council thirteen straight times.

Most important, the marriage brought him Frances Tasker. She too posed for one portrait: the artist provides her a long neck and full bosom, and the same facial features as George Washington in his most famous portraits—a truly beautiful woman, by eighteenth-century standards, already well-read, and ready-made for Southern society. Together, they returned to Nomony in the spring of 1754—giving up, for the time being, on Williamsburg and whatever friction remained there. They bore children, sometimes with breathtakingly short pauses between births and conceptions: Benjamin in 1756, Robert Bladen in 1759, Priscilla in 1760, Anne Tasker in 1762, Rebecca (who died at birth) ten months later in 1762, Frances in 1764, Betty Landon in 1765, Mary in 1767, Harriot Lucy in 1768, Amelia Churchill in 1769, Rebecca Dulany in 1770, and John Tasker in 1772.

Carter enmeshed himself in the tobacco trade, the staple of most planters' fortunes, and proved himself shrewd and well connected: despite a dramatic depression in tobacco prices during the French and Indian War, he turned surprising profits in Liverpool in the late 1750s by storing his crops while others sold and selling them when others didn't plant. Like other gentry planters, however, his economic correspondence began to be haunted by debt and instability: "I have experienced that the produce of my land and Negroes will scarce pay the demand requisite to keep them," he told one correspondent. In 1758, Carter was named to a seat on the Governor's Council, which sat in session when the House of Burgesses met, in a room in the opposite wing of the capitol building in Williamsburg. It was no electoral triumph: Thomas Bladen wrote Carter that some friends on the Board of Trade recommended him to Lord Halifax, who recommended the preferment to the king, the Carter name still carrying weight with the royal court. Having learned from experience that political preference was a fragile thing, however, Carter took no chances with the appointment: "Send it by the first king's ship that sails for North America," he wrote his London agent regarding the mandamuses certifying his appointment. "If it should miscarry, apply to the office for a second and send it as advised before. The matter is of great consequence to me."

At first, he approached Williamsburg again with caution: he attended only eight of forty-three sessions in 1759. By 1760, however, he was attending regular sessions, and in 1761, he moved his family there. He purchased a house on two acres from his cousin Robert Carter Nicholas; it was a sprawling white frame structure right next door to the governor's palace. Still haunted by debt and instability, Robert Carter nevertheless began to make immense purchases. He acquired silver plate with the family crest, the same counterfeit with which King Carter had smoothed his ascent. He remodeled the house, buying new curtains and wallpaper, and replacing the old wooden floors with new planks that concealed the nail heads. He moved the bedrooms upstairs and broke with the provincial tradition of separate bedrooms for husband and wife. He sectioned off three rooms as parlors, and began hosting: Washington, among others, "Dind" and "supped" there. He bought lottery tickets, raced horses, ordered dancing lessons for the children, and allowed the dance instructor to beat them if they missed their steps.

He doted on his clothing. Like many of his peers, he didn't care what he received as long as it was considered fashionable in London, and he trusted his merchant there to make the distinction, as much as he trusted another English merchant to price his tobacco properly: he ordered "sack if worn, if not fashionable, a fashionable undress to cost fifteen pounds sterling," and "glass" for a mirror "to be in many pieces agreeable to the present fashion." Frances Carter, when she wasn't pregnant or recovering from childbirth, insisted on stunning clothing: she bought a silver negligee, a black velvet cloak with a black silk lining, and reams of fine fabrics and needles.

Attending a palace party in 1767, she wore a suit of silk and satin that cost twenty-two pounds—the same sum her husband would have to spend to build fifteen slave cabins.

Carter, meanwhile, bought musical instruments: a harpsichord, a guitar, a flute, a piano, an organ, and one of Ben Franklin's few "harmonicas," a curious invention consisting of fine glass bowls that produced high, pure notes when rubbed by deft fingers. He purchased books: law books and divinities, but also novels (*Clarissa* and *Tristram Shandy*) and Samuel Johnson's famous *Dictionary*. He began to read voraciously, particularly in law, history, and philosophy, and introduced himself to the well-regarded royal governor, Francis Fauquier, who received the post, it was rumored, because the aplomb with which he gambled away his family fortune had impressed the powerful lord whom he paid in full. Fauquier quickly adopted Carter as a protégé: they visited Charleston together, and New York. As well, Carter befriended William Small, the erudite, Scottish-born professor of mathematics and natural philosophy at William and Mary; George Wythe, the revered law professor; Thomas Jefferson, fifteen years his junior; and John Blair, who became president of the Council.

Together, they dined frequently at the royal palace, evenings where Jefferson later claimed that he "heard more good sense, more rational and philosophical conversations than in all my life besides." While Wythe and Small were brilliant, Fauquier also proved to be a fearless thinker, republican enough to argue that "White, Red, or Black; polished or unpolished; . . . Men are Men." From these conversations, Page noted, Carter "derived great advantages" and "his understanding was . . . enlarged." And he became a seasoned musician. He played his harpsichord or German flute in weekly concerts alongside Jefferson and John Tyler (whose son would become president), with John Randolph or Fauquier himself on first violin. Sometimes, he even played his harmonica in public, immune to the nervous headaches its impossibly high, beautiful tones produced in many listeners.

As well, he acquired Williamsburg's contradictory politics. In 1758, he "sold part" of his "land and slaves" to repay the merchants who helped maintain his gentility. On April 29, 1767, he deported "Mary Anna," a slave seamstress "reared in my nursery," to Jamaica, as punishment for "cruelly Beating one of my Children"; he was content to take "Bullion, or Madeira Wine," in exchange for her. At the same time, he was persuaded by arguments in favor of American liberty: Page wrote that Carter "discovered the cruel tyranical designs of the British government," and he was among the councillors who sided with the House of Burgesses against the Stamp Act. But his membership on the Council left him on the anachronistic side of the Virginian government: if the House of Burgesses produced the leaders of the Revolution in Virginia, the royally appointed Council produced outright Tories, men who spent the war in suspiciously disloyal retirements, men who oversaw the decline of their family fortunes, and only one individual, John Page, who would inhabit a prominent position in the Revolutionary elite.

And so he balanced himself, as if on a knife edge, between the old generation of aristocrats only beginning to contemplate their obsolescence, and the new generation of radicals only beginning to contemplate their power. By the mid-1760s, his letters even acquire a faint diplomatic sense, and he was performing suave government services, writing the "fame" that the Council sent to the king to thank him for repealing the Stamp Act:

> As Duty and Affection to your Majesty are fixed and unalterable principles in us, we feel the Impressions of them so Strong and lively in our Breasts, that we cannot omit to lay hold of this Opportunity to renew our most sincere Protestations of our constant and inviolable Fidelity: And we do with Zeal and Firmness never to be Shaken, promise your Majesty, that we will at all Times exert ourselves in the Defence of your Majesty's sacred Person and Government, at the Risque of our Lives and Fortunes.

Not words, one suspects, that would age well, or make a place for the writer in American history. In 1765, however, they had to be said, and it was telling that Carter was the man asked to say them, that in ten years he had gone from being shunned to being the ideal intermediary between crown and colony.

5

In trying to understand the bond between the early years of Robert Carter's life and the Deed of Gift four decades later, one must confront the mystery of Carter's personality at its most perplexing point: how does someone so completely destined to represent aristocratic principles subsequently acquire the desire to subvert them? It is a remarkable question, in part because it forces us to consider other remarkable questions that we don't ask about the founders. As Edmund Morgan observes in the conclusion of *American Slavery, American Freedom,* we don't know where men such as Thomas Jefferson, James Madison, and George Washington acquired their republican ideals, either—nor do we inquire about it, due to the abundantly self-evident fact that they *had* republican ideals and, roughly speaking, the same set of republican ideals.

The mystery of Robert Carter, in this context, doubles: what were the sources of the spirit of liberty that moved an entire generation of slaveholding Virginians, and what was Robert Carter's relationship to those sources that led him down his eccentric path? Morgan offers three compelling possibilities for the sources that guided the Virginian leadership as they shaped their political ideals: first, their libraries, well stocked with law books, Roman and Greek history, philosophy, and drama, the great political thinkers of Enlightenment Europe—Locke, Rousseau, and Montesquieu most prominent—and "modern" playwrights, moralists, and satirists such as Shakespeare, Milton, Swift, and Voltaire; second, the dissenting religions in Virginia, small sects such as the Presbyterians, the Quakers, and the Baptists, whose ministers argued for equality among men and women, whites and blacks, rich and poor; and third, the House of Burgesses, whom one early royal governor described as "very much in a Republican way of Thinking."

In fact, Robert Carter's relationship to these sources, even in the first few decades of his life, was already veering down the eccentric path. He acquired the library, but read alone: there would never be a tutor to tell him what to think of Locke, Rousseau, or the ancients. As for the House of Burgesses, he never participated in their "Republican way of Thinking": he sat in the councillor's room on the opposite wing of the assembly house as men such as Jefferson, Washington, Page, Henry, and Madison configured their ideals and their temperaments to one another. Carter's relationship with the men and women of the Presbyterian, Methodist, and Baptist churches was unusually close for a man of his stature, however, so much so that rumors circulated around Williamsburg that Carter still remained a coarse and dangerous Virginian: "Will a complaining of some parts of the present liturgy used by the church of england create an atheist?" he asked in a letter from 1764 in which he wondered about the theft of the "good name" that he had spent a full decade building from scratch.

Carter, of course, was no atheist. During the mid-1760s, however, he struck a series of positions in political debates that distanced himself from his peers on matters of religion in particular. In 1764, for instance, Carter voted in the minority on the Council on a court case regarding the "Parsons' Cause," a landmark case that tested the power of local aristocrats and freemen against royally appointed Anglican ministers, and which would have forced ministers to take their salaries in the unstable (and then depressed) commodity of tobacco: Carter instead voted that they should receive stable salaries independent of the tobacco markets.

Then, in July 1766, he expressed disgust with his fellow councillors' response to a murder case in Cumberland County, where John Criswell, a gentleman deep in debt, started a drunken fight with Robert Routledge, a merchant, called him a "Presbyterian fellow," and ran him through with a sword. Blair, Byrd, and a third councillor, Peter Thornton, allowed Criswell bail and were preparing to dismiss the charges when a public outcry humiliated them and the defendant, who committed suicide in his cell. Carter, once again, set himself against his peers, but this time he took the people's side, condemning Blair, Byrd, and Thornton: "The contrariety of opinion as to the fact is very alarming; but I hope the whole truth will come out. . . ."

Eventually, Carter would receive credit for responses such as this, developing a reputation for an unflinching faith in law that bordered on incorruptibility: George Mason, a decade later, would call him "an honest Man." Similarly, he would earn the regard of dissenting Virginians. When John Craig, a frontier Presbyterian minister from Augusta County, was given charge of an emaciated, homesick Muslim prisoner-of-war who had escaped Mohawk custody at the end of the French and Indian War, he wrote Carter, appealed to the latter's reputation for "beneficence to the poor and afflicted," and asked the councillor to help "Selim the Algerine" return to Algiers—a task Carter undertook with such generosity that Selim, upon returning to America several years later, traveled directly to Nomony to seek Carter's renewed assistance.

At the same time, Carter recognized that his decisions were regarded by his peers, and even his family, as rebellious: not only was his uncle Landon one of the leaders of the Parsons' Cause, but, like many gentry, Landon considered dissenters to be "religious villains" and "horrid hellish rogues." But even that consideration undoubtedly satisfied Carter. As a member of Virginian society now, he maintained a lively correspondence, but the distance between himself and his family that began in his youth did not abate: he did not mention visits to his mother, or stepfather, and rarely corresponded with his sister or powerful uncles save for business matters. When the time came to name his children, names from his wife's family would dominate: he would even hesitate about continuing his own line, calling his first son Benjamin (after his father-in-law) before calling his second son Robert Bladen, a hybrid of his own name and that of his wife's uncle that ensured that there would be no Robert IV. Other names he gave his children, such as Tasker and Anne, also paid tribute to his in-laws and not his own blood relatives.

His correspondence, in turn, was as reverent to his in-laws as it was cool to his own kin. He told Thomas Bladen, who helped place him on the Council, "I have not forgotten one moment, & hope I never shall, the personal favors thou hast honoured me with." He solicited political advice from Benjamin Tasker, shyly speaking of his "Inquisitiveness to know your Sentiment," and hoping that the older man would "excuse it." On his father-in-law's behalf, he even pursued a lawsuit against his uncle Charles, seeking reimbursement of a fifty-three pound debt: "Col: Carter hath not been within the jurisdiction of York, James City . . . Courts since you directed that he should be sued. . . . I despair of catching him in either of those courts."

In fact, Robert Carter III simply picked up where King Carter left off, the disaffection and contradiction that his grandfather expressed in the last years of his life transformed into the first thing Robert Carter breathed in the air at Corotoman. King Carter too had tried to balance contempt for wealth with pursuit of wealth, and he had begun to move toward dissenting churches as a way of expressing his contempt for "muckworms": he wrote warm words to Quaker merchants and hired a tutor for his children from a dissenting church—something his grandson was about to do as well, with famous results. Likewise, the Carters had long understood that a certain legalistic rectitude, combined with some unnameable sympathy for the very people they exploited, was satisfying conduct: John Carter had liberated slaves and provided them land, livestock, and homestead in his will, an uncommon bequest in seventeenth-century Virginia, and King

Carter was regarded as a trustworthy benefactor who helped freed blacks stay free. Even Robert Carter III's detachment from his family was almost philosophical, his own version of his grandfather's self-estrangement. He didn't dislike his family. But he wanted to free himself from what they represented, and from what he knew he represented most of all: an intense abstraction of power and entitlement hopelessly entwined with early Virginian history, with a certain church, and with a certain style of life.

In itself, this was no small revolution: if one could learn to walk away from the name one was given, especially when that name came attached to great privilege, then there was no limit to the other things one might be capable of walking away from later in life. By 1768, however, Carter had begun to lose his balance, in part because the old Virginia that had made the balance possible was dying, and in part because the two men to whom he turned as father figures proved themselves as mortal as the actual father and grandfather who had left Carter orphaned and adrift four decades earlier. In August, Francis Fauquier passed slowly, and badly: he suffered "numerous + painful Infirmities," and his body wasted away gradually. In public, he maintained his decorum, and his erudition: he was a member of the Royal Society, a man who measured the diameter of balls of hail and sent the information home to his brother in England for the cause of science, and a certain Enlightenment stoicism ran deep in him. In private, however, he was shocked that his life would end so bitterly. In his will, he took his body to task: he called it "my infecting Carcass" and instructed that "it be Deposited in the Earth or Sea as I shall happen to fall."

Carter observed closely. He scrutinized the doctors, and sent letters notifying relatives of the death. He meditated on the funeral, which he revered for its unfashionable austerity:

> His burial was not pompous for his last testament directs that the ceremony should be performed at as little expense as decency can possibly permit. He believing that the present mode of funeral obsequies was contrary to the spirit of Christ's religion.

And he meditated, as well, on Fauquier's will, which was an astonishing document. Fauquier named four executors—Carter, George Wythe, William Nelson, and Peyton Randolph—and left them "single stone Brilliant Diamond Rings" to wear "in Remembrance of a Man who once loved them and dies in the belief that they loved him." More important, Fauquier left an unusual codicil in his will regarding his slaves: he stipulated that they be given "liberty to choose their own Masters," who could then purchase them at three-quarters of their market value. He also forbade his executors from separating mothers and their children: "Can I expect mercy from an offended God," he asked, "if I have not myself shewn mercy to those dependant on me?" To modern readers, this sounds, at best, like a mild form of noblesse oblige. In Virginia in 1768, however, manumission was illegal, except in extraordinary individual cases, and even Fauquier's measured terms of generosity were exceptional charity. Few white men in Williamsburg even contemplated emancipation: when Richard Bland, a veteran Burgess, proposed in 1769 that masters should be allowed to free their slaves whenever they chose, he was called "an enemy of his country," and his bill, composed and seconded by Thomas Jefferson, was never even put to a vote.

Fauquier's bequeathments, however, clearly touched Carter. And when Benjamin Tasker died in the autumn—Carter wrote that his father-in-law was a man whom he "sincerely loved & respected," words, again, he never used to describe his uncles, his father, or his grandfather—Carter fell into depression and confusion. Tasker's will left his property to his wife, but left his deceased son's property in control of Tasker's daughter Anne Ogle, his son-in-law Christopher Lowndes, and Carter. Carter rapidly took control of several matters regarding Tasker's estate and took control of the sale and distribution of the son's estate. But then he delayed the sale of land and slaves. He repeatedly recommended patience: "That Estate should not be sold hastily," he told Anne Ogle. He lost his copy of the will, leaving it behind in Baltimore, and he let four months pass before requesting a new one.

When Ogle complained, however, Carter hotly denied having advised delay: "Facts do evince my Readiness to fulfill the duty, & contradict the Idea of Slowness." He claimed, instead, that every single letter he sent had disappeared in bad weather: "I fear that every Letter, which I have written (since I saw you) touching your mother's Business & my joint Trusteship with you is lost." He even claimed that he was never given control of the estate's affairs, denying the existence of several letters to the contrary. As affairs deteriorated, he pled innocence, wondering what he had done wrong—

> I have lately reviewed my negotiations respecting those objects &
> do not discover any impropriety therein—but if in any future
> transactions I shall comit Blunders, or omissions, I beg leave to say
> that they will happen from mistake & not design.

And finally, he asked what might recover his name: "If these Endeavours do not evince you," he wrote Dulany, "be pleased to mention to me the Doubt, that I may strive to dispel the Cloud which envelops the Truth."

By summer, Carter and the Tasker family would take each other to court. Eighteen years later, Carter would still be exchanging both civilities and writs with their children. Anne Ogle would write him coruscating letters, telling him that the delays were ruining her and starving the slaves. Carter was ordinarily an astute businessman. And, as George Mason observed, he was not a liar. But the slowness here was telling, as was the confusion and hurt feelings. In late 1768, Dulany wrote Carter and reported that the Tasker sisters in Maryland wanted to draw "Lotts" for the "Bell-Air" slaves, each sister to "dispose as they please, of the Negroes that shall fall to them." Dulany, however, refused to participate: "I can have no Concern in the Business—the Distress is intolerable." In early 1769, Carter agreed:

> Mrs. Carter and I rejoice at your great humanity, and hope that the
> Negroes who have alliances at 'Bel Air' may not be sold till those
> slaves be, and that the Negroes be sold with wife and husband. . . .
> When that lottery shall be drawn, be pleased to inform me how
> many of the male and female Negroes belong to me, their ages and
> qualifications, and estimate the whole. My wife and I had rather
> let those slaves chuse masters in Maryland than send them to
> plantations.

Fauquier's influence was plain: Carter was unwilling to participate in a slave auction that did not at least partially acknowledge the will and desire of the slaves themselves. By 1769, he had clearly shown Virginia that he sympathized with religious dissenters. And he had certainly acquired a reputation for "beneficence to the poor and afflicted." But this was the first real signal that his sympathies might extend to African-Americans as well, and that whatever fragment of legalistic empathy for the freedom of blacks that lived within his great-grandfather, grandfather, and mentor in Williamsburg lived within him as well, and might be nurtured into something vital.

It is a small sign. But the key to understanding what Robert Carter wanted and what Robert Carter did, as Philip Fithian suggested, is not to look at his words. One must look elsewhere—in this case, at the Taskers' frustration with him, which tells us that his hesitancy blocked something crucial to their desires and their sense of themselves: the easy transformation of their black servants into portable forms of ready money. Faced with their reproach, Carter apologized, explained, grieved, but did not relent. Instead, he pursued ideals that few men of his time recognized: even George Washington, who moved quietly and with great dignity through Williamsburg society, served as sponsor to at least one slave auction in 1769, the same year that Carter declined the same role. Decades later, Washington would, like Carter, contort the labor configurations of his plantations rather than separate slave families. At the cusp of the Revolutionary 1770s, however, as Carter alienated his wife's family rather than tear slave children away from their parents, Washington was still buying teenage girls away from their parents and their homes in order to stock Mount Vernon: "not exceeding . . . 16" years old, he admonished his agent in the West Indies, in 1772, as he traded Virginia flour for Caribbean breeding women.

Unlike Washington, Carter had a stocked plantation. And unlike Washington, Carter had a past that both liberated him and dictated his destiny. As Robert Carter III, the grandson of a "king," he was too moneyed and titled to let anyone tell him which forms of liberty to love and which to shun. He could ally himself with dissenters; and when asked to choose between the welfare of his family and that of his slaves, he could choose his slaves. As Robert Carter III, the grandson of a "king," however, he was also too moneyed and titled to ever be associated with the destiny of a rising people. It was the same dilemma that deranged his grandfather in his later years, and even in his early years, the grandson began to look for actions and gestures that could resolve the inner conflict before it deranged him, too. That was why Fauquier's last will and testament was a milestone for him. When men such as Washington and Jefferson heard the voice of liberty, they acknowledged not only European influences but also their own power, an eloquent kind of self-assertion attuned to futurity.

When Carter heard the voice of liberty, his ear was turned backward, to the royal governor who taught him that some link existed between antislavery and the pre-Revolutionary elite, buried beneath the surface of the smooth, repressive aristocracy—and even further backward, to the visionary and troubled grandfather who taught him too early for speech that owning all the wealth, land, and slaves in Virginia could not make a man free.

It was a politics of nostalgia and sadness, deeply personal, and it too would set Carter apart, and would lead to the Deed of Gift, as surely as any positive assertion of antislavery sentiment. Washington and Jefferson knew this politics: Washington, who never bore children, and Jefferson, who lost his wife and four of his six children between the Boston Tea Party and the Constitutional Convention, grieved over incomplete families as they fought a revolution and built a union. But they did not embrace loss like Carter, who often seemed to engage himself with other men and women just so he could part with them. In its way, Robert Carter's pulse, which oscillated between extreme enthusiasm and extreme detachment, was probably set early, probably when his father and grandfather, whom he was destined to emulate, left him as the sole member of an elite imaginary fraternity. But once that pulse was set, everything beat to it: father figures were found and lost, new families were recruited and tossed aside, astonishing numbers of children were born, and astonishing numbers of children would die. He had more slaves than almost anyone, and he would free more slaves than anyone. Slaves were family, too; every benign slaveholder knew that. And Carter was used to watching families come and go.

CHAPTER II

Dance or Die

[1768–1774]

"Is he as grave as you?"

—FRANCES TASKER CARTER, 1774

Philip Vickers Fithian awoke to the sound of guns being fired.

It was Christmas Day 1773, and these guns were good news, just as when wealthy young Virginians went courting, one might reasonably expect a cannonball through the window. But Fithian, a stranger here, was tentative in his joy. He had just ridden down from New Jersey in late October, having missed commencement at Princeton in order to prepare for the journey. Henry Lee, who came from these parts, had been there, and had worn a suit of gold lace, refusing to be outdone sartorially by the royal governor of New Jersey. Fithian, however, had no gold lace. He had a black suit and a tied tongue. In fact, his austere childhood and training for the Presbyterian ministry had left him temperamentally unfit for polite Virginian society: he had attended his first dance that December and had declined every invitation to "step a Minuet," hot with embarrassment, standing to the side in his dark suit, joining with the other young men and women only when they played their kissing games.

It was a mistake, really, that Fithian was even here. His parents had both died the year before, and he was melancholy and drifting. He had allowed a year to pass after his own graduation without taking the ministry exam. As his peers hurried into careers in law or the ministry, he wondered why they were so impatient to surrender their youth: "Poor Boys!" he wrote in his journal that July. "Hard they push to be in the midst of Tumult, & Labour." When he learned of teaching opportunities in Virginia, he pondered the details (sixty-five pounds per annum, light teaching duties, the use of a library and horse, the ministrations of his own personal slave), consulted John Witherspoon, the Scottish-born minister who governed Princeton, and accepted an offer to be the family tutor for Robert Carter of Nomony Hall.

Immediately, he began to lose sleep. One long turbulent night followed another. He thought about death. He prayed for his own soul and for the strength to resist the temptations that Virginia, by reputation, was bound to offer. He wrote long letters to Elizabeth Beatty, a woman he called his "fair Laura." Notes from friends spoke a little too candidly of her beauty, however, and Fithian began to regret that he had agreed to leave her society for a year. He asked Witherspoon to release him from his obligation. Witherspoon declined to even answer personally.

Usually, Fithian required no help waking. If he stood at sunrise at the window of his room on the second floor of Robert Carter's schoolhouse, he could see the sun glint off the wide Potomac and cast a smoky glaze across the woods of Maryland in the far distance. He could follow the Potomac in his imagination, let it flow to Beatty—a geography of eighteenth-century affections that made sense on no map but momentarily solved his loneliness. On this morning, though, he was still in bed when Nelson appeared at his door—in nothing more than his shirt and his pants, incredibly—made Fithian a fire, blacked his shoes, straightened his room, and wished him a good Christmas.

Fithian gave him half a bit: a quarter of a pistareen, worth a little less than a shilling.

The journey to Virginia had begun well. Carter's library was enormous: Fithian called it "over-grown," and he was delighted with the use of it. Fithian's hours were reasonable: school was in session from roughly seven in the morning until a sixty-pound bell rang breakfast at eight-thirty, then again from nine-thirty until noon, and then again from three-thirty until five. And the Carter children seemed docile. Fithian thought the Carters were an unusually well-regulated family, and he was particularly impressed with the fact that Frances and Robert Carter "never pass over an occasion of reproof." Meanwhile, the Carters and their friends treated Fithian with extreme hospitality. He was terrified of saying the wrong thing, because he had readily gathered how one wrong utterance could ruin one's reputation in this society. But he never said the wrong thing: he might be blamed for being too grave, but a dark suit and a silent manner, he soon realized, passed for honesty here.

And then there were the kissing games. There was something in Virginian women that made him giddy. He loved Laura, but Mrs. Carter could pass for twenty, and she was already taking him for long walks, inviting him to stay for several years. There were already rumors of pairing him with Betsy Lee, and he didn't love Beatty so much that he would fail to appraise the opportunity to marry into that particular fortune. And there was Priscilla, the Carters' oldest daughter: it was only December, but he was already preparing his valentine, a poem that would balloon into 130 lines by the time it was completed in February.

Another servant came to the door. This was the man who tended the fires in the schoolroom. He was dressed formally in green, made several broad obsequious bows (from which Fithian deduced that he was already almost drunk), and wished Fithian a good Christmas.

Fithian gave him a full bit and searched his room for more coins.

Still, the Virginians bewildered him. The men brawled for little or no reason: they all knew how to box and how to use a "small-sword." And despite the new austerity that depression and political turmoil had made fashionable, they partied endlessly: a ball might run four days, drinking and dancing until three in the morning, coffee on an empty stomach at half past eight, then cards and races, and the whole thing all over again, until the guests had to excuse themselves and go home to nurse the fevers and agues that sometimes consumed them entirely. And the pressure to participate was almost political: it was dance or die, Fithian thought.

Likewise, he knew that Carter was regarded as "by far the most Humane to his Slaves of any in these parts," but he could not reconcile that reputation with the one peck of corn and one pound of meat per week that Carter allocated to each of his tithables. And there were others, far worse, who thought that their recipes for the torture and domination of African servants were topics for polite conversation. "To get a secret from a Negro," a man named Morgan told him in early December, "take the following method—Lay upon your Floor a large thick plank, having a peg about eighteen Inches long, of hard wood, & very Sharp, on the upper end, fixed fast in the plank—then strip the Negro, tie the Cord to a staple in the Ceiling, so as that his foot may just rest on the sharpened Peg, then turn him briskly round."

"You would laugh," Morgan concluded.

Inhuman infidel, Fithian thought to himself, but he said nothing, and eventually chose to wait for a righteous God to visit for these things. On this Christmas morning, his first and only Christmas in Virginia, he hoped for something of grace and comfort, something he thought the Carters could provide. But the Carters were fascinating and elusive, as always. Mr. Carter offered him his horse, and his newspaper, then took dinner in his bedroom, and passed up supper as well, playing instead on the pianoforte in another room. In time, Fithian would come to respect the inscrutable personality of his host: he would even begin to mimic it, taking meals in his own room, declining polite offers of society, eventually acknowledging that the best way to maintain his own dignity in this brash, beautiful place was to go where Mr. Carter went, stay as long as Mr. Carter stayed, and leave when Mr. Carter left. On this day, though, Carter's unnerving zeal for privacy left Fithian as the man of the house, forced to carve the meat, provide the toasts, and work through his shyness by keeping up his share of the repartee. And Mrs. Carter was merciless. She turned the conversation to marriage, and said that if she were a widow, she would marry any man alive, because she had "grown old when the world is thronged with blooming, ripening Virgins."

Fithian missed this broad flirtation by a mile. By the light of the fine, bright spermaceti candles in his room, though, he would acknowledge that she was a beautiful woman. The next day, he took her to church, while Mr. Carter stayed at home. There were so few people in attendance that the minister cancelled the sacrament and preached for only fifteen minutes, on the subject of "For unto us a child is Born &c." Very fashionable, Fithian thought. But not comforting. The next morning, like so many others, Fithian turned to his window, gazed at the Potomac, and wondered if he would ever follow it homeward.

Until he did—he would return to New Jersey a year later, in October 1774—he had pen and paper for solace. Night after night, he dipped a quill, and wrote his thoughts in a bold cursive across the crisp, amber paper his host provided. Some nights, he wrote little. Other nights, he stayed up late and wrote a thousand words with such candor and precision that, more than two hundred years later, his journals have earned him celebrity among historians that far exceeds that of the family who provided his inspiration.

Still, the compulsion that drove his pen remained unsatisfied. The Carters simply didn't tell him enough. He didn't know, for instance, that in an eleven-month period in 1771 and 1772, three of the Carter daughters— Mary, Amelia Churchill, and Rebecca Dulany—died of unknown causes, none of them seeing their fifth birthdays. He couldn't possibly know: the family never mentioned the girls in public, never left any sign of lament. That was how Virginians mourned: Thomas Jefferson responded to the death of his wife in 1782 by disappearing from public life for two months, and by burning her letters, so that no record of an emotional attachment might remain for posterity.

And Fithian didn't know, at least at first, how insecure the Carters really were. He didn't know how their carefully mannered plantation idyll had begun barely eighteen months before his arrival: in May 1772, Carter had suddenly moved his family from Williamsburg, put up the house on Palace Street for sale, and placed an enormous order of luxury goods to James Gildart in Liverpool—125 items, everything from cinnamon to lamb mittens to "3 dozen sortable hair Combs"—to stock the new home. No one could possibly know, of course, because Carter was Delphic, if not downright deceitful: he told Peyton Randolph that he was leaving Williamsburg because the house had gotten too small for a growing family, even one that had just lost three children.

Fithian did recognize that the man at the center was uncomfortable with the role of patriarch. But he couldn't recognize why. What, exactly, made Robert Carter the "most Humane 'man' in these parts"? Was he committed to slavery but regarded as a compassionate master? Or was there something in his constitution, and something within the constitution of his plantation family, that pointed toward a deeper antipathy toward slavery, and a deeper commitment to liberty that could not be answered even as the country marched toward a war in liberty's name?

2

Years later, Carter would write in his own private journal that he left Williamsburg because "a new system of politicks in british north america, began to prevail, generally" in "the first part of the year 1772." It was a many-sided phrase: Carter surely meant that the new "system" that repelled him was the more aggressive policies of the British government in suppressing independence in the colonies. But he implied, as well, that it might be the more incendiary radicalism of Sons of Liberty in the House of Burgesses, in Boston, and elsewhere. In truth, though, it was both: he could not live with the widening gap between crown and colony, and with the fact that the political space in the middle that he personally occupied was disappearing.

For Carter, Williamsburg by 1772 was a place heavy with personal mourning and political distress. Unquestionably, the loss of three young children would devastate even parents who regarded their children as replaceable entities, as did many eighteenth-century families. Carter, however, was also tiring of the public life of Williamsburg. He was weary, for instance, of its licentiousness, deciding against sending his sons to William and Mary, the sight of its professors gambling in taverns or drunkenly strolling the streets convincing him that no "useful Education" was available there.

He wearied also of depression and debt. The European tobacco markets had collapsed again in the early 1770s, and the economic effects in America were felt most profoundly in Virginia: white Virginians owed merchants in Great Britain almost half of America's overall debt, 1.4 million pounds out of a total of 3 million pounds. Further, that debt was concentrated among the most powerful men in the colony: at least fifty-five members of the House of Burgesses owed five hundred pounds or more apiece, and some owed more than five thousand pounds, huge sums that simply dwarfed the value of what they could send to England any given year. It made them think of themselves as dependents, even, as slaves, to Great Britain: when Thomas Jefferson wrote that "the planters were a species of property annexed to certain mercantile houses of London," he was only one of many Virginian voices who framed his own fight for freedom in this awkward metaphor.

While his peers compiled debts to British merchants, however, Carter was asking for balances to be sent back to him. As Fithian wrote, Carter may well have possessed "the clearest fortune . . . of any man in Virginia": there were Virginian planters who were wealthier than ninety-nine out of every one hundred white Americans, and Carter was forty or fifty times richer than they were. Carter borrowed: everyone did. But he lent far more. And so he walked the streets of Williamsburg, carrying with him the reputation as "the Benevolent, the Generous, the Honorable the Rich Mr Carter," as one Williamsburg resident wrote—one adjective too many for comfort. He lent money to everyone: Peyton Randolph, Benjamin Harrison, Thomas Jefferson. And when he tried to recover it, he was admonished—by John Dixon, editor of the *Virginia Gazette*, no less—that a "Rattle-Snake is wont to give Warning before he strikes."

Mostly, however, Carter had grown weary of growing political extremism. In the face of Townshend Act taxes on paper, glass, tea, and lead, the transport of political prisoners to England for trial, the erosion of the right to trial by jury, and clashes between British soldiers and American dissenters in New York and Boston, Virginian leaders had grown more radical. They organized economic boycotts and committees of correspondence, and in 1769 composed in the House of Burgesses a set of incendiary resolutions, sharply criticizing the British king and Parliament, and arguing that the only government that could tax Virginians was composed of Virginians.

On the other side, there was a new royal governor: John Murray, Lord Dunmore, a dark-eyed, dark-haired Scottish nobleman with a soldierly bearing. While only slightly less worldly than his predecessors, Dunmore was gruff, authoritarian, and more candidly entranced by the idea of the fortune he might glean in patronage from his new position. He attempted to seize control of political appointments traditionally reserved for local officials, and closed sessions of the Assembly with patronizing sermons on hard work and thrift: "Infuse that Spirit of Industry," he told them, and "abolish that Spirit of Gaming."

For Carter, who revered Fauquier's republican suavity, and was good friends with Fauquier's first replacement, the Baron de Botetourt, Dunmore was an ominous sign of British intent. But Carter disliked as much the rebellious spirit of his peers in the Virginia government. He grew angry at the House of Burgesses when they rebelled against Dunmore by convening on February 6, even though Dunmore was stranded in heavy rains outside of Williamsburg and was unable to deliver the ceremonial inauguration: Carter filled an entire journal with his legal arguments for why the session should be struck from the record, even though the Burgesses did nothing that day except make the symbolic point that they did not require royal permission to meet.

Of course, Carter kept the journal to himself—he would no sooner complain to the Burgesses than to the governor, his new neighbor, to whom he was also now lending money. Still looking backward, still practicing the liberal spirit he had acquired under Fauquier's tutelage, Carter saw the new blunt politics as a violation of what he called his "Plan of Life," which still revolved around the Enlightenment gentleman's virtue of "moderation." Further, he was simply too rich to feel threatened. He still thought highly of his friends in England. And he felt few concerns about his slaves. Most powerful Virginians, however, felt otherwise, seeing in their servants the mirror image of their own rebellion. Throughout February and March of that year, the minutes of the House of Burgesses were full of reports of individual slaves gone amok, physically assaulting their masters, defying armed overseers, and inspiring reactionary violence among whites in isolated Virginian counties. These concerns led Carter's peers to seize both high-minded and desperate reforms to their system. The House of Burgesses, for instance, petitioned the king to curtail the importation of slaves, arguing that slavery "greatly retards the Settlement of the Colonies." In February, the House also took up "An engrossed Bill to amend the Act, intituled An Act directing the Trials of Slaves," which gave "outlying" slaves greater benefit of clergy but also made it easier for a judge to order their executions. The bill was sent to the Council for amendment, who in turn passed the bill to a committee of three of its members, Carter among them.

The following day, February 12, the Council returned their recommendations to the House. They had significantly toughened the bill: in their view, a judge should be able to issue "a proclamation against any slave, to kill or destroy such slave" not merely if it "be first proved" that he had caused mischief, but if it "shall appear" that he had caused mischief. They also removed the clause that required the judge to have witnesses testifying to the existence of "mischief" before issuing such proclamations, and widened the definition of "mischief" to include any slave who "hath been outlying for the Space of ten Days," whether or not he had committed an act of violence or theft. Refusing only this last revision, the House passed the bill in its amended form, which gave local authorities the power to execute slaves merely suspected of doing wrong.

It is entirely possible that Carter approved these changes. But there are also three good reasons to believe that he was a distressed minority on that committee, and that this event, as much as the deaths of three daughters, the rise of rebellious native politics, Dunmore's arrival in Williamsburg, and the proliferation of debt and drink, convinced him to retire from public life. First, there is that testy, defiant journal calling into question the right of the House of Burgesses to convene itself: Carter wrote the journal on February 28 referring to events that occurred on February 6, as if something that occurred between these two dates had inspired discomfort with the Burgesses' sense of their own power. Second, the debate on the slave bill was the last Council committee on which Carter would ever serve: he continued to attend their sessions for two more years, but his name ceased to appear anywhere in the journals of the Council, except in its attendance rolls. Third, when he returned to Nomony, he made sure that his slaves received "due process." When two slaves were accused of stealing corn in March 1777, for instance, Carter convened a court at his plantation and held a trial. He was the judge. The slaves were convicted, and sentenced to be "scourged with scratches on their bare Backs," a cruel sentence Carter minded less since the protocols of law, evidently, had been honored.

3

Nomony Hall was an immense white rectangle, brick covered with stucco, two stories high, seventy-seven by forty-four feet, comprising more than six thousand square feet of living room. There were four rooms to a floor: the girls slept in one large bedroom, the Carters in another, the female house slaves in one called a "nursery." The boys slept in the schoolhouse, or in the living room if they wanted, and had breakfast with the housekeeper in the kitchen if they chose.

The black walnut marble staircase impressed visitors but required cleaning or repair so often that the family and slaves often used a second, less glamorous staircase in the back of the house. There was a large study for Carter on the first floor, and an even larger ballroom. Where there was excess, it dwelled in the more prosaic details of the place: the windows and doors were latticed with incredible numbers of panes of glass (forty-two on some windows, sixteen on some doors), and there were five chimneys, within which the Carters maintained so many fires that they could burn four cartloads of wood in a single day, and not necessarily a winter day.

From a distance, this "great house" would be the first thing a stranger might see: it was set high on a prospect, dazzling white, and two rows of tall poplars marked the lane to its front entrance. Upon entering the grounds, however, that same stranger might find his or her attention drawn away from the great house, and drawn toward the adjacent buildings, four large brick edifices that sat at the corners of Nomony Hall: schoolhouse, stable, washhouse, and coach house. An outdoor kitchen sat just outside the back of the house. Fine grassy lawns, gardens, a cemetery, and a bowling green entwined with these buildings. The Carters used burned oyster shells for paving stones on their paths, and tall shrubs were strategically planted to both obscure and reveal sight lines, to create the sense of privacy without the reality.

On one side of the great house, one could walk along a path for about a quarter mile and reach Carter's mill, which sat on a fork of the Nomony River. Carter had dammed the river and built a landing so that boats could land and deliver (or pick up) everything from bar iron to books and silks. On the other side of the great house, and at a slight distance, one could find what Fithian called a "little handsome street," composed of washhouse, stable, coach house, kitchen, bake house, dairy, storehouse, and several slave quarters. Robert Carter strictly guarded who might and might not enter the great house, but out here it was a different matter. In the morning, or on cool evenings, or on Sunday, this district was an urban swarm, where slaves, white employees, and the Carters commingled. Most of the men and women contributing to this buzz of activity, of course, were of African descent. They tilled potatoes, raised chickens, built their own houses, played at cockfights, and worshipped. The whites watched them.

Within the great house, Robert Carter attempted to construct an orderly and urbane space. He locked himself in his study for hours (all important men did: "The Great Man retiring to his study after breakfast," an English guest wrote of Washington), and kept a chamber pot in there so he wouldn't be interrupted. He read newspapers and periodicals, which he ordered from Philadelphia as well as Williamsburg. He practiced obsessively on one of his six ornate musical instruments. Mrs. Carter, in turn, led the family conversations. When the idea of living without slavery first got a public airing, for instance, it occurred at the Nomony supper table one evening in April 1774, and she was the one who suggested it. Sell the slaves, she advised, let the lands lie "uncultivated," and the interest from the revenue on the slave auctions would "be a much greater yearly income

than what is now received . . . making no allowance at all for the trouble &
Risk of the Masters as to the Crops, & Negroes."

Mostly, however, conversations fluctuated among forced lightness,
quick, teasing banter, and what must have been incomprehensibly dull
small talk: Carter and Fithian spent one July afternoon debating whether
a rower's efficiency was increased if more of his oar extended over the water
or over the boat. When there were guests, the Carters would prepare three
or four different entrees, and leave entire muttons untouched. When there
were no guests, the meals were often simple and economical: milk and
hominy for breakfast, with coffee and sage tea; coffee and bread and butter or oysters for supper; dinners comprised crabs and strawberries and
cream, or artichokes, huckleberries, and milk; broth when the weather was
cold, peaches when they were fresh.

Within this environment, Carter moved like he was untouchable. Writing to a friend in New Jersey, Fithian was fascinated by the personalities of
the patriarchs he met: "Such amazing property," he observed, "no matter
how deep it is involved, blows up the owners to an imagination, which is
visible in all. . . . they are exalted above other Men in worth & precedency."
But Fithian also observed that Carter was an exception to this rule because
he fulfilled it so completely: he hid himself from almost everyone. It was
not merely the dinners missed so he could practice pianoforte, nor the
church services he evaded. He often ate alone and also spent long after-
noons reading. When thunderstorms rolled through and slaves and family
scattered for cover, Carter would sit unmoved and take in the storm. He
left those endless balls early—"copy Mr. Carter" on this matter, Fithian
advised John Peck, his replacement—but never criticized the ethos of hospitality and frivolity that inspired their excesses. He measured things: he
bought thermometers and barometers, spent solitary hours with surveying
equipment and a telescope. He invented things: an instrument that tuned
a pianoforte, a gauge that converted between Maryland and Virginian currencies. Sometimes, he sounded like he was anyone but one of the largest
slaveholders in Virginia: returning from a visit to a neighboring plantation,
he was unable to dismiss the vision of a slave coachman chained to his
post. Sometimes, he sounded like he was traveling mystical planes: it was
not beyond him to interrupt an idle summer conversation and wonder
aloud whether or not life existed on other planets.

Fithian said that Carter was "discreet, and sensible," but this was something more than judicious detachment. Grief over their lost children had followed the Carters from Williamsburg, where it mixed with new fears. Smallpox was sweeping through Philadelphia, killing three hundred, acting with prejudice against children. Reports of malaria had begun to be heard from nearby Westmoreland County plantations. Carter was frequently sick, as were his children and his wife, and the illnesses were almost always sudden and perturbing. Two daughters might awake one morning with pustules on their arms and faces, or an employee might suddenly be infected by an uncontrollable pain in his jaw. And since the early symptoms of fatal diseases such as smallpox matched the symptoms of the common flu, there was no way of knowing which sickness might lift and which might accelerate, who might be dancing at a ball the next day or whose turn to die was next.

The Carters prepared themselves, followed their three lost children halfway into the next world. Carter began to speak of his burial plans. He would make his own coffin and "use it for a Chest til its Proper use shall be required," this proper use consisting of a burial underneath a "shady Tree," where he imagined himself "undisturbed," sleeping "in peace & obscurity," no marker designating the grave site. He imagined death like a "retirement," a word that also began to pepper his jokes and his reflections. He bragged that he could compose his will in five minutes. He even knew how he wanted to die: a fever that would take two days, "convince him that it would be fatal," and "gradually increase till it affected a Dissolution."

Listening to him describe it, one imagines that he believed he could will the nature of his passing, or order it from London. But Frances Carter, too, obsessed about mortality, and spoke freely of it in witty, elliptical phrases that barely contained their nightmarish origins in the child mortality that had struck her family. In warm weather, she would say, "This hot weather takes away all my life." On long walks, she claimed that life would be too "tedious to endure" if it wasn't for the aesthetic pleasures afforded by "Groves, Fields, or Meadows." On one dinner in May, the topic of the "Souls of Women" was raised, and she commented—with layers of irony too thick to sift through—that she had heard that women have no souls. And she too planned her own burial. Unlike her husband, she wanted a marker. In an odd twist upon his desire for anonymity, however, she wanted the name "Ann Tasker Carter" etched upon it—a cross between her mother's name, her own name, and the name of one of her daughters,

as if she had momentarily forgotten who she was, or whom she was bury-
ing.

But even the youngest Carters talked about death like it was imminent.
In his little school, Fithian noted, it was "a Subject for continual Specu-
lation." When Frances Carter commented that she refused to leave Williamsburg for Nomony until her husband built her a park and stocked it,
her daughter Priscilla interrupted her, laughing, and said, "Why Mama,
you plan and talk of these things as though you should never die." Cousin
Harry Willis, who attended Fithian's classes, was even bolder: he "signified
a Wish that his turn may be next." Fithian parried this wonderfully, telling
Harry he imagined he must be ready for "the business of the other world,"
since he wasn't ready for the business of this one. But Fithian, who had just
lost his parents, was at home here, his black suit and melancholy a perfect
match for this family so metaphorically dressed in mourning. "Last year,"
he told himself, "I had not the most remote expectation of being here in
Virginia! Perhaps by the next I shall have made a longer and more important Remove, from this to the World of Spirits."

Odd, ironic deaths were everywhere in the air. Nearby farmers were
dying suddenly, leaving behind Shakespearean parting words like *"Now I
must die."* Unlike debt or revolution, however, there was nothing Robert
Carter could really do about this, nothing his money or name could do to
protect his hold on this planet. Throughout the summers of 1773 and 1774,
Virginia pulsated: there were July nights where his family sat in the parlor
sweltering, and July nights where they sat shivering. No one stopped
throwing those elaborate balls, even if they produced as much influenza as
pleasure, and nothing stopped his defiant children from wanting to go to
them. Gradually, though only briefly, his children ceased dying, and he
grew inured to the persistent sight of spots on their faces, sudden evacua-
tions of blood, fainting spells. But the empire he governed, which was otherwise so opulent and so rapturously well maintained, was also a broken,
otherworldly, death-obsessed place, and he was having a hard time pretending otherwise. One summer day, with two daughters (Priscilla and
Harriot) suffering from an "eruptive Fever," one son (John Tasker) also
feverish, and Fithian complaining of being in "such Ferment to Day that I
cannot sit nor Walk," Mrs. Carter observed that the air had the feel of November, and proposed that a fire be lit. "There is not a single Person on this
whole Continent," Carter answered, with the simultaneously rational and

surreal air that characterized so many of his deepest thoughts, "who is not to day, in a greater or less Degree affected with a Fever!"

4

As the summer of 1773 turned into autumn, events moved quickly across the Eastern Seaboard, and the vague array of political, economic, and cultural resentments that roiled places such as Williamsburg began to coalesce into an irresistible urging among many Americans to leave the British empire. In December 1773, a well-organized mob dressed perfunctorily as Mohawks, protesting a new tax, dumped ninety thousand pounds of imported tea into Boston Harbor. In response to the Boston Tea Party, the British Parliament passed four Coercive Acts, which gave the royal governor and British Army broad, punitive control over the Massachusetts legislature, as well as town meetings, trials, and private property. In New York, Sons of Liberty responded with their own tea party. In Virginia, the House of Burgesses, led by Richard Henry Lee, called for a day of fasting and prayer in solidarity with their Bostonian brothers, half expecting that Lord Dunmore would respond angrily, as he subsequently did, shutting down the House of Burgesses on May 26. Gathering in the Apollo Room of Raleigh's Tavern (for neither the first nor the last time) in Williamsburg on the next day, eighty-nine burgesses signed an "association" stating their shared opposition to a "Determined system . . . formed and pressed for reducing the inhabitants of British America to slavery," and they subsequently issued a call for a continental congress. In August, this association reconvened, appointed a delegation for that congress (Washington, Peyton Randolph, Richard Bland, Henry Lee, Edmund Pendleton, and Benjamin Harrison, another one of King Carter's grandsons), and began contemplating what measures they might take to embargo commerce between Virginia and England.

At Nomony, however, the warning sounds of Revolution were distant and muffled. It was an age of mixed messages, of detachments and enthusiasms. Carter referred to his new life as a "retirement," but he only meant that he had retired from politics; he exchanged public life for a commitment to what he excitedly called "trade." He sent out letters to new merchants, renewed correspondences with the agents who managed his rented lands, dredged swamps to improve navigation around Nomony. He built a granary and a bakery, advertised for a baker and miller, and looked all over for wheat, vast amounts of it, some to trade, some to bake: "I purpose to manufacture about Eight Thousand bushels of James river Wheat at my mills here," he told David Patterson in 1773.

The depression that had begun in the middle of 1772 had not lifted by 1774, however, and Carter was seeing its effects in a whole new light. From Williamsburg, it was easier to believe that his holdings were in order, that economic disruptions touched others but not him. He had never shown any great attachment, for instance, to the signature crop of Virginia, tobacco, which still ruled the pride of many large planters, despite its instability as a cash crop. Carter had switched many of his lands from tobacco to wheat in the two decades prior to the Revolution, on roughly the same schedule as George Washington, the founder most conspicuously interested in crop diversification as a political act. Like other Northern Neck planters, he had built his own textile mill as well, and was producing cloth for market in the early 1770s. Unlike other Virginia planters, however, Carter had industrialized his empire in dramatic fashion, not only purchasing the Taskers' share of the Baltimore Iron Works but also shipping tons of bar and pig iron up and down the Chesapeake on a sloop he named after his daughter Harriot. When the tobacco market convulsed in the early 1770s, further troubling many free Virginians, Carter remained serene, even more confident of his fortune than he had been a decade before.

Once he arrived at Nomony, however, he rapidly understood that he had been missing something crucial. He was amazed at how few of his tenants were paying their rent, asking one of his agents, John Hough, for tenant records dating back to the 1760s. He didn't know the price of anything, and requests for market details began to perform ceremonial functions in his letters, like salutations:

> What is the Current price of Bar-iron pr Ton
> What is the Current price of Pig-iron p Ton

he asked Clement Brooke at the Iron Works in November 1773.

He grew short, frustrated, the sourness of the economic climate finally catching up to him. He saw deceit infecting his dealings with other gentlemen, even within his family: "there has been a fraud Comitted in this

Affair," he told Robert Prentis, describing a draft of money that his uncle Daniel Dulany claimed he never received, "Be Attentive and Mark well his Expressions." Among his tenants, he saw interlopers who stole his live-stock, broke up his fences for firewood, and left their rents years in arrears. In March 1773, he instructed his steward William Taylor to paint numbers on the sides of his oxen at his Coles Point plantation. In November, he wrote a furious note to Andrew Reid, protesting Reid's construction of a fish dam across the Nomony River: "You know that every work tending to obstruct Navigation up to my mill is hurtful to me," he lamented.

Few people even responded to Carter's entreaties, however. Hough never answered his requests for written records, and Carter boiled: "I do not Recollect that even one idle, impertinent-blamable Tenant has been driven off my land, Since you acted for me," he told him in June of 1774. Meanwhile, he grew wheat-obsessed: "I must have wheat," he pleaded with Prentis in August. Lacking either wheat or cash, but convinced that a market existed for whatever he produced, Carter borrowed the money, and soon realized the mistake he had made. He was now a true debtor, caught in the crosshairs of dependency like men with only ordinary fortunes: "I have bought large quantities of wheat lately," he told Christopher Lowndes, his brother-in-law, in trying to collect an old debt of 126 pounds, "which purchase, compels me to call on severall persons to make speedy pay-ments." Subsequently, he got his bakery up and running, but found him-self playing the role of salesman, dependent not merely upon the men to whom he owed money but also to the abstraction of the marketplace, which he now supplicated like a street vendor. "I have Bread and Flower to sell, here," he told one correspondent. "The very best brown bread," he told another.

It was another language Carter would never quite acquire. He could not negotiate with those he considered beneath him, but he didn't know what else to do: dealing for Indian corn in February 1773, he ended a letter to Williamson Ball without completing a sentence that began: "If you insist on One Shilling more than the selling price here," unable to imagine any-thing but his price, and equally unable to imagine what the next step might be should Ball refuse his price. Astounded that his credit was shaken, he put his prestige on the line, and printed his own money, curt little "Paral-lelogram[s]" that "entitle(d) the Bearer hereof to receive Bills of Exchange, payable in <u>London</u>, or <u>Gold</u> and <u>Silver</u>." He did not stop buying luxuries, but his tastes shifted slightly downmarket, to cheddar cheeses, mahogany bed frames, and Fithian. And he was once again conscious of his debt to British factors now: "I have been constrained lately to draw largely on my Correspondents in Great Britain to satisfy Demands against, on Account of Wheat." His letters acquired the aggrieved and unsympathetic tone of the chronically unsatisfied landlord. He made tart jokes about the inadequacies of hired help: "That Sett of Mechanicks, have rated their Labour so Highly, that one days work will enable them to idle 5 days." And the rhythmic salutations that inquired about market conditions bloomed into poems about crop failure:

> The Crop of Wheat is not cut—
> Not one Straw of the Crop of Rye is cut
> The Corn is foul—
> By Mannagement very blamable neither Wheat
> nor Rye is made at Old-Ordinary-Quarter this year,
> it is then very presumable that the Crop of Corn and
> Tobacco, there, are suffering . . .

Even as the economy of the Northern Neck slid into prewar confusion, however, Carter tried to maintain his sense of gentlemanly moderation. He rarely sued and rarely evicted: "I had rather be generous than ridged," he told Rowland and Hunt of London. He did not raise rents, and accepted diverse forms of currency and barter even when other wealthy landowners on the Northern Neck, men such as Richard Henry Lee, compelled their tenants to produce gold or silver specie to pay their rent. He honed his philanthropy, trying to find the voice that balanced his newfound sense of financial urgency with his aristocratic sense of moral obligation to the poor: when a widow named Mary Johnson asked him to forgive her debts, he told William Carr to "for bear," unless there were other lenders who would foreclose on her—in which case he instructed Carr to tell Johnson to auction off her possessions, and he would buy the share that paid off her debts to him, and then return them to her.

He also watched, warily, as poor whites tried to protect their own economic security by taking from neighboring blacks the few privileges they possessed. When his overseers combined the allotments of grain allowed to slaves and livestock, underfeeding slaves so that cattle might grow fat,

Carter restructured the allotments. When a tenant asked if he could rent the land Carter had reserved for the use of his slaves, Carter refused, stating that they had little enough land already.

Mostly, however, he kept his own counsel, "pleased with taciturnity," as he told Frances. He monitored the political battles, subscribing to the *Pennsylvania Gazette* so he could follow the Continental Congress, and ordering copies of the *Parliamentary Register* and the *Journals of the House of Burgesses:* "I read all the late political performances that come in my way," he told the merchant John Hyndman in London. When the Continental Congress, in October 1774, passed an association banning imports and exports between America and England, he ordered six copies. When the day of fasting and prayer was announced, however, Carter forbade any member of his family from fasting or going to church. Fithian observed that "by this . . . I conclude he is a courtier," but wished that the councillor would actually say something that could tell the tutor which side he was on. Others came to the same nervous conclusion: when a visiting inspector sitting at the Carters' table decided to make a toast, he looked around nervously, sized up the family, and made a halting salute to the king, not the patriots.

He needn't have worried: the Carters were amiable to guests who toasted the Sons of Liberty, or the king, or both sides. Such cautious neutrality was common even among patriots: Jefferson, in 1775, still spoke favorably, though privately, of "dependance on Great Britain, properly limited." To Carter, this was the only way he could be an honest man. He had left Williamsburg because of politics, after all, seeing dissolution where others saw possibilities, the unraveling of the social order interwoven with personal grief. But now he was almost paralyzed, still believing that a "moderate" solution was inevitable as long as powerful men in both crown and colony kept their heads. One week after the Virginia Convention called for a ban on tobacco exports in August 1774, for instance, Carter told an employee that "to persevere in growing tobacco . . . I apprehend Would be thought a mark of folly." If the gesture displayed solidarity with his rebel friends, however, Carter withheld his motives: was the "folly" betraying Revolutionary ideals, or economic common sense, or was it revealing himself as a Tory sympathizer by planting what no good American should be planting, and risking a local backlash that included tarring and feathering for merchants who refused to sever their British ties?

By the end of 1774, though, Carter chose a side. He distributed his six copies of the Continental Association to his agents, instructing them to honor their terms to the letter: "I hope and expect that every individual among us will be influenced accordingly," he told William Mathis on November 14, 1774. And once the Continental Association formalized its ban on exports and imports, Carter swung his plantations into new configurations, turning a tobacco storehouse into a textile factory, training slaves for seamstress work, and diversifying his crops even further, calling for vast fields of flax and hemp to be planted and even moving toward cotton production, all steps designed to produce economic autonomy from British interests for himself and his neighbors and to be completed on a schedule vastly more enthusiastic in support of that cause than most of his neighbors could manage.

The mixed messages, in other words, were no longer mixed. Throughout summer and fall of 1774, the Carters honored the continental boycott on imported tea, drinking mostly coffee. On one evening in September 1774, Frances Carter, clearly playing, brought her husband a cup of tea. Carter smelled it, took a sip, looked at it, said "What's this," and tossed out the contents. There was no audience to see this except Fithian, and no caution slowing Carter's instinct. By 1774, Robert Carter was a patriot. He just didn't want anyone to notice.

5

Meanwhile, his slaves toiled. Like many slaves—and many non-slaves—their bodies were battlefields: sprains, bruises, even broken bones were usually treated with more work, until vertebrae fused, fingers became unusable, enduring arthritis grew where the untreated contusion began. The diversification of Carter's crops was no courtesy to them: it simply meant that they could now work on one crop while another grew to harvest.

Tobacco was the hardest crop to grow: In the spring, slaves made seedbeds, planting the minuscule seeds in the wettest possible ground. In late spring and early summer, they painstakingly weeded these beds, until late May and June, when they built in the fields little mounds about three feet from each other, and placed the fledgling plants in these mounds. This was work best done in the rain, by piling a small hill of mud around one's leg, then carefully lifting that leg and placing the seedling within the hole that remained, roughly sixty times an hour, for fifteen hours a day, if Robert Carter's slaves kept pace with George Washington's. For the rest of the summer, they tilled and weeded, checked the plants constantly for worms, cut off the tops of the plants to prevent the flowering that discouraged new leaves, and cut off the shoots that did the same.

Growing hemp was easier, until the hemp was harvested: then slaves drenched the hemp in water, allowing it to decay, then left out the plant to dry, after which they painstakingly beat and combed the stalks, and then beat and combed them again, and again, until the filaments loosened. When Carter switched more of his land to wheat, on the other hand, the slaves must have regarded the transition as a kind of blessing. The overseers still sent them out to work in terrible weather—in this case, the fierce heat of an early July in Virginia—but all they needed to do was cut the wheat, if they were men, or gather it, if they were women and children, and thresh it, which a horse could do simply by walking on it. And all each one of Robert Carter's slaves needed to cut and thresh every day, if he kept pace with Thomas Jefferson's, was three acres.

After the wheat was harvested, the slaves returned to the tobacco plants. They cut them down and left them out in the field to dry, and when they were dry enough, they brought them to a tobacco warehouse to be hung up to dry some more and then pressed into the hogsheads. Meanwhile, there were cart men, and coachmen, and seamstresses, brick-makers, sailors, blacksmiths, and house-servants. There were four "well instructed" slaves who waited on guests at fine dinners, dressed in red and white lace and blue broadcloth, like good British servants. There were four more slaves to act as oarsmen, pushing the Carters' longboat down Nomony Creek and along the Potomac, sometimes for twenty or thirty miles. There were two butchers, James and Tom. There was Tom Henry, just turned twenty, good with horses and trusted enough to be promoted from hostler to coachman.

Some slaves were experts with livestock; others knew how to keep children entertained. Others provided "a good breast of milk" to the Carter infants, or were leased out to nurse the newly born babies of neighboring farmers. Many performed more than one job: Samuel Harrison was Carter's valet, and had been since Williamsburg, but he also worked as a doctor, treating agues and fevers as they swept through the slave quarters, killing his own young son at the tail end of the boiling summer of 1774. Nelson, who kept Fithian's fires tended and played with the older boys when no one else wanted, was sent to Williamsburg in 1774 to train as a barber. Prince Johnston, a thirty-year-old man for whom Carter bragged that he would not take "500 pounds ready cash," made shoes as well as bricks, and gathered corn when the field gangs were shorthanded.

In the bakery, five or six slaves operated Carter's enormous ovens, which were little more than holes knocked into thick stone walls: they set the fires, waited for the fires to die, swept the ashes into a ring, placed the dough inside the ring, and then baked, over and over. In the blacksmith's cabin, slaves took fine slivers of molten hot iron, fixed them within vises, and gave each sliver four or five supple blows with a hammer until the shape of a nail emerged, a new nail every twenty seconds when they worked fast. Up in Baltimore, meanwhile, six of Carter's slaves—part of his contractual agreement with the Iron Works—chopped wood, carted it to the forge, and kept the fires running, sometimes through the night. It was hard work, under close observation, and Carter saved it for slaves he could not otherwise control.

Carter counted on the expertise of his slaves, and even admired it. They were his guides and his mailmen. They reported thefts, especially when they could implicate an overseer: George Hull, according to a report from "Brutus" to Carter in the fall of 1773, is fattening his hogs on your grain, and stealing your "pine Planks" as well. They did "overwork": when his dam threatened to burst in September 1774, Carter offered rum and a shilling to any slave who would work on Sunday to secure it. In exchange, Carter gave them measured servings of independence. He allowed them to supervise his enterprises: "Solomon Miller," who was also "Solomon Dixon," oversaw Carter's valuable double mill. He let them build their own quarters, which saved him money and also gave them freedom to design their own homes. He rarely whipped them, or allowed them to be whipped. And he favored their versions of events: when a gelding died in September 1773, Carter's white employee William Taylor and his black "Servant Thomas" blamed each other, and Carter did not even bother to write down Taylor's account, preferring instead to report what "Thomas believes." A supplicant slave entering the main passage of Nomony had to kneel slowly and carefully before Carter, clasp his hands together as if in prayer, and then begin to speak to the master. But the slave often got his way—especially if his criticism was directed toward a third party, some agent, small farmer, or overseer, as it usually was.

Outside the great house, Carter's slaves had as much freedom as any in Virginia. They married one another for love, trained their children for their own occupations: Natt Single inherited the role of livestock tender from his father. One slave father managed to enroll his son in Fithian's little "school" (although it is doubtful he was given enough free time to learn much). Individual slaves sometimes spoke boldly: when Fithian told Thomas "Dadda" Gumby that he did not go to church one Sunday because it was "too hot," Gumby scolded the divinity student until Fithian's conscience burned: "I shall affront you, Master," Gumby said carefully. "Too hot to serve the Lord!" But when Fithian transcribed onto paper Gumby's verbal account of his family tree, the slave insisted on providing the tutor with fresh eggs, apples, and potatoes.

Most slaves needed every extra hen and every moment of independence Carter allowed in order to survive, however. The peck of corn and pound of meat that Carter provided his slaves each week was just slightly on the generous side of the spectrum: slaves could live on a heaping peck, but not a well-measured, sifted one, and Carter's were heaping. Carter's journals also listed the meat provided to his slaves as "pork." If he was like other planters, he gave them the head of the pig, the feet, the entrails—which, if they were like other slaves, they placed in the iron pots that were often one of their few possessions and let simmer all day while they worked, so they had small viscous stews ready by sundown, eaten alongside haphazard servings of milk, eggs, corn, or whatever else was surplus that particular night. In all likelihood, they ate alone, when they could, while others worked, and slept fitfully, at best, on mattresses made of straw or on hard dirt floors: a century later, Booker T. Washington would observe that he never slept in a bed until the Emancipation Proclamation.

Inside the great house, one would scarcely believe that the slaves even existed, or that manual labor was to be done. Books were everywhere: Carter ordered Bibles by the six dozen. There were books strewn across the sofa in the "long room." And everyone was expected to read. Carter offered to bet that his wife had read more than the local minister, and the taunt had as much to do with respect for her as it did with contempt for the parson. Carter bought sheafs of paper, copybooks, grammars, and at least ten or fifteen books every time he contacted a merchant. He took particular notice when one of his daughters bested one of his sons at some scholastic task—as often happened. If it was pride in their achievement, he didn't say, but he was spending a great deal more time riding out with his daughters than his sons, no surprise given the fact that he had just lost three daughters.

Probably, though, it wasn't pride: he only really cared about goading the boys, making a sharp point to Robert Bladen when Priscilla beat him at arithmetic. He kept them guessing, off balance. He told them that he wasn't going to give his estate to the firstborn, and he wasn't going to divide it equally, but he was going to endow it to the one son who would be most capable in business. Or to the one son who was going to best serve the public good. Or to the one son who did whatever Robert Carter, on that particular day, believed to be the essence of gentlemanliness.

It was his paternal duty to do so. As Fithian said, the apex of good child-rearing was shame and criticism.

The days were aimless and sober. Some mornings, he wrote six or seven letters, or copied out a long affidavit in one of his many lawsuits, using a small folding writing desk made of dark brown oak covered with felt, a hinge across the middle forcing him to plant his pen with care, a hollow on the upper-right-hand corner of the desk for an inkwell. The rite was simple. Crush ink (which was delivered in small, solid blocks, when not home-made) into water and perhaps vinegar. Dip pen, and compose, or call for an agent or son to take the letter. Write and dip pen, write and dip pen. Pull, don't push, and with a light touch, barely connecting the letters. The pen was everything: one cherished a good quill, kept it clean, kept the long cut from drying and splitting. With a good quill, one could write twenty-five words without stopping, and without smudging.

Write a clean copy, if revision was required, or if the pen had smudged. Write an extra copy (Jefferson had a machine for this that he called his polygraph), and place the copy within a broad, bound "letterbook" for safe-keeping. Fold the letter, heat the wax, press the seal containing the initials "R C" with the flourish. Scan the latest periodicals for items of interest, and when one is found, copy it out, sometimes into a letter, sometimes into the pages of the letter book itself, more often than not without attribution, making the letter book a commonplace book as well. At night, there was another book, a "daybook," in which two or three important details of the preceding day might be recorded: the number of men in the "gang" that built a fence; the price of a gallon of rum offered by a traveling salesman.

He transcribed music. He composed enlightened thoughts: mastery of

English grammar was the highest of scholarly pursuits. The social compact between employer and employee was benign and conducive of order. The best months of the year were October, November, and December. His library helped him compose these thoughts, and more. Like most planters, he was miles from any urban center, and almost every kind of specialized professional assistance—medical, legal, agricultural—was scarce. For the Aristotelian moments, he stocked his library with ancient Latin and Roman works, and enough scholarly tomes to supply a small law library, seminary, or government office. But he also bought the eighteenth-century equivalent of how-to books, a vital resource for the isolated country patriarch, ranging from *The Compleat French Master for Ladies and Gentlemen* to *Mrs. Glasse's Cookery* to Jacques Daran's *On the Disorders of the Urethra.* He bought geographies and astronomies, treatises on civil architecture, thesauruses and dictionaries. He bought the poems of John Donne and Alexander Pope, and collected Molière, Milton, Newton, Montesquieu, Congreve, Longinus, and Machiavelli. He owned a copy of the *Canterbury Tales,* and another of the *Odyssey.* He owned reams of sheet music. He owned a copy of the Marquis d'Argens's *Jewish Spy.* He had a set of Locke's works that he had borrowed from the Council's library and had forgotten to return.

It would have been his greatest pride, no doubt, to have a scholar for a son. But Fithian was the closest he had, and Fithian was not going to stay one week longer than necessary. Further, Nomony was not turning out to be the fine, mannerly British import that he had half hoped it would be, either. Mrs. Carter, it was true, was still a beauty and a wit. She traveled as much as he did, often alone, coerced Fithian out the door for walks in the garden, and kept up her share (and often, her husband's share) of their social obligations. She passed free hours in the library among her husband's books, and her tastes in literature were not light: she knew government, and she knew religion. And despite the fact that she was nearing forty and her husband was nearing fifty, and that she was often sick (her symptom was fever), she bore another child, Sarah Fairfax, in April 1773.

The move to Westmoreland County had not brought her any particular comfort, however. She was quite clearly bored on the plantation, complaining with justification that the men in her family were dour and private. But she was not interested in the frivolity of rural life, either. Like her husband, she left the balls early, and not always when he did. Unlike her husband, though, she had lived most of her life in cities, and there was something missing for her at Nomony—not enough urban flavor, not enough good conversationalists. Eventually, the rhythms of rural life, the rhythms of childbirth, the fevers, the dying children, all these dispirited her. More and more, she grew to fear the worst. When Ben got sick—with Ben, it was pains in the chest, "uneasiness," and fever—she grew anxious, and forced him back into the great house, where she could watch him. When she felt pain in her own chest, she threw out the stays in her dress and walked the house uncorseted, worried that she had cancer.

And each time a thunderstorm passed Nomony—and, in the summer months, great thunderstorms might pass Nomony several times in a week, "incessant, bright, and awful," as Fithian noted—she experienced something approaching existential grief. As the winds blew and the sky turned gray, her conversation grew quiet, and she would be unable to either serve or eat or drink: "Ben child," she would tell her son, if he was in the room, "take my seat & fill out the Coffee." As the storm struck, and her husband watched unmoved, she would excuse herself and shut herself in her room for the duration of the storm, sometimes longer, sometimes missing supper.

If it was night, her fear was even more uncontrollable. On September 2, 1774, she spent the entire night walking through the house, "without *rest* or *pleasure*," as thunder and lightning struck the Northern Neck. She ordered the girls' beds "removed as far as possible from the Chimneys," but that didn't comfort her. Then she ordered lights placed in the house's main passage, but that didn't help, either. "I wandered through the house silent & lonely like a disturbed Ghost," she told the table at breakfast, as if they hadn't noticed.

As bad as the storms might be, however, they cleared the air, and she often insisted on exercise or good conversations in their aftermath. Fithian found her extremely appealing at these moments, but he didn't know his own mind on the subject: "I love to see her in such distress," he told himself, but when he gave the emotion its official airing, it somehow transformed into affection for her "Temper, Oconomy, & whole management." The daughters, unquestionably, took after her. Like her, like most Carter women, they were bright and well educated. But they acquired, as well, their mother's restlessness. Fanny might take off her stockings in public, the kind of amiable adolescent undressing reserved for male children. Priscilla would ignore Fithian for days if she perceived a slight—if he accidentally brushed her head in a way she might interpret as a slap, like the slaps of the dance master when she missed a step (that cumbersome valentine, evidently, had not done its office). And one July afternoon in 1774, Nancy shaved off her eyebrows. It was a meaningful gesture: a good pair of eyebrows was what distinguished a beautiful woman from a plain one on the Northern Neck. Nancy denied doing it: she claimed instead that "some mischievous person has done it when She was sleeping."

The boys, however, were far wilder. Carter said that he hadn't made up his mind over which son he would favor, but Ben had the patrilineal advantages, and was regarded as the smartest of the sons as well. He complained frequently of sickness, and Robert Carter didn't entirely believe him: he joked that the boy was a "valetudinarian," and when Ben took bed rest, wondered if he had "retired from the World." Carter had good reason to suspect that Ben was insincere, or confused: he spent many of his nights somewhere other than his bed in the schoolhouse, even on the nights when he was ill. Eventually, Frances Carter insisted that he move back into the great house: she wanted to keep track of him, make sure he took his medicine and stayed in bed. And even then, he didn't: he still disappeared, his fevers and "uneasiness" insufficient deterrence to prevent him from seeking pleasure elsewhere.

But where did Ben go? The question stirred Nomony. He rode off on his horse in the evening, and returned in the morning on foot, the horse having disappeared, and the rumors were that he spent the night among the slave cabins or locked in the stable for hours with Sukey, a sixteen-year-old house slave that Fithian described as a "young likely Negro Girl maid." He responded to his father's obsession with harpsichord and pianoforte (and harmonica, guitar, organ, and German flute) with his own musical obsession: when the schoolhouse was closed for the evening, and the family had retired, Ben and Cousin Harry gathered with slaves in the classroom to play fiddle and banjo, and dance deep into the morning. Carter, who forbade slaves from entering the great house without permission, turned a blind eye to these dances: it was, in fact, Fithian who was startled by them, and who felt compelled to punish for them.

Sometimes, Ben grew even bolder. On the night of September 5, 1774, a commotion awoke the household. Sukey, this time, told the story, before it could be told about her. She awoke in the middle of the night and felt something brushing against her side. It was a man, Sukey said, or something that took the shape of a man, because it wore breeches. This was, of course, taboo—Carter kept the windows and doors of the "Nursery" locked at night to avoid precisely this kind of trespass. Sukey cried out, and the "Man" or "Spirit"—at this point, the house slaves providing witness argued that no human could have breached the locks—tickled her and said *"whish whish."* Sukey left her bed and went to Sally, the housekeeper, while the man, or spirit, rose, stamped its feet, shook the bed frame, and went downstairs. Immediately, Sally went to Ben Carter, and he led an investigation that showed that a series of doors and windows were left open. At first, suspicion alighted on "one of the warm-blooded, well fed young Negroes, trying for the company of buxom *Sukey.*" Carter was outraged, and the next morning, he threatened to "cause to be hanged" any stranger of any color found inside the house at night.

Within several days, however, everyone seemed to understand that it had been Ben, and no one wanted to talk about it. His crude, adolescent stratagem fooled no one, and threatened no one. There were white boys like him throughout Virginia, who preferred the music of slaves to the music of European composers. There were men, as well: Thomas Jefferson's brother Randolph often ran off to the slave cabins to "play the fiddle and dance half the night," as one Monticello slave recalled. Robert Carter himself had his "Man" play the fiddle at entertainments. What his son did in the schoolhouse was not a shock, and what he did in the nursery was not a surprise. Sally, with whom Ben often breakfasted instead of eating with his own family, clearly understood it: there was wisdom in her decision to go to Ben and ask him to investigate the trespass, a way of absolving and blaming him at the same time. Sukey understood it, too, as did the other house slaves: there was wisdom, as well, in blaming a spirit, which was vastly safer than actually blaming anyone who lived and breathed.

Carter understood, too. He probably did not personally exploit his slaves sexually. Slaves never engaged his passions, and Frances clearly did. Faced with his own son's sexual exploits, however, he was satisfied with an investigation that convicted nobody. In all likelihood, all he wanted Ben to know was that there were things he could not do in the great house that he could do elsewhere. That same week, the Northern Neck was disrupted by the news that three slaves had entered the bedroom of their master, a man named Sorrels, and were preparing to murder him, when suddenly he awoke and dispersed them with a rifle. All Ben had done, in contrast, was use the black community of Nomony for his own pleasure. He had not made any trouble the family could not manage.

There was another son, though, who did. Robert Bladen Carter was skinny, restless, and idle, although he had the best penmanship in his family, which he demonstrated by filling the margins of his grammar with the names of local belles. He cut school, rode his horse too hard, stripped off his clothes to go swimming regardless of the occasion or the company. He slandered, making claims of sexual transgress and deceit, sometimes in front of company. He beat his sisters, and probably the servants. He disappeared for days at a time: he showed up unannounced at Landon Carter's Sabine Hall one day, and Landon wondered if anyone was even keeping track of the boy anymore.

They were: he was Cain to Ben's Abel. The family told a story about him, and how, as a child, he had insisted on sleeping with a dog in his bed. The story stuck to him like a talisman, as did Ben's insistence that there was a biblical taboo against such behavior, and that Bob, only fifteen, was already damned. Unlike Ben, Bob Carter was not sexually exploitative: he spread the word about what Ben was doing, shocked (and perhaps a little jealous) that Ben was getting away with it. Similarly, he was indifferent to the appeal of the fiddle and banjo at night: if he ever attended those night-time dances, he was never caught there. Bob's instinct, rather, was incoherently, adolescently political. Over and over, he simply committed raw, pure acts of rebellion, turning the world upside down, too easily "pleased with the Society of persons much below his Family, and Estate." Unlike Ben, however, he was punished brutally for it. And yet he couldn't stop.

Fithian claimed that there were a "thousand" examples to illustrate Bob's "particular Taste." When a visitor to the plantation asked where the master of the house could be found, Bob Carter pointed to his father's clerk; when the visitor asked where the master's clerk could be found, Bob pointed to his father. One cold, rainy night in March, a drunken white stranger knocked on the door of Nomony and asked in a belligerent voice for shelter. Robert Carter offered him the kitchen. After the family retired, however, Bob moved the man into the schoolhouse, brought in a "Negro Fellow, his Papas Postilion," and spent the night sleeping between the two underneath a single blanket.

Perhaps most amazing, however, was his affinity for the poetry of Phillis Wheatley, the Bostonian slave whose erudite poetry had caused a sensation, shattering many pro-slavery arguments degrading the intelligence of African-Americans. On one evening in March 1774, Fithian dispassionately read reviews of her work aloud to Bob Carter. It was no surprise that Fithian, an antislavery Presbyterian, was interested in Wheatley. What was more striking, however, was that Bob was rapt: Fithian described him in "astonishment." Bob told Fithian he wanted "to see her." Ordinarily disinterested in *his* own education, he began to ask Fithian questions about Wheatley's "Latin" and "grammer." And then he said something that startled Fithian: "Good God! I wish I was in Heaven!" At first, Fithian may have thought that Bob Carter, like so many of his family, was simply obsessed with his own death. In his journal the following day, however, Fithian copied the climactic couplet from Wheatley's most famous poem of the day, and provided a telling clue about what heaven Bob Carter was conceiving: "Remember, christians," Wheatley wrote, "Negroes, black as Cain/ May be refin'd, & join the Angelic Train."

Fithian had no answers for this: Bob Carter didn't act like other boys on the Northern Neck, and he didn't act like Fithian's antislavery colleagues back in New Jersey. Robert Carter had a solution, however. Sometimes, he liked this son. When he heard that Bob had identified the clerk as the master of Nomony and demoted the master down to clerk, Carter was clearly amused, even if the joke diminished his authority: it spoke to his own self-deprecating humors. Sometimes, however, he loathed this son. His other children received occasional physical punishments when they were disorderly, an occasional slap or a blow to the head. But Bob was horsewhipped again and again. Fithian did it; he didn't want to, but he soon grew used to "horsing" the boy at every opportunity. He was horsed for oversleeping, for being late for class, for being reticent in his schoolwork. And the other Carter children made sure the punishment stuck: they spread the word around the neighborhood that Bob had received this chastisement ordinarily reserved for the coarser classes, doubling Bob's pain with public humiliation.

Neighbors watched with curiosity; the slaves, one suspects, watched with wonder. It was a curious inversion: on other plantations, there were whippings conducted for "shame," but they were usually reserved for servants. But Nomony was different all around. There was no doubt that the opinion of his peers, as recorded by Fithian, was correct: Robert Carter was an unusually "humane" slaveholder. The rate of population growth on his properties, a good raw measure of health among slaves, was roughly twice that found on the average Virginia plantation. They were listed by family, not plantation, in Carter's censuses, when he bothered to compose censuses, and their names tended to be those that slaves chose for one another, not those that masters chose for their slaves: slave sons were often named after slave fathers, for instance. When his slaves asked to keep their families together, Carter routinely responded with sympathy: "Negro Argy of Cancer Plantation requested of me that I would consent to his removal from said Plantation, and to be hired to Mr. Richard Neale of Loudon who has a Negro Woman, his Wife—I do agree. . . ." While his neighbors woke up to armed slaves standing over their beds, or lost barns to suspicious arsons, Carter never once confronted an event of slave violence more serious than a stolen turkey. Instead, his daybooks were laced with examples of cash transactions between himself and his slaves, a practice that the Virginia legislature eventually outlawed, believing that it emboldened slaves to see themselves as agents of their own entrepreneurial destiny.

At the same time, Carter was something other than just a "liberal slaveholder." Most of his actions, such as his refusal to buy or sell slaves and his efforts to maintain slave nuclear families, were the routine, mannered kindnesses of the benign patriarch. All the Great Men did something: Jefferson all but banned physical punishment—"I love industry and abhor severity," he noted in 1805—and he offered extra wages he called "encouragement," "donation," or "gratuity" for extra work. Washington, who ran his plantations with the fierce discipline of a military man, refused to allow any overseer to whip a slave without first receiving his written permission to do so. But Great and Lesser Men also found slaveholding an absorbing occupation: Washington, when not cloistered in his study, would "ride round my farms" from the time he finished breakfast to the time he had "to dress for dinner," watching his slaves labor, even timing them at their tasks, expecting that they would "be at their work as soon as it is light" and "work 'till it is dark." Jefferson calculated the labor patterns on his plantation with fanatical detail in his voluminous farm books: one graph, entitled "Estimate on the actual work of the autumn of 1794," shows him monitoring the scales at his nail factory on a daily basis, and noting how much iron each slave "wasted" to produce one hundred nails.

What made Carter singular, however, was his lack of enthusiasm for the intellectual challenges and, one might say haltingly, the pleasures of being a master. Unlike even liberal slaveholders, for instance, Carter almost never "rode out," because he seemed to barely care what his slaves were doing, and seemed to take no satisfaction—even the scrupulous satisfactions of Washington in this regard—in seeing his position at the peak of the social pyramid confirmed by the visible sweat of toiling Africans, what the early slaveholder William Fitzhugh perilously called "the secret & pleasant enjoyment of your self." And unlike other plantation owners, he merely recorded, not dictated, how much labor his slaves performed—and even then, with no great enthusiasm. Until the war, in fact, his rebellion against the peculiar institution was measured best by the absence of a certain sadistic note that other slaveholders took for granted, the proof that they knew how to handle their slaves and possessed the power to implement what they willed. His uncle Landon, for instance, believed that "every day I discover, the sordidness of a Slave," and laced his diaries with notes such as "I have ordered the wench to be tyed up and severely slashed to keep her care if possible; but I am afraid it will not be long enough remembered." Charles Carroll, the Maryland grandee, advised his son, "Correct but seldom but when you do correct, let not the correction be a trifling one." Henry Laurens, who served after John Hancock as president of the Continental Congress, and who seriously considered freeing his own slaves, frequently recommended their "chastise(ment)," and spoke of unsold slaves as "refuse." It is only gradually that the reader of Carter's massive and languid correspondence begins to realize that his tone toward blacks is dramatically different, that there are one hundred complaints regarding the inconstancy of his white tenants, business associates, and neighbors for every one time he wrote "these outlying Negroes are too unruly." Fithian saw the difference: other slaveholders at the party gathered together to discuss their recipes for the torture of their slaves. Carter, Fithian wrote, left the party early, tight-lipped but imperial, because he would rather "ride to a certain Stump" than join such conversation.

Of course, this neutrality too was a family inheritance: his grandfather pursued sadism as a business practice, not as an avocation, and never hesitated to treat his slaves humanely if it advanced his interests. And such indifference did not necessarily constitute kindness: like Thomas Jefferson, Carter did not order whippings, but he also did little to control the overseers who wielded the whip on distant plantations. Still, the fact that Robert Carter III was so uninterested in the displays of power and violence that provided so many other slaveholders both pleasure and security made it all the more curious that he had his son beaten with such regularity and for such small transgressions—and, most significant, as public humiliation. In young Robin, Robert Carter III saw his own shade, and was desperate to prevent the young man from turning into the rogue that he himself had once been. That prewar summer, however, Bob Carter was also the uncontrollable voice of Carter's own troubled conscience, and that made matters even more complicated.

Only three short years, after all, would pass between the moment when Bob Carter shared a blanket with a white vagrant and a slave and the moment when Robert Carter would take his own leap of faith, turn away from the religion of the planter class, and begin taking communion alongside his tenants and slaves. Perhaps the son was his father's mirror, reflecting back to the older man the radical thoughts he was already having—had been having all along—but was not yet prepared to recognize. One might get a good beating for that. But perhaps the son illuminated the way for the father, crossing the line between indifference toward one's slaves and the anarchic embrace of their cause. That, of course, would be unforgivable. When Bob said that he wished he could be in heaven with Phillis Wheatley, in fact, he said too much: that was Baptist talk, and told anyone who was listening where Bob Carter had been spending his evenings while Ben locked himself in the barn with Sukey. To neighbors, Bob Carter was the signal that there were two Nomonys, and Frances Carter wasn't the only one roaming through the night, looking to rearrange whatever only seemed to work during the daytime. As Robert Carter pondered his sons, pondered his wife, lamented his lost children and his torn country, as he gazed at lightning strikes and plumbed his books, he began to leave signals that he preferred the role of rebel to that of king. But he left no signal, no signal yet, that he too might be preparing to turn night into day.

CHAPTER III

Heavenly Confusion
[1774–1778]

"RC—& his servant Negro Sam—received tokens and they did both Comune."

—ROBERT CARTER,
Religious Notes, March 15, 1778

Even his enemies called him the Wonderful Boy. From the time Lewis Lunsford acquired that nickname at the age of seventeen, he had grown used to the mobs, the pranks, the arrests. It didn't matter: he knew the saving grace of God. When the sheriff of Lancaster County threw him in prison in 1775 for creating a disturbance to public order, he posted a bond, accepted a twelve-month banishment from that county, and preached elsewhere. When a mob broke up his sermon in August 1778, and tore down the stage upon which he spoke, he gathered his followers and renewed the sermon the next day. His indefatigability was legendary. It was said that he once traveled fifty consecutive hours to reach a service on time, and that in order to reach a meeting where he was scheduled to speak, he had once rowed three miles across a river using a garden pail as an oar. If he was scheduled to deliver a sermon in the day, he traveled by night. If he was scheduled to deliver a sermon in the evening, he traveled by day. He spoke in meetinghouses. He spoke in fields. He spoke in barns. He spoke in the rain. He spoke at night, holding a candle aloft to illuminate his face. And he spoke to anyone who would listen.

How could he not? Like the other Baptist preachers who came to Virginia in the 1760s and 1770s—the Regular Baptists who gravitated south through Maryland, and the more rebellious Separate Baptists, New Englanders who came circuitously north from the sandhills of North Carolina—Lunsford had struck a nerve. Men and women often traveled thirty or forty miles to see them speak, and turned up by the hundreds, sometimes by the thousands, despite the fact that no established church recognized their authority and that they sought no church's approval. Unlike the ministers of the Anglican Church, they used their bodies in extraordinary ways, jerking, twisting, as if God possessed them. Their voices were like instruments of a higher calling, as well: their most famous vocal technique was the "holy whine," a high keening that produced spectacular effects. They chanted. They shocked their listeners by addressing them in the second person. And they swore, or at least it seemed like they swore: they said "hell," and "damned," and it sounded like swearing to the genteel men and women who had begun to trickle into crowds otherwise dominated by the poor and the enslaved.

Even among this group, though, Lunsford was something special: one observer said that he was more angel than man, that a light emanated from his face when he spoke of God's love. He was auburn-haired and blue-eyed, wore no beard, and had a way of rebuking people where they hardly felt the rebuke. It was, perhaps, this gentleness of countenance that allowed Lunsford to be the first Baptist minister to crash the aristocratic, Anglican Northern Neck, where a few wealthy families controlled the parish vestries that controlled the churches. King Carter's Christ Church was here, an imposing cross-shaped brick edifice whose pews and pulpit ensured that the poor had to gaze at the minister over the heads of the wealthy, and that everyone together had to gaze upward at the minister as he spoke from an elevated perch.

In contrast, Lunsford founded the first Baptist church in the Northern Neck in 1778 in a home in Lancaster County, and "strolled" the peninsula. When Henry Self, the Revolutionary Army lieutenant who led the mob that stole his stage, asked him by what authority he claimed the right to preach, Lunsford recited the sixteenth article of the Declaration of Rights that the Virginia Convention passed in 1776, James Madison's fierce defense of the "free exercise of religion" suddenly given blood.

Gradually, Lunsford even began to attract a few gentlemen to his faith, despite the fact that his teachings were not kind to aristocracy, nor to their pleasures. He even attracted one convert of such substance and reputation that his very presence within the Baptist Church was almost impossible to imagine: on September 6, 1778, Lunsford baptized Robert Carter III, one of the two or three wealthiest men in the colony, in the waters of Totuskey Creek, in front of four hundred men and women, and then sent him "Home rejoicing on his way."

In turn, Carter became Lunsford's great patron: he donated the land underneath Lunsford's newly constructed church, donated the labor of the carpenter and the wood and bricks, organized the subscription that paid Lunsford's living, and invited the minister and his family to live on his own property. But what Carter meant to Lunsford, and to the Baptists, tran-scended money. At the start of the Revolution, there were roughly ten thousand adherents to the faith in Virginia, and they were overwhelmingly poor, overwhelmingly enslaved, a community of the disenfranchised and the lost: the minister Samuel Davies, in 1757, wrote, "Many of them only seem to desire to be, they know not what: they feel themselves uneasy in their present condition, and therefore desire change."

Carter, however, was a great and loving anomaly, a convert so shocking he altered the shape of the church, and America with it. Perhaps Lunsford recognized the irony: if the Baptist Church offered hope to those who had no hope in this world, as Davies suggested, then what force compelled one such as Carter, one of the richest and most powerful Virginians of all, to find solace in the same faith? Was he a courageous man, dedicated to liberty body and soul? Or was he a desperate one, broken in two by a Revolution he could neither oppose nor celebrate?

2

There had been signs all along that Carter, for a "churchman," was unusu-ally tolerant of dissenting religions. But there was a crucial difference be-tween rational disgust for intolerance and actually joining the dissent, and there was no question which position Carter reflected. Years later, he would say that he believed that religions were mere "political Con-trivance," and the Bible was written by man, for "temporary advantages only." He would identify himself—only retrospectively, of course—as a "Deist," which told his correspondents only what they already knew: that

Carter, alongside men such as Jefferson and George Wythe, had acquired in the 1760s that cerebral worldview that argued God's existence from design and rejected the idea of revealed truth. When Carter disdained the Fast Day in 1774, for instance, he did so not because he opposed the Revolution but because he disliked the notion that God could be employed to lend force to certain political positions. God, Carter believed, was like Carter: he didn't take sides.

It was an enlightened stance. Parson Thomas Smith was a good minister—a frequent dinner guest and an adviser to George Washington—but the services at Cople Parish, like so many across Virginia, had long ago lost whatever spiritual core they might have once possessed. Fithian described Sunday at Smith's church as a three-part affair:

> Before Service giving & receiving letters of business, reading Advertisements, consulting about the price of Tobacco, Grain &c settling either the lineage, Age, or qualities of favourite Horses 2. In the Church at Service, prayers read over in haste, a Sermon seldom under & never over twenty minutes . . . 3. After Service is over three quarters of an hour spent in strolling the Church among the Crowd, in which time you will be invited by several different Gentlemen home with them to dinner.

By contrast, the services performed among the dissenting churches struck liberal gentlemen as sincere if uncouth, and undeserving of violence. James Madison, who, like Fithian, had studied under John Witherspoon at the College of New Jersey, expressed perplexity that both illegal mobs and county officials could mobilize so stridently against men and women whose religious views were essentially "very orthodox." Patrick Henry found edgier rhetoric to describe the injustice: "Did I hear an expression," he was reputed to have asked in a Fredericksburg courthouse, where three Baptist ministers stood charged with creating public disorder, "that these men, whom your worships are about to try for a misdemeanor, are charged with,—with—what? Preaching the gospel of the Son of God?"

From the benign distance offered by Deist beliefs, the problem could be seen as political, a matter of interests and "human advantage," but no great dispute over the nature of God and the world. Thomas Jefferson understood the conflict in those terms, commenting that the dispute arose because "although a majority of our citizens were dissenters . . . a majority of the legislature were churchmen." Reasonable gentlemen did what they could: Henry anonymously paid the jail fees that freed John Weatherford from Chesterfield jail in 1773, and Madison, a new college graduate, returned to his native Orange County in 1771 and immediately began to defend Baptists in courts there. But, as Jefferson argued, there were surprisingly few reasonable gentlemen on this matter. In the late 1760s and early 1770s, Baptist ministers were whipped, jailed for months at a time, cruelly dunked in mock baptisms. Roughs waited outside their meetinghouses with guns, or with playing cards, either to disrupt the services or to deride them by turning their pulpits into whist tables. At times, the persecutions attained a kind of biblical depth. Live snakes and hornets' nests were thrown into meetings. A minister named Elijah Baker was arrested for vagrancy while preaching, then kidnapped from prison and impressed upon a ship bound for Europe. James Ireland, jailed for five months in a prison he labeled in letters as "my Palace in Culpeper," wrote in his memoir that his food was poisoned, that "miscreants" "made their water" in his face as he preached through the prison grate, and that the air in his cell was sometimes made unbreathable by a smoke concoction devised by his jailers out of brimstone and Indian pepper.

Circumventing county officials and parish vestries, the Baptists sought relief from the colony itself: in February and March 1772, Baptist churches in Lunenburg, Mecklenburg, Sussex, and Caroline counties sent petitions to the House of Burgesses "praying that they may be treated with the same kind Indulgence, in religious Matters, as *Quakers, Presbyterians* and other Protestant dissenters enjoy." But the Burgesses were unsympathetic, isolating not only Baptists but also the few legislators—Madison and Jefferson prominent among them—who believed that violence against dissenters was a greater threat to public order than the dissenters themselves. The Burgesses exchanged tales of subversive, illiterate preachers sowing anarchy: "such incredible and extravagant stories were told in the House of the monstrous effects of the Enthusiasm prevalent among the Sectaries," Madison told William Bradford. By April, they responded to the petitions by composing Acts of Toleration that instead questioned the loyalty of the dissenters and stiffened statutes against meetings out of doors, slave participation in services, and worship in the "night time." Dunmore, recognizing that the bill broke British legal precedent on religious freedom that had stood for a century, dismissed the session rather than allowing the Burgesses to act. In response, the Burgesses published the bill in the *Virginia Gazette* on March 26, 1772, hoping that an advertisement of their intent might make their alienation toward religious liberty custom, if not law.

There is little question that Carter stood with Jefferson, Madison, and Henry in the minority. In this matter as well, the springtime months of 1772 were the moment when Robert Carter decided that the political climate in Williamsburg had become intolerable. Characteristically, Carter, unlike Henry or Madison, left little correspondence that would have made clear his position in these sectarian debates. But he returned to Nomony with a profound antipathy for the established clergy: his absences from church, his mocking wager on his wife's reading acumen, his open distaste for the faculty at William and Mary and for Fast Day, all constituted a pattern of derision that bordered on the immoderate. By 1776, he had even resigned from the Cople Parish Vestry, on which he sat alongside Richard Henry Lee and John Augustine Washington, a clear sign that he was dissatisfied with the established church.

By 1776, however, the established church was only one of Carter's concerns. Without a doubt, the start of the American Revolution constituted the great crisis of Robert Carter's life. He was already a haunted and troubled man in the early 1770s, grappling with the loss of several of his children and with the eerie diseases that swept suddenly into (and out of) his family. Every disruption to his family's serenity, in turn, was matched by deepening disorder in the body politic: a depression and debt crisis that created conditions of economic uncertainty, a smallpox epidemic, and a widening and increasingly violent political crisis.

Throughout Virginia, in fact, the certainties upon which gentleman planters had built their sense of themselves were being swept aside. Despite new laws against "outlawry," slave uprisings began to increase in number and scale. Revolutionary documents, Gordon S. Wood writes, persistently "struck out at the power of family and hereditary privilege." Importation bans required the planting and harvesting of new, unfamiliar crops. New monies circulated, their values wildly unstable, while more reliable currencies vanished: "Our new Traders have left us Pennyless, I mean gold & silver Specie," Carter told one correspondent. "As to Continental & Provincial Bills of Credit, there are of those Currencies abundantly." When Dunmore shut down the House of Burgesses in April 1774, the courts of Virginia closed their doors in sympathy, and the mechanism by which debt suits could be brought, and rent collections enforced through legal means, also closed, turning the empires of landed gentlemen such as Carter into squatter's havens.

And when Dunmore seized the gunpowder stores outside Richmond on April 21, 1775, two days after Lexington and Concord, convincing many Virginians that a British attack was imminent, the situation worsened. George Washington, who had already purchased a military uniform, was given command of the new American forces. Patrick Henry, whom Dunmore now regarded as an enemy of the state, traveled everywhere with a consort of armed volunteers by his side. Militias formed across Virginia: some bore government sanction, but in some cases, plain folks, often dressed in defiantly egalitarian uniforms consisting of hunting shirts or leather leggings, simply began to arm themselves and march in groups, waiting for action.

No one knew how far this Revolution would go, or whose power it would overthrow. In a political climate where even celebrated, pro-independence legislators such as George Mason could be almost turned out of the House of Burgesses by suddenly bold small freeholders, however, many of Virginia's gentlemen came to believe that they were the ones being overthrown. For many, tories and patriots both, the tension was unendurable. Mason, for instance, was so disturbed by the disorder in Williamsburg that he retired to his bed for days. Robert Beverley, one of Virginia's wealthiest and most conservative landholders, believed he was witnessing "the World . . . drawing to an End." William Byrd III, who, like Carter, bore heavily the third generation of a legendary Virginian name, put a bullet in his own head on New Year's Day 1777, rather than face irretrievable debts and the inchoate threat to his social position that the Revolution represented.

Even the Council itself, who had ruled the colony only a generation before, lost their poise amid the flood of sentiment that now regarded them as the "meanest creatures and tools" of the prime minister of England. In a broadside distributed across Virginia, they told "the good people of Virginia" that they could "no longer forbear to express our Abhorrence and Detestation of that licentious and ungovernable Spirit that is gone forth, and misleads the once happy People of this Country." By the third paragraph of the statement, however, they began pleading for tolerance for themselves, asking that "they may be considered not as a separate body of Men . . . but in the Light in which they have always regarded themselves, as the watchful Guardians of the Rights of the People, as well as of the Prerogative of the Crown." "They have families," the Council concluded defensively, "and they trust they have Integrity too."

Carter shared the opinion of the Council, lamenting the fact that one could no longer stand for both crown and colony. He still did not share their anxiety, however. He had always loved newspapers, but now his interest in events was so intense that he began buying them for others and distributing them through his own servants, even though his neighbors "murmur[ed], saying that a News Paper was a very uncommon thing among them." He calmly turned his empire to the service of the new militias, fulfilling demands for bread and flour from the army ranging from four hundred to four thousand pounds: "Your orders . . . will be strickly furnished," he told Captain Richard Parker. And he now openly disdained Dunmore: having disappeared from the legislative activities of the Council in 1772, he disappeared from their attendance rolls completely after June 17, 1774, the day that Dunmore demanded their "loyalty" in his political skirmishes with the House of Burgesses.

He even experienced, during the summer and fall of 1775, an unexpected period of political relevancy. In June, as rumors of British marines and sailors in the harbor circulated around Williamsburg, and Dunmore hid offshore from angry and increasingly well-armed Virginians, the Burgesses appointed Carter as the "manager" of a committee to row out to Dunmore and negotiate assurances about the security of the city. That same month, he tried to divert the colony from revolution by composing a speech for the Virginia Assembly featuring a guarded recommendation to accept Lord North's compromise proposal of that spring. Ignoring the political debate, Carter analyzed North's proposal—which offered to stop taxing all colonies that paid their share of the burden for defense and essential government expenses—as a financial matter, and argued that the colonies could accept the offer if North and Parliament calculated equitably. The House of Burgesses, however, disagreed, and sent Jefferson to the Continental Congress with the news that Virginia refused to compromise.

At the same time, Carter clearly felt what Beverley and so many other Americans, both rich and poor, also felt: that he was watching the end of the world. Small events that took on apocalyptic significance began to dot his notebooks. He observed an earthquake (Landon Carter mocked him here, claiming that his nephew felt nothing more than a strong wind). Minor disasters at Nomony acquired portent, and substituted for larger events: he fixated on a "Memorable Rain" that fell on September 2, 1775, making "a breach in the Dam," which grew for months, until by 1776 he called it a "Mighty Casm." Left unmentioned, however, was that the first real armed conflict in Virginia began when that memorable rain left several British vessels foundering near Norfolk.

He watched the Revolution with devouring interest, maintaining his devotion to newspapers and trips down to Williamsburg on public business, noting in his journals and letters the sacking of Norfolk by the British Navy, the call for minutemen brigades in Westmoreland, and the appointments of friends and peers to the Continental Congress and the Revolutionary Army. His daybooks marked the events of the conflict in cryptic epigrams:

> Pamphlet styled Comon Sense . . .
> About twenty sail Vessels part of the British fleet burnt—
> Great mortality among the british fleet while in Potomack River—
> Sun rising—

On his plantations, meanwhile, Carter continued the transformation that had begun only three years before, turning Nomony and its environs into a small manufacturing town and diversifying his crops in accordance with calls for economic independence. In November 1774, he ordered his overseers to switch even more fields to flax and hemp, began planting more Irish potatoes and Indian corn, and traded more actively with his own slaves: chickens and cotton for rum, sugar, cash. He began to build a textile mill and factory, allocated ten young girls to spin thread, hired a local "spinster" named Mary Odriscal to teach them and a local Irishman named Daniel Sullivan to supervise them. Anticipating increasing demand for the products from his grain mill, he hired another Irishman, Hugh Burnie, to teach his ten black carpenters how to make "flower Casks."

But he also acted as if the war were little more than an annoyance to him. He continued to purchase what he considered to be the "real necessaries" of life for his family, which included not only hair curls but also Barbados rum, sugar, and a startling number of "the Best" chamber pots. He arranged for Robert Mitchell, one of his agents, to be excused from active duty, citing an exemption in the enlistment code for "overseers of 4 tithables," and made connections with merchants in Philadelphia to replace the "Social commerce" he was no longer allowed with England. His daybooks began to fill with homespun Enlightenment wisdom, the mark of someone hunkering down: "Olive oil, disolves sulfur and Wax, wch acids will not touch," he told himself. "A single grain of <u>Arsenic</u> will turn a pound of Copper into a beautiful white Mettal like <u>silver</u>—" But he refused to budge much more than what hunkering down required of him. When Mrs. Thomas Nelson told him to move back to Williamsburg from Nomony in order to get out of the way of the invading British Navy, Carter declined, diffidently telling her on October 25, 1775, that "our Situation, here, is full as safe as Williamsburg; therefore we Shall not remove . . ." Instead, he sent Robert Prentis down to Williamsburg, to stuff valuable possessions—including "Furniture & Liquor" and the complete works of Montesquieu—into a strongbox.

Slowly, however, Carter was coming to understand that what had worked for him in 1772 would not work in 1776. There could be no stately withdrawal this time. His mail was being opened, his beloved newspapers misdelivered. His family was an explicit target of patriotic rage: Virginian voters turned out Robert Wormeley Carter, Carter Braxton, and two Charles Carters, and narrowly returned Robert Carter Nicholas on the condition that he cast a vote for independence. Then, on November 7, Dunmore did something he knew would terrify and enrage white Virginians: he freed their slaves and their servants, on the condition that they crossed battle lines and made themselves servants to the British war effort. Dunmore's "emancipation proclamation" (as it is sometimes wryly called), Edward Rutledge wrote, did more "to work an eternal separation between Great Britain and the Colonies,—than any other expedient, which could possibly have been thought of." Virginians loyal to the crown became even more suspect, or became patriots. The Continental Congress authorized the construction of a naval task force to defeat Dunmore before he even got started, sharing George Washington's belief that the royal governor of Virginia would become "the most formidable enemy America has" if he "is not crushed before spring."

As Dunmore and the Revolutionaries dueled, the disintegration of Carter's immediate family fell into lockstep with the oncoming British armies. On September 25, 1775, while British militias surrounded Boston, Carter and his wife lost yet another daughter, Judith, one week after she was born. As George III authorized the seizure of American ships and sailors and his forces burned down Falmouth, Maine, and as the Continental Congress passed regulations on everything from road repair to the wearing of leather, Carter's son Ben's health deteriorated, and his wife, Frances, was spitting up blood. Finally, the war reached Carter. Like Washington, he devoured Tom Paine's *Common Sense* in the early weeks of 1776; but unlike the general, whom Paine moved to argue openly for independence for the first time, Carter's dawning sympathies with American independence bore a more eccentric, egalitarian flavor. He meditated upon the links between his new country and the Jews of the Bible, an idea that resonated more strongly among the vast, unnamed populations of dissenters than all but the most devout members of the Continental Congress: "Kings they had none," Carter observed, "it was held sinful to acknowledge any Being under that title but the Lord of Hosts."

Shortly after, on February 1, 1776, he shaved his head: given that Baptists and Revolutionary War soldiers were the ones who cropped their hair unfashionably short, the sympathies implied in this gesture made it no inconsequential haircut. Most strikingly, he renamed several of his plantations after the signs of the zodiac, a gesture as arcane then as now. Gentlemen might see omens, might privately ponder astrological conditions as they surveyed their empires. But such open tribute to the zodiac was reserved for almanacs, the kinds of books written for laborers and small farmers who bought only one book in a year, and even then—as anyone who read Franklin's *Poor Richard's Almanack* knew—regarded the stars with a measure of ironic distance.

As British armies entered Virginia, and American militias began their work in earnest, Carter searched wildly for a tone to match the extraordinary occasion. He spent March ordering his blacksmiths to make bayonets for the Westmoreland militia, and agonizing over whether or not to allow his children to join: he nullified nephew Harry's enlistment, telling Captain Richard Barnet that the boy was only fifteen and technically his servant, and citing an exemption against any servant who enlisted without "the consent of his master in Writing." But he allowed irresponsible Robert Bladen and invalid Ben to enlist, his sense of civic responsibility too intense to allow him to purchase the substitutes he could easily afford.

Then he spent April and May taunting imperial power: when the maverick American general William Lee occupied the royal governor's palace in Williamsburg in April—a gesture that struck even many within the army as excessively provocative—Carter sent Lee bedsheets and pillowcases to make his stay more commodious. When Lord Fairfax, residing in Maryland, wrote Carter on May 15 to request payment of a debt for 721 pounds, Carter pleaded poverty: "The whole amount of payments which fall into my hands . . . is not sufficient." And then he reminded Fairfax that Dunmore owed Carter 1,070 pounds, more than enough to reimburse Fairfax, if only all lords acted liked lords.

By June, however, as the debate over independence waxed into a concrete debate over the Declaration of Independence, Carter also refused to enlist himself within the nascent American government. When Richard Henry Lee, writing on behalf of the Virginia Convention, invited him to join the new state government in June 1776—in all likelihood, as a member of the Council of State, a variant of the old Council—he thanked Lee, so gratified by political acceptance two decades after his electoral humiliations that he wrote that "this very late Inclination of my Country man, to place me in an exalted office . . . fills my mind with joy." But he declined, telling Lee that his advancing years and a "numerous Family . . . makes the private Station most elligible."

Instead, he traveled to his Coles Point plantation where, on July 13, he made the second (and last) speech of his Revolutionary career—not to the Virginia Assembly this time, but to an assembly of his slaves. Gesturing in the direction of the Potomac, he told his slaves what they already knew: that British warships were sailing nearby, and that they were armed with Lord Dunmore's "black" declaration of the previous November, which offered them freedom if they betrayed their American masters and fled to the British. The British are liars, Carter warned his slaves; they carry smallpox (an accurate claim, given the grotesque mounds of decaying bodies that had been reported at British campsites), and sell runaways into the cruel sugar plantations of the West Indies. He then asked his slaves if they "dislike" their "present Condition of life as do wish to enter into Lord D's service, & trust to the Concequences"; unsurprisingly, they answered, as one, that they "fully intend to serve you our Master and we do now promise to use our whole might & force to execute your Comands." He then made them swear their allegiance to himself and the "13 United provinces," and gave them advice that, doubtless, came straight from his heart: if British troops land and "demand Provisions," he told both slaves and overseers, "refuse money or any other Consideration." Do not fight them, he told them, but flee to the "private places" that he knew they all had. "Advise me at what Place ye are gotten too," he added, able to comprehend that his slaves might want to escape, but unable, as yet, to imagine that his slaves might want to escape from *him*.

At times, he was the old Carter, his aristocratic obliviousness to the spirit of '76 so maladroit as to be almost marvelous. In August, two Richard Lees traveled from Virginia to Philadelphia on important matters: one, Richard Henry Lee, carried an urgent letter from Thomas Jefferson to the Continental Congress. Another, Richard Bland Lee, Richard Henry's fifteen-year-old cousin, carried "Sample of hair & measure," having been asked by Carter to purchase "two setts of curls for my daughters Priscilla & Nancy." In October of that same year, shortly after Thomas Jefferson arrived home to Monticello after composing the Declaration of Independence and fighting for its passage, Carter sent his collection agent with a bill for a small unpaid loan, a little more than thirty-six pounds with interest. The loan was repaid (Jefferson was diligent in this regard), and the message, no doubt, delivered: you may think you are independent of the king of England, Tom, but you are still dependent on me.

By fall, though, Carter had no escape himself: he turned his back confidently to the rebels, but he loathed and feared the British Army, whom he now saw in an apocalyptic light. He watched, increasingly nervous, as British and American troops, circulating up and down the Eastern Seaboard, throughout the Chesapeake, and down the Potomac, during 1776 and early 1777, brought smallpox from Boston and Philadelphia. As yet, Virginia was barely touched, but the news was ominous, and personal: epidemics had already claimed hundreds of lives, including that of Philip Vickers Fithian, who died of dysentery in an army camp in the aftermath of the Battle of White Plains, only two winters after he wondered if he might only live one more winter. For Carter, the presence of disease among these troops almost constituted a larger threat than the arms they carried: he called British forces "Speckled t[r]oops," an unkind tribute to the skin pustules the virus caused—and possibly a crude reference to the British Army's newly interracial composition. By November, though, as the epidemics reached his outlying plantations, Carter was transfixed. He noted thirty-seven slaves with smallpox in the Forest Quarter that month, jotting down phrases such as "Negro Martha, of Coles point Plantation, died 19th September 1776" in his daybooks, alongside descriptions of how the bark of a chestnut oak patriotically made good shoe leather, or how egg yolks dissolved gums and rosins.

By December, he applied for a special license to have his slaves inoculated. It was an unusual and expensive choice: inoculation, which required time and money, was a gentleman's prerogative, and had been so traditionally unpopular among Virginians that men such as Thomas Jefferson had been required to leave the colony to receive preventive treatment. By the end of the month, Carter ordered medicines for his slaves, and put them into the hands of "Negroe John": jalap, cream of tartar, salt, and five pennyweight of "Ipecacuan," the powerful diuretic. The procedure, which the slaves underwent in December and January, was comparatively straightforward. First, they were "reduced" through a diet of milk and ipecac and, in many cases, enough mercury to make their teeth ache and rattle as though they might fall out on the floor. They were then infected with a small dose of smallpox, placed inside gashes made in their arms. In ideal circumstances, inoculants suffered a mild form of the illness, from which, after a period of retirement, they would recover fully immune to subsequent infection. In less ideal circumstances, the smallpox raged in their bodies, leaving scars or permanent disabilities, or even killing them—a fact that provides a less humanitarian explanation for why Carter ordered inoculations for his slaves before taking the dose himself.

By 1777, the inoculated slaves were recovering, but the tension otherwise was unsustainable, the sense of disaster immanent in the very air. British forces had chased Washington and his armies south through New Jersey, although American victories at Trenton and Princeton had staved off the anticipated rout. January was brutally cold, and the fires at Nomony were not doing their work: "Water frose in my study," Carter wrote some mornings; "Urine water frose in my study," he wrote others. At the end of the month, Frances, incredibly, delivered another child, their fifteenth, a son named George. A change of inflection entered Carter's letters: where "order" was the key word in older letters, the word "peace" began to emerge in its place, as though the aristocrat who once believed he maintained social order was now willing to settle for anything short of total war. But peace was a lost cause now. Carter collapsed on April 3, simply fell down where he stood in the common parlor: he woke up four minutes later, vomited, and was helped to his feet by his "Wife and others."

Two weeks later, he made one final, poignant attempt to carve out for himself a place above the conflict: he took the vaguely treasonable step of sneaking correspondence to England against congressional mandate by using a deported traitor as messenger. But the purpose of his message was not espionage: he wanted to repay a small debt to the merchant Hyndman, a gesture that becomes even more striking when one considers his refusal to repay Fairfax. He wanted to pay one debt, get one letter through the blockade, tell everyone that he played by a higher set of rules. "Letter writers, on both Sides of the water," he told Hyndman, choosing evenhanded language with great care, "who were endeavouring to justify the late new Doctrines, grievous to great Britain and America," deserved to have their correspondence seized. But "all Letters toutching on matters of trade, only," he added, insisting that one could be a cosmopolite entrepreneur and a patriot at the same time, "ought not to have been distroyed."

His letter, however, was seized as well. By May, sudden frosts killed the peach blossoms, then the strawberries, and smallpox was general throughout the Northern Neck. Carter decided it was time to inoculate himself and his family. He found a celebrated doctor: Gustavus Brown, who would later tend to George Washington on his deathbed. But Carter was still convinced that this might be his death knell. One of his final daybook entries prior to departing for Maryland observed that the clerk of Westmoreland Court had died of smallpox, and that he "took the Disorder by inoculation." On the morning of May 16, just before embarking, Carter ordered "a full & complete Inventory" of all goods at Nomony: as he had vowed, he wanted to be prepared to dictate his will in five minutes. In the afternoon, he left for Maryland, taking with him his son, John Tasker, his daughters, Priscilla and Nancy, and his servant, "Negro Sam." On May 31, he took the cure, as did John Tasker, Priscilla, Nancy, and Sam, all treated by two doctors, Mrs. Ford, and Mrs. Ford's daughter Peggy.

If the two weeks that passed between their departure for Mrs. Ford's and their inoculation is any indication, it is likely that the Carters were well "prepared" for the inoculation. It is also likely that the Carters and their servant Sam received a sophisticated evolution of the inoculation, one that had been circulating among certain constituencies in America since it was devised by a British doctor named Sutton a decade before—there would have been little sense in seeking out Gustavus Brown otherwise. The gash in the arm within which the virus was inserted was not so deep as that endured by his slaves, the dose of the infection not so strong, and the bed rest and quarantine more wisely administered. A patient would experience a milder fever, and the fever would pass, leaving, at worst, only a few light scars across the patient's face and arms.

Carter's fever, however, lingered, and took on a life of its own. By June 8, when his wife arrived, he was in what he later described as "a Fever Heat—indicating that the inoculation was effectual." Four days later, he experienced what he called a "most gracious Illumination," where he felt "the truth contained in the followi[n]g scripture, where Paul declares—'That he, Paul was alive without the Law once: but when the Comandment came, sin revived, and he died.'" It is tempting to say that the smallpox had struck him hard, and took him to the brink of the death that had circulated all around him since his debut at Corotoman, that had struck his family with intense prejudice since the start of the decade, and that seemed to be hunting him now in the guise of the violent demise of every social marker that had defined him and the way of life he exemplified. From such a place, one imagines, a glimpse of Jesus could be obtained. Years later, on December 4, 1789, he would congratulate his son George for taking an inoculation: "Many, many of the human race, make their exit through that gate," he told George, as if he had seen the gate and measured the lock. From this moment on, in fact, he talked about the afterlife with remarkable certainty, albeit in confused phrases that never really possessed any kind of coherence that could be recognized, at least on earth: "a Continuation of Life," he told one of his sons-in-law in 1794, "in Substantial bodies, in a perfect Human form—"

Which is all conjecture. All that can be confirmed—and even then, through his testimony alone—is that, when Robert Carter believed he saw God, he was experiencing an effectual fever heat.

4

Carter returned to Nomony Hall from St. Mary's County, Maryland, on July 4, 1777. In Philadelphia, the first anniversary of the Declaration of Independence was being celebrated with a grand impromptu carnival: Congress took the day off, bells were rung, and the sounds of small firearms filled the streets. At Nomony, Robert Carter gathered together his family, around seven in the evening. In the past, he acknowledged to them, they had not gathered to read parts of the Bible and talk about "fundamental Christian doctrine." But now they would do it daily, "so that Hearers, each and every one, may examin whether they had experienced similar Exercises"—"til," he added, already thinking of the laws against certain forms of religious practice, "it should be forbidden."

In this way, Robert Carter celebrated the first Independence Day in American history. Turning away from the Revolution, he turned to the revolution in his soul, a conflict that—as his last, portentous phrase suggested—he saw as no less political. He still conducted business: three days later, on July 7, he went back to work, advertising for a slave who could build African-style "mud Walls." And he had not turned tory: on July 29 of the same month, he took his loyalty oath at the Westmoreland County Courthouse, alongside Richard Henry Lee and John Augustine Washington, and the ceremony pleased him so much that he wrote down every detail: "My Signature stands thus—Robt Carter, a British-Whig, or Revolutioner." If Carter returned a new man from St. Mary's County, however, he regarded his new self as someone who violated laws for higher purposes, not someone who found that laws constituted the core of social order. He was no longer someone who merely sympathized with the outsiders. Now he feared—and thrilled to the prospect—that he might have become one, a man who still might be legislated out of existence, but now as a true believer in heretical doctrines, a martyr, not as a fallen aristocrat and master of slaves.

The next fifteen months were the most energetic passage in Carter's life, a notion made more astounding by the fact that he was almost fifty and recovering from smallpox. Carter tested every major faith, ordered dozens of religious books, and traveled the countryside, sometimes journeying alone on horseback for hundreds of miles in order to hear Methodist,

Baptist, and Presbyterian preachers and exhorters proclaim the truth of the "new birth." He began by convening family prayers on July 6, and searching his Bible for precedents when middle-aged men found God: "Jesus, about 30 years old when baptized." On July 12, he stood up at Nomony Church and announced that "I . . . doubted, till very lately, of the Divinity of Jesus Christ—I thank Almighty God, that, that Doubt, is removed." And then he made this invitation:

> If there be any among this assembly of People, who have not a lively belief of J.C's Divinity, I wish to see such thereof, at my Mansion House, comonly called Nomony Hall.

These were false starts, however. Carter's family rapidly rejected his authority: he wrote that "the females have the outward form of Religion, but they are yet Strangers to the vital part thereof," but the larger truth was that Frances preferred Parson Smith's more conservative teachings. The "males," in turn, failed to even acquire the outward forms: "At present Robin does not Shew a pious Disposition," he wrote to a professor at William and Mary in early 1778, planning a curriculum for the boy that included subjects such as "Human Nature in its Primitive Integrity, Entire Depravation Begun Recovery & Consumate Happiness or Misery."

Similarly, Carter's familiar church was not welcoming. On August 6, Carter met with Parson Smith and spoke to him about becoming a minister. Smith rebuffed him, doubtless with great politeness: he "does not recommend his own Profession," Carter wrote. But Carter yearned to be heard, and he rapidly perceived that his fortune provided him with his own sort of pulpit, and his own sort of church. While he had always tacitly supported his servants when they protested against mistreatment, he now began to defend his servants more openly: "I am informed," Carter wrote to a neighbor in August 1777, "that an Iron pott in the house of negroe George, Carpernter at my plantation now Called Aries, was taken & carried to Your house, yesterday." Not questioning the word of "Negroe George," nor waiting to hear defense from the propertied white slaveholder accused of theft, Carter wrote as if he assumed that his social peer would not mind acknowledging his guilt to the face of the slave himself: "I hope you will deliver it [the pot] to the Bearer George." Three months later, he composed an emotional letter to John Augustine Washington on

November 10, 1777, demanding restitution on behalf of a white indentured servant tied up and whipped by a patrol of American soldiers: "I do presume that a violent Trepas has been committed against a mans Person; therefore I appear on the part of the injured Man."

As Carter composed these small but passionate defenses of the poor and enslaved, he continued his search for a spiritual home. On October 3, he wrote a printer in Williamsburg and ordered twenty-two books of theology:

> 1 Copy of a Companion for the Festivals & Fasts of the Church of England by Robert Nelson
> Ditto of a Brief Exposition of the Apostles Creed according to Bishop Pearson, by way of Paraphrase & Anotation, By Bishop Kenet—
> 1 Copy of the Acceptable Sacrifice, By William Tilly, D, D—

He still saw small apocalypses in the everyday landscape, but the nature of his vision grew warmer, more affirming, than the earthquakes and chasms of the previous winter. On December 19, he saw "a Great Light . . . in the Sky, towards the East of a deep red-colour." The following June, he observed an evening where "the Horns of the Moon pointed Northwards."

He began keeping religious daybooks, filled with labyrinthine meditations on religion and the spirit, laden with footnotes. Unsurprisingly, he gravitated toward the idea of rebirth, and the notion that earthly power might precede revelation:

> Dead Bodies, naturally, putrify 72 hours
> after Death, wherein ye Revolution of
> humours is accomplished—Hamond Page
> 337—Verse 37—
> Synesius was made a Bishop, before he
> Believed in the Doctrine of the Resurrection
> Hamond's Anotations Page 510—C2—

Suddenly creative, he composed his own prayers for family use, no less labyrinthine: in "An Evening prayer," Carter asked God to "have pity upon all Jews, Turks, Infidels & Hereticks," to "reform all things amiss in these united states," to "bless the Majestrates of every denomination," and, in a final peroration, to provide "thy afflicted servants . . . a joyful deliverance out of all their troubles." "In thy good time," he added, not yet wanting to rush the Almighty in this regard.

For the first time, however, the modern reader of Carter's writings could also see what John Page meant when he insisted that the councillor's mind was "confused" by a life of study without teachers. He read like an addict, going so far as to write the widows of freshly demised gentlemen to see what books their estate libraries might yield. He could refuse no religion, and no concatenation of religious ideas, absorbing so much doctrine with such rapidity that he began to maintain lists of who said what:

> Roman Catholicks, adopt arminianism—
> Doctor Whitby—favors the doctrine of Arminianism
> Stackhouse—Ditto Ditto
> Arminianism, the Doctrine of Free Will & Universal
> Redemption . . .

In his journals, ideas ricocheted off one another: he would tell himself that Deuteronomy 23:25 should be used "to teach People to be Neighbourly—, & not to insist upon Property in a small matter," put up his pen briefly, and then write, "O Lord, our Flesh trembleth for Fear of thee."

The war, meantime, briefly receded from Virginia. In February 1778, Dunmore's ships sailed down the Potomac again, gathering slaves—including three of George Washington's—but passing Carter's Coles Point farm for the second time without incident. Carter, however, now enmeshed himself more deeply in the Revolutionary cause. The bakery he had built so avidly in 1772, an enormous project featuring two ovens that could take twenty-five thousand bushels of wheat per year and bake one hundred pounds of bread at once, finally hummed with activity. His grain mill received so much corn and wheat that its wheels turned sometimes for eighteen hours a day. His textile factory, at the plantation now known as Aries, was completed, and he began selling stockings to his overseers and his neighbors. He took over salt production in Westmoreland County, addressing one of the most dire wartime shortages.

Perhaps most significant, however, the Baltimore Works, in which Carter maintained one-fifth ownership, began selling its pig and "barr" iron to new large buyers like Fredericksburg munitions maker James Hunter, the most important provider of weaponry to Washington's army. What iron remained Carter had shipped back to Nomony, where he sold it to his neighbors alongside food and clothing in the small, unspectacular forms of plows, axes, nails, and hoes, for small, unspectacular sums: twenty shilling "per hundred" for the very best brown bread, one pound per thousand ten penny nails, eighteen pence per pair of stockings, as little as twenty-seven and as many as one hundred twenty pounds for every ton of bar iron.

However, like George Washington—who was forced to contemplate declaring bankruptcy during his first year as commander of the American armies—Carter found the wartime economy ruinously unstable. At the very least, war with Britain severed America's ties with the largest importer and exporter of its goods, closing down the traditional markets for certain commodities, most noticeably tobacco, and cutting off the supply of others, ranging from the critical (salt, woolens) to the frivolous (tea sets, fine rugs). As important, however, war revealed, for Virginia gentlemen perhaps more than anyone, how much American assertions of political independence were contradicted by economic realities. As of 1776, the colonies of America did not host a single bank, filtering most of their accounts through European institutions to which they were suddenly denied access. Most financial transactions that required cash utilized combinations of foreign currencies, sometimes cut, like Fithian's half a pistareen, to make new pseudo-currencies. Once war was declared, however, new state legislatures as well as the Continental Congress were compelled to create the infrastructure of an economy as much as they were compelled to create the infrastructure of a political system.

Faced with new, fragile currencies, funded by uncertain promises of future redemptions and rates of depreciation, Carter, like most Americans, struggled. Alongside the Bible citations and lists of sermons attended, he filled his journals with currency conversion tables, trying to reckon with not just one new form of paper money but a baker's dozen: "A Dollar passes in the Province of Maryland at 7s/6. . . . A Dollar passes in the Colony of Virginia at 5/9." Facing inflationary spirals that, in three short years, would increase the price of a pound of bacon from six pence to ten shillings, a pound of sugar from two shillings to twenty, a gallon of rum from one pound to eight, Carter unsuccessfully tried to set his own prices at pre–Stamp Act levels: "Balance is to be satisfyed by the payment of 80 pounds in Gold or Silver Money, or Country Produce valuing the said Produce at the time of Payment as they sold for in the Course of the year 1765—"

Perhaps most difficult, however, was the fact that the old, stable currencies were still circulating, forcing every merchant and landlord in America to choose between patriotically accepting the new, fragile, almost worthless Virginia paper, or insisting upon payment in pounds, guineas, moidores, double pistoles, louis d'ors, crowns, or Portuguese joes, or any other form of European gold or silver specie that had dominated prewar America. Even patriots often made the wrong choice: Richard Henry Lee eventually faced censure for forcing his tenants to pay him in pounds. On this matter, Carter was a patriot, accepting whatever form of currency his tenants offered. On other matters, however, his willingness to sacrifice during wartime was far more limited. As Washington's troops drilled and built themselves huts in the bitter cold of Valley Forge, Ben and Robert Bladen were being marked "absent fm mustering," and subsequently "delinquent." On December 3, Richard Parker of the Westmoreland Militia, who once worked for Carter, now gave Carter's sons three days to report "completely armed" and with blankets and food, to help defend the Northern Neck against an anticipated "Landing" of "British Troops." Carter surveyed their situation, and told them, his tone self-consciously neutral, that they would be expected to "fire upon & endeavor to kill white & black Men, who ye Captain or chief Officer . . . should call an Enemy." Both sons listened carefully, and immediately became conscientious objectors, Ben saying that he "would not take up Arms in the present War, nor in any other War," and Robert Bladen concurring.

On December 9, however, three days after Parker's deadline, an "occasional Serjant" named Mahundro and five privates appeared at Nomony to collect Ben and Robin. But their rehearsed pacifism proved inappropriate to the occasion. Mahundro immediately provided Ben with an exemption due to his status as an "invalid." Robert Bladen, threatened with "30 Daies" in "Confinement" if he failed to muster, commented that he would find imprisonment "very irksome," and tentatively agreed to serve. When the soldiers left Nomony, Carter was so relieved that he fainted: "I fainted & fell down," he recorded, "but retained my Senses."

By January, he rededicated himself to religious pilgrimage and began attending religious meetings led by preachers of every dissenting denomination. He saw Lunsford several times, lending him money and clothing, and urging him to lead meetings at Nomony and his other plantations. But he also attended sermons by Presbyterian and Methodist ministers, and both Separate and Regular Baptists. From January 8 to January 13, he went to meetings three times, paying particular attention when Separate Baptist John Sutton visited Nomony and preached, "How shall we escape if we neglect so great Salvation." And when the weather warmed ("a Bright Sun," Carter noted on March 4), Carter began his pilgrimage in earnest. On March 15, he set out for the courthouse in neighboring Lancaster County, where he heard two sermons, took the sacrament, and shared bread and wine with the men and women who gathered there. Then he collapsed again, after which he dined and slept at the house of a local gentleman.

"Comune with your own Heart, & in your Chamber, & be still," he wrote that evening, citing the Book of Psalms. The illness that followed his collapse kept him at Nomony for a week. By March 24, though, he returned to meetings; he heard two sermons that day. On March 28, he went to two different services; he did the same the following day. Throughout April and early May, he traversed the Northern Neck, often attending one meeting during the day and another at night. On April 23, he watched rapt as John Turner came to Nomony and addressed his slaves and his daughters directly, and described to them the importance of the first Psalm. Carter noted:

> He spoke to the Negroes, particularly—
> He spoke to my Daughters, particularly—

On May 3, he stood in a field among 350 people and listened to Turner preach from John 3:7, "Ye must be born again."

Two days later, he mounted his horse and rode to the meeting of the General Association of Baptists in Buckingham County, a journey of more than one hundred miles that took him ten days to traverse. Once there, he commingled with crowds twice as large as any he had yet witnessed, "Whites & Blacks," who listened for hours as groups of four or five preachers, followed by exhorters, led them into religious ecstasies, "cr[ying] out in the Praise of <u>Jesus Christ</u>": "Such a heavenly confusion among the preachers, and such a celestial discord among the people," John Leland, one of Virginia's most politically agile Baptist leaders, wrote of such events. By May 24, when Carter opened up the weaving factory at his Aries plantation to religious meeting, and listened to a Presbyterian minister named James Crawford preach to several hundred people, he had attended twenty-eight different religious services in sixty-nine days, and heard more than forty different sermons and exhortations. On June 18, Carter received correspondence from Thomas Jefferson, a Virginian so well esteemed that he was shortly to be elected governor of the new commonwealth. Carter put aside the letter, however: he occupied himself that day constructing lists that told him which ministers he had heard were Baptists, which were Presbyterians, and which were Methodists.

It was, in its way, a beautiful confusion, as if the real, unavoidable lesson of his "illumination" was that grace was everywhere, and transcended the categories by which mankind conducted its business: Carter's religious daybook for March 15, 1778, read, "RC—& his servant Negro Sam—received Tokens and they did both Comune," a selection of detail strongly suggesting that what Carter found extraordinary about the meeting that day was the company he was keeping. At the same time, Carter went from preacher to preacher, from book to book, because he was also deeply struggling with doubt. While he never doubted his moment of divine vision, he seemed disappointed, even despondent, that it hadn't constituted his inauguration into a life where he routinely experienced exalted feelings. He must have been a striking figure at those meetings, which were, in themselves, extraordinary events: contemporary eyewitnesses describe waves of emotion, outbreaks of crying, even feverish and mystical scenes where hundreds of men and women lay inert on the ground, as if the life had left their limbs, as preacher and exhorters alternately thundered about the eternal fires of hell and soothed about the undying love of Christ. But there is something missing from Carter's journals—something he would surely have recorded—that still suggests a certain detachment. It was not he who was roiling on the ground, quaking, feeling the loss of his limbs. He did not cry out. By his own witness, he did not even speak. Yet because he believed (possibly because his own "illumination" convinced him) that what these men and women experienced were authentic expressions of the divine touch, he could be equally convinced that God was now hiding from him, perhaps testing him, or waiting for him in the next tome, or in the keening words of the next itinerant preacher.

As spring turned into summer, as the war deepened, Carter wandered through his personal wilderness. On April 14, he wrote a letter to a Baltimore man named Henry Goff, whom Carter had heard possessed "a pretty general Acquaintance amongst Gosple Preachers," and asked him to deliver "a Methodist, or a Dessenting Preacher" to the Northern Neck. He continued to attend sermons, some of which seemed almost suspiciously meant for his ears: on July 16, 1778, the Presbyterian minister David Rice visited Nomony, and preached the prodigal son, a parable within which Carter could empathize with the father *or* the son. But his despair grew. On June 29, he awoke with a yellow film on his eyes, which dissolved gradually over the next few days, during which he washed his eyes with rose water and Madeira wine. He felt it as a portent, an emblem of his failure of vision. He composed a formal poem, a stilted yet heartfelt psalm entitled "The Assaulted Christian leaving Recourse to Divine Mercy," whose first two lines declared that

> My soul is beclouded and heavy my heart
> When Jesus the Spring of my joys disappears.

One week later, on July 8, he listened to Samuel Templeman preach Job 23:3. In his journal that night, he excerpted this quotation from the text: "O that I knew where I might find Him! That I might come even to his Seat—" He was Job, tested.

What Carter was gradually coming to understand, however, was that his divine illumination required something of him that he was not yet capable of doing. He thought he was Job, but in fact he was Jonah, struggling in that awful interregnum between the moment when the authoritative voice tells one what to do and the moment when one realizes that one no longer has the choice to do otherwise. What he could recognize, almost unconsciously at first, but with increasing discernment as the year passed, was that the vision he had experienced was one that he shared with the poor, the persecuted, and the enslaved: when he perceived that great light in the sky in December, he wrote in his journals that his servant "Sarah Stanhope & Negro Harry-Ditcher" also saw what he saw, seeking corroboration not merely that the great light occurred but also that it had been witnessed by the people who suddenly mattered to him.

He hesitated, however, to acknowledge the extraordinary reversal implicit in such small moments. The men and women whose testimony would have been discounted in American courts became, for Carter, the arbiters of true experience. As important, he could not admit to himself the more shocking possibility that part of him wanted this all along, that the restlessness of his spirit and the manic egalitarian energies of his actions possessed an earthbound origin in his prewar, pre-illumination self. He could not understand that the fact that so many poor men and women, and so many blacks among them, were rattling and shaking may have had more to do with cultural roots, and with a desire to break free from a stultified public culture within which aristocrats such as Carter had always sounded the keynote, than with the fact that God was selectively distributing divine guidance. But his willful innocence was his revolutionary fulcrum: his refusal to discount either their religiosity, or his own, his stilted, relentlessly honest inability to see more complex motives, compelled him to regard the political world of Revolutionary America through this startling new lens wherein his slaves were the leading citizens of the world to which he wanted to belong.

Throughout the summer and the fall, he took two measures of his newly evolving place in the culture of the colony. To his old friends, the peers of his days in Williamsburg, he offered gracious, rambling repudiations of the values they shared—not enough to create social estrangement, which he did not want, but enough to make it plain that he now saw the world in a fundamentally different way: "it does not appear fit to mention, here, the probable motives that lead to . . . deistical Opinion," Carter wrote Thomas Jefferson on July 27. "I do now disclaim it and do testify that Jesus Christ is the Son of god; that through him mankind can be saved only—" With Jefferson, Carter was polite, concealing the fact that those "motives" were the fruit of many evenings spent sharing Francis Fauquier's hospitality and guidance, when their friendship was strong. Jefferson, doubtless, understood the refusal as much as he understood the civility: responding to an invitation to visit Monticello, Carter wrote only, "I fear my Situation will not allow me to visit you at your house shortly." In private, however, Carter worried deeply about the soul of his old friend, hiding feelings that would have made such a visit unthinkable: "I fear, many good natured Deists will perish . . . & my heart is wounded with the sad Apprehension of it."

While Carter was declining the company of men such as Jefferson, however, he was spending more time among his slaves and servants, whom he watched carefully, startled, amazed, a kind of fetish, but with an equanimity in his observations that marked the birth of his true revolutionary self. On April 21, he recorded what seemed to be the preconscious, involuntary religious conversion of his laundry maid, Sarah, who attended a sermon at Carter's Aries plantation by the Presbyterian John Wright, and began shaking as the first verse of one of Isaac Watts's familiar hymns was sung out:

> My heart, how dreadful hard it is!
> How Heavy here it lyes;
> Heavy and cold within my breast,
> Just like a rock of ice!

She continued shaking until she "was carried upon a Bed," from where she asked that another hymn be "give[n] out." Then she continued "quarking" through "the greatest part of this Night." Carter was clearly moved. The next day, he attended another sermon by John Wright, at a private house near Nomony. That evening, he departed from his conventional religious daybook notation and neglected to record the subject of Wright's sermon: "Sarah landry Maid attended" was all he wrote.

When he woke up the following day, Carter was still amazed. He attended another meeting, and still watching Sarah, wrote that "Negro Sarah Landy Maid Weeped bitterly & quaked a little." He began to fixate upon the religious regeneration of other slaves: "Negro Tom of Coles-Point Plantation showed great Contrition for his Sins"; "Negro Lucy of Billingsgate aged 54 was baptized at Mrs Browns by the Reverend Mr Lunsford, Baptist—" He continued to seek out new preachers, and to listen attentively to Lunsford in particular: on August 30, one week before he received baptism, he traveled to a stage mounted near the Rappahannock Bridge and listened to the Wonderful Boy preach "If ye then be risen with Christ, seek those things which are above." But when he finally decided to testify, the events that shaped his decision were not sermons, nor were they new manifestations of the "most gracious Illumination." He was still waiting for a sign from God: "O that I may have a saving knowledge of sin & Christ; and that I may have an assurance of God's love to my Soul," he wrote in his journal that evening, underneath a list of new books to order.

Rather, Carter's decision to be baptized, and his singular choice to join

Lunsford's fledgling Morattico Baptist Church, were inspired by feelings about whose side he was on, and whose witness he would trust. From that moment on July 4, 1777, when he assumed that his new voice might be a forbidden one, this was an inevitable choice, and probably a self-dramatizing one. In part, it was slumming for a man whose wealth and name, even during a revolution, still made him untouchable, a way of transforming self-pity regarding his broken social status into pride in being an "Assaulted Christian." But the risks of persecution were real: Eleazer Clay, probably the second wealthiest man in Virginia to convert to the Baptist Church during the decade, had his life threatened at gunpoint several times by men who would never have challenged him otherwise. Moreover, every indication suggests that Carter made his decision to convert precisely when he understood that the risk of persecution was real: in the three weeks before he testified at Morattico, he attended two different services that were attacked by armed mobs led by Revolutionary War soldiers, including the assault where Lunsford claimed what Madison had called "free Liberty of Conscience."

Carter found the experience of being the assaulted one so powerful that he devoted several pages in his journal to describing the details of the night: he wrote down, word for word, Lunsford's demand that "he hoped & expected that the Civil Power would countenance & protect every denomination of Christains, within the State of Virginia." Carter now understood where he stood, and who now spoke for him. Everything he felt, his ambivalence toward the Revolution itself, his ingrained love of reason and his newfound love of passion, came together in this convoluted moment when American soldiers fighting for political revolution fought against religious liberty, and Madison's words merged with Lunsford's voice in defiant response. Carter, experiencing catharsis without vision, did not wait long after. In his journal, he meditated upon the story of "Sarah Howey . . . between 8 & 9 years old," the third of three Sarahs that marked the stages in his conversion. She too had been awakened by a powerful sermon, and like the Sarah before her, made an inspired request regarding the next religious performance: "Miss—S- H- desired that a Sermon might be preached on the preciousness of time," Carter wrote.

Time now precious, he took the stage himself, and gave out his testimony. More significant, he testified at a Baptist meeting—a choice that might have been as astounding and counterintuitive as the divine illumination itself. If Carter had joined a Methodist congregation, he could have stayed in the established church (within which his wife and children remained), and prayed alongside congregants with whom he shared many doctrinal ideals. The Presbyterian ministers were bookish and intellectual, like him, and had established themselves on the Northern Neck. There were Quaker meetings all over the Chesapeake, if what Carter sought was an egalitarian, antislavery community. And if he had remained a Deist, he would have found powerful allies whose thirst for justice, even self-deprecating justice, approximated his: while sitting as the Committee of the Revisors for the Virginia Constitution, Edmund Pendleton and Carter's old friends Thomas Jefferson and George Wythe composed, then shelved, a bill that would have freed all slaves born after its passage, educated them, and then removed them to "such place as the circumstances of the time should render most proper."

The Baptists, on the other hand, were reputed to be illiterate, even sexually licentious, as fixated on spontaneity and the spoken word as Carter had been upon lawbooks and sheet music. The Separates, in particular, rejected all authority but the Bible, and their church charters carried such subversive canons as "Black Member to be dealt with as a White One." They were the religion of the slave cabins and the heavenly confusion, of wild gesticulations, laying on hands, and free-form hymnals that might go deep into the morning. By 1778, they were also the only dissenting sect that still endured persecution. And unlike the slaves in the Revisors' proposal, they weren't going anywhere. From the moment Carter let the Wonderful Boy push him gently into Totuskey Creek, in other words, he made the most profound commitment possible to turn his old self inside out. In the course of three short years, he had turned away from the religion of Thomas Jefferson, and embraced the religion of Thomas Jefferson's slaves.

Once a rich man made a choice like that, anything was possible.

PART II

REVOLUTION

CHAPTER IV

Inglorious Connexions
[1778–1789]

"It unanswerably follows that original sin and hereditary succession are parallels. Dishonourable rank! Inglorious connexion!"

—TOM PAINE, *Common Sense*

or five years, the congregants of the Morattico Baptist Church had met in private homes, on public stages, alongside creeks and bridges, and even in mansions. Sometimes they met at Kilmarnock, down in Lancaster County. They had built a small brick church there: the land falling away in soft folds in every direction, amid open fields, it was an austerely beautiful place. And sometimes, they met in a place they called Lunsford's Meeting House. It was a capacious building on Robert Carter's Aries plantation that was also called "the Factory," for the plainest of reasons. It was, in all likelihood, not even austerely beautiful. But when a minister such as Lunsford or William Fristoe preached the "Real heart religion," as they called it, seven or eight hundred men and women would fill its great wide floor and doorways to overflowing.

Inside the building, now, roughly thirty men and women gathered. They were almost all men, and almost all white. They dressed themselves in blacks and grays. Their expressions, no doubt, bore something of shell shock, and something of relief. They had endured war, persecution, and poverty to purchase this redoubt of tranquility and grace.

The February 27, 1783, business meeting of the Morattico Baptist Church was called to order: Lewis Lunsford, elder, and William Hazard and Henry O'Hagan presiding.

Brother Robert Carter was chosen as clerk, and he duly recorded the presence of "about 24 Brothers and 4 Sisters" in attendance—not as many as a few years before, when four or five score of "Brothers and Sisters" could be expected to attend, but still a goodly number.

At fifty-four, Carter was still lean, but he was also graver, slower, than the man he had been in prewar times. He wore somber colors from head to foot, and his coat "easy" around the elbows and shoulders, to accommodate his stiffening joints. He wore no jewelry, but employed two tailors, and never lost his appetite for small fine curios, such as a timepiece handmade to his own peculiar and dreamy visions of how time passed: "one hand only pointing to the hours and parts thereof." Sitting behind the modest desk provided by the church, meekly recording the minutes of its business, he had embraced the role of Brother. But he was also the wealthiest man in the room, and men and women still deferred to him. The Morattico Baptist Church supported itself through subscription among its congregation, gathering a combination of Indian corn, tobacco, bacon, and negotiable paper currency. Carter provided most of the currency: forty-seven precious English pounds in 1782 alone. Thomas Downing, another gentleman, provided twelve pounds. The remainder of the congregation provided the corn, tobacco, and bacon.

Now Carter rose and began the meeting. He spoke at length, a formal speech about the "great importance of good education," culminating in a request to raise money for the incorporation of a Baptist College in Providence. The church rapidly assented, and a paper was circulated, to which the brothers and sisters could affix their names alongside a promise to donate money.

Brother Carter sat down. Brother John Wright, a recent convert, rose, and announced that Negro Sam, "property of Elizabeth Davis, widow," had confessed himself guilty of adultery. The meeting voted swiftly to excommunicate the slave.

Brother John Wright sat down. Brother Thomas Downing rose: Negro James, "the property of Mr. Spencer M. Ball," had confessed to the crime of stealing a "young hog" from his master. Excommunicated, the clerk wrote in bold script.

Brother Downing continued. Word had reached the congregation that Negro Solomon had committed adultery: an "Inquiry" was launched. Brother Downing sat down. Then Brother John Rust rose, and reported that "Molly Bennett was a Common Swearer + that she Use Abusive language": another inquiry was launched. Brother Rust sat down.

Lunsford watched quietly. At times like this, he may have wondered if this was his church anymore, and if it ever was. He could reflect on literally hundreds of occasions where he led flocks of Americans, both black and white, into frantic ecstasies, where one inspired phrase could make men or women, rich or poor, fall down like they had died. He could also recall, however, other, less celebratory occasions: as late as 1780, four years into a revolution that Baptists had been zealous in supporting, Lunsford still faced mobs. Blood literally ran on the floor of Morattico. It was almost unbearable.

This, then—this February chill, the calming trivialities of church business—was surely better than facing an angry mob, or leading one. He still strolled the peninsula, but more often than not, he did so to collect rents from Robert Carter's tenants. He was not good at the work—few were—but Carter didn't seem to care. And the war was almost over: only three weeks earlier, British authorities had formally recognized the cessation of hostilities, having vacated their last camp on the continent, in the port of Savannah.

Moreover, Lunsford's personal share of the conflict was also winding down to a peaceable end. In the century prior to the Revolution, no colony had a more established church than Virginia. By the time the Constitutional Convention convened in 1787, however, no state had gone further in guaranteeing religious liberty and separation between church and state. Jefferson later called the debates over religious liberty in Virginia "the severest contests in which I have ever been engaged." Lunsford would undoubtedly agree: no sect had fought harder than the Baptists, who fervently believed that their faith would thrive without government assistance as much as without government persecution, and fought for ideals of freedom so pristine that they found themselves shoulder to shoulder with civil libertarians such as Jefferson and Madison.

By 1783, however, those battles were almost over: it had been three years since Lunsford had suffered the invasion of a state-sanctioned mob during one of his sermons, and it would be only three years more before he could celebrate the passage of Jefferson's groundbreaking Act on Religious Freedom in the Virginia Assembly. There was little spirit of persecution left in the Virginia populace, and there were no more British armies. He had only a family to protect now, and a farm to manage—also supplied by Carter— and those rents to collect.

Still, though, there was a little fire left.

Lunsford himself now rose and began to speak about a brawl between a man named Benjamin Marsh and Brother Rawley Hazard. Hazard did not deny that Marsh had attacked him, nor did he deny that he had fought back, injuring his attacker. The church disapproved and instructed Lunsford to officially "admonish" Hazard, "saying that his defense . . . was irregular."

Lunsford sat down. Brother Hazard now rose, unbowed, and asked the Church's permission for a license to preach. Not granted, wrote the clerk.

The meeting now quickened. Someone announced that "Mr. Alexander Hunton . . . refused to serve" as deacon: the church voted to find a new one. Someone else proposed that the following Wednesday should be reserved for "prayer and fasting": the church, again, voted in the affirmative. Lunsford then rose again, and formally delivered to the clerk a "Letter of Dismission" for Henry O'Hagan, which would allow him to join other churches. "When joined," the clerk noted, "he is no longer a member with us."

The meeting quieted. One final proposal was offered: that Lunsford "notify on the first Lord's day he may preach" that Negro Sam and Negro James are "Excommunicated." The motion carried, and the congregation spilled out into the chill February air.

And what did Robert Carter think, as he too left the church and entered the chill air, and began the ride back to Nomony? Like most Virginia gentlemen, the war and the changes that war brought had shocked and altered him: he was humbled by the assault on aristocratic privilege that lowered men such as him to the status of mere citizens, and that had broken to bits fortunes nearly as large as his. He was humiliated, like many Virginians, by a lengthy and frightening military occupation of Virginia during the last days of the war, led by the traitor Benedict Arnold. His family was smaller, sicker, and wilder than ever—his sons, in particular, seemed to have been born only to dash whatever dreams of empire he might have inherited from his imperial, visionary grandfather.

Unlike other Virginia gentlemen, however, Carter had developed a taste for humility, and regretted only that there was not more to taste. In his own way, Carter's deepest complaint about postwar America was the private equivalent of the plaints uttered publicly by such great rebels as George Mason, Patrick Henry, and Richard Henry Lee: that the spirit of '76, with its fervid love of liberty, was disappearing from the nation alongside those British brigades. In Carter's case, it had been five years since he had been graciously illuminated during a smallpox fever, and he was still seeking ways to make that flash of revelation sustain itself as a way of life. The little rituals of Morattico soothed him in this regard. But he couldn't miss the problem, in large part because he was the problem: slowly but surely, Morattico was shrinking, and its poor and enslaved members were either being excommunicated, or being compelled to defer to the landed and wealthy.

As he rode back to Nomony on February 27, 1783, in other words, he was likely thinking about the war: everyone was. And he may well have been thinking about that Baptist College in Providence, and a service it might provide him before the decade was over. As likely, however, he was thinking about the two slaves that Morattico had just excommunicated, and how he had joined the Baptist Church in large part because his slaves had found religion within its doors. And if he had brought his coachman Tom Henry with him, and now fixed his eyes upon him, Carter might have been reminded of one other piece of recent news: the new House of Delegates, in its May 1782 session, had passed "An Act to Authorize the Manumission of Slaves," the most liberal antislavery bill in its history, a law allowing private slaveholders for the first time to liberate their slaves without special permission, provided that two witnesses certified the "instrument of emancipation" in county court, that five shillings be paid, and that all freed slaves that were either too young, too old, or too infirm be maintained by their former owners.

Having joined his soul with those of many of his slaves—having declared to himself that all men are equal in the hereafter, if not here— Carter must have surely considered that this law might allow his gracious illumination to grow flesh and bone. For nine years, however, until 1791, he would wait. For nine years, his slaves would also wait, knowing full well how Carter worshipped, knowing full well how he was not like other slaveholders, even liberal ones, all asking the same question Tom Henry now perhaps asked himself, as he drove his master home from church: What was Robert Carter waiting for?

2

At first, other wealthy men rushed through the breach that Carter opened. "Within a month" of Carter's baptism in 1778, according to a British observer, three other Westmoreland planters placed their names below Carter's (which, in turn, resided below the names of several slaves, at the sixty-first spot) on the charter of the Morattico Baptist Church. Petitions circulated: on October 9, one month and three days after Carter was baptized, the vestry of Cople Parish delivered one to the Committee on Religion of the House of Delegates. They were unfailingly polite, not willing to "engross much of the time of the Legislature," and "only beg[ging] its attention for a few moments." They were concerned about efforts to "overthrow the Established Church," which, they believed, would "throw this State in particular into Commotion, and thereby prejudice the common cause" of the war. The words, however, were boilerplate: Lunenburg and Mecklenburg counties had sent nearly identical petitions to the House of Delegates in 1777. Carter was not mentioned by name. But suddenly, Cople Parish had discovered a reason to join their voices with those of other churches in Virginia that felt threatened by the revolution from within.

Carter, however, was inattentive to their protests. When Parson Smith delivered a strong denunciation of the dissenters, Carter was already missing from his pews, and he only heard about the sermon secondhand from his gardener. Instead, he threw himself into his new faith with extraordinary enthusiasm. In his correspondence, not just his personal journals, he now interrupted turgid letters with emotional phrases, understanding his new life as a permanent crisis of faith and restlessness: "That God would give me the desire of my Heart!" he called out to an unnamed correspondent. "That he would grant me the Thing which I long for!" A certain mysticism that had also lain half dormant as he stared through his telescope and contemplated life on other planets also emerged: he began talking openly about "the time world" and "the material world." In his journals, he copied or composed pages full of fragmented religious thoughts, "Confessions" or "Sundry Remarks," and entire essays citing one biblical quote after another, the only editorial intrusion being the haphazard underlines that he employed to emphasize certain ideas: "The Want of original Righteousness" struck him as an important matter, as did the idea that "in this World we have no abiding place."

With no less enthusiasm, he also immersed himself in the business of the church. He continued to provide homes and land for ministers, donated the ground upon which churches were built, and sponsored the education of young men who could provide compelling evidence that they had "experience[s] of grace"—when necessary, he sent a slave to compensate for the menial work that the young man would have done. Further, despite having joined the Baptists, he continued to respond to requests for donations from other churches. He provided the funds that repaired a damaged Quaker meetinghouse in Baltimore, provided books for an itinerant Presbyterian minister, and constructed stone steps for a Baptist church in Richmond. On one day in 1778, he gave Lunsford a pair of stockings, three pounds to a lay preacher named Francis Hill, and nine pounds to the Methodist layman John Turner. The pilgrim not trumping the businessman, Carter made note that the pants he gave Lunsford were worth two pounds, two shillings.

At Morattico, Carter acclimated to the small labors of an egalitarian community. He took notes in his own rolling handwriting, monitored attendance, prepared letters for "Black sister Betty Bell" and other brethren incapable of writing themselves. He loved seconding motions, and he participated in the "inquiries" with which the church punished individual members for the sins of adultery, fornication, "drunkenness," disobedience, violence (even self-defense), and the suggestive "walking disorderly." He signed off repeatedly on subscriptions that entailed him to pay the minister and the warden, repair the church, and even reimburse the lenders of church members who died in debt. He even attended meetings where the elders discussed the possibility of sharing their wealth in common, and fought for a proposal that would construct lists of private property that would help realize that ideal.

Away from the church, he reinforced its precepts. He delivered more polite repudiations of Deism and secular politics to the peers of his young adulthood. To George Wythe, he said what he was unwilling to say to Jefferson: "I do in behalf of your immortal soul, call on you to Supplicate the throne of Grace, to comunicate to your Soul experimental Religion." He stopped playing musical instruments, despite the fact that he had described them as his "darling Amusement." He discontinued dancing at Nomony, telling the dance master Francis Christian something else he would never tell Jefferson: "I believe it would not be difficult to prove that in every civil Government customs are permitted, which are in them Selves sinful."

Rejecting a culture that mocked an individual if he missed a dance step, Carter, in turn, fully adopted the Baptist love for the unrehearsed. He threw open the doors of his mansion's ballroom to church meetings, encouraging all those who had been saved—an unpredictable group that included his own employees, tenants, and slaves—to command the space. By day, his factory at Aries turned out wool and cotton goods; by night and on Sundays, it hosted church services and prayer meetings attended by hundreds. He reviewed ministers as if they were musicians, and disdained those who read from prepared texts: "I wish he would lay aside his notes," Carter wrote of a Presbyterian named Montgomery, observing that other ministers in that sect would be "more Zealous and Pathetic" if they did the same.

It was as a transformed man, then, that Carter faced the crises of 1779 and 1780, ones that would have forced him to be humble and soul-searching were he not already so inclined. In May 1779, he endured what was surely one of the most sorrowful months of his entire life. On May 6, Carter's firstborn son, Ben, who had been showing "alarming" symptoms, finally did "retire from this world," dying of tuberculosis while visiting Loudon County. Carter, who had rushed to Ben's deathbed, expressed his grief regarding his son's death in the gentlemanly fashion of his old life: his corresponding pen, which sent out several letters a week, sometimes a day, composed nothing for a month and more.

When he resumed correspondence, however, he found himself facing an economic crisis inspired by laws the House of Delegates had passed while he had been stricken by mourning. Responding to the debilitating failure of taxes on personal property, interest, "cash on hand," and salaries announced in 1777 and 1778 to cover their expenses, the legislature increased land taxes and decided that owners of slaves would pay an additional five pounds per tithable. Due to the shortage of gold and silver specie, and the unreliability of their own paper money, they also instructed that taxes could be paid in the form of tobacco and tobacco certificates.

The taxes on property and slaves, as well as the designated modes of payment, reversed the economic advantage Carter had taken for granted for decades. More than almost anyone in Virginia, he possessed an extraordinary wealth of land, personal possessions, and slaves. Now that vast empire was transformed into a vast tax burden, literally hundreds of pounds of precious specie, or dozens of tons of tobacco per year. Like most gentry, Carter lacked "cash on hand," either to be taxed or to pay taxes. Unlike most landed gentry, however, he had also stopped planting tobacco, in large part because he had honored congressional calls to diversify his crops: "Previous to that tax," Carter explained, "my intention was to make grain at my Plantations. . . . I was almost without any Tobacco when said Tax was Collecting—"

The new rules tested Carter's resourcefulness. Years later, writing to a recalcitrant tenant, he would call himself both a "rich man" and a "poor man," trying to explain how he could be among the wealthiest men in Virginia yet dependent upon others to collect the staples required to fulfill his civic duty: "If the yearly payments therefrom do exceed the necessary demands," he told Abraham Vaughan, "then it may be said that I am Rich—but if the yearly Demands exceed the payments than may it be said that I am poor." Carter felt malaise, a certain "heaviness": in letters, he referred to the "heavy public claim," or the "heavy Demand this Commonwealth is now making on me." But he honored the tax bill. He did not profiteer to make up the difference; instead he hardened his opposition to the idea of profit itself: "the Notion of Profits I can't bare," he wrote bitterly, rejecting the offer of reimbursement for a gift he presented to the French war hero de Grasse. He declined to sell slaves, despite the fact that the proceeds from the sale of one slave could settle the yearly tax bill of most Virginia gentlemen of the era. He also refused to use them to reimburse his tax burden, despite the fact that the House of Delegates subsequently designated slaves as legal tender for this purpose.

Rather, Carter traded his harpsichord to the Lees for Indian corn. He turned more and more to the "barrs" of "pigg iron" that were forged in Baltimore, and which now became the salvation of his family: he shipped them to Norfolk in exchange for more Indian corn, and to Williamsburg to pay tuition on the education that Robert Bladen, like his father before him, was squandering. His situation, however, still worsened. When he applied for an exemption for interstate commerce in September, in order to provide his share of supplies to the Iron Works, the Council of State that he had rejected in turn rejected him—"This Resolution . . . is singularly hard on me," he noted. Finally, he borrowed: sixty-five thousand pounds of tobacco in 1779 alone, bought at the seller's price and at "considerable loss."

Even these emergency steps, however, barely slowed the anarchy that was increasingly enveloping Carter's plantations. In October 1779, Frances, who had given birth to their sixteenth child, Sophia, the previous November, was pronounced an invalid: the Carter family physician, one "Doctor Todd," recommended that she take rest away from Nomony, a prescription that, two centuries later, speaks loudly to the estrangement that entered their marriage as Carter turned his plantation into a revival camp. Carter's businesses, meanwhile, faltered. Inflation continued rampant, and made a mockery of his efforts to conduct "trade." And Carter's religious proclivities were also biting into his fortune. He began introducing religious homily into his business practices in remarkable ways: to an overseer seeking authority to collect unpaid rents, Carter wrote that "the present time is not a time for litigation," and cited biblical precedent on forgiveness.

Even more remarkably, he began hiring ministers for the most unlikely of tasks: as rent and debt collectors. He hired John Sutton as his agent, despite the fact that Sutton's only recommendation for the position was his preaching skill. He also hired Henry Toler, a preternaturally eloquent teenager whom Carter had sent to an academy in Philadelphia to study "God & Literature," not trade or mathematics. Even Lunsford received lists of unpaid debts from Carter, long detailed graphs that the older man could compose from memory and which simply befuddled the Wonderful Boy.

By the spring months of 1780, in other words, it became clear that the Revolution without was being trumped by the revolution within. Carter felt deep antipathy for British sympathizers: he fired one employee, the loyalist Thomas Dudley, telling him that "you may never expect either Countenance or protection from me . . . for your offences against god and your Country." But he kept his distance from the heroes of the war as well: when offered an opportunity to ally himself with the Washingtons— a proposal of marriage made to his daughter Priscilla from George Washington, the general's nephew—Carter responded with almost complete indifference: "I am apprehensive," he wrote on February 2, 1780, "however if her-self + mother should think otherwise—I shall not refuse to let Priscilla marry." He now regarded himself as a pacifist, one whose moral objections to war itself grew as the War went on: even after his sons were cleared of service (Robert Bladen had received a "Ticket marked Clear" in a military lottery), Carter wrote James Madison, the minister who governed William and Mary, and asked for biblical citations "forbiding Hostilities."

Moreover, he continued to recognize his deepening empathy with his slaves. By 1780, he began refusing to allow runaway slaves to be flogged, and told several of his overseers that they could no longer beat his slaves under any circumstances: "I do forbid you," he wrote Thomas Olive, who worked at Nomony, "to correct, in any manner what ever, either old or young negro belonging to me." He also began expanding economic protection to his slaves. When James Ireland, released from his "Palace in Culpeper," received a ministry in Frederick County, Carter reserved a home for him and insisted that paying white tenants on surrounding lands "provide themselves plantations elsewhere," and turned over their farms to his slaves instead, despite revenue increases passed in the March 1780 Assembly session that forced him to sell valuable pig iron "to discharge publick taxes."

The Church, meanwhile, provided him with fresh reminders that he had aligned himself with the outcasts of the new American society. On September 18, he was sitting in the pews at worship when yet another mob of roughs and soldiers invaded Morattico, crippling two of the parishioners, including a young boy named Pitman, and inciting so much anger among the others that a counter-riot ensued in which one of the invading mob was murdered. Carter simply melted into the crowd and disappeared so completely that Lunsford sent a worried note to Nomony that evening, making sure that his benefactor had gotten out alive.

As autumn turned to winter, however, Carter, like most Virginians, found it impossible to hide. On December 30, British troops, led by Benedict Arnold, landed at Jamestown, and spent the early months of 1781 rifling westward through Virginia, chasing the state government from Richmond to Charlottesville, and from Charlottesville to Staunton, facing so little resistance and revealing so many loyalists in the commonwealth that the national response was withering. At the same time, military leaders believed that the Virginia soldiery were near collapse: "few men in the field; not a sixth part of what is called for, a greater number without arms—the greatest part of whom live day to day upon food that is injurious to their health—" the Marquis de Lafayette told Thomas Nelson, governor of Virginia, in 1781.

Facing economic and military disaster, the Virginia government in June 1781 ordered the printing of twenty million nearly useless Virginia dollars, and passed legislation so authoritarian that one minor legislator actually called for the appointment of a "dictator" to expedite the functions of government—which now included the seizure of property "as may be wanted," the right to jail "any person and persons whatsoever" without court hearing, the declaration of martial law within twenty miles of any military personnel, and death sentences for any loyalist who refused to leave the country, and any soldier who deserted and took his rifle with him.

At Nomony, the effects of the British military presence and the altered political climate left Carter, like many Virginians, virtually helpless, his property all but forfeit. On January 12, the local recruiting officer for the Westmoreland Militia, "armed with a Sword," and accompanied by "3 white Men," invaded Carter's Aries textile mill, kidnapped "Negro Will," then released him when they came upon "Negro Prince"—Prince Johnson, a teenage weaver—whom they described as the "Person they wanted." They then held Prince as ransom for 2,065 pounds they claimed Carter owed the militia in payment for the failure of a recruit he provided to pass muster. Carter was stunned: he sought immediate assurances that the soldiers would not harm Prince, and offered them loan certificates in exchange for his safety, despite the fact that, even amid inflationary spirals, no healthy male slave was worth more than two hundred pounds.

Then, in the first week of April, two British ships, the *Trimmer* and the *Surprise*, stopped three times at Carter's Coles Point plantation and left with thirty-three slaves on board. The incident troubled Carter, not only because he loathed the British incursion but because he suspected that the slaves had voluntarily "put themselves under the Care and direction of some officers in the Service of George the third." In June, as British forces were flushing the state government out of Charlottesville, the American Army began confiscating Carter's property as well, beginning with his "horned cattle": he referred abjectly to a "heavy loss both to Individuals and to the State."

In turn, Carter still fought the war within. In April and May of 1781, Carter clashed genteelly with Richard Henry Lee, by breaking a labor law designed to limit the freedom of movement of black workers. He sent "Bearer Negro Tom . . . and his Team" to retrieve a supply of corn, and Lee turned them away, insisting that Carter send instead "two white men and one Black man"; Carter, in turn, sent two more black servants. In June and July, he scolded his overseer Thomas Olive again, compelling him to return a pot that two of his slaves, "Joan" and "Patty," claimed he stole, not once but twice, to boil salt. But these small dramas meant little amid the larger chaos that now engulfed most Virginians. As Washington's troops encircled Cornwallis at Yorktown at the end of summer, Virginians were relieved and triumphant. But they were angry. The House of Delegates immediately began impeachment proceedings against ex-governor Jefferson, for allowing the British Army to occupy the heart of the state too easily; and against his successor, young Thomas Nelson, for the opposite sin of prosecuting the war at the expense of the civil liberties for which the war was being fought.

And when this sense of self-directed outrage dissipated—both proceedings collapsed by the end of 1781—resentment against the new national government bloomed. Embittered by what they perceived as lack of military support from the Continental Army during the British military occupation of 1780–81, and by congressional negotiations dominated by Northern states that called upon Virginia to surrender its claim to western lands and to provide a cumbersome share of national debt relief, many Virginians simply transferred the pride they felt in overthrowing one overweening government into distrust of the new central authority in Philadelphia: "Our people still retain their opinions of the importance of this State," Joseph Jones wrote to James Madison in June 1783, and "its superiority in the Union."

In this regard, Carter remained a true Virginian, and a tentative American. He loathed paying taxes, what he called "the public claims demanded of me." He loathed the inflation that compelled him to exchange one dollar's worth of gold or silver specie for 167 of the paper dollars authorized by the Continental Congress. He longed for the recovery of his absent slaves: he wrote to the "Comanding officers . . . at Portsmouth, York, & Gloucester" on October 30, and told them to locate any recaptured slaves that identified him as their master. Mostly, though, he resented the clumsy force of the young American government: on December 11, 1781, as Jefferson's impeachment trial was collapsing, Carter was telling Clement Brooke how the navy had impressed his sloop, the *Atwell*, and then sunk it—"Government disappointed me," he wrote simply. A war that was about repelling coercive government had in his eyes constructed a coercive government in its stead, one that persecuted him and his fellow Baptists, took his property, and rewarded profiteers and those of his peers who continued to plant tobacco out of pride or lack of imagination, or who would sell slaves to retire their debts rather than worship alongside them. "I nither give nor Sell Negroes," Carter instead told bidders, defying the economic logic of his predicament, ignoring the forgiving loopholes of government policy, and gradually forcing the issue of what, exactly, he would do with slaves he could not afford, refused to sell, and did not want to master.

3

The luxuries continued to land at the dock at Nomony, though their arrivals slowed to a trickle: two pairs white satin shoes, three bunches artificial flowers, "1 stamped Tiffany hankerchief," "4 Groce best Velvet Corks." And new children continued to replace the ones who were lost: Frances gave birth to Julia in 1783, the seventeenth Carter child, when she was forty-five years old and more or less permanently bedridden. Otherwise, however, Carter's home plantation was an altered place. Not only was Ben dead, but Robert Bladen had been moved out: Carter, with some trepidation, launched his second-born son by giving him "possession & profits" of a 1,200-acre plantation named Billingsgate, "Slaves and Stock," and the occasional services of the malevolent overseer Thomas Olive. Robert Carter's daughters, in turn, began to marry: Frances married a man named Thomas Jones in 1782; Anne Tasker married John Peck, who had replaced Fithian as the family tutor eight years before. Carter, who had spurned Washingtons (and would later spurn Lees) in order to bring these anonymous men into the bloodline, gave each couple a farm, livestock, and ten slaves.

Out in the fields, in his gardens and factories, Carter's slaves still toiled. But their lives were also changed. Thirty-three had left on British ships to uncertain fates. Some had undoubtedly died of smallpox; others were enslaved by new masters. Some few may have remained in the British Navy, joined exile communities forming in distant locales like Nova Scotia, or melted into the free-black communities of the North. For the most part, Carter decided to heed George Washington's calculated indifference: "Several of my own are with the Enemy," Washington observed, "but I scarce ever bestowed a thought on them." But when Carter received word that individual slaves were bound to other plantations, he employed agents to recover them and sell them for the apostasy of trying to escape from him.

Those slaves who remained worked at new tasks, and with new measures of authority. Because of the war, and because of Carter's unusual respect for the intelligence and responsibility of his slaves (a respect that served his wallet as well as his soul), Nomony had industrialized: there were five times more slaves working as carpenters, spinners, bricklayers, shoemakers, blacksmiths, and artisans than as domestic servants. Daniel Sullivan, the Irishman who trained Robert Carter's teenage weavers, stayed through the decade to take "Care + Management of the Negro weavers." Otherwise, though, Carter usually kept white artisans around only long enough to train his slaves. Slave craftsmen produced clothing, shoes, and other goods for blacks as well as whites, slaves as well as freemen, often using the same materials and the same processes, and often within arrangements that mocked the ideals of freedom and capitalism by mimicking them. A slave named Jack Smith, for instance, was the blacksmith: he shoed horses and hammered out nails for whites and blacks throughout Westmoreland, was paid for his efforts, and turned over his wages to Carter.

Meanwhile, the slave population of his plantations kept growing: what had been 184 slaves in 1773 exceeded 400 by 1785. And so, while some families were divided to make up dowries for the Carter daughters, and some were forced to follow Robert Bladen, and some "men of gallantry" were shipped north to cut and haul wood for the furnace at the Baltimore Iron Works, Nomony remained a stable, even overpopulated community. Grandfathers and grandmothers were moved so they could take care of grandchildren, or receive care if they were invalid. Prince Johnston, Carter's favorite, became a tanner. Tom Henry, the coachman, began to practice medicine. Sam Harrison, who took communion alongside Carter in 1777, continued to care for Master's wig, and shave Master's face. Sukey, who in 1774 had chased off Ben Carter like the ghost he would become, married Solomon Dixon, the miller, and bore eight slave children:

Fanny, Billy, Moses, Nutty, Elijah, Solomon, Jemima, and Flora. By 1781, she was also complaining of "fits"—history will never tell us whether life at the heart of the Carter household was too much for her, or whether she had invented a nervous ailment to recuse herself from serving them.

Carter, meantime, emerged from war brokenhearted and yet still hungering for fulfillment, convinced that the Revolution had gone both too far and not far enough. He was not remotely the only Virginian who suffered personal loss and civic malaise at the same time, not remotely the only Virginian less than elated with the uncertain new world that the triumph of Washington's armies brought into being. Throughout the thirteen states, in fact, there was a widespread sense that the new country was nearing what Alexander Hamilton, in the *Federalist Papers,* called "the last stage of national humiliation," an era marked by depressions, uncertain sovereignties, and a troubling reprisal of the patterns of debt that had shaped so much prewar political feeling: "Our trade was never more compleatly monopolised by G.B.," James Madison told James Monroe on June 21, 1785, "when it was under the direction of the British Parliament than it is at this moment." "Times are Verry dull here," Richard Lemmon, one of Robert Carter's agents, told his employer that same month. "Money verry Scarce."

Carter saw his share of the "national humiliation" all around him. He continued to experience cash shortages: "Gold & Silver I have not," he lamented. He sought out new ways to generate income: he leased out his stallions to "cover" local mares, for instance, one and a half dollars for the first "leap," seventy-five cents for every "leap" after. He clearly believed that "Abuses" were "too frequent among Tenants," as George Mason acknowledged to him in 1781. But he acknowledged as well that "I am more defective in collecting money than most persons." He scolded John Sutton, itinerant preacher turned rent collector, for not seeking enough "excuses" from his tenants for not paying their rents. Sutton, in turn, continued to mismanage Carter's affairs. When he neglected to pay property taxes on Carter's lands in Loudon County for three years, the sheriff of that county seized the farms, an event that so formally embarrassed Carter—and which would never have happened before the war—that he rushed payment within a week.

Carter fared even worse among close friends and relatives than among his tenants. Other Virginia families no longer paid him the same homage he enjoyed in the prewar period: when Carter, in 1785, begged Philip Lee for an extension of unpaid tobacco debt, Lee curtly refused. He sued Dunmore twice, trying to recover the bond he had extended to the Scottish lord in 1772, before he became America's most formidable enemy. His own relatives, in turn, kept suing him: his cousin Charles, whose father Carter had once offered to have arrested, over lands near his birthplace at Corotoman in a tract called the Frying Pan; and his in-laws especially, the Ogles, Lowndeses, Taskers, and Dulanys, over a variety of aggrievements that never seemed to dissipate their momentum. With great deference, he asked Patrick Henry and George Mason to intervene: both demurred.

Perhaps most embarrassing, though, were the actions of his own son, Robert Bladen. Like his father, Bob Carter avoided formal schooling, and spent more than he could afford. And like his father, Bob Carter fled to England at the first opportunity. Unlike his father, however, Bob Carter never deviated from the path of the reprobate. By February 1783, he had lost control of his taxes, his spending, and his gambling debts. Displaying that the radical intuitions that had inspired his infatuation with Phillis Wheatley had horribly withered, he started selling teenage girls at Billingsgate away from their families. When his father heard that Bob had sold fifteen-year-old Lucy to a family overseer, he interceded to stop the sale. When Bob sold her sister Nanney in April 1784, however, Carter did not intercede. By June, it became clear why: Robert Bladen had accumulated roughly seventy different creditors, and owed taxes and gaming debts worth more than eighty tons of tobacco. Rather than settle his debts, Bob fled to England again. And rather than acquire them, his father ordered an auction of land, livestock, and thirty-seven slaves.

Carter distanced himself from the auction, just as he wanted to distance himself from his son. On July 4, 1783 (yet another ironic Independence Day), he turned over its conduct to local agents, providing only one guideline: they were allowed to sell only what would reimburse the debts, and nothing else. The agents then did what Carter must have known they would do: they commandeered the slaves, advertised their sale, and divided husbands and wives, mothers and children, according to the wills of the highest bidder. Carter never forgave his son. He began criticizing him again, as much as when Bob was a wild gentry teen. He acidly sabotaged a marriage proposal from the young man to a "Mrs. Baylor": "I think advisable to inform you," he warned, "that Mr Bladen's Conduct has been very blamable therefore a Caution is requisite." And he tightened his son's budget beyond what might be considered gentlemanly: when Bob returned to Virginia, he could not even order a suit of clothes and "3 pair of Worsted Stockings" without first receiving his father's permission.

But Carter himself clearly regarded the sold slaves with a guilty conscience. When two sold Billingsgate slaves, "Negro Winny . . . forward with Child," and a black man named either "Talbot" or "Tabbard," ran away from Stephens Thomson Mason, Carter intervened to protect them against the inevitable retribution. Winny "Surrendered herself up" at one of his plantations, but Talbot had wounded two white overseers who attempted to capture him, and Carter thought it was "probable . . . he will be Shot." Instead, Carter arranged the capture of Talbot unharmed, and sent him unpunished back to Mason, scolding him that "no outlawry was published." Carter then added, "Your people are both, almost, without Shoes," and told Mason that his own black servant, "Will," would deliver the two servants back to their home plantation, with "provision from hence for himself & your people." If Mason missed Carter's inference that Talbot's life was unnecessarily threatened, he could not ignore the statement Carter made by returning the two slaves with provisions, and even new shoes, led by one (and only one) of his own black servants.

What was most striking about the loss of deference Carter was experiencing, however, was how much it suited him. He savored his new monkish form: "That State has been productive of humiliation," he would later write, "which growth is glorious—" And ironically, that new monkish form was providing him with a new kind of prestige. By 1785, he was established as a national figure in the austere Baptist Church, one who participated in major doctrinal debates, who corresponded with its most eminent ministers and historians, who served on its General Association, and who had helped seed so many Baptist churches in the Northern Neck that well into the twentieth century there remained ten Baptist congregations within ten miles of the site on which his plantation once stood. In fact, Carter, by 1785, had acquired something more than a reputation for beneficence and erudition: the entire drama of his conversion—the man of privilege, wealth, and learnedness who had allowed the Baptist ministry to blast his pride—had acquired national celebrity among the disenfranchised and eclectic populations to whom the dissenters appealed.

To the new visitors at Nomony, Carter remained enigmatic but inspiring. Some were poor, and they responded to Carter's reputation as a figure who bridged the divide between the powerless and the powerful: "we are mostly Illiterate and understand you have Communication with Religious persons of Emminant charrecters," a man named William Briscoe, traveling to Nomony from Kentucky, told him, seeking support for "a youth By the Name of Jesse Bledsoe who has Imbraced Religion Now being twelve years old." Others were international figures who had heard of Carter as far away as Europe. Francis Asbury, the legendary British minister and antislavery activist, "waited on Colonel Carter, a Baptist," at Nomony on May 14, 1785. He was so pleased by Carter's "free conversation on the subjects of religion, Churches, and slavery" that he returned on Christmas Eve to spend the sacred day with the "counselor," whom he described as "a man of a most excellent spirit."

On his plantations, Carter continued to winnow the distinctions that made him a master and made other men slaves. Just as the servant "Negro Sam" became "Samuel Harrison" on the rolls of Morattico, so too did slaves such as "Negro Will" become "black Brother Will" in Carter's private correspondence. But the alteration was more than rhetorical. In its amended version of the Acts of Toleration in 1772, the House of Burgesses had particularly exerted itself to sever dissenting ministries from slave unrest: they stipulated that any minister who caused a slave to "neglect or forsake the service or employment of his, her, or their master or owner, under the pretence of religious worship" could be imprisoned without bail for one full year. Carter, however, turned this fear on its end: he employed the ministers who preached this neglect, and was the master whose authority was undermined. Carter urged his new preacherly agents to seek conversion among his slaves: "It affords very pleasing feelings in me," he told Sutton on July 12, 1781, "that some of the Black family have Satisfyed you that they are now Subjects for Baptism." In turn, he instructed his more secular agents that his black brothers and sisters should be allowed to attend any religious service they chose, at any time or place: "I Never Refuse to Let wone of the people goo to meeting If they Ast my Leafe," the overseer at Forest Quarter reassured him. At times, however, the line between "asking" and "leaving" blurred, and Carter left no doubt that he sided with the slave who sought spontaneous religious experience, even if that search meant unraveling the authority of the slave economy: "I understand by Suckey that she has Leafe of you to Stay at home & wash hir Cloathes at Any time she pleases or to goo to Eviry place to meeting in the week,"

Samuel Straughan fumed. "She Let the worke bee in what Condition it will."

In this way, the Baptist Church helped Carter undo his plantations while he still ran them. As always, Carter's slaves knew they could negotiate with Carter. When "Ralph" told Carter that his house was in a "ruinous state," Carter ordered the construction of a new log cabin. When "Dennis" married a woman living at a distant plantation, Carter arranged for the slave to be transferred to Taurus, the plantation nearest the one belonging to his wife's master. With the exception of the thirty-three Coles Point servants who left on British frigates in 1782, slaves still escaped to Carter, not from him: "Charles" ran after being severely beaten; "Old Abraham + his wife + too Children" ran, they told one overseer, because "they were too Old to Worke." Similarly, Carter continued to favor the versions of events told him by his slaves, often without appeal or challenge: to Straughan, he wrote that "Negro Jerry of Forest plantation informs me that you Stripped him this morning, and with Switches whipped him on his bare back yet the offense you Charged him with was a matter in his own house."

Now, however, he was trusting his slaves more, and providing them with even more autonomy. Prior to the Revolution, for instance, Carter dispatched his own doctors to treat ailing slaves. By 1782, however, he was allowing slaves to choose their own doctors, even slave doctors, approvingly citing the recommendation of "Negro Michael" that "black Hannah," a slave servant of one of Carter's neighbors, was an expert in treating the kind of "fits" that afflicted "Negro Suckey." More remarkable, however, he was also compelling merchants, sea captains, tenants, lawyers, and neighbors to see black faces and hear black voices represent his power and his fortune. His sloop, delivering goods up and down the Chesapeake and Potomac, was guided by a mulatto skipper, a man named William Laurence. His favorite messengers were black men as well: Tom Henry, the coachman, was sent to Portsmouth at the end of 1781 to negotiate with army officers for the return of slaves his master had lost on the *Trimmer* and *Surprise*. "Black Billy," an elderly slave around sixty years old, converted to the Baptist faith, became "Baptist Billy," and became Carter's most trusted emissary, traveling up and down the Northern Neck, exchanging cash and legal papers among government officials, planters, and Carter's white tenants, agents, and overseers.

Repeatedly, Carter would decline or curtail social invitations, using consideration for his slaves as an excuse. He scolded his overseers for making slave messengers ride to Nomony in two days when three or four was more humane, and cut short letters by saying that "Negro Joe is impatient to be dispatched—" He issued harvest instructions to white overseers based upon reports provided by slaves visiting Nomony, Carter's voice and those of his slaves merging into one authoritative testimony: "Presley informs that the Barley is ripe for Cutting, and he expects that the rye and Wheat will continue on the harvest without any interruption." He let his slaves use his fine riding chair, even though the practice required explanation: "It is no uncustomary thing," he scolded one suspicious neighbor. And over and over, he interceded to protect small objects that belonged to slaves who belonged to him—not only Negro George's iron pot, but Negro Harry's meal bags, or Negro Willoughby's pound of yarn. Small things suddenly mattered, implied powerful new equalities. Having to scrabble for hard currency had evidently done wonders for Robert Carter's soul.

But he didn't yet free his slaves. And he could have. The war had altered the Virginian consensus on slavery: while thirty thousand slaves (according to Jefferson's estimate) had left their masters for uncertain fates on Dunmore's ships, many other slaves had served during the Revolution as patriots. Virginians knew about the success of the Rhode Island Plan, which in 1777 had created entire regiments from the ranks of Northern slaves—regiments that led the assault on Cornwallis's besieged troops at Yorktown. Moreover, many powerful Virginians felt sympathy for the bold vision of John Laurens of South Carolina, who repeatedly petitioned George Washington, the Continental Congress, and the South Carolina legislature to approve the enlistment and subsequent emancipation of Southern slaves. After the war, they watched as states such as Pennsylvania enacted legislation that gradually freed thousands of Northern slaves and compensated slaveowners at public expense. Touring Virginia, the French nobleman Marquis de Chastellux observed that emancipation had already won a rhetorical triumph, if not a legislative one: Virginians, he wrote, are "grieved at having slaves, and are constantly talking about abolishing slavery."

And from the moment that the House of Delegates finally honored persistent petitions by Quaker and Methodist meetings by passing "An Act to Authorize the Manumission of Slaves," many small and middle-class slaveholders began to release their slaves, in numbers that rapidly entered the thousands. By 1785, petitions for general emancipations, also inspired by Quaker and other dissenting Protestant sects, had been delivered to the House of Delegates for consideration. Throughout the state, in fact, dissenting Protestants had been sculpting their antislavery positions for a decade and more: the Quaker Robert Pleasants, whose father had tried to free his slaves in 1771, when the practice was still illegal, now tried to entice George Washington and Patrick Henry into placing their crucial signatures on antislavery petitions. Baptist ministers, in turn, told audiences of slaves that God sympathized with their bondage and their suffering, and told white audiences, as did David Rice (whom Carter hosted whenever he could), that they should practice "Self Examination" if they sought to reach heaven.

As with the battle over religious liberty, the battle over slavery provided opportunities for alliances between radical Protestant sects and liberal, well-educated gentlemen. In 1783, Jefferson drafted another emancipation plan for the Virginia Constitution, and the following year presented to the Congress a "Plan of Government for the Western Territory," which would have forbidden the expansion of slavery into new states after 1800. Washington and Henry, while declining to append their signatures to the dissenting petitions, offered words of adamant sympathy in private. Throughout the 1780s, in fact, the Virginia legislature produced a startling collection of laws designed to encourage the liberation of individual slaves. Having banned the slave trade in their first legislative session in 1778—becoming the first government in the Western hemisphere to do so—the House of Delegates in 1785 voted that all slaves transported into the state and kept there for one year "shall be free." Subsequent bills simplified the means by which individual slaves might sue for freedom, including having the government pay all court costs on behalf of the slave, providing counsel at no charge, and banning from jury service any white man who bore a financial interest in the continued servitude of the plaintiff.

From the moment the Manumission Act of 1782 was passed, however, the state legislature also received vituperative counterpetitions from those counties where slavery remained strongest: "this Permission to buy and inherit Bond-men and Bond-maids . . . continued through all the Revolutions of the Jewish Government, down to the Advent of our Lord," several hundred residents of Amelia, Mecklenburg, and Pittsylvania counties argued, "And we do not find, that either he or his Apostles abridged it." In the legislature itself, all efforts to extend the Manumission Act were met with overwhelming opposition, and even derision: when the celebrated Methodist petition of 1785 was presented in the House of Delegates, a "motion was made to throw it under the table," Madison reported to George Washington, and a bill that would have repealed the 1782 Manumission Act nearly passed in its stead.

Similarly, Jefferson's second emancipation proposal, like the first, never received a hearing in the House of Delegates: there were "men of virtue enough to propose" emancipation, Jefferson observed, but "the moment of doing it with success" was "not yet arrived." In the counties, reformers were also met with derision, and fought back in ways that ministers such as Lunsford had once lamented: "We, however, came off with whole bones," Francis Asbury wrote in his journal on April 30, 1785, describing a fight between a pro-slavery "Colonel Bedford" on the one hand and a man Asbury called "brother O'Kelly" on the other.

By 1785, Carter clearly held antislavery opinions: on November 8 and 10 of that year, he spoke with favor of the Methodist "Petition of sundry persons" for "general emancipation," and lamented its curt dismissal, eventually writing in frustration to one correspondent that emancipation was "a Subject that our Legislature will not take up." He ordered a copy of the House of Delegates minutes, and began buying and distributing newspapers to his neighbors again, a sign that he thought the historical moment was a crucial one. Like Jefferson and other genteel slaveholders, however, Carter argued that "Judgements will follow us so long as the Bar is held up," and yet did nothing. Like other progressive planters, like Virginia itself, he had merely found a formula that would allow him to maintain slavery and a belief in his own moral probity at the same time. By training slaves in practical crafts, for instance, he created a large pool of black artisans at Nomony, ignoring the misgivings of other slaveholders who believed that educated slaves were more likely to escape or foment discontent. In so doing, however, he also created a pool of sophisticated laborers that, unlike white wage servants, he did not have to pay—white millers and bakers made twenty-five pounds per year, black ones made nothing—and over whom he possessed significant legal control.

Similarly, Carter's white employees understood that while their authority was limited, they did maintain authority of the most vicious kind. Carter offered no opposition to the idea that slaves could be "a good deal beaten and bruised," refusing only to sanction anything more than "Moderate Correction in every Case." And when overseers disobeyed, Carter tormented them, but did not dismiss them. When Thomas Olive refused to honor Carter's commands to refrain from physically punishing slaves, and ordered the whipping of "Vincent" in September 1784, a small delegation of slaves—Kate, "with Child," Winney, "compelled to come here, by Sickness," and "Abraham, foreman, Tom, boy, Cartman, Vincent three men of Billingsgate"—fled to Nomony and reported the transgression to Carter. Carter then authored the strongest conceivable humiliation for Olive he could imagine. "The Overseer," Carter reported, "asked in the presence of Abraham if he had not full power & Authority to beat strip & whip all the Negroes." In the presence of Abraham, Carter said, "I did not allow him to use his pleasure in such a manner," and called him as "violent, now, as formerly, when I took the power of Correction from him."

But Carter did not fire Olive, and two months later, the overseer claimed that a ten-year-old boy named "Joshua" knew who stole a turkey, and whipped him "on his bare back" until he identified "Negro Toby" as the thief. Olive then ignored the confession and instead "surprised" a slave named "Tom-boy," accused him of the theft, "put a Rope round both his Wrists—striped his Body bare—hoisted & whipped him severely—" Again, a delegation fled to Nomony. Again, Carter believed their accounts without contradiction. Again, Carter chastised Olive. And again, he did not fire him. Carter was still practicing, still more entranced with the reiterative drama of his own righteousness than with the righteous act itself.

4

By 1785, Robert Carter knew that his revolution was not over, that there remained conflict both without and within. Similarly, he understood that slavery was the most visible manifestation of that conflict, if not the cause itself. Economy, religion, politics, and family, however, now all urged compromise, even retreat. By 1785, Virginia had fallen into a profound postwar depression, as the prices of staples such as wheat and corn fluctuated and fell, the value of slaves declined sharply, and the tobacco market entered what looked like its death spiral. Unlike the prewar period, however, Virginians were now also required to pay taxes that made the duties that had inspired the Revolution in the first place look like minor irritations.

Among smaller farmers, unrest was pervasive: two county courthouses burned in suspicious arsons, and sheriffs, those civil servants most responsible for tax collection, acquired the reputation (to use Patrick Henry's words) of "unfeeling bloodsuckers." When combined with the erosion of arable lands in old settled areas such as the Northern Neck, and the inevitable growth of slave populations on the more benignly operated plantations, slaveholding itself, for many large planters, began to look like an anachronism. Carter himself observed that "the Profits arising on land Cultivated by Negroes in this State . . . do not enable proprieters of the like Estates to pay the present taxes—and other Necessary Charges."

Rather than free their slaves, as many small and middle-class planters had done, however, most of Carter's peers chose a different strategy: they sold their slaves by the thousands to planters in Georgia, South Carolina, Kentucky, and western Virginia, forcing their servants to acquire new labor skills in harsh climates. On any given plantation, the removals could be both massive and disruptive, often tearing apart families that had been united for generations: although the population of Monticello never exceeded roughly three hundred, for instance, Thomas Jefferson still sold or gave away more than one hundred sixty slaves from 1784 to 1794, and conducted the sales like a man who preferred to keep families together but regarded the relief of his debts as a larger concern.

On his own plantations, Carter struggled with the same combination of high ideals and economic exigency that he had practiced throughout the decade. He continued to refuse all suitors for his slaves. Instead, he tried to disperse them himself, undertaking a massive, unkempt removal of scores of slaves from his overpopulated plantations on the Northern Neck to unsettled properties on the "Shenandoe" River—"being well satisfyed," he noted in 1787, "that my lands below will not Support those and others who are to remain." In 1784, he composed a list of thirty slaves to be sent to "Libra," but the list promised disaster: eager to keep families together, he sent dozens of children and elderly slaves alongside able-bodied men and women, a population mix poorly designed to settle a wilderness. Moreover, he sent John Sutton, whose "irregular Conduct" now simply "grieve[d]" him, but who could be relied upon to protect the spiritual lives of distant slaves. Within a year, however, so many slaves had fled back to Nomony, complaining of poor work conditions and unmanageable overseers, that only three slaves—two of them children—remained on the Shenandoah tract. Carter declined to punish the runaways, and honored petitions from older slaves to return to less rigorous work conditions on settled plantations. But he persisted with the removals: he sent twenty-eight slaves to Libra and a new plantation, Scorpio, in 1785, where they struggled with illness. Then, in 1787, he sent forty-eight more slaves up the river aboard his ship named the *Mayflower,* where they settled plantations named Capricorn, Sagittarius, and Aquarius.

At Nomony, Carter struggled for funds, a new edge of desperation that exceeded even the heaviness of the war years entering his correspondence. On May 18, 1785, he tried to recover four pounds he sent to a wine merchant named Henry Hill in 1772 for an unfulfilled order for a "parcel of Earthern Bowls" for his harmonica. He sent letters inside letters in order to save postage. He began selling assets: he sold his share of the Baltimore Iron Works to Abraham Van Bibber, a Dutchman who had conducted espionage and diplomacy in the West Indies for the state of Virginia during the Revolutionary War, for twenty thousand pounds. He relinquished control of most of his plantations, arranging long-term leases with agents he trusted only slightly more than his tenants, leaving only two—Nomony itself and the neighboring Aries—under his direct control by 1788. He rented his corn and flour mill, his enormous bakery and wheat mill, and his textile factory, arranging in the last case detailed instructions that guaranteed to the slaves food, clothing, medical care, and "a Garden for each Tenement."

Morattico, meanwhile, offered him less and less solace. While the General Committee of the Baptist Church passed a motion in 1785 that declared "hereditary slavery to be contrary to the word of God," a "tumult" ensued when brethren at the Ketocton Association meeting in 1787 actually tried to compose a gradual emancipation plan. In church after church, the increasing conservatism of the Baptist Church altered the way that individual congregations and their pastors managed their small, daring communities. Morattico had always been radical in this regard: the names of slaves, free blacks, and whites intermingled on their charters and petitions, on their committee assignments, and on their letters of dismission. As the 1780s progressed, however, Morattico, like most other churches in the sect, began to segregate its meetings, finally permitting only "free male members"—a distinction that briefly tortured the powers that governed the Baptist Church—to vote on all church matters.

These changes frustrated Carter, both as a political matter and as a reflection of his inner spiritual conflict. He knew he was important to the Baptist Church. But he also knew that he was vastly more eloquent as an anomalous example of God's diffuse grace than as a voice describing that grace. He never fully surrendered his aristocratic distance from the spontaneity of Baptist religious services, as much as he sometimes wanted: he never approved of laying on hands, never wanted to be touched by the disenfranchised men and women whose fellowship he had otherwise embraced. He tried to exhort once, alongside the bridge at the Rappahannock Creek, one May day in 1785 when the scheduled preacher did not appear. He never tried again, and the only witness to record the event used the word "Disappointment."

He recognized that his stiffness was a failing, keeping a quote from a religious tome carefully cited in one daybook to remind him that his redemption was imperfect: "There is much stupidity of Mind, & Hardness of Heart, remaining unmortified in the Best of Saints . . . Burket-p-108.-1 Column." Itinerant ministers, who loved and feared Carter, sought to comfort him on this point: "Because we cannot dive to the bottom & drink the sea dry," Henry Toler, still a teenager, advised him, "that is no reason we should not drink part." But Carter still wanted to drink the whole sea. By 1785, he began drifting from the Baptist Church, arguing so emotionally with the sect elders and his fellow brethren that it became disturbing: "the Company of each must have been distressing to each other," Toler wrote after one such argument. He scolded correspondents who suggested that God chose some to be saved and some to be lost: "Where is it written?" he asked, almost rhetorically. "I cannot find it in the Word of God." He even grew tart with Lunsford. Where formerly he had signed his letters "Yours in gospel bonds," he now composed disputatious salutations: "from a Pilgrim not satisfied with the Assurance of Salvation from the guilded Doctrine of Eternal Justification," he signed off one letter, to the minister who led him into the sect a decade before.

The compromises within the Baptist Church, however, merely reflected a growing national consensus on the practical applications of ideals of liberty. By the end of the 1780s, many Virginian leaders and citizens— including Madison, most openly—increasingly believed that consolidation of the power of the states was the solution to national woes. Others felt that a stronger federal government represented an abandonment of the promises of the Revolution, and they became national leaders of the fight against the Constitution. Richard Henry Lee argued that the federal government proposed in the Constitution would be led by "a coalition of Monarchy men, Military Men, Aristocrats, and Drones whose noise, impudence, & zeal exceeds all belief." George Mason worried about a "Monarchy, or a corrupt oppressive Aristocracy." Patrick Henry questioned the authority of the Constitutional Convention itself—"What right had they to say, 'We, the People'?"—and compared his new defiance to his stand against the Stamp Act two decades before:

> I have lived long enough to become an old fashioned fellow: Perhaps an invincible attachment to the dearest rights of man may, in these refined enlightened days, be deemed old fashioned: If so, I am contented to be so . . .

Ironically, Carter would not become an anti-federalist, as those political leaders who opposed the Constitution were called. In fact, he expressed his pleasure that his "Neighbours" had "marked all Antifederalists," savoring the use of epithet, and even mob intimidation, against those who opposed the Constitution. But he shared the anti-federalist's disappointment in the moral and economic condition of the new country, and shared, as well, Henry's belief that the new national culture had defied the independent "soul of Virginia." Moreover, he watched the Constitutional debates with unease: he understood what someone such as George Washington meant when he observed that "I can foresee no evil greater, than disunion," and yet hoped that "union" could be purchased without Constitutional commitments to the future of slavery and without the ongoing political potency of slaveholding Southern planters such as himself.

In private, men such as Washington lamented the spirit of "deference and concession" with which pro-slavery demands from Georgia and South Carolina were knit into the Constitution: a twenty-year extension of the slave trade, and extra representation for the South, in exchange for slaveholders' support of articles that allowed economic legislation to be more easily enacted. Even contemporary observers noted how the final document evaded the issue altogether, and how the word "slave" never appeared in its contents, the presence of African labor in America instead buried verbally among "other persons." The delegates, William Paterson observed, were simply "ashamed."

The great Virginians, without a doubt, were troubled, and began to contemplate measures that might ameliorate slavery, at least in their own hearts and on their own plantations. George Wythe eventually liberated several of his slaves, and provided them rents and interest in trust, a plan so generous that the grandnephew with whom the liberated slaves would share his estate placed arsenic in his coffee. Washington began to speak—in private—about schemes that might "make the Adults among them as easy & as comfortable in their circumstances" and "to lay a foundation to prepare the rising generation for a destiny different from that in which they were born." Jefferson, too, wrote of placing his slaves "ultimately on an easier footing," and considered importing German farmers to lease his lands in fifty-acre tenancies, "intermingled" with his slaves, and employing them as free labor in the manner of European peasants.

Carter, too, turned inward. His rhetoric bore no hint of compromise: "tolerating Slavery indicates great depravity," he wrote curtly in 1788, as the Constitutional ratification debate raged. But what set Carter apart was his astonishing treatment of his family. By the middle of the decade, Carter's sons and sons-in-law had provided ample evidence that they would be, at best, average slaveholders, unwilling to part with the wealth represented by African bodies, and equally unable to mend their ways to be more responsible patriarchs themselves. John Peck, the Princeton student who married Anne Tasker, took his new wife north in 1785, but first insisted that her dowry slaves be sold for "Cash or Tobacco" to "any Purchaser." Then, in June 1786, Robert Bladen returned to Nomony from England ready to make amends and accept whatever employment his father offered. But as he sat in his father's study, rehearsing what he might say, he grew frightened, panicked, and fled, not stopping until he had returned to London. He sent a note a few days later, telling his father that

> it has and ever will be the case I am afraid, when before you; in my serious reflections, I have observed a stoppage in my Throat and intellects vastly confused; what it proceeds from God only knows.

Carter understood the problem clearly: as much as any slaveholder in paternalistic times, he knew that he was "father" not only to his biological children but also to his slaves, for whom he was expected to provide subsistence, labor, discipline, protection, and even, incredibly, love. In his letters, like many slaveholders, he referred to "the Whites & black[s] in our families here." For other slaveholders, especially liberal ones, this anomaly was a Gordian knot, impossible to cut. To free one's slaves might fulfill one's responsibilities to that share of the "Whites & black[s] in our families here." But emancipation undermined the fundamental duty of every slaveholder to the other shade of child, to "launch," as William Fitzhugh wrote, one's real sons and daughters "out into some happy subsistence" by protecting their inheritance.

Carter, however, tried a third path, one that he might have conceived as early as that chilly February meeting in Morattico in 1783. Shortly after the aborted meeting with Robert Bladen in the library, he sent his two younger sons, J.T. and George, to the Baptist seminary in Providence that he had helped finance "till each of them arrive to the Age of 21 years." As he did so, he cited one reason, and one reason only: he told James Manning, the seminary's president, that the "most abject State of Slavery in this Common-Wealth" had inspired a choice almost unique among Virginian slaveholders.

For the rest of the decade, Carter tried to make his children Northerners—or, at least, tried to liberate them from the need to be cared for, and supported by, slave labor. In November 1788, he also sent three of his four unmarried daughters away to Baltimore (ironically, the same city to which he often sent unruly slaves), to live with a middle-class Baptist family of Carter's acquaintance, providing instructions for their hosts that the "Girls are not to act by a Maid, but by themselves"—by which he meant that they would live with no help from the slave that Carter sent as barter for their room and board. When Sarah Fairfax, the fourth daughter, announced her engagement, Carter said that her dowry would consist of "one thousand Pounds," and not the "Land, negroes, and Stock, which each of her Sisters hath received," a clear indication that he remembered that John Peck and Anne had sold their slaves for cash.

Perhaps the most extraordinary example of how deeply Carter's feelings toward slavery became enmeshed with his family, however, resided in his treatment of his youngest son. J.T. was clearly a disappointment—"Literature he detests, and [he turns] to dissipation"—so Carter proposed to James Manning that J.T. "be entered immediately with an approved farmer in your Neighbourhood, and Articles passed to give the farmer a right to his Service" with "the Privilege of Eating at his Masters table."

J.T. never became an indentured servant, even one who could eat at the master's table: Carter instead found a place for this dissolute son in an academy in Philadelphia, living with the minister who governed the school. For the most part, however, Carter sternly enforced his new rules for his children. He refused every request his children made to come home: "I cannot consent that either of my Sons should Visit here," he wrote Manning on September 24, 1787. "Such a Vacation would be attended with bad Consequences." As he honored requests from slaves to keep their families intact, he forced his own family apart—he told Manning to enforce "a Separation of my two Sons"—scattered them across the Eastern Seaboard, and declined *their* appeals for reunion. He refused social invitations in inclement weather when he was afraid his coachman would catch cold: "I cannot think of exposing my Servants," he told William Dawson. But when George took sick in the Rhode Island cold, and doctors recommended that the boy be sent to Wilmington in North Carolina "as proper temperature of Air for Geo: to live in," Carter refused, instructing that his son "should wear a Garment under his Shirt affording a Covering for his Body Arms and Thighs" all through the following winter rather than allow him to live among slaves in a balmier climate.

If his sons, those would-be masters of men, could have challenged Carter—if they could, unlike Robert Bladen, unstop their throats in that austere, authoritarian presence—one imagines that the elder man would have been prepared to respond. He would have told them, if he could unstop his own throat, that perpetually repressed instrument, that there was a principle at work, and whatever insults and confusion that his children endured spoke to the strength of his desire to create an heir he could trust. He might have told them that the only slaves he had separated from their families since the war ended were the slaves he had given to his children, and that fact frustrated him. As well, Carter might have reminded them of his own sacrifices: that he had surrendered control of his plantations, that he had abandoned profitable as well as unprofitable enterprises, that he had foresworn a church that he had sacrificed great authority and prestige to join.

It is unlikely, however, that any such conversation would have met with their approbation, or that they would have thanked their father for trying to cleanse from their futures what Tom Paine had called "inglorious connexion." On the last day of October 1787, Frances Carter, having spent sev-

eral years as an invalid, finally passed away. As she declined during the
summer and early autumn, Carter had regarded her with detached yet
puppyish longing, he at Nomony, she at Bladensburg: he sent her one mis-
sive after another, complaining that "no letter from you to us by post has
come to hand," and wondering when she was going to return to Virginia.
And when she died, he threw himself into sorrow with marked aban-
don: he bought thirty-seven items of mourning, the word "black" reiterat-
ing itself in almost every entry ("29 yd black bombazeen 2 yd fine black
Durants . . . 3 pair black leather gloves 2 pair black morocco Shoes 1 pair
Ditto Ditto Slippers," four "mourning fans," and six pounds of chocolate),
and buried her, not quite as she requested, underneath a plain red brick in
the family garden.

Carter told friends that he had lost his "Old companion and helpmate,"
and that her "Soul was full of Love"—like many gentry, she had converted
to the Baptist Church during a great revival in 1786, almost exactly when
he began to contemplate leaving it. And he wrote Henry Toler, the teenage
Baptist prodigy, and urged him to attend the "private" funeral. But he
banned his sons from the service, refusing to allow them to leave Rhode
Island, and explicitly casting slavery as the reason: "The Example and
Custom in this Neighborhood I take to be very destructive both to the
Morals and advancement of youth," he told Robert Rogers, "Master of an
Academy at Newport," on December 7, 1787. One doubts George and J.T.
understood him, or forgave him.

5

Seen as a public matter, 1788 might have been Robert Carter's last sane
year, the last moment before he succumbed to the same confusion that
marked his grandfather's last years on earth, that disease the elder King
had called "the madness of the people"—the inability to resolve the will to
power with the will to rebel against power. Unlike his grandfather, however, Carter was ingenious in this last tempestuous moment. He crafted
an organizational scheme that, he hoped, might transform the Baptist
Church into a more truly egalitarian institution: he composed a charter for
the Yeocomico Church that insisted that "a majority shall determine every
question that may be proposed in Church meetings," and hoped that it

might be "offered to the consideration of all the Churches, now in union," as a template for churches throughout America. And then he left Morattico for this splinter church, signing his name to the Yeocomico charter underneath the signatures of Samuel Harrison, Jemima Redman, Hannah Turner, Phillis Lavender, and other slaves, and taking his place as the members of this new congregation celebrated their newfound "union and fellowship to each other" by "rising and joining hands in a circle."

Even more remarkably, he made an effort to rejoin the government, running for office for the first time in nearly thirty-five years. As the Constitution, which had been completed in September 1787, moved to the individual states for their ratification conventions, Carter found the debate so "interesting and important" that he decided in November to end his self-imposed political exile and "offer himself a Candidate" for the Virginia ratification convention. He gathered a list of the freeholders available to vote, divided the county into four "Classes," and asked four men to circulate among those electors, asking them in turn to sign a petition indicating that they would vote for him—without telling either his agents or the freeholders how he would vote if they sent him to the ratification convention.

Whether or not this odd, detached campaign strategy indicated that Carter remained stung by his losses in 1752 and 1754 and did not want to run unless he was sure he would not lose, or that, despite his religious conversion, he had not otherwise shed an aristocratic temperament entirely unsuited for participatory politics, he did not serve, and the Constitution as a topic disappeared from his correspondence. In a like manner, he refused to invest the bulk of his spiritual hopes at Yeocomico: in January 1788, Carter received a visitor he called "Mr Moyce," and his visitor spoke with such enthusiasm about Baron Emanuel Swedenborg, whose Church of the New Jerusalem was so small that only a handful of copies of its publications could be found in America, that Carter wrote the word "Swedenburgh" in bold letters along the left margin of his journal.

Before he could act on this advice, though, or more deeply absorb himself in the "circle" at Yeocomico, Carter grew ill, and withdrawn. There was "a late trying season" sometime in early 1788. He became increasingly insomniac, telling Toler on one occasion that "a very little Sleep has possessed my eyes since I saw you," falling into what he called a "watchful state" laden with opportunities for "contemplation." He transcribed lengthy, arcane folk remedies into journals, his faith in Enlightenment medical practices fading:

> Take 2 qts rye bran, 6 Spoonful of Clean Tar, 1 qt hony 7 qts Stagnated water Stir all to gether and Simmer them all together in a Clean iron Vessel till reduced to one half, let it stand till Cool . . . this has Cured dangerous Consumptions in a fortnight.

He began to speak of "Agues, which were succeeded by fevers." Finally, he died, or seemed to: "We have been alarmed with the news of your death," Lunsford told him on December 11, 1789, "but have happily heard it contradicted."

That Carter might lose heart at this passage in history was neither surprising nor unique: weariness with the anarchy of the postwar economy and its politics was something he shared with even devoted Federalists such as Alexander Hamilton, who would write, "This American world was not made for me." Undoubtedly, the loss of his wife had scored him, turned him briefly outward to Yeocomico and the ratification convention, and left him more susceptible to those unnameable "agues." As well, he missed his children, even as he compelled them to stay away from Virginia: he told Rogers in Newport that he was "deny[ing] myself the pleasure of the sight and conversation of my Sons now in the State of Rhode island," and asked his daughter Sarah Fairfax in April 1789 to return to Nomony and to bring "whomever of your acquaintances that may favour you with their company to this place."

As well, however, Carter was tried by the failure of the great public compromises of the late 1780s to yield a resolution that spoke to his ethical sensibility. Like Jefferson, who composed one emancipation proposal after another, and who felt great and genuine frustration when they failed to inspire consensus, Carter hoped that the will of Virginia would settle the issue of slavery for him: in August 1788, he told a Baptist elder in Britain that "the latest petition before the house of Delegates, praying for Liberation, was rejected by a great Majority." Unlike Jefferson, however, he was growing impatient: "Let us then Unite in prayer," he added, "to Correct this Error."

By 1788, Carter was also struggling to keep his slaves fed and clothed. He told John Leland on April 9, 1788, that "the present deficiency of Corn in this County is alarming—and duty calls on me to be more active in the field." The same slaves who once fled to Nomony to seek protection from violent overseers now arrived to report that they were underclothed, and to request new shirts, shoes, and blankets. On December 15, 1789, "Negro Jesse" visited Carter from Old Ordinary, and gave him the names of "nine . . . negroes" who were "bear of Cloathing." Carter responded with promptness and a new parsimony: he wrote that same day to the overseer Solomon Nash, and told him that "should . . . you think that cloathing is absolutely necessary, . . . inform Major Muse," the local storekeeper, "that he may consider me as a ready money dealer." He even began to circulate advertisements asking for the reimbursement of his outstanding debts, a strategy that suggests how desperate he was for cash, and for closure: "Robert Carter requests the favor of all Persons in this County who owes him either Cash, Tobacco or Grain to pay off said demands immediately."

Seen from another angle, however, 1788 may have been Carter's *first* sane year, the first moment where the cure for the madness of the people began to really possess him, and transform his business, spiritual, and political practices. His economic emergencies, in many ways, remained largely self-imposed, a symptom of resolution, not desperation: despite his protestations, he always produced hard money when it mattered, and had managed to maintain the rough contours and size of the Nomony fortune without relying on the sale (or even the hire) of slaves. Moreover, the pattern of withdrawals that marked his entrepreneurial life during the latter part of the decade began to bear resemblance to a conscious design with a conscious motive. A decade and a half of identifying with his slaves, and of learning to respect their acumen, had not brought him any closer to freeing them. And a decade and a half within the Baptist Church had not produced a second gracious illumination to match the first. But what Carter taught himself instead was that slavery, like all sin, was intertwined in every major institution of his life, and that withdrawal from the slaveholder's life required, as well, withdrawal from the fine mesh of ideas and beliefs upon which slavery depended, including those ideas and beliefs that wore the most benign façades.

By 1789, in other words, Carter had readied the ground for yet another reinvention, one that might finally unify right thought with right action: that lost fortnight in December 1789 when he "died" could not have been better, or more symbolically, timed. In later letters, Carter would often refer to what he called his "first life," as if there were a second, even a third and a fourth: "Disappointments in our first Life are common to all," he told one of his sons-in-law, Thomas Jones, in 1794. In fact, Carter could look back at 1754, and 1777, and observe that his life had been constructed as a series of new beginnings, where disappointments both within and without had grown so unmanageable that nothing less than ritual rebirth would keep the vast incongruities of his personality in synchronicity.

In Anglican and Baptist church histories, Carter is described unsurprisingly as a failed and dissatisfied servant of the Lord: "Once a man get wrong," Robert Baylor Semple, the prominent early-nineteenth-century historian of the Baptist Church, stated in regard to the councillor, "it is impossible to foresee where he will stop." It is tempting to argue, as did Semple, that Carter simply possessed "an unstable disposition": at the very least, Carter's life affirms William James's maxim in his classic *Varieties of Religious Experience* that "a religious life, exclusively pursued, does tend to make the person exceptional and eccentric." But Carter's religious restlessness was madness with a method, his instinct for the radical act blossoming into a rebellion against all institutions that settled for anything less. Just as Carter left the Anglican Church in 1777 for a persecuted church with impoverished and enslaved members—in fact choosing the most disenfranchised church he could find—he left that church just as a new revival led many landed gentry into its fold. By 1790, the Baptist Church could claim twenty thousand adherents in Virginia: "I have never seen anything more like taking the kingdom by violence than this," Jesse Lee observed in 1788. By 1800, the Baptist Church was one of the two largest sects in Virginia, their ministers had discontinued the practice of "odd tones, disgusting whoops and awkward gestures," and any politician who dared speak out against religious liberty, as Leland wrote, could "no more be popular."

As the Baptist Church grew more popular, of course, it also grew more pro-slavery. By 1793, the General Association of the Baptist Church in Virginia voted "by a large majority" to cease all debate on the subject, "believing it belongs to the legislative body." By 1802, the General Association expanded this restriction and simply banned all blacks from voting at church meetings. Within a decade, church records began to include assigned, segregated seating charts, barring as well the possibility that slaves, free blacks, and whites could sit next to one another in Baptist churches any more than they could within the starchy pre-Revolution Anglican churches that the dissenters had rendered irrelevant to American life.

Carter recognized the reversal: he had not joined the Baptist Church to sit in segregated pews and talk tobacco with the local gentry. While he continued to oppose the laying on of hands, which the General Association fully approved in 1792, his most passionate disputes revolved around both practical and doctrinal disagreements where he was eager to be more egalitarian than they could support. From his own perspective, he fell away from a church that doled out salvation in unequal portions, and insisted that men and women could not transcend the history trapped inside their bodies. As early as 1781, in fact, he was calling the idea of "universal restoration" a "heretical doctrine," almost with a thrill of pleasure in his voice, as if he had found the radical seed from which his rejection of all worldly hierarchies might grow. He refused to believe that some men and women, once they were saved, could do no wrong, could not forfeit their saved position: "A true believer may finally fall" was a sentiment that earned paragraphs in his untitled religious notes. Likewise, he rejected the idea that men and women lacked the will and the agency to alter their destinies: "Man is somewhat more than a mere inannimate Statue," he told Manning near the end of 1789.

At such times, it seemed clear how much Carter was speaking about himself, about his urgent private desire to transcend the history trapped inside himself, and the history revolving all around him. But the achievement of Robert Carter's decade within the Baptist Church lay in the fact that he increasingly believed that he could transcend history only by transcending slavery, a belief that compelled him to identify the liberation of his slaves with the liberation of his own spirit. That he remained one of the largest slaveholders in Virginia during this period also indicates the extent to which the contradiction within the Baptist Church paralleled the contradiction within himself: his conscience, like theirs, could still be sated by bright displays of moral doctrine, and could overlook what compromises lay buried in the church minutes, or the Nomony daybooks.

Increasingly, however, Carter grasped the earthbound implications of his doctrine. Among conservative gentlemen who were unable to adapt to revolutionary realities, radical gentlemen who deftly balanced revolutionary sentiments with a very real desire to maintain social order in the new nation, and radical gentlemen who looked back nostalgically to 1776, Carter crafted an original course. As the great founders grew more important, more central to the new country, he joyously marginalized himself, as a matter of principle and a matter of faith: "We Seem to be detached from the world," he wrote one son-in-law in 1786. "We do presume you have written letters to us." Instead, he meditated elegiacally about secular power: "Upon examination it may be found that there are Popes against Popes—Councils against Councils," he wrote in 1787, "a Consent of Fathers of one Age, against a consent of fathers of another Age." Increasingly, as well, he used the Church as a prism through which he could transcend "nation" and, incidentally, salve the spirit broken when the ties between crown and colony were sundered with firearms: "We believe that Christ's Church in her miletant state is not <u>national</u>," he insisted, "but <u>congregational</u>." Carter's spirituality, in other words, became the vehicle with which he could distance himself from the new nation founded in compromises he could not bear. Just as heretical religious doctrines provided the means by which Carter could criticize the Baptist Church in its secular forms, so too could they provide the means by which Carter, still a gentleman of the old style and a friend of the Revolution, could express profound criticisms of the new era of American politics without seeming to do so.

It was this mild but principled antinational bias that would become an essential prerequisite for the composition of an emancipation plan when most of the new country's leaders believed that freeing the slaves would undo the republic. From the moment that Carter watched military men dismantle Lunsford's stage, a part of him ceased to believe that the security of the new United States was worth every sacrifice of freedom. But he described his sense of difference as a religious difference, not a political one: the fatal pride of Deism, according to Carter, was that its proponents believed that "the Regulation of social Life is the only end of Religion." That many of those Deists governed the new nation, however, constituted a fact that Carter left unstated. Instead, a form of alienation blossomed implicitly toward his peers, a sense that he considered their political and religious vision somehow inauthentic: the word "real" began to enter his letters, and rarely without a sarcastic sting, as in "I delight in real Believers." Carter had chosen revelation over reason, and he looked at the men and women who had chosen reason as if they had made a terrible, lethal mistake, both here and for the hereafter, as if political compromise and religious compromise were both symptoms of the same lack of passion and faith about what kinds of truth and what kinds of change were possible. It was, finally, this increasingly radical and otherworldly stance to American politics that endured with him, one where his religious dissent and his political dissent shared the same voice, spoke the same language of uncontrollable faith in the individual. In 1790, Carter wrote the Baptist elder John Rippon and complained of ministers who seemed to offer "universality of redemption for all," when they were prepared to commit only to "partial Election before Creation." He wrote these words in the wake of a special convention in Virginia that met—without him—and voted to ratify a national Constitution that argued in its preface for equality among men but, in the small prim print of Article 1, Section 2, defined each one of his black brothers and sisters as three-fifths of a person.

For Carter, it was more important to keep alive the spirit of the Revolution than keep a new country united. And he did not act to free his slaves until it was absolutely clear that the men running the country, its capitols, and its churches, felt otherwise.

CHAPTER V

Deed of Gift
[1789–1804]

"A man has almost as good a right to set fire to his own building, though his neighbours is to be destroyed by it, as to free his Slaves."

—Anonymous correspondent to
Robert Carter, August 5, 1796

There is a story, passed down through the descendants of Robert Carter's freed slaves, that Carter emancipated his slaves with a grand gesture, a speech made from a "great big pulpit" on his front lawn on some slow, hot August morning in 1791. It is entirely possible that such a scene took place, although Carter himself does not record the event. At the same time, what makes this story noteworthy is that it constitutes the only narrative of Robert Carter's life that has been told and retold, and therefore constitutes the only passage in his entire life to which anything approximating the shaping power of fiction has had the chance to accrete. In 1791, however, Robert Carter was sixty-three years old, his slaves were distributed on almost twenty plantations across a broad swath of Virginia, and the details of his emancipation plan—who was released from servitude, and when—were so detailed that he would have been required to stand for hours on platform after platform reciting from the deed to make its meaning clear. The story of Robert Carter and the great big pulpit speaks to our belief that the gift of freedom is a grand gesture that requires a grand staging.

In the short run, however, the story does not account for the gradualism of Carter's approach, the extent to which he remained deferential to the goodwill of his white neighbors, or somehow still fearful of the implications of his act. In the long run, it does not account for the idea that Carter's Deed of Gift was anything more than a dramatic gesture, and the beginning of a commitment to the freedom and prosperity of those slaves who would survive his own lifetime.

If there is a single reason why Robert Carter is so difficult to resurrect in this century, it lies in the sheer counterintuitive shape of his life story, and the fact that his one great burst of freedom fighting, when it finally came, was the product of a genius for withdrawal and aloofness as much as for empathy. Theoretically, it should be possible to tell the story of Robert Carter's life as a redemption song. One should be able to speak of his astute Baltimore wife and the iron mill she brought with her, and how he had been persuaded away from the agrarian ideal that enchanted other Virginia patriarchs. One should be able to speak of the spiritual revelation he experienced in 1777, and his subsequent conversion to the antislavery Baptist Church. Perhaps most important, one should be able to speak of the democratic spirit of the age, of the new Constitution, the First Congress, and the rise of a federal government that would allow proud Virginians to regard themselves also as strong, free Americans.

This interpretation makes sense if we accept a simple explanation of Carter's conduct, that he committed a good act because he became a good man, and that he became a good man because he was influenced by good institutions: a strong marriage, an active church, and an egalitarian government. But Carter did not emancipate his slaves until four years after his wife died, and until three years after he left the Baptist Church. Similarly, Carter's relationship to the democratic fervor of the era grew no warmer in the years following his uncomfortable declaration in 1776 that "a new system of politicks, began to prevail" in "british north america," and his substantially less ambivalent declaration in 1781 that "Government disappointed me." By 1789, the same year that George Washington took office as the first president of the United States, Robert Carter lived virtually alone in the huge square mansion at Nomony. He was accompanied only by his daughter Sarah Fairfax—whose proposed marriage to Richard Bland Lee was being squelched by Carter—a handful of domestic slaves, and one trusted agent. He was surrounded by indifferently used slave quarters—the populations of several plantations had been reduced by more than fifty percent, while others were dominated by surprisingly large numbers of children less than ten years old—and mills and factories that he no longer governed. Within a short coach ride lay fields to which he had ceded control, and churches that he had once enthusiastically sponsored but that now disseminated creeds he believed denied the possibility of second lives. His oldest son, Robert Bladen, had lit out once again for England, sailing out of Baltimore in late November. Even Dunmore had paid him back. Through the exertions of his will and against what must have constituted the force of his desire, Carter's home plantation had been transformed into a landscape of nostalgia and loss, and quite possibly regret.

It was also a blank slate, however, and Enlightenment men often did their best work on blank slates. From certain perspectives, emancipation, by 1791, had never seemed more sensible, more tangible. Since the passage of the 1782 Manumission Act, ten thousand Virginian slaves had been freed, and with few visible disruptions to the body politic. Virginians could also reflect upon the fact that the price of slaves had reached a twenty-year low, and that the census of 1790 reported that the percentage of the population of the commonwealth listed as "black, tithable" had fallen to slightly more than forty percent, lower than at any other point in the eighteenth century, and conclude that the peculiar institution was dying of its own accord, at least in their enlightened districts. At the same time, schemes for gradual emancipation had never been given more credibility: Ferdinando Fairfax, a slaveholder close to George Washington, published a "Plan for Liberating the Negroes Within the United States" in the Philadelphia-based journal *American Museum*. Carter's own hopes rose: he himself expected that a gradual emancipation plan would pass through Virginia's legislature sometime in 1790, and he described the plan, in detail, to a British friend in a letter written on July 22, 1789:

> I apprehend that an Act should pass, here, declaring that all Persons, male & Female, were free, born of Women in Slavery in this State from the date of the Act of Parliament declaring that the thirteen united States were free and independent States—; that the People so liberated should serve to the age of thirty five years, only—

By 1791, however, it became clear that Carter's hopes were misplaced. The 1789 petition, like so many others, never received a hearing in the House of Delegates. Moreover, Virginian ambivalence on slavery was becoming national policy: in February 1790, when the debate over gradual emancipation threatened to engulf the first Congress of the United States, Virginians claimed the leadership roles for both sides. Warner Mifflin, a Quaker reformer from the northern shore of the Potomac, presented one of two Quaker proposals to end the slave trade, and provided eloquent support for the Pennsylvania Abolition Society's petition for emancipation. And James Madison labored most avidly to bury the proposal, to bury, in fact, the idea that Constitutional language about the "general welfare" might ever prove to be the trigger of a congressional act to end slavery. "Whoever brings forward in the Respective States, some General, rational and Liberal plan, for the Gradual Emancipation of Slaves, will deserve Well of his Country," fellow Virginian Thomas Pleasants wrote, four months after a 29-to-25 vote in March approved a committee report that buried the issue for three-quarters of a century, until cannons at Fort Sumter reopened it, "yet I think it was very improper, at this time, to introduce it in Congress."

Carter watched carefully: in the aftermath of the congressional debate, he copied into his journals a set of twenty-six "Queres" that argued that emancipation was unthinkable, that the economic issues were overwhelming, that relocation of the freed slaves was essential (both Jefferson and Fairfax, and almost all future composers of emancipation schemes, insisted on this point), that everything he was about to try to do in microcosm was impossible. But it was not the only debate he was watching carefully: even as he withdrew from what his neighbors and peers regarded as the provinces of the rational world, Robert Carter remained an exemplar of how the civic life of the nation seeps into the lives of even those citizens who most disavow politics. For instance, it was no coincidence that Carter's first religious conversion took place in the wake of the Declaration of Independence, and that his second took place in the wake of the ratification of the Constitution: the timing of his great changes always coincided with great changes in the life of the new nation. He even shared their vocabulary: he called the charter he designed for the Yeocomico Church in 1788 its "constitution."

Most important, he shared their aspirations, which in the early 1790s revolved around the nature of liberty, and bore an excited character. In August 1791, as Carter wrote the Deed of Gift, the Assembly of France compelled King Louis XVI to sign into law a new constitution, and enthusiasm for the French Revolution became, briefly, a canon of American politics, nowhere more than among the freedom-loving planters of Virginia: "I like a little rebellion now and then," Jefferson wrote from Paris. "It is like a storm in the Atmosphere." That same month, slaves outside the Haitian capital of Le Cap, led by a voodoo priest named Boukman, began killing and dispossessing French planters, who, as they washed ashore as refugees, told stories that brought "terror" to those Southern patriarchs who could pass as their American cousins. On American soil, meanwhile, the politics only seemed less dramatic, the debate over gradual emancipation only one means through which Americans tested the new Constitution. By August 1794, in fact, when farmers in western Pennsylvania rioted and armed, refusing to pay a new excise tax on whiskey, George Washington began to consider the possibility that the same "Democratic societies" inspired by both American and French Revolutions were now spawning a spirit of anarchy on this side of the Atlantic.

As always, Carter was prepared to go further than his planter peers, was prepared to follow the implication of their almost spiritual affection for liberty to its dangerous but logical end. Entranced by the same egalitarian implications of the French Revolution that enraptured Jefferson, he began to tell correspondents to address him not as "Councillor," nor as "Honorable," but as "Citizen Robert Carter": "I apprehend, 'Honorable,' does not appertain to Robt Carter—" he claimed. He wore other new, hopeful symbols: he began to sign letters "Friend to Man I Am," where he used to sign them "Your Humble and Obedient Servant" or "Your brother in unworthy gospel bonds."

Most significant, however, he became a devotee of the writings of Emanuel Swedenborg. Like Carter, Swedenborg was an aristocrat, and a pure product of the Enlightenment: he attended college alongside Linnaeus in Stockholm, taught himself chemistry, astronomy, mathematics, poetry, and several European languages, invented dozens of small machines (including a remarkable little airplane), and served the Royal Court of Sweden as an engineer and the intellectual leader of that nation's powerful Board of Mines. Like Carter, Swedenborg experienced a religious illumination late in middle age, an intense "shivering" over several days in April 1744 that was soothed when, he believed, he saw Jesus on the cross and placed his arms around him.

Unlike Carter, however, Swedenborg was almost incomprehensibly voluble, composing one huge volume after another to explain the world and its wonders, each bearing a confident title such as *Heaven and Its Wonders from Things Heard and Seen, True Christian Religion, Apocalypse Explained,* or *Apocalypse Revealed.* While Carter tortured himself because, he believed, God had visited him only once, Swedenborg believed that he routinely conversed with angels and devils, and that the channels between the physical and spiritual worlds were open wide. He said clearly what Carter could never fully articulate, that one moment with Jesus made the exaltation of "reason" and "understanding" at the core of the Enlightenment seem like the lesser path to real wisdom:

> In the end it was given me of the Spirit's grace to obtain faith without reasoning, an assurance about it. Then I saw my thoughts that confirmed it, as it were under me; I laughed in my mind at them, and much more at those that rebutted them and were contrary.

From this new faith "without reasoning," he created a theology that even Thomas Jefferson in his Deist mode might have embraced: that "heaven is never closed"; that, while Christianity was the perfect religion, good men and women of every sect and theology resided there; that "it is not so difficult to live the life of heaven as some believe"; and that men and women in the afterlife were not cast into heaven or hell after a thunderous judgment, but lived in the heavens or hells that they made for themselves when they lived.

As Ralph Waldo Emerson later noted, however, Swedenborg's theology also possessed a "deranged balance." He was no Bosch, nor Blake: his "heavens and hells" were "dull," his angels were "all country parsons." Further, he never stopped being a scientist, a man of numbers and literal meanings, and he turned manically to the "mystical and Hebraic" to explain the "fine secret that little explains large, and large, little." He practiced numerology: "The number 'twelve' signifies all, and is predicate of truths from good," he wrote in *Apocalypse Revealed.* He believed that the images from certain dreams were divinely coded: "Saw that a boy ran away with a shirt of mine and I ran after him. *May mean that I had not washed my feet.*" Not only did he believe that he conversed with angels and devils, but he also believed that he had traveled to other planets and conversed with the men and women of Mercury, Saturn ("they are upright, and they are modest"), Venus, and the inhabitants of "a second earth beyond our solar system." Most significant, he believed that the Apocalypse had already happened, sometime in July 1757: "The coming of the Lord is not a coming to destroy the visible heaven and the habitable earth, according to the opinions of many," he wrote. His God did not want "to destroy any thing, but to build up," and consequently came to earth gently but abstractly, "not in person, but in the Word," to initiate a new Jerusalem in the minds of men.

Unsurprisingly, Carter was impressed by both sides of Swedenborg's "deranged balance." By 1790, he was allowing merchants to reimburse him with volumes of Swedenborg's works rather than cash. He wrote Francis Bailey in London, and inquired about Swedenborgian societies there, convinced that he had fallen upon a religion that was sweeping Europe. And when he discovered that the Church of the New Jerusalem (also called the New Church) possessed few members (seven "attentive readers" alone in Baltimore), and that Swedenborg was "frequently announced to the world" as "a madman," he only grew more enthusiastic. He paid two hundred and fifty pounds to a pair of Baltimore printers with the familiar names of Samuel and John Adams to print one thousand copies of the liturgy of the New Church "in an elegant manner." His journals began to fill with long essays cataloging God's visitations to man, and detailed graphs explaining the symbols in dreams:

> by an Olive-tree
> Vine—   } are meant the goodness & truth
> a Cedar   } of the Church; under their different
> a Poplar   } Characters—of Celestial—
> an Oak—   } Spiritual

He discovered numerology, and announced that the key to the future of America lay in the federal government's introduction of dimes: "<u>Ten</u> or <u>Tenths</u>," he wrote, "signify duration of States to the full."

What might have been madness in some particulars, however, wasn't necessarily madness in the aggregate. A modern reader might consider the possibility that Robert Carter freed his slaves because a certain concatenation of numbers gathered themselves on a page in his ledger, or symbols appeared to him in a dream: "We find that the Lord did sometimes discover his will in Dreams," he observed in 1791. But Swedenborg left no codes for "emancipation." If anything, Swedenborg served Carter because, unlike the Baptist ministers Carter had previously loved, the Swedish baron offered a theology that had no foundation in the physical realities of American life. His universe, which revolved around an immense, ecumenical heaven with gates open wide, was a radical democracy. For Carter, true devotion was now only a matter of bringing earth into conformity with the politics of the divinity, a surprisingly abstract yet principled affair that required that he hold no hands, experience no paralysed collapse in the cornfields and barns of yet another revival.

Moreover, Swedenborg provided Carter with one important idea in particular that entranced him, and convinced him that anything was possible. In 1791 and 1792, as Carter, still a resident of Virginia, contemplated, wrote, and executed the Deed of Gift, he focused upon one particular tenet of the Church of the New Jerusalem, Swedenborg's belief that the Apocalypse had already occurred: "The second Advent of the Lord now is," Carter insisted. In the early 1790s, most Americans believed that they lived in an extraordinary and delicate time: as Herbert J. Storing has noted, both Federalists and Anti-Federalists, as they debated the Constitution, recognized that the new country faced a "critical period" in its existence. Many citizens of the new nation believed even more than that, however: they believed they lived in a millennial moment, and that the dawn of the new century might very well coincide with a convulsive social revolution (begun in France, not America), and even a celestial last judgment. They filled the newspapers and broadsides of the new country with prophecies of transformation and doom, often surprisingly dull by contemporary standards: "In the year 1810," an anonymous author in the *Maryland Journal* promised, "a new form of government will take place" in America, "in the manner of the . . . Seven United Provinces of Holland."

Only a handful of Americans, however—a few dozen, isolated mostly in Baltimore and Philadelphia—believed that the last judgment had already happened, that the convulsive social revolution had already begun, and that the latter was but the visible manifestation of the former. To a Swedenborgian, wondrous things were not about to happen. They were already happening: "The Instances you mention of Divine Influence," Thomas Jones wrote Carter three days before the Deed of Gift was submitted to the Northumberland District Court, "are not more recent than common in this illumined Age." Evidently, among those numbers and dream symbols, Carter had been searching for proof that one more wonder would not be out of place. The mystic had done his office. But would the Enlightenment man be able to do his?

2

If Carter is the anti-Jefferson, the man who did not lack the will to free his own slaves but who did lack the vision and clarity to make his love of freedom eloquent, then the Deed of Gift is the anti–Declaration of Independence, a document that makes liberty look dull but which is so absent of loopholes and contradictions that no result but liberty could prevail.

In his first paragraph, Carter wrote, "I have for some time past been convinced that to retain them in Slavery is contrary to the true Principles of Religion and Justice, and that therefor it was my Duty to manumit them," but this statement constitutes the limit of his willingness to explain himself, or to aspire to rhetorical flourish for the occasion. Instead, he seems more interested in the manumission as a practical matter, one made difficult by what he conceived as his responsibility to the white community of northern Virginia: "I have with great Care and Attention endeavoured to discover that Mode of Manumission from Slavery which can be effected consonant to Law and with the Least possible Disadvantage to my fellow Citizens." His solution was an "immediate but a gradual Emancipation," fifteen slaves freed every January 1 ("unless when that happens on a Sunday and then on the next succeeding Day"), with a series of painstaking amendments: first, that "the Oldest of my Slaves be the first emancipated"; second, that all "Male and Female Slaves . . . under the Ages of 21 and 18 Years" will be automatically freed when they attain those ages; third, that all children born to his slaves during 1791 will be manumitted as well, when the males turn twenty-one and the females turn eighteen.

In the official public document, which still resides in the land records office of the Northumberland County Courts building, Carter also filled three pages with the names of 452 of his slaves, their home plantations, and their ages. In his private copy, however, which fills an entire volume in his correspondence, Carter constructed dozens of pages of schedules and censuses, often with information duplicated but seen from different angles: amid these cross-referenced, redundant charts, the reader begins to sense that Carter wanted to make sure there would be no slave denied his freedom, or given his freedom one day before Carter himself had designated.

As always, Carter concealed the inner drama. Not one letter described clear intent to free his slaves. Only one loose journal entry even came close to pondering the finances of such an act. His daybook for September 5, 1791, the day he submitted the Deed of Gift to the Northumberland District Court, did not mention the event, which was effaced by another innovation at Nomony:

> This day Mr William Spearman brought a sample of Brandy 15 Gallons of which is equal to 17 Gallons of the Rum now in the House. Note. Mr. Spearman is to bring 20 Gallons of such Brandy mentioned above, the price of which is to be fixed according to the proof by Mr Thomas Collins and Mr Francis Smith.

When Carter awoke the next morning, he thought briefly about freedom, not rum: he wrote Charles Jones, overseer at Cancer, and told him that "Negroe Jerry," who had received "Stripes" from Samuel Straughan four years before, would be "free on the 2d day of January next," and that "Sukey" and "May" would receive their freedom in 1795 and 1801, respectively.

Having announced the future liberation of these individuals, however, he then put aside the Deed of Gift altogether. For three months, he sent tobacco to Bordeaux, organized more "Gang[s]" to be sent to his plantations on the Shenandoah, and watched guardedly as two of his daughters fell ill in Baltimore. But he did not mention the Deed of Gift in his correspondence for three months, until two days after Christmas, five days before the first group of slaves were due to be freed. When January 2, 1792, arrived, Negro Jerry, and others scheduled to be freed, were not freed. No legal mechanisms had been organized or contemplated. Despite the story of the grand platform, it is likely that most of the slaves scheduled to be liberated did not even know.

It is a strange pause, as if Carter required autumn to absorb the implications of his promise, that he feared the response of the "citizens" of Virginia, or that, more subtly, he shared their public indifference. On September 28, the *Virginia Gazette* published a one-sentence acknowledgment of the Deed of Gift on its third page, blended with other social news: "We are informed that Mr. Robert Carter, of Nominy, has emancipated FOUR HUNDRED and FORTY-TWO SLAVES," the editor noted, before announcing that "Our theatre opens on Monday the 17th of October, with a Comedy Call'd THE FOUNDLING." That short notice, however, constituted the entirety of written reference to Carter's act in the newspapers of the state, the records of its government, and the letters of its most celebrated statesmen.

In the waning days of 1791, however, and the first week of the new year, as the date for the first emancipations passed, Carter took the first hesitant steps toward actually freeing his slaves. Beginning on December 26, 1791, he opened a complicated correspondence with the clerk of the Westmoreland County Court, Thomas Edwards, about how much he should pay for recording the Deed of Gift: Carter, apologizing for having composed the Deed in "haste," wanted to pay ten dollars for the entire document; Edwards, with great studied deference, argued that Carter would need to pay five shillings for a deed of gift for each individual slave. Carter then began a series of debates with his lawyer, John James Maund—a dashing, garrulous state senator, and the only one of his sons or sons-in-law to openly share his antislavery sensibilities—about whether each individual slave would require an individual deed, whether the law required that manumitted slaves register in their counties of residence across Virginia or at Carter's home county courthouse in Westmoreland, and whether a freed slave could purchase other slaves, a crucial strategy for reconstituting the families that Carter's schedule for freeing slaves by age would divide.

Carter's concerns now were pragmatic ones. When the Virginia Assembly passed the 1782 Manumission Act, its members simply did not conceive that someone such as Robert Carter might invoke its liberties: the act did not provide guidelines for how to conduct an emancipation so large that it would take place in more than one county, for instance, nor so complicated that one intimate, familial list might not comprehend the will of the master. In the last days of January, however, Carter began to look less like a man who was loath to free his slaves and more like one who didn't want the manumission to begin until it was foolproof. On January 29, he wrote Edwards a short letter in which he agreed to pay ten dollars to register the Deed of Gift; the following day, he wrote Edwards a second letter, rushed, unrevised, and changed his mind, vowing instead that he would pay for the individual deeds of gift: "the Charge of 5/- for each Extract is proper," he conceded.

As February dawned, he began to test the idea of emancipation by degrees. On the first day of that month, he announced that the fifteen slaves scheduled to be freed in 1792 would be allowed to "bargain for themselves": they would be able to lease out their own labor, and keep their wages. On February 10, he settled the residency issue: his patriarchal instinct still lively, Carter decided that the "residency of Slaves I apprehend is to be where Master wills it," and required that his removed slaves would have to return to Westmoreland to receive their freedom.

One week later, on February 13, he began to offer wage contracts and leases to several of his most trusted servants, striking terms that showed how deeply he was divided between the desire to maintain his mastery, or be rid of it. He rented farms to Prince Johnston and Samuel Harrison, allowed them to reconstitute their still-enslaved families, provided them livestock and poultry, and gave them jobs that paid off a year's rent with several weeks of work. Simultaneously, he forced these men to "hire" their wives and children, and wrote clauses into their leases that obliged them to remain part-time slaves: "Prince also Agrees to receive + deliver Grain as heretofore without any compensation."

Finally, on February 28, 1792, two months behind schedule, he undertook the largest private emancipation in American history. A small group of slaves from the 1792 schedule, not even the entire list for that year, were escorted to the courthouse in Montross. They waited while the judges sifted through the court calendar, which featured cases of "drunkenness," "fornication," and "Seling Liquor above the Rates Established by the Court." Then their turn arrived: they were "examined" to ascertain that "all & every of the aforesaid Negroes are of Sound Minds & Bodies," received the certificates that the state of Virginia required them to possess and carry with them at all times, and departed the courthouse as freed men and women.

The response was shockingly quick. One week later—barely enough time for word-of-mouth to cross the Northern Neck—John Peck, the

New Jersey–born tutor who had married Carter's daughter Anne, flew into a rage and told "Abram," an elderly slave on the 1792 schedule, that he would not "Victual & Clothe him any longer for his labour." By May, Carter also began receiving criticism from his tenants and overseers, more deferential and evasive than that offered by Peck. George Newman, Carter's overseer at Taurus, sent out a letter "to those whom it may concern," stating that "Robert Car[ter] is of opinion that" the court would not emancipate slaves at its May session, and ordering slaves scheduled to be freed in 1792 to remain at their plantations. It was a sentiment that directly contradicted correspondence in Carter's own hand during that same month preparing for emancipations at the May 29 session: Newman was trying to subvert the Deed of Gift through a secondhand act of forgery.

Faced with these first indications of resistance, Carter turned his complete attention to the Deed of Gift. If Peck intended protest by chasing off Abram, Carter profoundly disappointed him: he instructed his son-in-law to free Abram and his wife "in writing," and informed him civilly that they would be lodged at Nomony until their emancipations later that year. One week after Peck's rebellion, Carter wrote Christopher Collins, an overseer at his western plantations, as well as Newman, and addressed the transportation problems that had been created by his insistence that all slaves to be liberated had to travel to Westmoreland: he authorized the construction of a "common Stock" of money to "accommodate the said Negroes on their journey to the Courthouse." He also told his overseers to "Advise the Negroes" that they would be naming themselves at the court ceremony, surrendering any interest in composing those names himself.

Similarly, he responded to Newman's evasion with a remarkable strategy. He sent back two runaways from Sagittarius, "two Lads" named "Samuel and John," without punishment or escort, each wearing a new "Vest" and "pair of Preeches," and each having promised to "be diligent the remainder of the present year"—a curious, limited guarantee from slaves to master, given that neither "Lad" was scheduled to be freed until the latter part of the decade. In a variation of an old scheme from the first years of the war, however, when he tried to send a message to England using a deported traitor as postman, he presented Samuel and John with a written pass instructing them to stop at George Newman's plantation and deliver letters confirming that the slaves there should report to Westmoreland Courthouse in May: his returning runaway slaves were now also emissaries of freedom, employed to checkmate any of Newman's efforts to impede the emancipation.

More remarkable, however, he then sent another letter to Newman, instructing him to provide the same instructions to those same slaves: the overseer was now the "second channel," as Carter wrote, employed in the event that Samuel and John (Were these the proper names of liberty, Carter must have wondered, some mystic code designed to guide him into revolutionary altitudes?) failed to fulfill their charge. Littlebury Apperson, the tenant at Sagittarius plantation from whom Samuel and John had fled, was amazed: he wrote Carter a lengthy letter, warning his employer that "your negroes" were "flushed with notions of freedom," and recommending "some little rigour" to "excecerate their motions." But such sentiments only steeled Carter. When May 29 arrived, he went to the Westmoreland Courthouse himself, "presented to the Court his Instrument of Emancipation," and delivered certificates of freedom to eight slaves. He repeated the ritual on July 28, when he delivered certificates to six more slaves, and on August 4, when he delivered ten more.

For the remainder of 1792 and 1793, he clarified the Deed of Gift, tried to render it unassailable, and eventually sought to transform it into an engine of liberation that could function without his presence. He declined to alter the Deed of Gift in response to white protest, and often accelerated its purpose in response to such signals. At the same time, he disdained the excitement felt by many of his slaves, who now, unquestionably, understood that their freedom had been announced, if not delivered. For instance, he told slaves that they would have to pay the five-shilling fee for recording their deeds of freedom, and then lent them the money under strict terms: "Samson Robinson agrees to collect this money from the several persons mentioned above, to be answerable for it—" But then he allowed the debts to languish like the gentleman's bonds of the prewar era. Similarly, he rejected any alterations of the Deed of Gift to accommodate the separation of families, or sales of slaves to family members, heeding John Maund's distinction between a "free Man" and a "freed Man," and concluding that "an emancipated Slave cannot hold any person in Slavery unless a particular Law Should give him the Ability." But then he labored to accommodate requests that achieved the same purpose in practice, lowering the rents of white tenants so that freed slaves could hire the wives and children entangled within those leases: "I am very much inclined to come into Samson's proposal touching his wife & Children," he told John Latham, one of his tenants, as he made arrangements to deduct "the Hire of Rose," Robinson's wife, from the "Rent for the ensuing year—" On Christmas Eve 1792, he conducted an interview with "Jack" and "Dick," who had fled to Nomony, told them that their actions "did not comport with the expectation of men who were to become free," convinced them to tell him "that their Minds and Inclinations were ready," and sent them back to Libra plantation to wait until 1799 and 1800. One week later, however, he wrote a special deed of gift liberating thirty slaves over the age of forty-five who were not included in the original emancipation document, "every Expence arising on their Accounts . . . to be reimbursed by Robert Carter, or his Estate."

By the early months of 1793, when Carter wrote and delivered deeds for fifty-seven slaves, he was no longer behind schedule: he was ahead of schedule, having freed more than eighty men and women, when his original document had promised thirty. He freed Prince Johnston, Samuel Harrison, and Solomon Dixon together on February 27, 1793; he freed Sukey Dixon one day later, although she was scheduled to be freed in 1795, and freed Tom Henry on the same day. He was often meticulous: he offered to send Maund extra deeds of freedom if they were needed, and composed special letters freeing slaves whose circumstances made it difficult for them to reach the Westmoreland Courthouse, liberating "Bett," for instance, the slave he had sent to the Prestmans in Baltimore in exchange for providing a home for his two daughters. Many slaves, such as Prince Johnston and Samuel Harrison, continued in their old professions, but with new legal status: Gloucester Billy, for instance, continued to work as a sailor on Carter's ship, the *Betty*, but now worked as a freeman. Other freed slaves declined to continue to work for Carter, a fact that aggrieved him. One liveried servant declined his ex-master's invitation to continue waiting upon him as a free black: Solomon, Carter noted in his journals, "prefers to mould Bricks, than to Serve me—"

In turn, despite his promise to execute the Deed of Gift with "the least Possible Disadvantage" to his "Fellow citizens" of Virginia, Carter repudiated every effort by his white neighbors, tenants, and employees to find loopholes in the Deed of Gift. In response to tenants who wanted to remove "breeding women" from their plantations, presumably to procreate a new generation of slaves that would not be freed by the Deed of Gift,

Carter insisted that none of his slaves be moved. When a tenant named Mary Lane asked for Carter's help in recovering a runaway slave, Carter refused: "I cannot consistantly furnish Means to continue a practice manifestly Oppressive to Mistresses & Slaves." And while he lowered rents in order to honor requests from freed blacks, he refused all such petitions when they came from white tenants who believed that the value of their leased farms had declined as the slaves attached to those farms were emancipated: "It is not expected that the Diminution of the Negroes," Carter told Thomas Stowers, on May 3, 1793, "will Operate so as to lessen the Yearly Rent."

Most important, however—and most damaging, from the perspective of his white neighbors, who disliked emancipation but loathed emancipation without relocation—Carter arranged for large numbers of the freed slaves to settle on his lands and occupy "tenements" that had been constructed for the use of white men and women. Unquestionably, Carter had been considering such a policy before he recorded the Deed of Gift: in early 1791, he declined to rent his Scorpio plantation to Charles Mynn Thruston, a well-heeled Episcopalian minister, telling Thruston that his "present wish is to accommodate the Poor." But Thruston, like most of Carter's tenants and neighbors, could not have possibly imagined what would happen next. Carter evicted white tenants whom he considered "blameable," and replaced them with black tenants: he instructed Newman on August 27, 1792, to "dispossess" a "Mr. Holcomb" by the end of the year, and allow "Negroes Jo: Reid & Anthony Harris" to "become occupiers of the aforesaid Tenement." When Samson Robinson asked permission to rent an entire plantation in the Shenandoah Valley on behalf of his family and several other liberated slaves, Carter provided a "positive Grant," despite the misgivings of Christopher Collins, who told Carter, "I deemed it rather inexpedient to Rent it to them, and found . . . it gave considerable dissatisfaction to the . . . Neighbors around."

Throughout his properties, Carter then began offering such "positive Grants." By April 1793, eighteen freed slaves leased farms at Nomony, including one, "Negro Sarah," who occupied lands alongside the property belonging to Carter's wealthy neighbor, John Turberville. By 1797, entire plantations, such as Leo, were occupied by free blacks living on small farms. In response to one white tenant, who wanted to remove the "breeding women" from his farm to another state, Carter wrote, "Slaves are thought to be very prejudicial when permitted in a Country." When his white employees, tenants, and relatives made the same argument about the presence of free blacks in a "country," however, Carter gave their claims an imperial cold shoulder. If Carter regarded the will to freedom among his slaves with a certain measure of distanced propriety, he was absolutely dismissive in response to the conviction of his white neighbors that he was ruining their communities by creating whole villages of liberated black men and women in their midst.

3

Sometime in the early months of 1793, Robert Carter began looking for a new place to live. He first considered moving to the new "Foederal City," which at that point was little more than surveyors' lines, clearings, and fledgling constructions strewn across a square of forests and bluffs on the banks of the Potomac. While the new capitol enticed him, however, he doubted the value of the land upon which it was to be constructed. In January 1793, Carter learned of thirty lots for sale on "S. Capitol Street," and asked a proprietor and landowner named David Burnes "whether it is sufficient to build good brick houses," or a "certain Sum is to be paid." When Burnes responded that the lots were not free, Carter inquired instead about the cost of "five contiguous lots . . . between Pennsylvania and Massachusetts Ave." When Burnes told him that each lot cost one hundred pounds, however, Carter declined to purchase, and turned his attention to other cities. Five hundred pounds, he decided, was too much to spend for a mansion-sized tract in the heart of the District of Columbia.

Instead, on May 8, 1793, Carter sailed to Baltimore on the *Betty*, leaving behind Nomony Hall for good. He had left little notice that he was leaving: his son George Carter, for whom Carter was arranging an education in "business," wrote a letter from Philadelphia to Virginia that same day, telling his father, "It is a long time since I have heard from Nomony." In fact, Carter made the decision to move quickly: he left behind his papers, his ledgers, and his journals, all locked within a small building at Nomony that he called the "Library." He traveled light: he took only two servants with him, "Negro George" and "Negro Betty," and would spend the rest of the year sending to Nomony for "necessities," ranging from his coach—which Tom Henry delivered—to his books and butler. An observer might have assumed that he was traveling to Baltimore for a short visit, except that, two weeks before, on April 26, he leased Nomony and its servants to his son J.T., who had just turned twenty-one, and whom he still didn't entirely trust. Among the lease terms, Carter insisted that "an inventory of the furniture in the kitchen and dwelling House" were "to be taken," and held J.T. to strict adherence to the terms of the Deed of Gift, requiring this reprobate son to "deliver the Aforesaid Negroes Completely Clothed" to the Westmoreland County Courthouse on their scheduled days of emancipation.

At the same time, Baltimore beckoned appealingly. He had business interests and two daughters there, and there were those "attentive readers" of the works of Swedenborg, whose numbers, Carter was convinced, would imminently "encrease," and for whom he already felt authorized to speak: before leaving Virginia, he composed the preface to the edition of liturgy and hymns he had financed, a fine, concise essay only troubled, from a modern perspective, by Carter's failure to capitalize the words "united states." The journey started pleasantly: on the second night, the *Betty* stopped at the plantation landing of Corbin Washington, and Carter and his daughters dined that evening on a meal that featured "a plate of Butter and Milk from Mrs. Washington's Dairy" as their ship lay off White Point Bar. By May 12, however, both of Carter's daughters and "Black Betsy" had fallen sick, and thunder and lightning roiled the waters of the Chesapeake. And when Carter and his company landed at Baltimore, they were met there by a tragic report: Carter's son, Robert Bladen, had died in London three months before, as the result of wounds, a British coroner insisted, that had nothing to do with the fact that a city sheriff in pursuit of gambling debts had assaulted him in the street nine days before.

The information likely shook Carter: "I died at Mr George Prestman's—" he wrote in his diary on the evening of May 16, the missing "n" from "dined" a poignant mistake. But he scarcely mourned. On May 19, four days after he arrived there, he was among sixteen converts to Swedenborg's New Church to witness two infant baptisms at the house of James J. Wilmer, a converted Baptist minister. Three days later, he purchased a house on Green Street for 550 pounds (50 pounds more than what he refused to pay for several lots in the new city of Washington) and acquired, as well, a new set of neighbors, to replace Turbervilles, Washingtons, and Lees: carpenters, seamstresses, stonemasons, silversmiths, some of whom were white, some of whom were black, some of whom were both, and none of whom would be thought out of place in a Swedenborgian heaven.

Within weeks, he had made Baltimore his new home. He ordered a "Pent house" for the house on Green Street, and a "building to contain 2 Wheel Carriages and a Stable having 4 stalls." He built "Gutter[s]" made of brick, rebuilt foundation walls, reconstructed windows and doorways so that they were symmetrical. He ordered ducks, chicken, bacon, and firewood from Nomony, had his coach repainted, and strolled the streets of Baltimore, buying watermelons and bottles of beer at nine pence apiece. He received the first runaway slave from Nomony, a man named Ben-Chine who complained that John Tasker had beaten him for no reason, and made an effort to have the escaped slave "enter'd . . . with a street Comissioner—"

Most important, he worshipped as he had not for fifteen years. He went to two Swedenborgian services every Sunday, and "spoke at both places" in most cases. He joined a Swedenborgian New Church "reading group," noting to himself that he had renewed his dedication to worshipping alongside men and women who would have been considered his social inferiors:

> Mr Welfrahrt . . . lives with George Werner, Shoe-Maker . . . John McLeathery, Stone cutter . . . Joseph Starr—Schoolmaster . . . John Kerr Schoolmaster in Log-town—John Boyer, Carpenter, in Log-town—Daniel Lamott, Tanner near Log-town—

By July, he was attending as many as three services in a day, as well as "free conferences," and hosting meetings at odd hours and of uncertain beauty: "Meeting held at R C's House," he wrote in his journal on July 24, 1793, "Night—ended in Love—"

Nevertheless, as Carter recognized, removal to Baltimore reflected a kind of civic death as much as a kind of civic rebirth. It is possible, though not likely, that the white community of Virginia had intimidated Carter, and that he left for Maryland in a state of duress: scrawled across one page of his diary for the first days of May 1794 one can find the words "tarred and feathered" written three times in jagged script, but with no indication who suffered that most tender of civic humiliations, or when. Similarly, he spent the last years of his life refusing virtually every invitation to return to Virginia, often with more vigor than was necessary, and with allusion to some undescribed bias against travel there: he told son-in-law Hugh Quinlan on March, 18, 1798, for instance, that "several impediments . . . forbid me to attempt an excursion into Virginia, which hindrances do effectually suppress every Inclination to go thither." Six months later, "Carter's Meeting House," where the Yeocomico Baptist Church was founded, was burned down, as the man for whom it was named sat snugly in Baltimore.

More likely, however, Carter had remained untouchable, even if structures that bore his name were not, his critics stunned into silence by his wealth and his name, or by the inability to find a vindicatory rhetoric with which to dispute his actions. Carter saved one letter in his correspondence, for instance, which claimed to speak for "the vast majority of the community," and argued that "the consequences of the" Deed of Gift "are too injurious to do otherwise than complain of them," and that "a man has almost as good a right to set fire to his own building, though his neighbours is to be destroyed by it, as to free his Slaves."

In all likelihood, Carter understood the message—which he believed was composed by Charles Mynn Thruston, the minister from whom he had withheld lands reserved for free blacks—was accurate. He knew that there existed a wellspring of animosity toward the Deed of Gift beyond the deferential protests of his overseers and tenants, and the sudden rages of his sons and sons-in-law. He also knew that his tenant slaveholders would be working slave children harder to compensate for the loss of the labor of their free parents, and that his neighbors would be beating their slaves more frequently to keep the spirit of liberty from taking hold among their own slaves. He also would have recognized another remarkable effect of the Deed of Gift, that a "vastly greater number of these people," as his anonymous correspondent wrote, were "now passing as your free men than you ever own'd." But Carter also would not have ignored the fact that the author of the letter was too timid to sign his name, and too resigned to even ask Carter to stop freeing his slaves, although he was willing to propose that Carter remove them to Pennsylvania, whose "inhabitants," he wrote sarcastically, "seem anxious to have them."

That Carter left Virginia as a consequence of the Deed of Gift, however, was obvious. The decision reflected the natural culmination of the great retirements of the 1780s, which were founded in the desire to rid his life of all connections to slavery. But it reflected, as well, Carter's recognition that "public Acts discountenanc[ing] Slavery" (as he referred to the Deed of Gift) and the departure of the author of such public acts from the slaveholding community were inextricably linked. Three months before he set pen to the paper of the Deed of Gift, his Baptist friend John Leland also left Virginia, and in parting delivered a gorgeous antislavery sermon, his relief at finally being able to speak his mind palpable as he spilled page after page of revolutionary utterance, telling white residents of the state that "The names of master & slave" should once and for all "be buried."

Carter, undoubtedly, revered the sentiment: he copied the sermon, in full, into his journals. But he recognized, as well, Leland's precedent. To his neighbors, black and white, his children, and his peers in the slaveholding elite, Carter's removal to Baltimore must have looked like surrender, a clear indication that the Deed of Gift had just been another one of Carter's infatuations, or that he had been frightened by the threat of retribution or quietly devastated by the alienated silence that engulfed his life as a white citizen of the commonwealth. Carter, however, was vastly more hopeful. Baltimore was literally New Jerusalem, an afterlife of sorts, where his days and nights ended in "love." And Virginia, seen through this same spiritual prism, was a previous life, a cluttered, complicated place that had hosted the old revolution, but was not hosting the new one. Further, as Swedenborg taught—and Carter scarcely needed Swedenborg to teach him this lesson—it was a surprisingly free and easy undertaking to talk across "lives." In fact, Swedenborg's insistence that spirits walked the earth, that the heavenly world made its will known in the physical world, seemed to provide Carter inspiration about how he might govern the Deed of Gift from a distance, with the detached touch of one of the Baron's mundane angels.

For Carter, the "channel" between Baltimore and Nomony, the intermediary who would guard the Deed of Gift even as its author entered his eighth decade on earth, came in the form of an obscure Baptist minister named Benjamin Dawson, who first began working for Carter as a collection agent in 1789. By all accounts, Dawson was an indifferent preacher. His name does not appear in histories of the Baptist Church in Virginia that devote pages to ministers such as Lunsford or Toler. He was an uninspiring exhorter: "Not exercised with comfort or joy," Richard Dozier, one of Carter's Baptist overseers, wrote curtly after watching Dawson preach at

Carter's Meeting House in April 1790. Similarly, he was an inefficient and corrupt collection agent, as Carter would eventually discover.

Dawson, however, had one great administrative skill: "His Zeal in the Cause of Slavery Carried him beyond the Bounds of justice," Spencer Ball, yet another of Carter's frustrated sons-in-law, wrote of him. For Carter, as he made his plans to leave Nomony in April 1793, this was the only qualification that mattered. In the lease he composed for Nomony for John Tasker, his son received use of the farmlands, the "dwelling house," and almost all the auxiliary structures. But Dawson got the "library," where Carter left all his papers and all his books—and got, as well, the only key.

Carter had asked men of the cloth to manage his financial enterprises before, and refused to fire them even when they proved incompetent. But never before did he turn over primary control of those enterprises to a man whose only qualification to govern plantations was his single-minded willingness to free slaves. In September, Dawson began his work. He reminded Carter that he had offered to "execute Leases of Lots of ground to Sundry Negroes who have been freed exceeding 45 years old." By the beginning of 1794, however, as Carter failed to execute the next set of deeds of freedom, Dawson showed how seriously he took his charge: he waited until March 15, and then went to the Westmoreland County Courthouse himself to free Carter's slaves, using documents of his own composition and execution. And when he was turned away because the documents did not contain Carter's signature, Dawson arranged a "safe hand," Reverend Samuel Templeman, to take the deeds to Carter in Baltimore. There, his employer, abashed by Dawson's alacrity, rushed the signed deeds back to Dawson, and sent two notes to confirm their delivery: "Hope the said Letter got to hand in due time," he told Dawson on April 21, almost apologetically.

By the summer of 1794, the correspondence between the two men had developed a rhythm. Carter would write Dawson a long letter, reminding him to collect unpaid debts, and deliver a book, papers, or furniture from Nomony to the house on Green Street. In a closing paragraph, Carter would then return to the subject of the Deed of Gift, invariably expanding its scope, but without the systematic dedication he showed while he still lived in Virginia: on July 22, 1794, for instance, Carter finally acted on his promise to lease "tenements" to his older freed slaves, and compensated for his slowness by instead guaranteeing to them the houses "during their

Lives." In response, Dawson, who called Carter "respected friend," assured his employer that debt collections were proceeding apace, and delivered whatever Carter requested. He also kept Carter focused on his own schedule, reminding him to produce new deeds of emancipation in advance, asking Carter on August 15, 1794, for instance, for the "List of the Negroes that are to be Liberated on the first Day of January next."

By September 1795, Carter decided that Dawson was a better representative of his emancipatory will than he himself was. In a crucial letter written on the seventh of that month, Carter, acting with sudden, mysterious urgency, told Dawson that "this business requires expedition," sent him "List No 4" without prompting, authorized the minister to allow the slaves on the list to hire themselves out and apply their earnings "according to their own Will + Pleasure," and then reconsidered and proposed instead that a "Special Letter of Attorney" be sworn out providing Dawson with the unfettered authority to free Carter's slaves. Dawson, plainly excited, wrote back to Carter a month later, and told him that the County Clerk accepted the deeds without examination—a way of telling Carter that, after eighteen months of delays and harassments, the government of Westmoreland County had also accepted Dawson's authority to do Carter's work.

When Carter's sons and sons-in-law learned of their father's intention to provide the minister with a sweeping power of attorney, they responded as if they had been disowned. Maund, whom Carter had good reason to trust, immediately sent a letter to Baltimore, warning his father-in-law that Dawson was untrustworthy, that he disappeared for weeks at a time, and that he rode around in his coach spending Carter's money: "The Extravagance of this Man + his Brother exceeds description," Maund argued on October 6, 1795. John Tasker was furious for other reasons: "There is a manifest alteration in him for the worse," Dawson told Carter the following February, adding that J.T. was now threatening to sell his slaves "where they will never hear talk of freedom." Repeatedly, Carter's relatives in Virginia asked him to return there, believing that only his presence could right things: Maund, who disliked both Dawson and J.T., lamented that his father-in-law ever left, telling him that Nomony was now nothing more than a "large white House." In response to another son-in-law's request to return to the Northern Neck, however, Carter was dismissive: "I have no prospect of going into the Country," he told Spencer Ball on April 23, 1796, "having now one Gelding, only, for my use."

Instead, Carter devised a plan that would wipe the slate clean once and for all, simultaneously addressing his desires to invest Dawson with more authority, to calm the protests of his children, and to free himself from slaveholding for good. On August 16, 1796, Benjamin Dawson and a lawyer named John Wickham entered a room at Nomony and laid out two hats. In one hat they placed slips of paper upon which were written the names of Carter's children. In the other they placed slips of paper upon which were named tracts of land, roughly equal in value (Dawson having executed the surveys), comprising almost all of Carter's lands in Virginia. As Dawson matched slip of paper to slip of paper, Wickham began executing leasing and gift agreements that gave away Carter's lands to his children, requiring each one of them to pay him one hundred dollars each year while he lived, and protecting "leases for all the tenements now possessed by the liberated Negroes." On March 27, Carter then provided Dawson with a "true & lawful" power of attorney, entitling the minister to act "in my name" to "dispose of the said Remaining Negroes & their Issue . . . according to the Covenants . . . specified in the said Deed of Emancipation."

Carter's sons and sons-in-laws were almost completely frustrated: Spencer Ball wrote an emotional letter to Carter the following May, warning him that Dawson's "distribution of your Negroes" was out of control. J.T. informed his father that he had the "countenance" of "General Lee" to marry into that celebrated bloodline: if you give away our slaves, he seemed to tell his father, I will join a family of old Virginia that knows its place. In the end, however, the logic of Carter's swan song to Virginia must have seemed inexorable even to Carter, something he ordered but was executed by alien hands. On July 26, 1797, Dawson sent him a letter telling him that Wickham had "read and considered" the power of attorney, and believed that "a doubt may arise" when Dawson tried to free the slaves. In turn, Dawson recommended that Carter swear out a new "Deed of Trust . . . which will put it out of the power of any person, to prevent your plan being carried into full effect." Carter assented: in August, he began to execute a new agreement, formally selling Dawson his remaining slaves "in Consideration of the sum of one dollar." "The true intent & meaning of these presents," Carter wrote, was "to continue the powers of . . . Benjamin Dawson and his successors until a full and complete Emancipation of the beforementioned Slaves shall be effected."

Spencer Ball offered the last, most vivid protest: on November 6, 1797, he visited Dawson and "struck" him "several times." Maund was there, and escorted Ball away. It was, of course, a concession. On September 24, 1798, the new document, the Deed of Trust, was recorded at the Westmoreland County Court. Carter had previously given away his lands to his children. Now he had given away his slaves—and to the only white man he knew who hated slavery more than he did.

5

Liberty, as any person who ever held a certificate of freedom would likely acknowledge, is a frail possession from the instant it is rendered as a physical object. Like many of the business papers of the day, the certificates were slips of paper, not even entire sheets. Sometimes they were copied onto the backs of other documents, to conserve paper. Some courts developed forms, using plain, easily repeated language to promote what modern contract lawyers might call transparency. Some did not. If a white sponsor simply attested in writing to the freedom of a black man or woman, then the certificate was usually considered good, particularly if the sponsor also listed distinguishing "marks" identifying the free black: Mary Coleman, "five feet 4½ inches high, a scar on her right wrist"; Ann Grigg, "some tumours on her throat and neck"; Anne Gaskins, "twenty nine years old, five feet one inch high, some scars on each hand."

Certificates of freedom were easily hidden and, as Robert Carter's anonymous complainant argued, easily counterfeited by any slave who possessed the vastly less fragile possession known as literacy. But they were also easily lost, and even more easily stolen. And a freed black without a certificate of freedom, to any white man or woman who possessed the opportunity and lack of scruples, was found money. The language of emancipation always possessed a surreal buzz: when slaves ran away, masters said they "eloped"; when slaves were freed, or hired, or sold (it didn't matter which), masters used the word "disposed." But the language was merely the surreal reflection of the jurisprudence, which made the freedom of every single individual belonging to one race of American citizens, even when "certified," completely dependent upon the ongoing goodwill of every single individual belonging to another race of American citizens. The men and women who freed their slaves were sincere. But the law they used, like the language, was not.

As Robert Carter's slaves began to be freed, so too did they face obstacles to their continued freedom. They were easy targets for random violence: Sally Brutus charged a man named John Wilkes with assault in 1798; Anthony Harris was shot to death in a fight with another free black in 1803. In other cases, they were also easy targets for kidnappers and local jailers enthusiastic to charge traveling black men and women with the possession of forged certificates of freedom. Benjamin Taylor, freed in 1797, was "committed . . . as a Runaway" in 1800; Tom Richardson, whose name can be found on the 1794 emancipation list, was thrown in a jail in Havre de Grace, Maryland, in January 1803. Beverly Harrison, one of Samuel Harrison's sons, was impressed by the British Navy in a skirmish off the coast of Jamaica. Boatswain Bailey, who was nine years old when Carter sent him to the Shenandoah tracts with his parents, and twenty-one when he was freed, was arrested, and acquitted, for supplying an escaping slave with a copy of his certificate of freedom. Patty and Richard Johnston, traveling down a Maryland road near Bladensburg, were confronted by a man they described as "half Drunk," who confiscated their "Pass" and brought them to the local jail—Richard was taken away and Patty was put to work in the jail chopping wood.

From the moment in 1797 when Robert Carter ceased to own other human beings until the end of his life, he repeatedly intervened in individual cases where the freedom of one of the men or women listed on the Deed of Gift was stolen, or forgotten. He wrote letters confirming the free status of Benjamin Taylor and Tom Richardson. He wrote several letters in August 1801 trying to liberate Harrison: on August 12, he wrote James Madison (whom Carter addressed as "James Maddison"), then secretary of state of the United States, and requested federal intervention to extricate his former slave from the British Navy. In a like manner, he sent a letter to "Doctor McHenry" in Baltimore in 1800, and told him that the slave named "James" serving in his household was one of Carter's, who had drifted free of his plantations but was still scheduled to be freed in 1803; perspicaciously, he sent another letter in 1803 to confirm that James was given his "Full Freedom."

As always, he respected his schedules more than the freedom of his slaves: he spent part of July and August 1803 trying to locate and reenslave "More," a twelve-year-old runaway slave who was scheduled to be freed in 1812. And when Patty Johnston escaped to the home of Mordecai Miller, an antislavery Quaker, and Miller wrote Carter seeking assistance, Carter claimed that he could not confirm that the Johnstons had once belonged to him. Other times, however, he disregarded this caution, and insisted upon the freedom of slaves who could not be verified as Carter slaves: "Let it be remembered," he told Samuel Jay, who was adjudicating one such case, "the Black people mentioned in the Schedule added Sir-names generally when discharged."

Most remarkable, however, Carter turned against Dawson, whom he began to regard as a danger to the freedom of his slaves shortly after he had formally embraced him as the agent of their liberation. By the spring of 1800, less than two years after Carter had executed the Deed of Trust that sold his remaining slaves to the minister for one dollar, Carter began to find Dawson's management of his interests to be "a matter of lamentation," and then "a capital evil," and finally, most familiarly, "a great Disappointment." There is no question that Dawson was an inept and corrupt agent, one whose failure to deliver important papers to several Virginia courts that March was jeopardizing Carter's position in several crucial lawsuits. There was also no question that Dawson had failed to provide Carter with written accounts of his collections, and that, even more ominously, he was "hold[ing] . . . all my Cash, Tobacco, etc. collected by him since the 9th day of March in the Year 1798," six months before the Deed of Trust was recorded at the Westmoreland County Court.

What is most striking, however, is that Carter did not see this coming: he could scarcely be surprised that Dawson would not provide written accounts when Dawson had never provided written accounts, and when men who did, such as Maund, swore to him that Dawson was spending what did not belong to him. And yet he acted surprised, outraged. For several months, he sent letter after letter to Dawson. But Dawson, as Maund had warned Carter, had disappeared. On February 5, 1801, Carter sent his son, George, who presumably had completed his education in "business," to the minister's house at Nomony to search for any papers he could find. And when George found nothing, including the minister himself, Carter gave Dawson one month to provide a written statement describing the accounts of his tenants and the locations of his remaining slaves, and he provided an open-ended threat: "If you do not come forward with Satisfactory Information," he warned Dawson, without completing the sentence. On October 13, when Dawson did not answer, Carter turned over his affairs to a lawyer named Thomas Swann, whom he authorized "to ask, demand, sue for, recover and receive" what Dawson owed, "by attachment, arrest, distress or otherwise." On October 24, Carter went one step further: he sent Swann a copy of the Deed of Trust that gave Dawson the power to "dispose of certain Negroes and their Issue enumerated in a Schedule annexed to a Deed of Emancipation," and told the lawyer to free him from that ironclad agreement.

On the surface, this was not what Carter wanted, not the ending to his public career (or that of the Deed of Gift) that he had been composing with great earnestness. And yet, any student of his life could easily conclude that his career in the public arena had to end with an anticlimactic hiccup. By 1800, Carter was clearly exhausted, and convinced that he was really dying. In the early part of the 1790s, Carter, as always, spoke about death with almost superhuman calm: "The Dead remain as they die," he told Lady Harriet Essex in the summer of 1793. By the latter part of the decade, though, his meditations began to sound more concrete, more wedded to physical decay, though sometimes strangely cheerful: "May our internal + external fatigue, therein, give general Contentment," he told Dawson on August 9, 1798.

In a similar fashion, his thoughts regarding his own legacy grew increasingly dark as the decade and the century wound to a close, and as his body began to fail for good. In the 1790s, he reflected calmly on the difficulties he had endured in trade, or as a father: "The government of a family is an arduous attempt," he told Elizabeth Whiting in October 1797. By 1803, however, as his pen finally began to labor and still, he reached for a more comprehensive eulogy, one that forever condemned him, in his own eyes, as an outsider: "I do acknowledge," he told his daughter Harriot on March 3, "that my plans and advice have never been pleasing to the world."

In part, Carter believed that he had lived too long: he told a grandson that "real Christians" were grateful that "after 70 Year, that Life is mostly Labour," because "if the life of mankind was to be greatly lengthened, that the Wicked would be more troublesome, than at present." He had lived long enough to witness the deaths of two more daughters—thirty-six-year-old Anne dying in March of 1798 in "violent Convulsive fits" after delivering "a dead Child"—and several grandchildren. Lunsford, while still the pastor at Morattico and still living on Carter lands, had passed away at the age of forty, consumed by a fever he ignored in order to honor a promise to preach at a distant church, and dying on an isolated stretch of Virginia highway. Even Maund, whose letters to Carter never stopped radiating the enthusiasm of youth, collapsed in court one May day in 1799, was carried for succor to a nearby Montross tavern, and never revived.

In part, however, Carter's sense of his own failure was bred deep in his blood, and fulfilled by the infatuated, transient character of the choices he made as an old man, as much as when he was a younger one. At first, Carter had been exhilarated by his life in the New Jerusalem, and was convinced that he had joined a great and rising movement: "hearers encreasing," he wrote excitedly in his journal entries in the summer and fall of 1793. He made the usual obeisances: in June, he gave 167 dollars to the Baptist turned Swedenborgian minister James J. Wilmer, and hired him to work in the house at Green Street. Perhaps more important, he now preached as often as he practiced, fulfilling the dream he had presented to Parson Smith fifteen years before when he contemplated joining the ministry himself. Not only did he speak at the meetings ("R C—read sermon"), but he performed the most sacrosanct rituals of his faith: "R C—baptized John Kerr & Joseph Star."

By autumn, though, it was clear that the community of Swedenborgians was not fulfilling his spiritual hunger. Repeatedly, he invited New Church congregants to his house in the afternoon following a morning meeting. In October, however, he began to attend Quaker meetings, and they shocked him to his senses: as he wrote the words "Crouded Congregation" or "crouded House" alongside his journal entries for the "Friend's Meeting House," Carter seemed to realize that Swedenborg was not yet leading a great and rising movement after all. He began to worship by himself on days when no meeting was held: "This Morning R C performed duty at his own House both—Morning and Evening," he wrote on December 8, 1793. Soon, Wilmer, his newest minister-employee, would return to the Baptist Church, and Baltimore booksellers were telling Carter that sales of the New Church liturgy that he had financed and prefaced were "very slow here." But Carter persisted, until it was amply clear that there was no point: on February 9, 1794, he made his way to the old schoolhouse where the church met, despite the fact that he had just turned sixty-six, that the weather was bad, and that he had only recently recovered from fever. As in years before, he defied his own body when confronted with the yearning for spiritual community. But now he was the only one: the doors to the schoolhouse were shut, and no one else waited with him for them to open.

In the long term, Carter never gave up on Swedenborg's church. He continued to attend meetings, but sporadically, for several months. In late 1797, he even tried to found a splinter group, and wrote a charter encoding his restlessness as theology, encouraging hugely divergent views among the congregants and requiring, as a matter of orthodoxy, that the congregation disband after one year. Unsurprisingly, Carter's new church couldn't even last that long, falling apart in its very first meeting as its parishioners argued over "animal magnetism," "Baptizing infants," and, as always, "the Doctrine of universal Redemption."

In the short term, however, Carter knew what he had lost. He wandered Baltimore like a lonely man, a "passenger through Time + Space," as he now called himself, who understood that his inchoate dreams of community would find no fulfillment on earth. He filled his daybooks with a retiree's minutiae, rendered comic by the royal third person he continued to employ: "RC paid 2 pence for one Apple"; "RC received boiling coffee on the back of Left-hand." He fell back upon old, comfortable habits, touring Baltimore's churches, often with his youngest daughter, Julia, by his side. He doted on his other daughters in small ways: when Sarah Fairfax fell to an epidemic of yellow fever and told him that "nothing could please my taste so mutch as some Limes + Tamrons," he persisted for two months in trying to force a small parcel of fruit through a quarantine that surrounded the city. He tinkered with new wage structures for his freed slaves, every contract a prosaic microcosm of reparation and new political alignments. He brought his cook, Sarah Johnson, from Nomony, agreed to pay her six dollars and "67 Cents" a month and room and board, and then backdated her wages so that he was paying her, as well, for several months (but only several months) of her slavery.

Without even the iconoclastic "system" presented by Baron Swedenborg, however, Carter's travels on the spiritual plane turned chaotic. In late March 1794, he began filling pages in his daybooks with prophecies that declared an imminent end to the world. He was particularly fascinated with a report in the *Philadelphia Gazette* that a flagstone covered with Hebrew characters inlaid with gold had been unearthed in Paris under an "old wall." The characters, the *Gazette* claimed, foretold the onset of the French

Revolution with great accuracy, and predicted a cataclysmic "great Slaughter" in 1796, the appearance of a "Gog & Magog" in 1797, a "great Destruction that will thin the Inhabitants of the Earth" in 1798, and finally, by 1800, the union of "the Remnant of all Nations" under "One Religion, and no more wars amongst Men."

In May, he then monitored a "Congress of Jews" in Amsterdam with favor, convinced that "Some of the Rabbis" would acknowledge "Jesus Christ" as the "true Messiah," and acknowledge "that the Strange circumstances which have lately occurred prove that the Millenium is at hand." Within weeks, he displaced Swedenborg in his private cosmos with this political mysticism. On the twenty-ninth, he ordered twenty-one copies, at five dollars each, of a pamphlet entitled "Prophetic Conjectures on the French Revolution + Other Recent + Shortly Expected Events," the kind of order he reserved for religious texts that excited his spirit. Two weeks later, on June 15, he attended a Swedenborgian gathering, "read Some Remarks" about converted Jews, and "gave Notice" to the assembled worshipers that "Meetings at his house" would be "discontinued."

At first, Carter's new millennial vision liberated his freedom-loving spirit once again, and awoke him to the duties of the Deed of Gift at a time when his attention appeared to be drifting. He took notes approvingly as the French Assembly got the new millennium under way by emancipating slaves in the Caribbean and giving them the status of "citizens," an event that confirmed for Carter that the Deed of Gift meshed with the prophetic events spinning out from Paris. But it was Dawson who made the links between prophecy and powers of attorney explicit, by reminding Carter, as he reminded his employer of his languishing schedules, that "there appears to be great Darkness in the Councils of America which is to me an evident Token that the Lord is about to chastise us for our National Sin."

Carter approved the sentiment, which convinced him that he and Dawson had set their souls to the same celestial clock, and that Dawson would understand that the "business" that required "expedition" transcended politics and family. Carter was convinced that something big was about to happen: "Attend!" he shouted at his daughter Sarah Fairfax in the opening lines of a rambling letter dated May 12, 1795. And when the celestial clock failed—when Gog and Magog failed to show, when no divinely penned Deed of Gift was recorded to flatten the political map of the world—Dawson also failed. As Carter watched the century close not with a bang but with a whimper, he dwelled once again upon the idea that the Revolution had been a failure, and that the nation had not purged itself of its original sins: "After becoming an independent Nation," he told John Chinn on May 4, 1798, "it is apprehended that different considerations would have prevailed—but alas, the fact is otherwise." But the solution, as well, was a broken promise: Dawson was guilty of "manifest neglect." When Carter offered the minister his power of attorney, he hoped and expected that Dawson would "dispose" of the slaves judiciously, "each of them," he wrote, "to be paid . . . like fee as allowed to apprentices, by Law in Virginia," until their dates of emancipation. Instead, they seemed scattered and abandoned, leaving Carter, now well past seventy, with one last struggle against the incomplete dedication to freedom upon which his nation was founded.

It was a struggle he left unfinished and left, from his own perspective at least, in the wrong hands. When Robert Carter died, sometime in the late hours of March 10, 1804, he died quickly and unexpectedly. He kept his promise from three decades before: his will was, in fact, five minutes' work, and it merely confirmed the division of wealth to his children that he had already undertaken, named George Carter as its executor, and refused to allow any inventory of his possessions, so that there could be no fight over who would inherit them. Honoring his father's wishes, George arranged for his father's body to be transported back to Nomony, where it was buried in the garden. Just as there had been no witness, no deathbed scene, no autopsy to determine cause of death, there was no published obituary, no marker, no public ceremony. In a letter written the same day he announced his father's death to a family friend, however, George Carter also arranged to purchase new slaves to replace those who had been liberated from Nomony, which was now his possession. It was not the epitaph his father wanted, but perhaps one that he would have recognized. In his own final reckoning, Robert Carter at last identified himself with America. There was no New Jerusalem after all. The founders had tried and failed, and so had he.

5

Except that he hadn't. In response to Carter's numerous legal entreaties, Dawson simply maintained his disappearance: he never wrote Carter another letter, never provided the accounts or the backdated cash and to-bacco, never protested as Carter hired new lawyers and agents to represent his interests in Virginia, and never told Carter whom he had freed, and who remained in bondage and to whom they were hired. But he also never returned the Deed of Trust, nor stopped administering it. In the county of Frederick alone, from 1799 to 1803, Dawson freed more than seventy of Carter's slaves, at the same time that Carter himself had emissaries all over the state denying Dawson's authority to act on his behalf. And once Carter died, Dawson remained indefatigable, as if (as was doubtless the case) it simply did not matter to him whether or not Carter was there anymore: he executed the certificates of freedom for the 1804 list in April, one month after the author of the list had passed away.

Unsurprisingly, Carter's sons and sons-in-law saw the burial of their father as an opportunity to stop Dawson. First, they tried direct approaches: Robert Mitchell, one of Carter's sons-in-law, stopped the 1804 group on a Virginia road as they walked to the courthouse to be freed. But they simply ignored his offer to "protect" them. And when Mitchell asked Prince Johnston and Tom Henry, who had become leaders in the free-black community, to urge the 1804 group to surrender themselves to his plantation, they also refused, telling him that they "did not know that they had any Business with them—"

In 1805, George Carter tried his own second channel: he sued Dawson in the Virginia Court of Chancery to "take immediate possession (for as soon as it could be done) of the remainder of the Negroes, that are now in his possession." On April 3, 1805, Dawson arrived at the courthouse with thirteen slaves scheduled for freedom. But they were turned away by the "Gentlemen Justices of the Court of Frederick County"—led by Charles Mynn Thruston—who told Dawson that George Carter's active lawsuit provided reason for "not admitting to record a deed for the Emancipation of certain slaves."

Dawson persisted, suing the gentlemen justices themselves: on October 12, he returned to the courthouse, alongside the thirteen slaves now late for freedom, and read into the record relevant passages from Robert Carter's Deed of Trust. But the judges did not relent, "relying" instead "that the Laws of this Commonwealth will Justify such Conduct." For three years, the Deed of Gift was halted, while Dawson filed an appeal and George Carter's attorneys searched for arguments to stop the manumissions altogether. Eventually, they argued that the 1782 law required *"immediate"* emancipation, that it "must be by the master himself, and not through the intervention of another," and that Robert Carter had failed to file the Deed of Gift in the proper courthouse. Carter, of course, had considered that possibility, and knew the law better than his son. On March 24, 1808, the Virginia Court of Appeals granted Dawson's plea; the judges could find no legally actionable flaw in Carter's array of wills, deeds, and contracts. As for the justices of Frederick and their refusal to honor the Deed of Gift, the Appeals judges curtly noted that "the County Court erred," and authorized the liberation of the slaves held illegally in bondage.

George Carter now persisted: in 1812, he sent the lawyer John Wickham fifty dollars to press his case against Dawson in "The Federal Court." By 1815, though, he was fixated on other lawsuits, content to murmur airily about "a Deed without a Name." Dawson, however, was not finished. He sent George Carter a taunting note, reminding him that "Moin," who "has been living with you for some time past, is of age"—and signed himself "Benj. Dawson, Trustee for Robert Carter, deceased." He continued to write certificates of freedom throughout the 1810s and 1820s. He made custom what Carter had never actually made clear until the 1797 power of attorney, freeing the sons and daughters of slaves born after 1791 as well as the slaves themselves: Nancy Dickson, for instance, he wrote on August 12, 1826, was born free, "being the daughter of woman, that was emancipated by Robert Carter, deceased."

And when Dawson's name disappeared from the freedom register around 1826, other names replaced his: Thomas Buck and John Rust, listed as "Agents" for "Colonel Carter's Estate," helping Sarah Brutus certify her "freedom papers," so she could immigrate to Ohio; Steven Davis, certifying "Henry Allen, the bearer of this note . . . freed by Old Mr Carter, Commonly Called Councillor Carter." Even George Carter certified the freedom of men and women he had sued to enslave. Finally, the Deed of Gift had momentum of its own: as late as 1852, in the shadow of the Civil War, Carter's daughter Julia was still freeing the descendants of Carter's slaves under the terms of Carter's original document, as if the year were still 1792 and he were somehow still watching.

Of all the evasions, omissions, and repressions that guided Robert Carter's crazed yet gentlemanly walk through this world, his disavowal of Dawson in the last years of his life was, perhaps, the most incredible. It was, in all likelihood, a fiction, composed, like the best of Robert Carter's creative acts, from what was not there rather than what was: he never acknowledged that he knew Dawson was freeing his slaves, but after a short period he also made no effort to recover the Deed of Trust from him, even as he turned the remainder of his business interests over to a new collection of agents, lawyers, and merchants. It is easy to believe that he simply faltered, that he decided that he had given up too much control. Most likely, however, Carter simply stuck to the script to the very end. What appeared to be failure was only his fierce, principled, and self-deprecating belief that the search for higher meaning was doomed, and his supreme willingness to guard the sanctity of that belief by twisting reality into whatever forms were required. And yet, he never let the despondent self win: he might regret that he had chosen Dawson, but he still arranged matters so that the Deed of Gift would harden like the rock of ages. To the end, he knew the difference, composed a suave and strange political poetry out of the metaphysical conundrum in which he had trapped himself: how does one lead a revolution against oneself?

The irony, of course, is that it could have been far less complicated. Amid the heartbreaks and vacillations, the broadside mysticism and the fevers and agues, Carter had maintained a core of sanity and integrity, and spent the last years of his life surrounded by evidence that his nonconforming choices had been wise ones, and that the distance he kept from the mainstream of American politics was his own construction, one that he could dismantle at any moment with one truly unambivalent social act. Even at his most zealous, he balanced the rational and the visionary with more confidence than ever before: he told Sarah Fairfax that "the past is nothing, the present is nothing, and the future will be nothing, and confidence will vanish away, and each Nation return to Acts of Oppression," but only if men and women abandoned the precept that "whatever is necessary must be lawful." He was more civic-minded than ever before, uttering for the first time phrases that would have sounded comfortable coming from a candidate for public office: "Citizens of my Standing pass life of action, would be blameable to be Talkers only," he told Thomas Jones on October 13, 1798. In May 1794, he wrote Maund about matters including the Whiskey Rebellion, and the letter was so supportive of the young nation that Maund, upon being introduced to George Washington two months later, decided to fill an awkward silence by reading the letter aloud. "My prayers," Maund recited, "is that is the Bulk of the People in the US may cry out, Order—O! My Country." The president, Maund reported, "seemed greatly pleas'd"—in part because Maund, polite, deferential, even terrified by Washington's great passive dignity, omitted reading the private parts of the letter that pertained to freeing slaves.

It was a telling, calculated omission. Only two months before, Washington had written his own confidential letter to his secretary, Tobias Lear, about selling his western lands to raise capital: as "powerful" motive, Washington cited his desire to "liberate a certain species of property which I possess, very repugnantly to my own feelings." Over the next two years, Washington underwent the same transformation that had moved Carter in the previous decade: he watched with repulsion as young relations began selling the slaves they had inherited or received as dower, and he began planning an emancipation in response, hoping other relatives would agree to employ the slaves as free labor on plantations that Washington purchased for them. When this failed, Washington chose an option that showed what he did and did not share with Carter: unlike Carter, he did not free his slaves while he lived, but liberated them in his will, on the stipulation that they remain Mount Vernon slaves until Martha Washington passed away; but like Carter, and like few others, he did not require their removal from Virginia. To execute that will, he chose his nephew Bushrod, who had worked as a lawyer for Robert Carter during the early 1790s, helping the aging councillor settle his debts and his lawsuits, helping with almost everything except, remarkably, the Deed of Gift.

Maund's silence and indirection, in other words, remained the suave keynote for all matters regarding Robert Carter and his freed slaves. Just as Carter's critics derided the Deed of Gift but could not yet deride its author, Carter's friends found ways to praise him through diplomatic evasions: George Carter, reserving all his animosity toward the Deed of Gift for Dawson, insisted that his father's business practices were "perfectly Just, + Correct"; Richard Dozier, meditating in his journals about the fire at "Carter's Meeting House," wrote "O! What manner of buildings are there," and wished that "the man" would "be sanctified." Even Thomas Jefferson, with whom Carter had stopped corresponding, emphasized in a letter to Elizabeth Carter that she belonged to "a family *all* the members of which are *still* very dear to me" (italics mine).

In turn, Carter endorsed evasion, whether the silence was one constructed by friends or enemies, and lived life as a pariah and a respected recluse at the same time. He lived comfortably within the monkish contours upon which he had insisted for two decades. But any suggestions that he was impoverished—"If Five hundred Dollars were to be taken out of this Stock," he told John Tasker on May 19, 1800, "we could not live, even upon our present system of oeconomy"—were belied by the tens of thousands of dollars in debtor's bonds that he shuffled into and out of the Bank of Maryland every month. Frances Carter had been right two decades before: the real money in slavery was in giving it up. Even with Dawson's graft and inefficiency, Carter was flush with dollars he didn't want, from rents, hires, and interest income, and his willingness to put cash back into circulation gave him the respectability and deference afforded to any lending institution. He made large, civic-minded donations, providing "succour," for instance, to the "Cape Francois" refugees, those displaced Haitian planters. He "engaged to lend ten thousand Dollars" to the city of Baltimore to finance the construction of their city hall, negotiated real estate deals with the United States Bank, and received long, excited letters from the commissioners of the District of Columbia urging him to help finance the construction of the new capitol: "We have been informed that you have large Sums of money which you have no objection to loan," they told him on June 3, 1796, taking "the liberty of applying to you for any Sum you can conveniently spare."

In one last effort to involve Carter in the new capitol, in fact, Daniel Carroll in 1799 offered Carter a prime lot, in an "elegant" location, "near the President's House, on fine high dry ground"—in all likelihood, a spot somewhere around Seventeenth and G Streets. Carter, surely, must have understood how meaningful this offer was, how much it offered him a chance to recant three decades spent spinning out in eccentric orbits from the official politics of his time. It was an opportunity to finish where he had started back in Williamsburg, as a close neighbor of the chief executive of the community in which he claimed his citizenship, only an even grander community, and an even grander situation, in the city that the money men of his day in fact called the New Jerusalem, in a mansion adjacent to the nearly finished White House, soon to be occupied by an old friend, also of Williamsburg pedigree, to whom he may have had much to say, and much to share, since they last corresponded in 1778.

But Carter didn't even respond to the letter. This, instead, was the end he wanted: an unmarked grave. He had survived political and economic turmoil that had ruined most Virginia planters. He had retained a radical, egalitarian purpose even as many of the great heroes of the Revolution had settled into cushioned and conservative respectability. He had created an antislavery oasis in a society lurching (and lurching with a heavy conscience) toward a pro-slavery consensus. Most amazingly, he had even been forgiven all this political apostasy, and had been invited to spend his retirement as a privileged resident of the new beating heart of American power. But he would admit to no solace, nor satisfaction. He would stay in the modest house in Baltimore. He would repudiate Dawson. He would refuse to acknowledge that the Deed of Gift was effective, that its strange amalgam of the prudent and the mystical, the spontaneous and the planned, had made it something larger than he was. However, in protecting while also condemning Dawson, deftly creating a loophole through which his slaves might be freed and he might receive no credit, Carter proved to be something more than a brilliant, repressed rebel aristocrat torn straight down the middle. There are no words, really, to describe ambition this vast, modesty this sublime, or the cunning required to make it all stick. He wanted to be free. He wanted to transcend this material world, spirit himself off to some quiet, solitary place from which the rumble of American history would be but distant cannonade. In the end, he got what he wanted.

Plans and Advice

"All the value which attaches to Pythagoras, Paracelsus, Cornelius Agrippa, Cardan, Kepler, Swedenborg, Schelling, Oken, or any other who introduces questionable facts into his cosmogony, as angels, devils, magic, astrology, palmistry, mesmerism, and so on, is the certificate we have of departure from routine, and that here is a new witness. That also is the best success in conversation, the magic of liberty, which puts the world, like a ball, in our hands. How cheap even the liberty then seems; how mean to study, when an emotion communicates to the intellect the power to sap and upheave nature; how great the perspective! Nations, times, systems, enter and disappear . . ."

—RALPH WALDO EMERSON, "The Poet"

The Deed of Gift was a sound document, founded upon a sound political idea: that the American Revolution would not be complete until African-American slaves were free. There were emancipations that worked more rapidly: Martha Washington, assisted by Bushrod Washington, freed more than 120 slaves belonging to her late husband in January of 1801, inspired not by liberatory impulses but by the possibility that they might murder her, a possibility created by the clause in her husband's will that freed them only after *her* death, not his. There were emancipations more deeply committed to the health and welfare of the freed slaves: Edward Coles, who worked as secretary to James Madison, took roughly twenty slaves with him to Illinois in 1819, and en route offered each family freedom and 160 acres of Northern soil. But there is something extraordinary about the scale, the character, the timing, and the geography of Carter's emancipation that makes it a recognizably important act, one that, by any measure, deserves a larger share of the national memory than it has yet received—and one that inspires, as well, a search for answers to why it has been so completely, compellingly, forgotten.

The symbolic value of the Deed of Gift, of course, is immense: authored by a man whose surname was synonymous with slaveholding power, and whose neighbors were guiding authors themselves of the national founding, Carter's act was a reversal of historical wrong planted at the symbolic birthplace of young America, a powerful repentant anti-federal impulse that, like the very best anti-federal impulses, juxtaposed the promise of America against the fulfillment of America, and sought vigorously to close the gap. But the true beauty of the Deed of Gift—and the heart of the great dilemma of its forgetting—lay in its practical implications. What any individual familiar with the debate over general emancipation—and Carter, unquestionably, was one such individual—would have easily recognized was that, with its age limits and complex schedules, Carter's Deed of Gift looked more like the gradual emancipation laws passed by the legislatures of Northern states than the intimate deeds of gift that freed the slaves of Virginia in small, familial numbers. Whether or not Carter intended, what he recorded at the Northumberland District Court looked as much like a pilot for general emancipation as any Southern state had yet witnessed, disdaining only the one codicil upon which virtually every other plan for emancipation insisted: the removal of the freed slaves from the Southern body politic to Africa, the western frontier, or the free North.

It is hard to declare that Carter's pilot was a success; but it is harder to declare it a failure. Carter's stiff, gradual schedules produced hardships that might have been saved by a more immediate emancipation. There were husbands who were freed but whose wives remained slaves, and there were free parents with slave children: Carter's schedule freed slaves according to age, not family ties. There were slaves who died before Carter's schedule turned to them, or who had been leased to masters who took them where no one had ever heard of the Deed of Gift: Carter had never liked "hiring out," believing that he could not control the treatment of slaves he had rented, but his Deed of Trust to Dawson now compelled such practices. And there were, inevitably, errors and deceits: there were slaves who received their freedom decades late, and freed men and women whose freedom was stolen from them. There were freed slaves who were made to pay rents they could never afford, and orphaned children who were evicted from the farms Carter promised to their parents only "during their Lives." There were freed slaves to whom farms were rented, but not farm tools, seed, or stock.

From 1792 to 1804, however, Carter and Dawson were diligent to the point of heroism. Westmoreland and Frederick county court records confirm more than 260 Carter manumissions at those two courthouses, even though Carter scheduled only 195 for that period. Certificates of freedom and court records from other counties confirm further emancipations. Other evidence—or the lack of it—lends strong support to the notion that numerous other emancipations also took place. No county records survive for 1794, for instance, even though slaves from that year's list can be found living as freemen by 1797. No record survives to confirm that the thirteen slaves that Dawson brought to court twice in 1805 were ever liberated, even though Dawson fought in court for three years to win, and a Virginia Court of Appeals ruling guaranteed, their liberation. No record survives to show that Baptist Billy was freed, but his children were freed. Perhaps most important, no record survives that can definitively link the first names on Carter's Deed of Gift to the newly named men and women listed on the freedom rolls of Westmoreland and Frederick counties, let alone the censuses in Ohio, Indiana, and other Northern states that received black émigrés from the South. Overall, in fact, there is far more evidence to suggest that the Deed of Gift, as Spencer Ball wrote, was executed with more "zeal" than caution: that slaves were freed faster than scheduled and sometimes without certificates, that they ran off and were not pursued, and that Carter did not receive money for the lease of their labor, as his Deed of Trust mandated, because Dawson was not leasing them at all, obeying instead Carter's earlier instruction to let them live and work "according to their own Will + Pleasure."

Further, there were also untold numbers of black men and women who gathered their freedom even though their names never appeared on the Deed of Gift. Many, as Carter's anonymous complainant wrote, forged their liberty by claiming to be his slaves: "They intended to pass as three of

Grand Papa's Emancipated negroes," Anne Maund wrote in 1808, describing an escape from a nearby plantation. Many more escaped to freedom through the legal loophole that freed the natural issue of the slaves on the Deed of Gift as well as those slaves themselves. Baptist Billy's daughter, Winney, for instance, was freed in 1795; she gave birth to a boy named Joseph in 1800, born free; Joseph married a woman named Hannah, who bore eleven children, all born free; and most of them married and bore numerous free children as well, creating by the 1850s a diffuse community of scores of free blacks from one line on Carter's Deed of Gift.

For these men and women, and for their ancestors whose names did appear on the Deed of Gift, there would be fewer humiliations, and fewer vulnerabilities. None of Robert Carter's freed slaves, at least, would have to endure the trauma felt by the slaves of Thomas Jefferson, who treated his slaves during life as well as any plantation owner, but could do nothing after his death to prevent their sale to the highest bidder in order to pay Monticello's immense debts, at a well-attended auction for five days in January 1827. Some made their way to the North, to the twilight of freedom that obtained there: Baptist Billy's great-grandchildren were born in Ohio, and one, Nimrod Burke, attained the rank of first sergeant in the Union Army. Most, however, stayed in the South. And where Carter's slaves were freed in large groups, as in Frederick and Westmoreland, they accidentally created some of the largest free interracial communities in the South. Their lives were difficult, dominated by menial labor and repressive laws, but none chose to return to slavery. Some ended up in jail, or destitute. Others found themselves and their children working in conditions little different from slavery. Others simply disappeared. But records also show that a large number of Robert Carter's freed slaves in Frederick—where Benjamin Dawson focused his efforts between 1799 and 1804—resided within a condition often nearer to freedom than slavery.

There are no censuses for hearts and minds, but we can here note that one Isaac Gray, a huckster, accumulated sixty-nine acres of comparatively good land by 1860; that street addresses of blacks and whites were clearly intermingled, showing residential integration; that many free black women owned slaves, in all likelihood relatives; and that a white man named, incredibly, John Mann, donated his own land for a black church, and then served the function of "one white man" required at black church meetings until his death, when he was buried in the crypt of the church. Anecdotal histories of the Northern Neck, in turn, argue that small parcel of land eluded much of the racial tumult of the nineteenth century: the peninsula was unofficially neutral during the Civil War, hosting little fighting, but it provided secret ports for boats smuggling people and goods across the lines between North and South; after the war, the Ku Klux Klan found little support there. Where Robert Carter's Deed of Gift was allowed critical mass, in other words, it promised a gentler American future, one where the South and North looked more like each other, and where the nineteenth-century dispute over slavery lost its edge and volatility, and never divided a nation or helped start a civil war that no one knew how to stop.

The Deed of Gift is not forgotten because it failed, however. It is forgotten because it succeeded. And it is not forgotten because it was meaningless. It is forgotten because it was meaningful. To find the trail gone cold, one might start (but only start) in the soil and the story of Virginia, that great conflicted homeland of so much idealism and confusion. The best route to Nomini Hall is to pass first through Monticello, preferably in mid-summer when the fifty- to sixty-minute wait in Virginia humidity will provide the appropriate counterpoint to the cool air inside the high cerebral dome that Jefferson built in the low mountains outside Charlottesville. This way, the small parks devoted to the birthplaces of George Washington and Robert E. Lee—roughly 120 miles east of Monticello—can be seen in context as well-managed and quiet backwaters of history, with no lines, and park service employees and volunteers who hope you will linger and talk to them so their days will pass a little more quickly. In the eighteenth and early nineteenth century, the Northern Neck yielded three future presidents and the Lees: the Potomac River ran along its northern edge like a Parisian boulevard, and sloops from Europe went door-to-door at the great plantations, creating a commerce of goods and ideas that gave the region the intellectual hum of a powerful city. In our century, however, it is one of America's forgotten places, a run of unsentimental small towns and achingly beautiful sunsets on a scenic loop between Fredericksburg and Williamsburg.

Nomini Hall is not open to the public. If you want to find Nomini, you will have to ask somebody, maybe several people, before you can get the following directions: go east on Route 202 out of Montross until you pass a Virginia Department of Transportation shed, and look for that rusting, wearied marker that commemorates the home of the "celebrated" Robert

Carter; make a right turn alongside that marker onto Beale's Mill Road, another right at the first stop sign, go about a mile, and look for a plain wooden fence on the right, entwined with flowers, upon which is mounted a small, peeling sign that reads "Nomini Hall Circa 1850." Once you are standing at that fence, though, there is no mistaking that you are standing at the threshold of something that was once epic. The two rows of giant poplars still stand, although several are gone, and the remainder are wilder, more beautiful, than they must have been when they led somewhere. The avenue that runs up the bluff to the great house is still there, too, though it is only gravel and a wash has cut it in two, and the wash is filled with dozens of tires. And the house is still there, and it is still tall, square, and white. But even from a quarter mile away and through a cloak of poplar leaves, one can see that this place is a modest echo of Carter's and Fithian's Nomony, built, as the sign indicates, in the middle of the nineteenth century, when flames destroyed what King Carter and his grandson had built in the eighteenth.

Despite outward appearances, there has been a renaissance at Nomini Hall in the last decade, but it has been a private matter for the people of Westmoreland County. In 1988, the Jerusalem Baptist Church placed a small marker alongside the old slave cemetery, across the road and a quarter mile down past the Nomini gate. It takes the help of a good guide to find this place, buried in deep forest, the ground covered in periwinkle and shallow depressions that mark the grave sites. On the other side of the road, the old South is being revived from an opposite angle. One of Robert Carter's granddaughters married a man named John Arnest, and the house and surrounding lands have stayed in the line ever since; but the estate that stretched for seventy-seven thousand acres in Robert Carter's time had been sold off in pieces over nearly two centuries, until the twenty-five-acre parcel surrounding the house was all that remained. In the last decade, however, Nomini has risen. An archaeology professor from Longwood University has brought his students to Nomini, and they have uncovered parts of the foundations of the old schoolhouse, the mansion, and perhaps even the cabin of Dadda Gumby, the elderly slave who scolded Philip Vickers Fithian for his lack of religiosity. The youngest living Arnest son has bought back Nomini and more than one hundred acres of the surrounding land: he keeps a postcard reproduction of the portrait of Robert Carter in a frame on a wall in the house, which he has restored and even stretched out, back near the seemingly lost foundation lines of the original plantation manse. The family cemetery has also been recovered, cleared of wild grass, and surrounded by a low brick wall. Here lie the remains of Robert Carter, in a grave so unmarked that the only way you can find him is to look for the plain red clay brick that marks the grave site of his wife and, facing south, turn to her right and look down at nothing.

The effacement must have begun early, as early as the first summer after the Deed of Gift was recorded in the Westmoreland District Court. Robert Carter's decision to free his slaves was made in the late 1780s and early 1790s, a period when Virginians, inspired by revolutionary democratic fervor and the rhetoric of egalitarian Baptists, Quakers, and Methodists, created a legal space within which the emancipation of African-Americans would be permitted. He freed his slaves, however, during the 1790s and 1800s, a period when white Virginians moved to contain the flow of emancipations, and to redefine a large free-black population as a threat to social order. In fact, it is plausible that Carter accelerated the emancipation of his slaves because he saw the door to their freedom shutting a little farther with every session of the Virginia legislature: a 1793 law requiring free blacks to obtain new certificates of freedom every three years; a second law, enacted that same year, banning free blacks from moving from another state into Virginia; and an act in 1794 levying a two-hundred-dollar penalty against anyone creating false freedom papers, and creating penalties against any person pretending to seek "justice toward persons unwarrantably held in slavery" by enmeshing honest masters in "unfounded law suits," or causing "great and alarming mischiefs." On the grassroots level, white Virginians in the 1790s increasingly treated the manumission of slaves like a civic sin. Publicly, they kept quiet, assigning to emancipation the aura of a taboo: Robert McColley has written that the "newspapers of the time avoided so delicate an issue, and there were no other forms of journalism practiced." Privately, they derided the emancipator: Warner Mifflin, who freed his slaves, wrote that "it was then circulated, that Mifflin had set free a parcel of lazy, worthless negroes, that he could make nothing by them, and therefore set them at liberty." Upon providing the freed slaves land and teams in exchange for half of their produce, "the tune was turned, and it was reported, that Mifflin was making more money by his Negroes now, than ever, and keeping them in more abject slavery, under the pretence of their being free."

In context, whether Carter heard similar "tunes" might be less relevant than whether the white community of northern Virginia chose to say anything at all. As a Quaker and antislavery activist, Mifflin was a radical, and an easy target. Robert Carter, however, offered a new startling fact: the Carters had built Virginia, and built it ruthlessly, and now one of them wanted to dismantle the social order that took a century to construct. For Carter, 1793 must have represented a kind of perverse annus mirabilis, one where his lifelong conflict with the racialized republicanism of the other Virginia planters reached an absurd pitch: his pen freed slaves, while the legislature to which he never belonged worked to restrict their movements. If he faced derision as well, leaving the state, and leaving Benjamin Dawson as an abolitionist time bomb ticking in its midst, must have seemed to be sensible options. For his peers and neighbors, however, 1793 represented the high-water mark in their tolerance of emancipation: as they digested the news of disarray in France and slave revolution in Haiti, and contemplated the increasing number of free blacks among their neighbors, Robert Carter in all likelihood began to look like both a danger and a luxury. As Conor Cruise O'Brien has noted, the great Virginia planters responded to the successful slave rebellion in Haiti by maintaining a public silence, while tightening the slave code in their own country. Faced with the fact that one (and only one) of the wealthiest men in Virginia showed no fear of free blacks during this period, the remainder likely found that silence and similar legislation were the best ways to "absorb" (to use Philip D. Morgan's words) the "severe contradictions" of their ethos implied by Carter's Deed of Gift.

In retrospect, Robert Carter freed his slaves during a brief interlude in the history of the antebellum South, when voluntary emancipation seemed like a real, if distant, possibility. If the institution of slavery in America had been somehow gradually and peacefully disbanded, Carter might be remembered as a pioneer. Instead, as McColley notes, slavery in Virginia was "fixed more securely" in 1815 than in 1776. As Edmund S. Morgan describes in *American Slavery, American Freedom*, "Virginia's republicans had the decency to be disturbed by the apparent inconsistency of what they were doing": in fact, virtually every Virginia planter who was also a public figure, or who dealt with international interests, knew that there existed occasions when the detestation of slavery was the moral *and* practical response. At the same time, as Morgan writes, "they were far more disturbed by the prospect of turning 200,000 slaves loose to find a place in their free society." In order to justify the contradiction between their stated democratic ideals and their practice of slaveholding, the gentry of the South increasingly argued that emancipation, while desirable, was impracticable. In *Construction Construed, and Constitutions Vindicated,* one of the most influential law books of the early nineteenth century, John Taylor instructed that "zeal to abolish slavery may find ample food, without hazarding the union upon the experiment." Virginian Samuel Goode, arguing on the floor of the House of Representatives, told Northern congressmen that calls for emancipation had the "tendency to create disquiet and jealousy." By 1831, in fact, a representative in the Virginia legislature was capable of describing emancipation as "a day dream." In defense of this notion, another representative in that same legislature described Jefferson's failure to free his slaves in his will as evidence that emancipation was impractical—"sufficient" evidence, in fact, "to put to flight all the conclusions that have been drawn from the expressions of his abstract opinions" in the Declaration of Independence. These were easy arguments for these men to make: one can almost hear the assured, disdainful pleasure in their voices. The best evidence that contradicted them, that argued that emancipation was practical and slavery was the daydream, was buried where no one would find it.

2

Perhaps, as this narrative suggests, the fact that Robert Carter remains buried in obscurity represents testimony to the resiliency of the old South in modern times: as Jim Crow replaced Dred Scott, Robert Carter remained a traitor to the heart of the white South, his Deed of Gift an awkward exception to the incrementalism upon which its caste system was built and maintained. But many stories that offend the sensibility of the old South have found their way into the national narrative. The forgetting of Robert Carter, rather, has been the work of the entire American community, as though there were many different reasons to keep him buried, or one holistic explanation that found its source in some passion we did not know we shared.

In addition to controverting pro-slavery claims that emancipation was impractical, for instance, Robert Carter's story offended nineteenth-century

Northern pride as well, which was founded, as the historian Joanne Pope Melish has recently written, in the belief that Northerners stood for "liberty," Southerners stood for its abstract opposite, and during the Civil War "New Englanders had marched south to end slavery," conquering a region infected by what George Washington Parke Custis called "a deadly disease . . . entailed upon them by the fault of their fathers." At the very least, Robert Carter stands as the exemplar of a group of men and women lost to history, whose heroic efforts undermine both Southern claims that emancipation was impossible and Northern claims that emancipation was something that only Northern morality and Northern will could make happen, through persuasion or by force: between 1782 and 1861, white men and women in the state of Virginia freed more than one hundred thousand slaves without compensation, and without the support of a public consensus that showed much patience for their efforts. During that same time period, gradual emancipation legislation throughout the Northern states liberated approximately only sixty thousand slaves, providing in most cases financial compensation (as well as political cover) to the masters.

At the very most, however, Carter represents the vision of America that disappeared as those complex, self-deprecating Virginians also disappeared. What Carter and the other Virginian emancipators did contradicted the history that was about to happen so precisely and so completely that it is a wonder we can even find traces and shadows of his (and their) existence: Southern leaders during the early nineteenth century would utilize state's-rights arguments to defend their slaveholding practices, arguing that Northern abolitionists and federal courts had no right to demand them to do what they conceived as both impossible and un-American— emancipate their property. Northern leaders, increasingly, would advocate abolition and federal power, increasingly forget that they once owned slaves, too, and would found their own sense of regional pride upon the idea that they were the only ones who could have put an end to slavery, and who, eventually, *did* put an end to slavery. That there might be Southerners who would (and, more important, who *could*) rise above "the fault of their fathers," on their own, without the intervention of federal armies or federal morals, was a fact that was ignored so that the lines on both sides might be drawn as they have been drawn. Instead, emancipation would become an event that required extralegal activity, national violence: the runaway slave, the great sacred war. And the idea that the path to liberation could be dull, voluntary, and effective disappeared from the American world, displaced by the idea that slavery—if not racial difference and inequality itself, something that might survive slavery—was crucial to nationhood, that it was economically and socially necessary to the very life of the United States.

Perhaps Emerson, who collected visionaries the way modern men collect stamps or model trains, took the measure of Carter better than we ever could: it has always been easy to recognize the "questionable facts" of Carter's "cosmogony," his "angels, devils, magic, astrology, palmistry, mesmerism," and so on, but those few historians who ever even bothered to consider Robert Carter erred when they concluded that those "questionable facts" were merely evidence of his eccentricity and irrelevancy. In general, religion has made it difficult to see Robert Carter amid the great founders: as James H. Hutson argues in *Religion and the Founding of the American Republic*, Virginian leaders such as Madison and Jefferson had political reasons to portray themselves as motivated by liberal ideals, not by religious fervor, and this portrayal has remained the prevalent historical perspective regarding what forms of intellectual activity catalyzed the Revolution and the great founding documents. In adopting the Baptists, Carter not only retreated from a public role in the American Revolution that might have canonized him as a minor founding father, but he also retreated from the nexus of intellectual ideals for which that generation would be celebrated by future generations—namely, that their political progress was inspired by the embrace of the "deistical opinions" on the nature of man and the role of religion in everyday life from which Carter tried to sway Jefferson. At first, the Baptist Church celebrated Carter: John Rippon's *Baptist Register* for 1791 waxed poetically and cautiously, noting, "It is said that *Mr. Robert Carter*, of Nominy, Virginia, . . . has emancipated 442 slaves . . . if this be true, vote him a *triumph*, crown him with laurels, and let the million listen while he sings—'I would not have a slave to till my ground.'" Once Carter repudiated the Baptists, however, he lost as well the love of historians who celebrate the role of religion in the Revolution: nineteenth- and twentieth-century Baptist scholars, in fact, treat him cruelly, dwelling like Semple upon his "unstable disposition." In turn, the histories of the Swedenborgian New Church are kinder—Marguerite Beck Block's *The New Church in the New World* even links Carter's Deed of Gift to his conversion to the Swedenborgian faith—but also struggle to describe Carter's falling away. As always, Carter closed all the trapdoors through which his historical reputation might have escaped to respectability.

Perhaps the problem, ironically, was that Carter was not eccentric enough, that he blended too easily into the middle distance. Like so many other wealthy, well-educated colonists before the Revolution, Carter imbibed what Gordon S. Wood calls the "enlightened Republicanism" of the day—the long-standing belief in virtue and egalitarian ethics that circulated around American capitals such as Williamsburg, and that marked the libraries and dinner conversations of America's leading men, the "basic principles" of which, according to Pauline Maier, "colonists could pick up from sermons or newspapers or even schoolbooks without ever reading a systematic work of political theory." Nor was Carter alone as he grazed intellectually across the rougher sources of revolutionary ferment that circulated through the American 1770s. Like many Americans, Carter celebrated the new ceremonial forms of patriotism and democracy with an ardor that seems naïve in modern times: so many of his small political fixations, ranging from his brief obsession with oath-taking in 1777 to his love of newspapers to his support of the exiled Haitian planters in 1794, were national fixations as well. And, like many Americans, Carter cheered patriot victories, but he often disagreed with new government policies and disliked the hardships the new government imposed upon him. In his awareness that antislavery politics tweaked the conscience of a new nation, in fact, he was not alone among the conservative aristocrats of the time: Robert Carter Nicholas, one of his more loyalist cousins, delayed the passage of the Declaration of Rights in the Virginia Convention for days in June 1776 by repeatedly challenging the delegates to consider whether their calls for equality included their slaves. But in his radical and sometimes mystical rejection of aristocratic privilege, Carter was also not alone: Benjamin Rush of Pennsylvania, for instance, was also fascinated by dreams and doctrines of universal salvation, and he championed antislavery, education for women, and humane treatment for the mentally ill, pursuing egalitarian visions that turned him, like Carter, against the power he represented, a kind of political love that trumped self-interest, as beautiful as it was convoluted.

If one focuses upon the gentlemen rebels of Virginia, and Virginia only, then the resemblances between Carter and the founders become even clearer. In the taciturnity of his patriarchal social skills, or the minutiae of his plantation operations, Carter was often indistinguishable from men such as Washington, Jefferson, or Richard Henry Lee. Carter learned both politics and manners from the same tutors as Jefferson, alongside Jefferson in the governor's palace in Williamsburg. Only Lee, perhaps, struggled more with his tenants than Carter. Washington was born four years after Carter, in a small house along the next inlet of the Potomac west of Nomini Bay. Both men went to Parson Smith's services; both men developed Deist bents early in their public careers. Both men devoured newspapers, educated themselves. Among Virginian planters still fixated on tobacco, Washington and Carter were crop diversifiers and tenant landlords. They both knew the same twisted paths of the Northern Neck; their families sailed their ships into the same creeks and rivers, knew the way home to be nearly identical. And if one looks at their journals side by side, one might note an extraordinary resemblance: both constitute exactly the kind of glorified commercial account books that Jan Lewis describes as characteristic of the mid-eighteenth-century planter, laden with the dry minutiae of weather, trade, illness, and other family matters, and with startling passages of evasion where what modern readers might call a subconscious threatens to rise to the surface.

Perhaps the reasons that Robert Carter and his Deed of Gift have been forgotten are essentially structural, having more to do with the kinds of resources he left for us to ponder as much as what those resources contain. Carter's story is flat, shapeless, lacking not only the words we need to attach to the bases of monuments but also the ascending arc of courage and self-discovery that we routinely associate with the biography of the self-sacrificing freedom fighter. Men such as Washington, Jefferson, Lee, and Madison might have left behind thousands of pages of mercantile journals and correspondence, but they also conducted a conversation with posterity, in the way they lived, and in the thousands of pages of public papers they also left behind. Carter hid, both by design and by accident: because he bought and sold slaves as rarely as any large slaveholder of his day, for instance, because he rarely "hired out" his slaves, and because he declined to "ride out" with any real frequency to watch his slaves work, he left behind fewer records of his interactions with slaves than did more famous men.

In the very shapelessness of his life story, however, lies the keystone to Carter's importance to American history. As much as Patrick Henry's speeches, or James Madison's treatises, or John Adams's letters to his wife, Abigail, constitute examples of American rhetoric that, in their style and substance, helped create a national political voice, so too does Carter's curious dry language of omissions and absences—which was, after all, no more and no less than the voice of those more revered men when they were not writing for history. To some extent, the fact that we remember Henry and Madison and Adams while forgetting Carter pays tribute to his instinct for the contrarian act: unlike those revered men, he chose to speak incontrovertibly about the one issue they themselves addressed through a language of omissions and absences. To some extent, however, the fact that we forget Carter while remembering founders toward whom he bore great resemblance pays backhanded tribute to the fact that we have forgotten the parts of the lives of the founders that they shared with Carter, in effect dividing their economic and religious lives from their political lives. When we need founding *heroes,* we use their exalted civic rhetoric as the core of their biographies—as anyone telling the story of an essentially political entity like a nation would inevitably do. When we are building not myth but anti-myth, on the other hand, when we want to prove that the founding of the United States was a hash of economic and societal trends that the founders merely reflected, not changed, not rose above—note, for instance, the title of Woody Holton's excellent *Forced Founders*—we use their account books, their tenant rolls.

In part, this division is specific to the issue at hand: the great Progressive histories of the Revolutionary period, volumes such as Charles A. Beard's *An Economic Interpretation of the Constitution of the United States* and J. Franklin Jameson's *The American Revolution Considered as a Social Movement,* were composed and published during the same decades that the Washington and Jefferson memorials were being contemplated and constructed. In part, however, this division is inevitable, germane to all biography, especially celebratory biography, of political figures: how, exactly, does a man have a political voice without a political office, or a record of political utterance? In this division, Carter suffers perhaps more than any other American of his time: Louis Morton, the only man who has ever cared enough about Carter's reputation to compose a book about him, argues that Carter wrote the Deed of Gift for financial reasons, more interested in "disposing" of his slaves during a twenty-year low in the slave market than in "freeing" them. It is, of course, an obvious conclusion, drawn from the disproportion in Carter's letters and journals between mercantile and political utterance. In contrasting economic activity with political activity, however, Morton implicitly denies the possibility that economic vision might be the inspiration for a startling political act, or vice versa. Similarly, just as modern historians rely upon secular (or narrowly parochial) interpretations of the role of religion in the founding of the United States, so too have modern economic historians since the mid-1970s focused, as Mark M. Smith writes, upon one particular question regarding antebellum slavery: "Was it essentially profitable" and "efficient," or was it "acommercial," "unprofitable, and largely inefficient"? Rarely in this surprisingly emotional debate, however, have recent scholars considered, as did Carter, a third variable, and a fourth: that slavery might be a psychological expense to the slaveholder, who in turn might have other ways to invest his capital that were more profitable than the overseer and the whip.

Similarly, recent scholars do not always provide the intellectual foundation within which Carter's economic vision might be seen as the corollary to political courage rather than its antithesis. Morton's argument (which is, in retrospect, a generous one) begs the question of why other slaveholders did not choose emancipation once it emerged as an easier and profitable alternative to slaveholding, and does not account for the fact that Carter actually accelerated the manumission of his slaves during the same decade that the introduction of the cotton gin dramatically enhanced the profitability of the slaveholding plantation. Nor does it do the work of juxtaposing Carter against those slaveholders who declined to free their slaves because, they claimed, they were saddled with debt. Robert Carter was also debt-ridden, but he was also more stubborn, preferring to count every bushel of corn rather than sell his slaves down South. When the time came, he paid what debts he could pay. Then he exchanged marginal luxuries in his own life and the lives of his children, as well as the goodwill of most of his white neighbors, for the freedom of his slaves. Many slaveholders, in fact, possessed this same option. Unsurprisingly, few chose it. There were men and women who were willing to risk economic sacrifices—and, as Carter's case proves, there may have been far less risk than we think, given that the fortune he left to his children was a substantial one. But few were willing, as was Robert Carter, to be shunned and forgotten for taking that risk. As David Brion Davis writes in *The Problem of Slavery in the Age of Revolution,* "All significant moral change springs from people who are in some sense deviant, at least insofar as they are willing to suffer the risk of continuing unpopularity." It is hard to imagine words that better apply to Robert Carter.

Such considerations might be less relevant if the forgetting or remembering of Robert Carter were a matter of political idealism. It is not: he is forgotten because his Deed of Gift drastically alters the map of what could and could not have been done during the founding period—not what should and should not have been done, about which there is little dispute. Robert Carter is forgotten because he both blended too well and contradicted too finely, because the difference between himself and his legendary neighbors, the animating justification for remembering him, lies as always in what he didn't do, didn't say, didn't need, and never justified. In other words, we forget Robert Carter because his song of liberty lacked the crescendo and the passion we assume precedes any stunning moral act. Of all the reasons that Robert Carter has been ignored, none is more disturbing than the most subtle: that we cannot imagine a version of American history where racial progress is made by ice, not fire. When Philip D. Morgan writes that "if manumission rates are a barometer for gauging the level of concern for slaves, then emotional attachments between masters and bondpeople may seem extremely shallow," he encapsulates a long-standing belief that racial progress comes from enhanced attachment between blacks and whites—from more dialogue, in the parlance of the day. Robert Carter met his slaves on the common ground of the dissenting church, but we make a mistake if we think only about what attachment formed there between them. Other slaveholders prayed with their slaves; other slaveholders probably "loved" their slaves better. Robert Carter freed his slaves because his heart was colder, because he lacked the passion for racism. His Deed of Gift was an act of profound detachment: he completed the phase of racial self-definition where whites defined themselves (and their liberty) against blacks, and where blacks were compelled to define themselves against whites in response. The men and women he freed, one imagines, understood: they rented his land and sold him their produce, but not one single emancipated slave took his last name at the manumission ceremony. Probably, it was the safe thing to do. They did not seem to love him or hate him: they were free, and that was better.

3

Ultimately, the reasons that Robert Carter disappeared, and remains disappeared, have less to do with what he did than with what others failed to do, less to do with the narrative of American history within which his story would fit than with the narratives of American history that his story contradicts. There were founders who felt little ambivalence toward slavery, one way or the other, men such as Massachusetts's John Adams, who never owned a single slave, or South Carolina's James Jackson, who believed that slavery was both productive and virtuous. The Deed of Gift, however, contradicted the ethos within which many powerful Virginians lived. In part, their response was emotional: as Jefferson's metaphor of the wolf suggests, the idea of a free black presence on Virginian soil provoked deep, primal fear among these enlightened gentlemen. In part, their response was political: they knew that no Virginian who opposed slavery could win an election in which the overwhelming majority of voters were slaveholders. Robert Carter knew this too, of course, but he had no office to lose.

What Robert Carter or anyone else could not have known, however, was how the ambivalence of the Virginian founders would evolve into an official national characteristic. In the decade after the American Revolution, Northern and Southern leaders argued vociferously about the morality of slavery, and about its economic necessity. But even New England's fiercest abolitionists agreed to shelve this volatile issue if there was no other practical option, if everyone believed that large emancipations were simply impossible, even if the laws had to be written to *make* them impossible. Perhaps Carter recognized this change when he wrote in 1795 that the Deed of Gift "requires expedition." Perhaps he sensed that the mood of the entire country was shifting permanently against the very idea of successful, voluntary emancipations. Perhaps he understood, as Thomas Pleasants wrote more suavely, that plans for emancipation were "improper": good-hearted, well-intentioned, but improper nonetheless, providing dangerous evidence that would unravel compromises that kept a fragile union stitched together.

What is most striking, however, is the extent to which evidence of successful emancipations has remained improper, even as the nation itself has grown more secure and more certain of its future. For instance, just as nineteenth-century Southern politicians claimed as a keystone argument in their defense of slavery that emancipation was impractical, twentieth-century historians continued to make the same argument as a keystone to the defense of the slaveholding practices of the Virginian founding fathers. This defense has two familiar parts. First, the founders should be judged not by contemporary political standards but by the standards of their day: as Andrew Burstein writes in *The Inner Jefferson*, "We should not expect his disengagement from the moral space he occupied." Second, the founders wanted to free their slaves, but no practical plan for emancipation existed: Richard Brookhiser, in *Founding Father*, quotes Washington as stating that emancipation "ought to be effected," and then observes, "But how was this to be done?" Douglas Freeman, in *Washington*, writes, "Had there been a practicable way by which he could dispossess himself of slaves, he would have done so long ago."

Robert Carter's Deed of Gift, of course, does substantial damage to these arguments. It becomes difficult to argue that the founding fathers acted liberally within their own moral universe when small slave owners up and down the Virginia coast were freeing their slaves. It becomes impossible, however, to make that argument when one of their peers commits the same radical act. Similarly, the argument that there existed no practical plan for a mass emancipation makes sense only if Robert Carter's Deed of Gift is suppressed from the historical record. Richard Norton Smith writes that Washington's last will and testament represented "the most humane yet practical solution possible," ignoring not only Carter's actions but also the fact that Martha Washington, in desperation, executed a swifter emancipation than he thought possible. Joseph Ellis, in *American Sphinx*, notes that Jefferson could find "no workable answer to the unavoidable question: what happens once the slaves are freed?" In fact, Jefferson was not looking for one. If the history of the founding fathers were written in a manner that accounted for Robert Carter, they might be that much less heroic, but they could be regarded that much more fully as active agents in their own destinies, as men who made choices—who knew, as McColley writes, that "the Virginia statesman who came out publicly against slavery would be very quickly retired to private life," and who, as John Quincy Adams once said, "had not the spirit of martyrdom."

Taken individually, however, none of these arguments explains an evasion this entrenched and poetic. Robert Carter has disappeared from the historical record not because he undermines certain tenets of history, and not because of a two-hundred-year-old series of strategic and partly conscious evasions by historians, politicians, and biographers. He has disappeared from the historical record because he did something that transcends our ability to listen to our own past: we are all talking the same language about the same limits, the same possibilities, and he belongs to an America we cannot imagine. Read through the histories of slavery, even the histories least invested in protecting the reputations of the founding fathers, and you will find certain kinds of phrases over and over. Some tell us that "slaveholders" only thought one thing, and thought as one: "slaveholders strenuously resisted emancipation." Other phrases insist upon the *unanimous* moral failure of the slaveholding elite: "the great Virginia liberals all agreed that Negroes, if freed, must be removed."

On one level, these locutions seem justified: as William W. Freehling has written, "No other New World slavocracy" but the American South "could muster as united a front against worldwide antislavery currents." And certainly, after two centuries of antebellum nostalgia, it is late in history to seek out new heroic slaveholders. On another level, however, these phrases reinforce something deep in the American grain, something that diminishes us: the belief that the powerful cannot also be radical, that the powerful never surrender that which makes them powerful. The demoniac Simon Legree helped Harriet Beecher Stowe sell millions of copies of *Uncle Tom's Cabin;* the noble, courtly Ashley Wilkes did the same for Margaret Mitchell. But Americans have made no place for the reformed slaveholder: the "master" has two parts to play in the American story, and in both, he keeps his power and his privilege until someone takes it away. No one waits for the modern equivalents of antebellum masters to surrender their patents, or to divide their incorporated selves among the third-world workers who, for pennies a day, stitch and sew and pick. If Robert Carter's story is any guide, we would be speechless if they even tried.

More than ever, in fact, Robert Carter is awkward evidence. Having undermined the logic of pro-slavery politicians before the Civil War, he does nothing to help heal the rift in the national story created fifty years ago, when the civil rights movement and *Brown v. Board of Education* helped black Americans emerge from the virtual apartheid of Jim Crow to join their history to that of the establishment. In the interest of promoting a multicultural (or at least bicultural) vision of American history, teachers, scholars, writers, politicians, and students alike have accepted what amounts to a schizophrenic version of our nation's founding. It is only a radical tenth on one edge of the political spectrum that refuses to acknowledge that Thomas Jefferson was a significant defender of the principles of freedom, and it is only another radical tenth on the other edge that refuses to acknowledge that his practice of keeping slaves was a stunning contradiction to his articulation of those principles. The rest of us inhabit a murky middle of the road where Jefferson and Washington, the signers of the Declaration of Independence and the writers of the Constitution, seem to have given us a riddle instead of a country: were they the best of men, or the best of hypocrites?

Because this perspective seems evenhanded, even sophisticated, we forget that it has been out in the open for four or five decades, and we have grown complacent with it. In this new mythos of American history, we *accept* that we are a people badly divided about race. Washington and Jefferson remain our founding fathers, even as we reveal the contradictions between what they said and what they did, precisely because we now accept those contradictions as our birthright: "the paradox is American," Edmund S. Morgan writes. It is even taught in the schools, more canonical now than the conservative view of the founders we all pretend is canonical: Ellis writes, "My own experience as a college teacher suggested that most students could be counted on to know two things about Thomas Jefferson: that he wrote the Declaration of Independence, and that he had been accused of an illicit affair with Sally Hemmings, a mulatto slave." In our current enshrinement of Thomas Jefferson—which does not lose momentum for being challenged, as Ellis suggests—we accept that the nation's founding inherently possesses this contradiction, that the idea of America has always promised more than Americans at any given time were willing to deliver: "Thomas Jefferson," Julian Bond writes, "embodies the conundrum on race . . . this gross imbalance between national promise and execution." We hope that our awareness of this schism will drive us over and

over to do the right thing, and for historical precedent we look to the
Emancipation Proclamation, women's suffrage, and the civil rights movement. But we lean heavily on this single interpretation of how we can
make our country a better place. We have rejected slavery, but not the incrementalism of mind and spirit that saved slavery over and over. As much
as ever, we aren't interested in someone who did not suffer from a "gross
imbalance" between promise and execution. There's no paradox there, only
more guilt for being so paradoxical ourselves.

The possibility exists, of course, that we are the most equitable generation of Americans that have ever existed, and that we have grown comfortable with this ambivalent telling of American history because it is the only
fair version. But we ought to consider the possibility that we are the
shapers of history now, and that we have made for ourselves the only Jefferson and the only Washington that seem at home amid the struggling
and contradictory progress toward racial equality of the last generation—
an age that, like the Revolutionary epoch, was thick with political voices
who knew how to say exactly what is right on matters of race but lacked
the will to implement any motion that might be perceived as extreme. It is
a sorry tribute we make to Jefferson, Washington, and the other founders
that we continue to insist that they were larger than life so that we can
blame implicitly our own confusion and ambivalence on the heroic power
of their legacy of confusion and ambivalence. But we tip our hand when
we continue to ignore Robert Carter, whose example is enough to remind
us that there existed men and women during the Revolutionary War who
knew what was right and who did not lack the personal will to act upon
that belief. The more one reads in the twenty-first century about someone
such as Robert Carter, the more one feels a sense of fury and frustration
that there were already men and women in Virginia in the 1780s prepared
to surrender money and power to bring a dull end to the institution of slavery, and that the whole thing—the Civil War, Jim Crow, the Ku Klux Klan,
two hundred years of relentless bitterness and division—could have whim-
pered and died in the Potomac tidewater. It is infuriating in the early
twenty-first century to consider this alternate history, in which Robert
Carter is the founding father of the only American Revolution we truly
lost. It is even more infuriating, however, to consider that we have been
unable to find a single use for Robert Carter. He does not soothe us, excuse

us, or help us explain ourselves. But what is most incriminating is that he does not even interest us, because that forces us to consider whether there now exist similar men and women, whose plain solutions to our national problems we find similarly boring, and whom we gladly ignore in exchange for the livelier fantasy of our heroic ambivalence.

ACKNOWLEDGMENTS

First, I wish to offer special thanks to three individuals: Frank Delano, for his vision and his intellectual courage; John Barden, for his diligent, accurate scholarship; and Dal Mallory, for his gregarious tours of Nomini Hall and its environs. Without these gentlemen, it would not have been possible to undertake this book. I also wish to thank the current residents of Nomini Hall for their hospitality.

I am grateful to the many individuals at research libraries who patiently responded to my numerous requests for assistance, including, especially, the entire staffs of the library at the Virginia Historical Society, and the Rare Books and Manuscripts Room at Duke University. Darlene Slater at the Virginia Baptist Historical Society also deserves recognition, as does the staff at the Library of Virginia, and the James House in Richmond. I am grateful to the research staffs at the Swem Library Special Collections annex of the College of William and Mary; the Rockefeller Library at Colonial Williamsburg; the Maryland State Archives; and the Maryland Historical Society. Frank Grizzard at the Washington Papers, University of Virginia, provided me guidance and access on short notice, and directed me to the staff at the Thomas Jefferson Papers at Princeton University, who also responded quickly and helpfully to my queries. And I owe a debt of thanks to the staff of the Westmoreland

County Historical Society for their gracious interest and assistance, and the staff of Historic Christ Church, as well.

My university provided immense support for this book. I am particularly thankful to William Watts, chair of English, Joe Kirsch and Paul Hanson, deans of Liberal Arts and Sciences, and Bill Berry, provost, for responding favorably to my requests for release time. I thank, as well, the Office of University Research Programs for their support. And Susan Berger and her staff at the Butler University Interlibrary Loan Office responded swiftly and creatively to my numerous requests, and convinced many libraries, I am quite certain, to lend what they did not want to lend.

Henry Burke provided an invaluable interview, as did Mark R. Wenger, Sarah Withrow, and Clare Rider. Dan Barden, Phil Baruth, John Darby, Susan and Ken Neville, and Steve Webb read the manuscript and pointed me in fruitful directions. Linda Ferreira provided extraordinary counsel. Sarah Owen, Anne Marshall, Courtney Clark, Kirstyn Brownson, and Annelise Pruitt were conscientious support staff. And Laura Navratil deserves gratitude for her indefatigable help with documentation.

I have a wonderful agent: Lydia Wills. She has been a brilliant mentor, indispensable reader, and good friend throughout. I also have a terrific editor: Jonathan Karp. He was serene in the face of my cacophonous first draft, and showed me the way, I hope, to a lucid final one. I am grateful to Ann Godoff and Scott Moyers for their initial interest in my book, and to David Ebershoff for his interim guidance of the project. Jonathan Jao, Jillian Quint, Janet Wygal, Mark Birkey, Simon Sullivan, Richard Elman, and Elena Schneider have all been thoughtful and resourceful in its support. And sincere thanks to Anne Fadiman and the *American Scholar*, who helped turn nothing into something.

My family has been warm and generous throughout: love, always, to my kin in Asheville, Philadelphia, Princeton, Plainsboro, and Ireland and England. And lastly, I wish to especially thank my wife, Siobhán, and my son, Aedan, for filling my life with passion, humor, wonder, and the best kind of chaos. This book is dedicated to you two, you know.

SELECT
BIBLIOGRAPHY

The richest source of Robert Carter III's letters, journals, and daybook ledgers is entitled "Robert Carter Papers," an eighteen-volume collection housed at Duke University. Significant resources, particularly for the last decade of Carter's life, are also found in the "Robert Carter Papers" in the Library of Congress. Other significant collections of Robert Carter I and Robert Carter III's letters and journals can be found within "Carter Family Papers, 1651–1861." This collection is housed in the Virginia Historical Society in Richmond, and also includes substantial archives of letters written to Robert Carter III. Some of Robert Carter I's letters have been collected: see *Letters of Robert Carter, 1720–1727*, Ed. Louis Wright. Most of George Carter's letters can be found in the "Carter Family Papers," or in the "George Carter Letterbook," Virginia Historical Society.

Valuable collections of Carter Papers are housed at the libraries of the Colonial Williamsburg Foundation, the College of William and Mary, and the Maryland Historical Society. Important individual items can be located in the New York Public Library, New York Historical Society, the Huntington Library in San Marino, California, and elsewhere. Court records regarding the Deed of Gift, and its execution, can be found in the archives of the Library of Virginia in Richmond, and the Land Records Office of the Northumberland County Courts Building in Heathsville, Virginia. Documents relating to

Robert Carter's life within the Baptist Church can be found in the "Robert
Carter Papers" in the Virginia Baptist Historical Society at the University of
Richmond, and in the *Morattico Baptist Church Minutes, 1778–1844,* available
at the Library of Virginia. Robert Carter's last will and testament is stored in
the Maryland State Archives in Annapolis. Secondary articles from the nineteenth and early twentieth centuries make reference to letters now lost, or
in private hands: see Moncure Daniel Conway, Blackmer, Rowland. "Washington Papers" refers to the George Washington Papers at the University of
Virginia in Charlottesville. A key to abbreviations for these archives is below.

As indicated in the provided introduction and notes, unpublished secondary materials currently provide a richer body of material about Robert
Carter III than do published materials: see especially Barden, but Kwilecki
and Ebert as well. Nonacademic historians Frank Delano, Henry Burke,
and Dal Mallory also provided valuable information not available in any
published source.

I have preserved and reproduced the spelling, punctuation, and syntax
of the original versions of Robert Carter's letters and papers, and those of
his correspondents and peers. Superscript abbreviations, and other abbreviations ("wch" for "which," for instance) were common, however, and I
have chosen to revise them for clarity. On extremely rare occasions, I have
revised original spelling or syntax for clarity, especially with proper names.
"Nomini," in Carter's day, was usually spelled "Nomony": I have preserved
the original spelling in all eighteenth- and early-nineteenth-century contexts, but used the modern spelling in more recent contexts. In the notes,
Robert Carter III is shortened to "RCIII," and Robert Carter I is "RCI."
Other Carter family names have also been abbreviated. Lastly, "Baptist
Church" is abbreviated as "BC" in all cases.

CFP: Carter Family Papers, 1651–1861, Virginia Historical Society
CWF: Robert Carter Letterbooks, Colonial Williamsburg Foundation,
     John D. Rockefeller Library
DU: Robert Carter Papers, Rare Book, Manuscript, and Special Collec-
    tions Library, Duke University
LC: Robert Carter Papers, Library of Congress
LV: Library of Virginia, Richmond, Virginia
MHS: Robert Carter Papers, and others, Maryland Historical Society

NYHS: New York Historical Society
NYPL: Robert Carter Papers, New York Public Library
VBHS: Robert Carter Papers, Virginia Baptist Historical Society, University of Richmond, Richmond, Virginia
VHS: Virginia Historical Society, Richmond, Virginia
WM: Robert Carter Papers, College of William and Mary

Documents

Barden, John Randolph. "The Carter Family Library: A Survey of Extant Volumes from the Libraries of Councillor Robert Carter of Nomony Hall and his Descendants." Presented to Virginia Historical Society, Richmond, Va., 1992.

Carter, Robert. Last will and testament. Maryland State Archives. Baltimore County Registry of Wills. Book 7, Folio 264.

Frederick County Deed Book 26.

Frederick County Deed Book 27.

Frederick County Deed Book 28.

Frederick County Free Negro and Slave Records.

Frederick County Minutes, 1801–5.

Frederick County Minutes, 1809–13.

Frederick County Order Book 30.

Frederick County Order Book 36.

Frederick County Superior Court Order Book, 1804–12, 1809–14.

Hening, William Waller, ed. *The Statutes At Large: Being a Collection of All the Laws of Virginia, from the First Session of the Legislature, in the Year 1619: Published Pursuant to an Act of the General Assembly of Virginia, Passed on the Fifth Day of February One Thousand Eight Hundred and Eight.* 13 vols. Richmond, Va., 1810–23.

———, and William Munford. *Reports of Cases Argued and Determined in the Supreme Court of Appeals of Virginia: with Select Cases Relating Chiefly to Points of Practice, Decided by the Superior Court of Chancery for the Richmond District.* 4 vols. Philadelphia, 1808–11.

Hillman, Benjamin, ed. *Executive Journals of the Council of Colonial Virginia.* Reprint ed. 6 vols. Richmond, Va., 1966.

Kennedy, John Pendleton, ed. *Journals of the House of Burgesses of Virginia, 1770–1772.* Richmond, Va., 1906.

————. *Journals of the House of Burgesses of Virginia, 1773–1776, Including the Records of the Committee of Correspondence.* Richmond, Va., 1905.

"List of Negroes To Whom Certificates of Emancipation Were Delivered by Robert Carter," January 1797, *Westmoreland County Papers.*

"List of Persons, To Whom Certificates of Emancipation Have Been Delivered, Manumitted by Robert Carter," 1795, *Westmoreland County Papers.*

"List of 24 Negroes, To Whom Certificates of Emancipation Were Delivered, by Robert Carter," January 1796, *Westmoreland County Papers.*

McIlwaine, H. R., ed. *Legislative Journals of the Council of Colonial Virginia.* 2nd ed. 3 vols. Richmond, Va., 1979.

Morattico Baptist Church Minutes, 1778–1844.

Northumberland County District Orders, Deeds, Etc., 1789–1825, part 1.

Shepherd, Samuel, ed. *The Statutes At Large of Virginia, from October Session 1792, to December Session 1806.* 3 vols. Reprint ed. New York, 1970.

Westmoreland County Deeds and Orders 19.

Westmoreland County Deeds and Wills 18.

Westmoreland County Deeds and Wills 21.

Westmoreland County Orders, 1790–95.

Westmoreland County Orders, 1797–99.

York County Records, Wills and Inventories 21.

Books

Andrews, Matthew Page. *Virginia: The Old Dominion.* Garden City, N.Y., 1937.

Arnebeck, Bob. *Through a Fiery Trial: Building Washington, 1790–1800.* New York, 1991.

Asbury, Francis. *The Journal and Letters of Francis Asbury.* 3 vols. Ed. Elmer T. Clark. London, 1958.

Bailyn, Bernard. *The Ideological Origins of the American Revolution.* Rev. ed. Cambridge, Mass., 1992.

Ballagh, James Curtis. *A History of Slavery in Virginia.* Baltimore, 1902.

Barnes, Robert, comp. *Marriages and Deaths from the Maryland Gazette, 1727–1839.* Baltimore, 1976.

Beard, Charles A. *An Economic Interpretation of the Constitution of the United States.* Intro. Forrest McDonald. Rev. ed. New York, 1986.

Berlin, Ira. *Many Thousands Gone: The First Two Centuries of Slavery in North America.* Cambridge, Mass., 1998.

———. *Slaves Without Masters: The Free Negro in the Antebellum South.* New York, 1974.

Berman, Eleanor Davidson. *Thomas Jefferson Among the Arts: An Essay in Early American Esthetics.* New York, 1947.

Betts, Edwin M., and James A. Bear, Jr., eds. *The Family Letters of Thomas Jefferson.* Columbia, Mo., 1966.

Bloch, Ruth H. *Visionary Republic: Millennial Themes in American Thought, 1756–1800.* New York, 1985.

Block, Marguerite Beck. *The New Church in the New World: A Study of Swedenborgianism in America.* Intro. Robert H. Kirven. Reprint ed. New York, 1984.

Bowers, Claude G. *The Young Jefferson, 1743–1789.* Boston, 1945.

Breen, T. H. *Tobacco Culture: The Mentality of the Great Tidewater Planters on the Eve of Revolution.* Rev. ed. Princeton, N.J., 2001.

Brinkley, M. Kent, and Gordon W. Chappell. *The Gardens of Colonial Williamsburg.* Williamsburg, Va., 1996.

Brodie, Fawn M. *Thomas Jefferson: An Intimate History.* New York, 1974.

Brookhiser, Richard. *Founding Father: Rediscovering George Washington.* New York, 1996.

Brown, Katharine L. *Robert "King" Carter: Builder of Christ Church.* Irvington, Va., 2001.

Brown, Kathleen M. *Good Wives, Nasty Wenches, and Anxious Patriarchs: Gender, Race, and Power in Colonial Virginia.* Chapel Hill, N.C., 1996.

Bruce, Philip Alexander. *The Virginia Plutarch.* Chapel Hill, N.C., 1929.

Buckley, Thomas E. *Church and State in Revolutionary Virginia, 1776–1787.* Charlottesville, Va., 1977.

Burnaby, Andrew. *Travels Through the Middle Settlements in North America, in the Years 1759 and 1760.* Ithaca, N.Y., 1963.

Burnett, Edmund C., ed. *Letters of Members of the Continental Congress.* Washington, D.C., 1921–36.

Burstein, Andrew. *The Inner Jefferson: Portrait of a Grieving Optimist.* Charlottesville, Va., 1995.

Butterfield, Fox. *All God's Children: The Bosket Family and the American Tradition of Violence.* New York, 1995.

Carson, Jane. *Colonial Virginians at Play.* Williamsburg, Va., 1989.

Carter, Landon. *The Diary of Colonel Landon Carter of Sabine Hall, 1752–1778.* Ed. Jack P. Greene. 2 vols. Charlottesville, Va., 1965.

Carter, Robert. *Letters of Robert Carter, 1720–1727: The Commercial Interests of a Virginia Gentleman.* Ed. Louis Wright. San Marino, Calif., 1940.

Chastellux, Marquis de. *Travels in North America, in the Years 1780, 1781, and 1782.* Ed. and trans. Howard C. Rice, Jr. 2 vols. Chapel Hill, N.C., 1963.

Colonial Williamsburg Official Guidebook. Williamsburg, Va., 1970.

Conway, Moncure Daniel. *Barons of the Potomack and Rappahannock.* New York, 1892.

Currer-Briggs, Noel. *The Carters of Virginia: Their English Ancestry.* Sussex, England, 1979.

Davis, David Brion. *The Problem of Slavery in the Age of Revolution, 1770–1823.* Rev. ed. New York, 1999.

Dole, George F., and Robert H. Kirven. *Scientist Explores Spirit: A Compact Biography of Emanuel Swedenborg with Key Concepts of Swedenborg's Theology.* New York, 1992.

Dowdey, Clifford. *The Virginia Dynasties: The Emergence of "King" Carter and the Golden Age.* Boston, 1969.

Edwards, Morgan. *Materials Toward a History of the Baptists in the Province of Virginia,* 1772. Manuscript.

Ellis, Joseph J. *American Sphinx: The Character of Thomas Jefferson.* New York, 1997.

———. *Founding Brothers: The Revolutionary Generation.* New York, 2001.

Emerson, Ralph Waldo. *Essays and Lectures.* Ed. Joel Porte. New York, 1983.

———. *Representative Men.* Ed. Pamela Schirmeister. New York, 1995.

Fenn, Elizabeth A. *Pox Americana: The Great Smallpox Epidemic of 1775–82.* New York, 2001.

Finkelman, Paul. *Slavery and the Founders: Race and Liberty in the Age of Jefferson.* 2nd ed. New York, 2001.

Fisher, Joshua Francis. *Recollections of Joshua Francis Fisher, Written in 1864.* Arr. Sophia Cadwalader. Boston, 1929.

Fithian, Philip Vickers. *Journal and Letters of Philip Vickers Fithian 1773–1774: A Plantation Tutor of the Old Dominion.* Ed. and intro. Hunter Dickinson Farish. 3rd ed. Charlottesville, Va., 1957.

Franklin, John Hope. "The Moral Legacy of the Founding Fathers," in *Race and History: Selected Essays, 1938–1988.* Baton Rouge, La., 1989.

Freehling, William W. *The Reintegration of American History: Slavery and the Civil War.* New York, 1994.

Freeman, Douglas Southall. *George Washington: A Biography.* New York, 1948.

———. *Washington.* Abr. Richard Harwell. New York, 1968.

Frey, Sylvia R. *Water from the Rock: Black Resistance in a Revolutionary Age.* Princeton, N.J., 1991.

Genovese, Eugene D. *Roll, Jordan, Roll: The World the Slaves Made.* 2nd ed. New York, 1976.

Gewehr, Wesley M. *The Great Awakening in Virginia, 1740–1790.* Reprint ed. Gloucester, Mass., 1965.

Glenn, Thomas Allen. *Some Colonial Mansions: And Those Who Lived in Them.* Philadelphia, 1899.

Godson, Susan H., Ludwell H. Johnson, and Richard B. Sherman. *The College of William and Mary: A History.* Williamsburg, Va., 1994.

Green, Bryan Clark, Calder Loth, and William M. S. Rasmussen. *Lost Virginia: Vanished Architecture of the Old Dominion.* Charlottesville, Va., 2001.

Hakim, Joy. *The History of Us.* Book 4: *The New Nation.* New York, 1994.

Hamilton, Alexander. *The Papers of Alexander Hamilton.* Ed. Harold C. Syrett. 27 vols. to date. New York, 1961–.

———. *Writings.* Ed. Joanne Freeman. New York, 2001.

Heath, Barbara J. *Hidden Lives: The Archaeology of Slave Life at Thomas Jefferson's Poplar Forest.* Charlottesville, Va., 1999.

Hirschfeld, Fritz. *George Washington and Slavery: A Documentary Portrayal.* Columbia, Mo., 1997.

Holton, Woody. *Forced Founders: Indians, Debtors, Slaves, and the Making of the American Revolution in Virginia.* Chapel Hill, N.C., 1999.

Hutson, James H. *Religion and the Founding of the American Republic.* Washington, D.C., 1998.

Isaac, Rhys. *The Transformation of Virginia: 1740–1790.* Rev. ed. Chapel Hill, N.C., 1999.

James, Charles F. *Documentary History of the Struggle for Religious Liberty in Virginia.* Reprint ed. New York, 1971.

James, William. *The Varieties of Religious Experience.* Intro. Reinhold Niebuhr. New York, 1997.

Jameson, J. Franklin. *The American Revolution Considered as a Social Movement.* Intro. Frederick B. Tolles. Reprint ed. Princeton, N.J., 1967.

Jefferson, Thomas. *The Garden and Farm Books of Thomas Jefferson.* Ed. Robert C. Baron. Golden, Colo., 1987.

———. *Jefferson's Memorandum Books.* Eds. James A. Bear, Jr., and Lucia C. Stanton. 2 vols. Princeton, N.J., 1997.

———. *Notes on the State of Virginia.* Ed. William Peden. New York, 1982.

————. *The Papers of Thomas Jefferson.* Ed. Julian P. Boyd. 30 vols. to date. Princeton, N.J., 1950–.

————. *The Works of Thomas Jefferson.* Ed. Paul Leicester Ford. 12 vols. New York, 1904–5.

Johnson, Inez Selden. "Black History." In *Westmoreland County Virginia, 1653–1983.* Ed. Walter Biscoe Norris, Jr. Montross, Va., 1983.

Jones, Alice Hanson. *Wealth of a Nation to Be.* New York, 1980.

Jones, Joseph. *Letters of Joseph Jones of Virginia, 1777–1787.* Ed. Worthington Chauncey Ford. New York, 1971.

Jordan, Winthrop D. *White Over Black: American Attitudes Toward the Negro, 1550–1812.* Chapel Hill, N.C., 1968.

Justice, Hilda, comp. *The Life and Ancestry of Warner Mifflin.* Philadelphia, 1905.

Kimber, Edward. *History of the Life and Adventures of Mr. Anderson: Containing his Strange Varieties of Fortune in Europe and America, Compiled from his Own Papers.* Reprint ed. Glasgow, 1799.

————. *Itinerant Observations in America.* Ed. Kevin J. Hayes. Newark, Del., 1998.

Kolchin, Peter. *American Slavery, 1619–1877.* New York, 1993.

Kolp, John Gilman. *Gentlemen and Freeholders: Electoral Politics in Colonial Virginia.* Baltimore, 1998.

Kulikoff, Allan. *The Development of Southern Cultures in the Chesapeake, 1680–1800.* Chapel Hill, N.C., 1986.

Labaree, Benjamin Woods. *The Boston Tea Party.* New York, 1964.

Lafayette, Marquis de. *Lafayette in Virginia, Unpublished Letters.* Ed. Gilbert Chinard. Baltimore, 1928.

Laurens, Henry. *The Papers of Henry Laurens.* Ed. Philip M. Hamer. 16 vols. to date. Columbia, S.C., 1968–.

Lee, Richard Henry. *The Letters of Richard Henry Lee.* Ed. James Curtis Ballagh. 2 vols. New York, 1911.

Leland, John. "The Virginia Chronicle." In *The Writings of the Late Elder John Leland.* Ed. L. F. Greene. New York, 1845.

Leventhal, Herbert. *In the Shadow of the Enlightenment: Occultism and Renaissance Science in Eighteenth-Century America.* New York, 1976.

Lewis, Jan. *The Pursuit of Happiness: Family and Values in Jefferson's Virginia.* New York, 1983.

Lewis, Ronald L. *Coal, Iron, and Slaves: Industrial Slavery in Maryland and Virginia, 1715–1865.* Westport, Conn., 1979.

Little, Lewis Peyton. *Imprisoned Preachers and Religious Liberty in Virginia.* Lynchburg, Va., 1938.

Lockridge, Kenneth A. *On the Sources of Patriarchal Rage: The Commonplace Books of William Byrd and Thomas Jefferson and the Gendering of Power in the Eighteenth Century.* New York, 1993.

Loth, Calder, ed. *Virginia Landmarks of Black History.* Fore. Armstead L. Robinson. Charlottesville, Va., 1995.

MacLeod, Duncan J. *Slavery, Race and the American Revolution.* New York, 1974.

Madison, James. *The Papers of James Madison.* Eds. William T. Hutchinson and William M. F. Rachal. 17 vols. to date. Chicago, 1962–.

———. *The Writings of James Madison.* Ed. Gaillard Hunt. 9 vols. New York, 1900–10.

Maier, Pauline. *American Scripture: Making the Declaration of Independence.* New York, 1998.

Malone, Dumas. *Jefferson the Virginian.* Boston, 1948.

Mason, George. *The Papers of George Mason, 1725–1792.* Ed. Robert A. Rutland. 3 vols. Chapel Hill, N.C., 1970.

Mayer, Henry. *A Son of Thunder: Patrick Henry and the American Republic.* New York, 1991.

McColley, Robert. *Slavery and Jeffersonian Virginia.* Chicago, 1964.

Meade, William. *Old Churches, Ministers, and Families of Virginia.* 2 vols. Reprint ed. Bowie, Md., 1992.

Melish, Joanne Pope. *Disowning Slavery: Gradual Emancipation and "Race" in New England, 1780–1860.* Ithaca, N.Y., 1998.

Miller, John Chester. *The Wolf by the Ears: Thomas Jefferson and Slavery.* Rev. ed. Charlottesville, Va., 1991.

Morgan, Edmund S. *American Slavery, American Freedom: The Ordeal of Colonial Virginia.* New York, 1975.

Morgan, Philip D. *Slave Counterpoint: Black Culture in the Eighteenth-Century Chesapeake and Lowcountry.* Chapel Hill, N.C., 1998.

Morton, Louis. *Robert Carter of Nomini Hall: A Virginia Tobacco Planter of the Eighteenth Century.* Williamsburg, Va., 1941.

Mullin, Gerald W. *Flight and Rebellion: Slave Resistance in Eighteenth-Century Virginia.* New York, 1972.

Mullin, Michael. "British Caribbean and North American Slaves in an Era of War and Revolution, 1775–1807." In *The Southern Experience in the Ameri-*

can Revolution. Eds. Jeffrey J. Crow and Larry Tise. Chapel Hill, N.C., 1978.

Nash, Gary B. *Race and Revolution*. Lanham, Md., 1990.

Noonan, John T., Jr. *Persons and Masks of the Law: Cardozo, Holmes, Jefferson, and Wythe as Makers of the Masks*. Rev. ed. Berkeley, Calif., 2002.

Norton, May Beth, Herbert G. Gutman, and Ira Berlin, "The Afro-American Family in the Age of Revolution." In *Slavery and Freedom in the Age of the American Revolution*. Eds. Ira Berlin and Ronald Hoffman. 2nd ed. Urbana, Ill., 1986.

Oakes, James. *The Ruling Race: A History of American Slaveholders*. New York, 1983.

O'Brien, Conor Cruise. *The Long Affair: Thomas Jefferson and the French Revolution, 1785–1800*. Chicago, 1996.

Otis, James. *Rights of the British Colonies Asserted and Proved*. Boston, 1764.

Paine, Thomas. *Common Sense*. Reissue ed., intro. Isaac Kramnick. New York, 1976.

Papenfuse, Edward C., ed. *A Biographical Dictionary of the Maryland Legislature, 1635–1789*. Vol. 2. Baltimore, 1985.

Peterson, Merrill D. *The Jefferson Image in the American Mind*. New York, 1960.

Price, Andrew. *Selim the Algerine*. Marlinton, W.Va., 1924.

Ragsdale, Bruce A. *A Planter's Republic: The Search for Economic Independence in Revolutionary Virginia*. Madison, Wis., 1996.

Rippon, John. *The Baptist Annual Register for 1790, 1791, 1792, and Part of 1793*. 1793.

Rowland, Kate Mason. "The Carters of Virginia." In *Some Colonial Mansions and Those Who Lived in Them*. By Thomas Allen Glenn. Philadelphia, 1899.

Ryland, Garnett. *The Baptists of Virginia, 1699–1926*. Richmond, Va., 1955.

Salgo, Sandor. *Thomas Jefferson: Musician and Violinist*. Thomas Jefferson Memorial Foundation, 2000.

Schwarz, Philip J. *Migrants Against Slavery: Virginians and the Nation*. Charlottesville, Va., 2001.

Selby, John E. *Dunmore*. Williamsburg, Va., 1977.

———. *The Revolution in Virginia, 1775–1783*. Williamsburg, Va., 1988.

Semple, Robert Baylor. *A History of the Rise and Progress of the Baptists in Virginia*. Rev. ed. G. W. Beale. Richmond, Va., 1894.

Smith, Daniel Blake. *Inside the Great House: Planter Family Life in Eighteenth-Century Chesapeake Society*. Ithaca, N.Y., 1980.

Smith, Mark M. *Debating Slavery: Economy and Society in the Antebellum American South.* New York, 1998.

Smith, Richard Norton. *Patriarch: George Washington and the New American Nation.* New York, 1993.

Sobel, Mechal. *The World They Made Together: Black and White Values in Eighteenth-Century Virginia.* Princeton, N.J., 1987.

Stanton, Lucia. *Slavery at Monticello.* Pref. Julian Bond. Thomas Jefferson Memorial Foundation, 1996.

Stevenson, Brenda E. *Life in Black and White: Family and Community in the Slave South.* New York, 1996.

Storing, Herbert J., ed. *The Complete Anti-Federalist.* 7 vols. Chicago, 1981.

Storing, Herbert J. *What the Anti-Federalists Were For: The Political Thought of the Opponents of the Constitution.* Chicago, 1981.

Swedenborg, Emanuel. *A Compendium of the Theological Writings of Emanuel Swedenborg.* Ed. Samuel W. Warren. New York, 1974.

———. *Heaven and Its Wonders from Things Heard and Seen.* Trans. J. C. Ager. New York, 1964.

———. *Swedenborg's Journal of Dreams, 1743–1744.* Intro. Wilson Van Dusen. 2nd ed. Bryn Athyn, Pa., 1989.

———. *The Apocalypse Revealed, Wherein Are Disclosed the Arcana There Foretold Which Have Hitherto Remained Concealed.* Trans. John Whitehead. Vol. 1. New York, 1968.

———. *The True Christian Religion Containing the Universal Theology of the New Church.* New York, 1909.

Sydnor, Charles S. *American Revolutionaries in the Making: Political Practices in Washington's Virginia.* Rev. ed. New York, 1965.

Tate, Thad W. *The Negro in Eighteenth-Century Williamsburg.* Williamsburg, Va., 1965.

Taylor, James B. *Virginia Baptist Ministers.* Series 1. New York, 1859.

Thom, W. T. *The Struggle for Religious Freedom in Virginia: The Baptists.* Baltimore, 1900.

Tinling, Marion, ed. *The Correspondences of the Three William Byrds of Westover, Virginia, 1684–1776.* Fore. Louis B. Wright. Charlottesville, Va., 1977.

Washington, Booker T. *The Booker T. Washington Papers.* Ed. Louis R. Harlan. Vol. 1. Urbana, Ill., 1972–89.

Washington, George. *The Diaries of George Washington.* Ed. Donald Jackson. 6 vols. Charlottesville, Va., 1976–78.

———. *The Papers of George Washington, Colonial Series.* Ed. by W. W. Abbot. 10 vols. Charlottesville, Va., 1983–95.

———. *The Papers of George Washington, Confederation Series.* Eds. W. W. Abbot and Dorothy Twohig. 6 vols. to date. Charlottesville, Va., 1992–.

———. *The Papers of George Washington, Presidential Series.* Ed. Dorothy Twohig. 11 vols. to date. Charlottesville, Va., 1987–.

———. *The Papers of George Washington, Retirement Series.* Ed. Dorothy Twohig. 4 vols. to date. Charlottesville, Va., 1998–.

———. *The Writings of George Washington.* Ed. John C. Fitzpatrick. 39 vols. Washington, 1931–44.

Waterman, Thomas Tileston. *The Mansions of Virginia: 1706–1776.* Chapel Hill, N.C., 1946.

Wiencek, Henry. *An Imperfect God: George Washington, His Slaves, and the Creation of America.* New York, 2003.

Wirt, William. *Life of Patrick Henry.* Philadelphia, 1818.

Wood, Gordon S. *The American Revolution: A History.* New York, 2001.

———. *The Radicalism of the American Revolution.* New York, 1992.

Zilversmit, Arthur. *The First Emancipation: The Abolition of Slavery in the North.* Chicago, 1967.

Articles

Anderson, James LaVerne. "The Virginia Councillors and the American Revolution: The Demise of an Aristocratic Clique." *Virginia Magazine of History and Biography* 82 (Jan. 1974).

Barden, John Randolph. "Reflections of a Singular Mind: The Library of Robert Carter of Nomony Hall." *Virginia Magazine of History and Biography* 96 (Jan. 1988).

Blackmer, Horace B. "Col. Robert Carter and the First American New-Church Liturgy." *New-Church Review* 35 (1928).

Blair, John. "Diary of John Blair." *William and Mary Quarterly,* 1st series, 8 (July 1899).

Boyd, Julian P. "The Murder of George Wythe." *William and Mary Quarterly,* 3rd series, 12 (Oct. 1955).

Breen, T. H. "Horses and Gentlemen: The Cultural Significance of Gambling Among the Gentry of Virginia." *William and Mary Quarterly,* 3rd series, 34 (Apr. 1977).

Calhoon, Robert M. " 'A Sorrowful Spectator of These Tumultuous Times':

Robert Beverley Describes the Coming of the Revolution." *Virginia Magazine of History and Biography* 73 (1965).

Conway, Moncure Daniel. "The Recantation of Colonel Carter of Virginia." *Open Court* (1889–1890).

"Councillor Carter's Comments on the Baltimore Society of 1797." *New-Church Messenger* (1892).

Daniel, W. Harrison. "Virginia Baptists and the Negro in the Early Republic." *Virginia Magazine of History and Biography* 80 (1972).

Delano, Frank. "A Man of Conscience." *Fredericksburg Free Lance–Star.* 3 Mar. 2001.

Delano, Meriwether. "The Manumission: A Story of Slave and Master at Nomini." *St. Timothy's School Alumnae Bulletin* (Fall 1991).

Doyle, Christopher. "Judge St. George Tucker and the Case of Tom v. Roberts." *Virginia Magazine of History and Biography* 106 (Autumn 1998).

Dozier, Richard. "Richard Dozier's Historical Notes 1771–1818." Ed. John S. Moore. *Virginia Baptist Register* (1989).

Essig, James David. "A Very Wintry Season: Virginia Baptists and Slavery, 1785–1797." *Virginia Magazine of History and Biography* 88 (Apr. 1980).

Evans, Emory G. "Planter Indebtedness and the Coming of the Revolution in Virginia." *William and Mary Quarterly,* 3rd series, 19 (Oct. 1962).

Gardner, Robert G. "Virginia Baptists and Slavery, 1759–1790, Part II." *Virginia Baptist Register* 25 (1986).

Gipson, Lawrence H. "Virginia Planter Debts Before the American Revolution." *Virginia Magazine of History and Biography* 69 (1961).

Goodwin, Conrad H., Jr., and Henrietta G. Godwin. "Colonel Carter's Mansion Dwelling Burnt." *Northern Neck of Virginia Historical Magazine* (Dec. 1978).

Hazard, Ebenezer. "The Journal of Ebenezer Hazard in Virginia, 1777." Ed. Fred Shelley. *Virginia Magazine of History and Biography* 62 (Oct. 1954).

Holmes, Steven A. "Slave Owner's 1791 Act of Emancipation Endures." *The New York Times.* 29 July 1991.

Isaac, Rhys. "Evangelical Revolt: The Nature of the Baptists' Challenge to the Traditional Order in Virginia, 1765 to 1775." *William and Mary Quarterly,* 3rd series, 31 (July 1974).

"Journal of a French Traveler in the Colonies, 1765." *American Historical Review* 26 (July 1921).

Kelley, Jennifer Olsen, and J. Lawrence Angel. "The Workers of Catoctin Furnace." *Maryland Archeology* (1983).

212   *Select Bibliography*

Klebaner, Benjamin Joseph. "American Manumission Laws and the Responsibility for Supporting Slaves." *Virginia Magazine of History and Biography* 63 (Oct. 1955).

Latane, Lawrence. "Gift of Freedom: Tale Handed Down." *Richmond Times-Dispatch.* 21 July 1991.

Lumpkin, William. "Col. Robert Carter, a Baptist." *Virginia Baptist Register* 8 (1969).

McGroarty, William Buckner. "Experiments in Mass Emancipation." *William and Mary Quarterly,* 2nd series, 21 (July 1941).

Meyers, Harold Burton. "The Carter Who Shocked Virginia." *Colonial Williamsburg* (Aug. 1996).

Nicholson, Francis. "Statement by Nicholson as to Lightfoot and Carter," in "Papers Relating to the Administration of Governor Nicholson and to the Founding of William and Mary College." *Virginia Magazine of History and Biography* (July 1900).

Ohrmundt, Jan. "New Life for Nomini Hall: Old House Glows Again." *Westmoreland News.* 3 Apr. 2002.

Page, John. "Governor Page." *Virginia Historical Register* 3 (July 1850).

"Polls in Westmoreland County for Election of Burgesses." *William and Mary Quarterly,* 1st series, 8 (July 1899).

"The Proceedings of the Virginia Committee of Correspondence, 1764." *Virginia Magazine of History and Biography* 9 (1902).

Puente, Maria. "As Others Held On, He Freed Slaves." *USA Today.* 29 July 1991.

Quarles, Benjamin. "Lord Dunmore as Liberator." *William and Mary Quarterly,* 3rd series, 15 (Oct. 1958).

Riley, John P. "Written with My Own Hand: George Washington's Last Will and Testament." *Virginia Cavalcade* 48 (Autumn 1999).

Ringle, Ken. "The Day Slavery Bowed to Conscience." *The Washington Post.* 21 July 1991.

Rowland, Kate Mason. "Robert Carter of Virginia." *Magazine of American Biography* (Sept. 1893).

Schmidt, Fredrika Teute, and Barbara Ripel Wilhelm. "Early Proslavery Petitions in Virginia." *William and Mary Quarterly,* 3rd series, 30 (Jan. 1973).

Spencer, R. H. "The Honorable Daniel Dulany, 1722–97." *Maryland Historical Society Magazine* 13 (June 1918).

Tarter, Brent. "The New Virginia Bookshelf." *Virginia Magazine of History and Biography* 104 (Winter 1996).

Thompson, Mary V. "And Procure for Themselves a Few Amenities: The Private Life of George Washington's Slaves." *Virginia Cavalcade* 48 (Autumn 1999).

Turano, Kathryn Murray. "Nomini Hall Dig May Be 'Dadda' Gumby's House." *Westmoreland News.* 12 Nov. 1998.

———. "Probing the Past at Nomini." *Westmoreland News.* 9 Apr. 1998.

Wood, Gordon S. "Rhetoric and Reality in the American Revolution." *William and Mary Quarterly,* 3rd series, 23 (Jan. 1966).

Zwelling, Shomer S. "Robert Carter's Journey: From Colonial Patriarch to New Nation Mystic." *American Quarterly* 38.4 (Autumn 1986).

Miscellaneous

Albert, Peter J. "The Protean Institution: The Geography, Economy, and Ideology of Slavery in Post-Revolutionary Virginia." Diss., University of Maryland, 1976.

Armitage's Impartial List of the Ladies of Pleasure of Williamsburg, with a Preface by a Celebrated Wit. Reprint ed., n.d. Williamsburg, Va., 1775.

Arnest, Thomas Lee. Interview with author. Nomini Hall, Va., 7 July 1998.

Bagby, Ross Frederick. "The Randolph Slave Saga: Communities in Collision." Diss., Ohio State University, 1998.

Barden, John Randolph. " 'Flushed with Notions of Freedom': The Growth and Emancipation of a Virginia Slave Community, 1726–1812." Diss., Duke University, 1993.

———. " 'Innocent and Necessary': Music and Dancing in the Life of Robert Carter of Nomony Hall, 1728–1804." M.A. thesis, William and Mary, 1983.

Brown, Thomas. "Tom Brown's Memoirs." N.p., n.d.

Burke, Henry Robert. Telephone interview with author. 14 Apr. 2002.

Delano, Frank. E-mail to author. 26 Feb. 2001.

———. Interview with author. Warsaw, Va., 11 June 2000.

Ebert, Rebecca Aleene. "A Window on the Valley: A Study of the Free Black Community of Winchester and Frederick County, Virginia, 1785–1860." M.A. thesis, University of Maryland, 1986.

Iaccarino, Anthony Alfred. "Virginia and the National Contest over Slavery in the Early Republic, 1780–1833." Diss., UCLA, 1999.

Kwilecki, Susan. "Through the Needle's Eye: Religion in the Lives of Wealthy Colonial Americans." Diss., Stanford University, 1982.

Mallory, Dalton W. Interview and tour with author. Nomini Hall, Va. 7 July
    1998.
Rider, Clare. E-mail communication with author. 12 June 2003.
Teagle, Robert. Telephone conversation with author. Historic Christ Church,
    Lancaster County, Va., 20 Jan. 2005.
Wenger, Mark R. Interview and tour with author. Robert Carter House,
    Colonial Williamsburg, Williamsburg, Va., 5 June 2003.
Withrow, Sarah. E-mail interview with author. 1, 5, 12 July 2004.

Introduction

xi **"My plans and advice"** RCIII to H. L. Maund, 30 May 1803, LC.

xi **On September 5, 1791** RCIII to Charles Jones, 6 Sep. 1791, vol. 9, DU. Carter dated the document August 1, 1791. "Deed of Gift" was a common phrase in the eighteenth century, used to describe a transfer of property. The original public version of the Deed of Gift sits untended in the land records room of the County Courts Building in the tiny hamlet of Heathsville on the Northern Neck. One need only ask the clerk on duty for the book entitled *Orders, Deeds, etc., 1789–1825*, Part One of the Northumberland District Court, and turn to page 232. Characteristically, for Carter, the census of slave names precedes his preamble. The number 453 is written at the end of the census, but only 452 names are listed. A microfilm version is available in the Library of Virginia. Carter also copied out an extended version into his own notebooks: see chapter 5.

xi **And yet, Carter's document** During the Revolutionary era, no emancipation rivaled the size of Carter's, although several slaveholders (including George Washington and a Virginian named Joseph Mayo) freed large numbers. In the nineteenth century, there were two large recorded emancipations. See Ross Frederick Bagby, "The Randolph Slave Saga: Communities in Collision" (Ph.D. diss., Ohio State University, 1998), for a description of John

Randolph's liberation, in his will, of 383 Roanoke slaves. See page 143 (note, as well, that Bagby overlooks Carter): "The only manumission in American history perhaps larger than John Randolph's had resettled its freed blacks in Ohio . . . Samuel Gist, a British-born resident of Virginia. . . . The exact numbers of manumitted Gist slaves are uncertain—"

See William Buckner McGroarty, "Experiments in Mass Emancipation," *William and Mary Quarterly,* 2nd series, 21 (July 1941). See also Philip J. Schwarz, *Migrants Against Slavery: Virginians and the Nation* (Charlottesville, Va., 2001), 78–80, 124–40, for descriptions of the Randolph and Gist emancipations. Schwarz states that Gist freed 350 slaves.

xii **But as his friends** "Green" Street in Baltimore is now "Greene" Street. For a discussion of Carter's life in Baltimore, see chapter 5.

xii **Dig deeper** Philip D. Morgan, *Slave Counterpoint: Black Culture in the Eighteenth-Century Chesapeake and Lowcountry* (Chapel Hill, N.C., 1998), 679.

xii **"extraordinary, very, very exceptional"** Quoted in Ken Ringle, "The Day Slavery Bowed to Conscience," *The Washington Post,* 21 July 1991. Sec. F. Ira Berlin, *Many Thousands Gone: The First Two Centuries of Slavery in North America* (Cambridge, Mass., 1998).

xiii **It turned out, however** Fox Butterfield, *All God's Children: The Bosket Family and the American Tradition of Violence* (New York, 1995), 133.

xiii **the best sources about Robert Carter** Kate Mason Rowland, "Robert Carter of Virginia," *Magazine of American Biography* (Sep. 1893). John Randolph Barden, " 'Flushed with Notions of Freedom': The Growth and Emancipation of a Virginia Slave Community, 1732–1812" (Ph.D. diss., Duke University, 1993). Unless noted, all references to Barden cite this text. Louis Morton, *Robert Carter of Nomini Hall: A Virginia Tobacco Planter of the Eighteenth Century* (Williamsburg, Va., 1941). Morton writes that "the study was not written as a biography" (x). As its title suggests, "Flushed" focuses on the lives of the Nomony slaves during a period that includes the major events leading up to, and following from, the Deed of Gift. Barden has also composed an unpublished master's thesis on Robert Carter's musical interests, and a short published article on Carter's library, based on a bibliography of the contents of Carter's (and his descendants') library that he compiled and donated to the Virginia Historical Society. Lastly, and perhaps most remarkably, Barden has also transcribed the Carter Papers housed at Duke University, a transcription that can be found only at Duke—the original of the papers has been photographed, however, and is available in microfilm at libraries across the country. See chapter 2.

xiii **Shomer S. Zwelling published** Shomer S. Zwelling, "Robert Carter's Journey: From Colonial Patriarch to New Nation Mystic," *American Quarterly* 38.4 (Autumn 1986).

xiii **"Emancipated!"** Joy Hakim, *The History of Us*, Book 4: *The New Nation* (New York, 1994), 134.

xiii **Meriwether Delano composed** Meriwether Delano, "The Manumission: A Story of Slave and Master at Nomini," *St. Timothy's School Alumnae Bulletin* (Fall 1991).

xiii **The event drew a thousand people** Steven A. Holmes, "Slave Owner's 1791 Act of Emancipation Endures," *The New York Times*, 29 July 1991, sect. A. Ringle, F1, F4, F5. Maria Puente, "As Others Held On, He Freed Slaves," *USA Today*, 29 July 1991, sect. A. A file on the 1991 celebration, donated by Frank Delano, is housed in the Virginia Historical Society, featuring clippings, correspondence, letters, and even budget. Note also Harold Burton Meyers, "The Carter Who Shocked Virginia," *Colonial Williamsburg* (August 1996), a sound biographical sketch of Carter. Ringle, however, may be the best *published* account of the Deed of Gift available.

xiii **Let us try to quantify forgetting** Morton, 251–69.

xiii **The total number** In the notes and bibliography of this book, I have not cited every brief (i.e., one-sentence) reference to the Deed of Gift available. But I have attempted to cite all extended, published references to Robert Carter III and the Deed of Gift, or every source for which Robert Carter III or the Deed of Gift are the primary subject, with the exception of local Northern Neck newspapers.

xiv **"Nomony" became "Nomini"** Throughout Carter's correspondence, he uses "Nomony." However, "Nomini" was used during his lifetime. See Philip Vickers Fithian, *Journal and Letters of Philip*

Vickers Fithian 1773–1774: A Plantation Tutor of the Old Dominion, ed. and intro. Hunter Dickinson Farish, 3rd ed. (Charlottesville, Va., 1957), 80.

xiv **Berlin, in his groundbreaking** Ira Berlin, *Slaves Without Masters: The Free Negro in the Antebellum South* (New York, 1974), 59, 61, 101, 150. Brenda E. Stevenson, *Life in Black and White: Family and Community in the Slave South* (New York, 1996), also provides roughly two pages on the Deed of Gift in a four-hundred-page volume. See particularly 265–68 and 296–97.

xiv **From late-nineteenth** Philip Alexander Bruce, *The Virginia Plutarch* (Chapel Hill, N.C., 1929); Matthew Page Andrews, *Virginia: The Old Dominion* (Garden City, N.Y., 1937).

xiv **"unhappy" and "death-dreading"** William Meade, *Old Churches, Ministers, and Families of Virginia,* reprint ed. (Bowie, Md., 1992), vol. 2, 111–12.

xiv **In some books** For instance, Mechal Sobel, *The World They Made Together: Black and White Values in Eighteenth-Century Virginia* (Princeton, N.J., 1987).

xiv **In others** For instance, James Oakes, *The Ruling Race: A History of American Slaveholders* (New York, 1983).

xiv **"liberal"** *Colonial Williamsburg Official Guidebook* (Williamsburg, Va., 1970), 88.

xv **Authors for whom** Robert McColley, *Slavery and Jeffersonian Virginia* (Chicago, 1964). Rhys Isaac, *The Transformation of Virginia: 1740–1790,* rev. ed. (Chapel Hill, N.C., 1999). Gordon S. Wood, in "Rhetoric and Reality in the American Revolution," describes Carter's "strange religious conversions" as "only the most dramatic example of what was taking place less frenziedly elsewhere among the gentry"—an accurate description, but one that implies that the story of Robert Carter's religious career was readily familiar to his readers (*William and Mary Quarterly,* series 3, 23 [Jan. 1966], 29).

xv **When Genovese discusses private emancipations** Eugene D. Genovese, *Roll, Jordan, Roll: The World the Slaves Made,* 2nd ed. (New York, 1976), 17, 224, 599. Other authors use Carter not as an example of a liberal slaveholder but as an example of the mendacity of that occupation (for which, inevitably, his papers provide a wealth of evidence). See, for instance, David Brion Davis, *The*

Problem of Slavery in the Age of Revolution, 1770–1823 (New York, 1999; 1975), 278: "A Virginia planter like Robert Carter, thinking of himself as a benevolent patriarch . . ." See also Peter Kolchin, *American Slavery, 1619–1877* (New York, 1993), 33, 71. But Kolchin also illustrates the way that many authors intuitively downplay Carter's achievement: he claims that Carter freed his slaves in his will, "thereby securing emotional benefit without suffering financial loss" (77). He also claims that "legal complications . . . prevented most of . . . Carter's slaves from ever receiving their freedom" (77–78). The first statement is clearly incorrect; the second statement is almost certainly incorrect (see Conclusion).

To my knowledge, only one author combines all three potential approaches to Robert Carter III; that is, only one author details instances of his inevitable venality as a slaveholder, his status as an extraordinarily compassionate slaveholder, and the fact that he freed his slaves, within the same text. See Gerald W. Mullin, *Flight and Rebellion: Slave Resistance in Eighteenth-Century Virginia* (New York, 1972).

xv **He left no great edifice** Bryan Clark Green, Calder Loth, William M. S. Rasmussen, *Lost Virginia: Vanished Architecture of the Old Dominion* (Charlottesville, Va., 2001), 32. The "edifice" comment is attributed to Frank Delano, interview, 11 June 2000. Carter's house on Green Street in Baltimore is a ghost as well: the city block upon which it resided is now occupied by a VA hospital.

xv **"new system of politicks"** For descriptions of Carter's election "campaigns," see chapters 1 and 4. RCIII, vol. 13, DU.

xvi **"no Stone"** Fithian, 61.

xvi **"It is hard to know"** Ibid., 111.

xvi **"the least possible"** *Northumberland District Court Orders, Deeds, Etc., 1789–1825*, part 1, 236, LV.

xvii **"wolf by the ears"** Thomas Jefferson to John Holmes, 22 Apr. 1820. "Justice is in one scale, and self-preservation in the other," he added. *The Works of Thomas Jefferson*, ed. Paul Leicester Ford (New York, 1904–5), 12:159.

xvii **There has always been good evidence** See Berlin, *Slaves Without Masters*, or Davis, "What the Abolitionists Were Up Against," 39–83.

Chapter I

3 **"But where says some"** Thomas Paine, *Common Sense,* intro. Isaac Kramnick (New York, 1976), 98.

4 **When Carter stood** This portrait currently hangs in the Virginia House, a small, gracious museum overlooking the James River in Richmond.

4 **He had wealth** Barden, 26.

4 **"inconceivable illiterate"** John Page, "Governor Page," *Virginia Historical Register* 3 (July 1850), 146. A fine overview of Carter's early connections to his family, especially his parents, grandparents, and uncles, can be found in Morton, chapters 1 and 2.

4 **He read** Carter, for instance, owned a share in the Ohio Company (Morton, 68–69).

4 **He even played** Sandor Salgo, *Thomas Jefferson: Musician and Violinist* (Thomas Jefferson Memorial Foundation, 2000), 6.

5 **For John Carter . . . even less.** Morton, 3–4. Clifford Dowdey, *The Virginia Dynasties: The Emergence of "King" Carter and the Golden Age* (Boston, 1969), 10. Katharine L. Brown, *Robert "King" Carter: Builder of Christ Church* (Irvington, Va.), 3–5. Noel Currer-Briggs, *The Carters of Virginia: Their English Ancestry* (Sussex, England, 1979), 14–15. Brown and Morton cite different emigration dates for John Carter, and different pedigrees. I am using Brown and Currer-Briggs.

5 **They filled the new colony** Green, Loth, Rasmussen, 9–10.

5 **"a sinke"** Edmund S. Morgan, *American Slavery, American Freedom: The Ordeal of Colonial Virginia* (New York, 1975), 185, 236. See also Claude G. Bowers, *The Young Jefferson, 1743–1789* (Boston, 1945), 3.

5 **"twenty and odd"** Armstead L. Robinson, fore., in *Virginia Landmarks of Black History,* ed. Calder Loth (Charlottesville, Va., 1995), xi. See also James C. Ballagh, *A History of Slavery in Virginia* (Baltimore, 1902), 8.

5–6 **By 1641 . . . in England.** Brown, *King,* 4–5.

6 **He built . . . promised freedom.** Morton, 4–7. Brown, *King,* 5, 6, 8. Currer-Briggs, 18–19, 32.

6 **Upon his death . . . named Bailey.** Morton, 8–9. Dowdey, 95–96. Brown, *King,* 12.

6 **One look** Brown, *King,* 18–19.

6–7 **And when . . . recalled her charge.** Dowdey, 196–201. Morton, 11–12.

7 **Shuttling back . . . Rappahannock.** Brown, *King,* 62–63.

7 **By 1711** Morton, 16, 18. Brown, *King,* 57. Again, Brown and Morton use slightly different dates. I have used Brown. For a discussion of the proprietary in context, see Edmund S. Morgan, 244.

7 **By 1726 . . . Rappahannock waterfront.** Dowdey, 174. Brown, *King,* 20, 32–38.

7 **"a pennyworth"** Robert Carter I to Richard Perry, 13 July 1720, in Robert Carter I, *Letters of Robert Carter, 1720–1727: The Commercial Interests of a Virginia Gentleman,* ed. Louis Wright (San Marino, Calif., 1940), 3–4. See also Brown, *King,* 29.

8 **He used a coat of arms** Brown, *King,* 3. Currer-Briggs, 14–15, 32.

8 **"pray allow me"** RCI to Micajah Perry, 13 Feb. 1720/21, in *Letters,* 73.

8 **"the goods of felons"** RCI to William Cage, 19 July 1725, in ibid., 120.

8 **Similarly, when Virginians** For a description of the transition to slave labor, see Edmund S. Morgan, 295–304.

8 **Whenever possible, he saved** Dowdey, 212. Brown, *King,* 50.

8 **"cured many a negro"** Carter to Robert Jones, 10 Oct. 1727, quoted in Kathleen M. Brown, *Good Wives, Nasty Wenches, and Anxious Patriarchs: Gender, Race, and Power in Colonial Virginia* (Chapel Hill, N.C., 1996), 352. See also Edmund S. Morgan, 313.

8 **"King" . . . "Robin"** Francis Nicholson, "Statement by Nicholson as to Lightfoot and Carter," in "Papers Relating to the Administration of Governor Nicholson and to the Founding of William and Mary College," *Virginia Magazine of History and Biography* (July 1900), 56. Quoted in Morton, 10, and Dowdey, 203.

8 **"country"** Dowdey, 154.

8 **"terror"** RCI to Richard Perry, 13 July 1720, in *Letters,* 1.

8 **Across every western horizon** Dowdey, 150. See also Brown, *Good Wives,* 252, 256–57.

9 **While other slaveholders expected** RCI to Robert Jones, 10 Oct. 1727, quoted in Brown, *King,* 53.

9 **In a like manner, he ordered** RCI to Robert Jones, 10 Oct. 1727, quoted in Brown, *King,* 53.

9 **In his ledgers** Brown, *Good Wives,* 358.

9 **A lifetime of prodigious eating** Dowdey, 319. See 323–26 as well. Brown, *King,* 41–42.

9 **He tried crutches . . . decades afterward.** RCI to William Dawkins, 14 July 1720, in *Letters,* 27. RCI to John Carter, 3 Mar. 1720/21, in *Letters,* 84. RCI to Honorable Sir, 3 Mar. 1720/21, in *Letters,* 86–87.

9 **He married well . . . Rappahannock.** Morton, 27–28.

9 **"Thus you see"** RCI to Messrs. Perry, 22 July 1720, in *Letters,* 35.

10 **He wore a diamond ring** Dowdey, 372.

10 **"too great lovers" . . . "muckworms."** RCI to William Dawkins, 23 Feb. 1720/21, in *Letters,* 80–81.

10 **"sublunary blessings"** RCI to Messrs. Perry, 22 July 1720, in ibid., 35.

10 **"a crazy, disordered" . . . "sound mind."** RCI to Micajah Perry, 10 July 1732, quoted in Dowdey, 370.

10 **"madness of the people" . . . "It is an old adage"** RCI to Micajah Perry, 13 Feb. 1720/21, in *Letters,* 74, quoted in Dowdey, 360.

10 **"I have the blessing"** RCI to "Another Merchant," quoted in Dowdey, 351.

10 **"three Girls"** RCI to Honorable Sir, 21 May 1728, CFP.

10 **In early 1729** Conrad H. Goodwin, Jr., and Henrietta G. Godwin, "Colonel Carter's Mansion Dwelling Burnt," *Northern Neck of Virginia Historical Magazine* (December 1978). Dowdey, 352.

10 **"blood so divided"** Landon Carter, *The Diary of Colonel Landon Carter of Sabine Hall, 1752–1778,* ed. Jack P. Greene (Charlottesville, Va., 1965), 2:898: "I shall be cautious of it till I can be certain it contains nothing of opium in it; having from my Observation on 3 of my family seen the fatal effects of that medicine; all of them died by blood so divided and rarified as to finish life with an universal Mortification, (to wit), my brother Robert, next my Sister Page and last my Couzin John Carter of Cleve."

10 **"dearly beloved"** Quoted in Kate Mason Rowland, "The Carters of Virginia," in Thomas Allen Glenn, *Some Colonial Mansions:*

And Those Who Lived in Them (Philadelphia, 1899), 243. Morton, 29.

11 **"died of the Flux"** Quoted in Brown, *King*, 76.

11 **His will** Morton, 19.

11 *cum regiam* Brown, *King*, 83, and phone conversation with Robert Teagle, Historic Christ Church, 20 Jan. 2005.

11 **"Here lies Robin"** Rowland, "The Carters of Virginia," in Glenn, 234. Morton, 23–24.

11 **By his fourth birthday** Linda Baumgarten, *What Clothes Reveal: The Language of Clothing in Colonial and Federal America* (Williamsburg, Va., 2002), 142: see photo, "Cradle to the Coffin," and caption.

11 **Eventually, King Carter** See Brown, *King*, 1–2.

12 **"gust"** See, for instance, Edmund S. Morgan, 242.

12 **"wretch'd contrived affair"** Edward Kimber, *Itinerant Observations in America*, ed. Kevin J. Hayes (Newark, Del., 1998), 63.

12 **"They are all"** Quoted in Joshua Francis Fisher, *Recollections . . . Written in 1864*, arr. Sophia Cadwalader (Boston, 1929), 97. See Gordon S. Wood, *The Radicalism of the American Revolution* (New York, 1992), 115: "In Virginia about forty or so interrelated wealthy families dominated the society and practiced a Republican stewardship that rivaled that of the English squirearchy." This governing squirearchy is well detailed in John E. Selby, *The Revolution in Virginia, 1775–1783* (Williamsburg, Va., 1988), 38.

13 **"suffer death"** . . . **"whipping post."** *The Statutes At Large: Being a Collection of All the Laws of Virginia, from the First Session of the Legislature, in the Year 1619: Published Pursuant to an Act of the General Assembly of Virginia, Passed on the Fifth Day of February One Thousand Eight Hundred and Eight,* ed. William Waller Hening (Richmond, Va., 1810–23), 6:104–12; 4:127.

13 **One hundred twenty** Dumas Malone, *Jefferson the Virginian* (Boston, 1948), 10, 11, 12. Fawn M. Brodie, *Thomas Jefferson: An Intimate History* (New York, 1974), 34, 35. Bowers, 10.

13 **"filled"** RCI to William Dawkins, 25 Mar. 1721, in *Letters*, 91. Dowdey, 370.

13 **Then there were views** Dowdey, 174. Brown, *King*, 20, 32–38.

14 **As well, his material needs** Morton, 63. References to Landon Carter's bad temper and self-pity abound among the work of his-

torians of this era and region. See, for instance, Lewis, 24, where she describes him as "a planter who generally assumed that advantage was being taken of him." On 32, she calls him "an unusually bitter and bad-humored man."

14 **In 1735, she remarried** Morton, 28.

14 **"thrown on a wide world"** Jefferson to Thomas Jefferson Randolph, 24 Nov. 1808, in *The Family Letters of Thomas Jefferson,* eds. Edwin M. Betts and James A. Bear, Jr. (Columbia, Mo., 1966), 362.

14 **"Miss Betty Carter"** John Lewis to Lawrence Washington, 28 June 1742, reprinted in Daniel Moncure Conway, *Barons of the Potomack and Rappahannock* (New York, 1892), 161–63.

14 **They sent him** Morton, 32.

14 **Then they brought him** A conventional description of William and Mary in the mid-eighteenth century. See, for instance, *Colonial Williamsburg Official Guidebook,* 56: "The grammar school . . . admitted boys of about twelve who spent four years."

14 **"studied without"** Page, 146.

15 **he booked passage** Carter wrote that he "embarked on board the ship Everton, Captain James Kelly, then in York-River, bound to Liverpoole." RCIII, daybook, 9 Nov. 1778, vol. 14, DU. Kate Mason Rowland, "Robert Carter of Virginia," 116. Rowland, "The Carters of Virginia," in Glenn, 262. Morton, 34.

15 **"monster"** Landon Carter, 16 Mar. 1776, 2:1004.

15 **Carter pursued some** Clare Rider, e-mail communication with the author, 12 June 2003.

15 **"My gratifications"** RCIII to Samuel Athawes, 17 Feb. 1764, CWF.

15 **"the richest heir"** Edward Kimber, *History of the Life and Adventures of Mr. Anderson: Containing his Strange Varieties of Fortune in Europe and America, Compiled from his Own Papers,* reprint ed. (Glasgow, 1799), 39, 43, 227–31. I discovered this novel through T. H. Breen, *Tobacco Culture: The Mentality of the Great Tidewater Planters on the Eve of Revolution,* rev. ed. (Princeton, N.J., 2001), xxi–xxiii.

15 **"confused"** Page, 146.

16 **"I hear Mr. R. Carter"** "Diary of John Blair," *William and Mary Quarterly,* 1st series, 8 (July 1899), 8–9.

16 **"At that parting"** RCIII to Samuel Athawes, 17 Feb. 1764, CWF. See Zwelling, 614.

16 **In 1752 . . . beaten as ignored.** The results: on 20 Jan. 1752, John Bushrod received 262 votes, Robert Vaulx, 190, Richard Lee, 157, and Robert Carter, 34; on 12 Sept. 1754, Augustine Washington received 194 votes, Richard Lee, 130, and Robert Carter, 7. See "Polls in Westmoreland County for Election of Burgesses," *William and Mary Quarterly*, series 1, 8 (July 1899), 32. Morton, 41.

16 **By the 1750s** Brown, *Good Wives*, 364. Isaac, *Transformation*, 56.

16 **Landon Carter lost** Brown, *Good Wives*, 364.

16 **"As for myself"** Robert Wormeley Carter, diary, 1 Apr. 1776, CWF, quoted in Charles S. Sydnor, *American Revolutionaries in the Making: Political Practices in Washington's Virginia*, rev. ed. (New York, 1965), 49.

16–17 **If losing one . . . president's Cabinet.** Sydnor, 98.

17 **If anything . . . *his* second election.** Ibid., 96.

17 **Nor was it** Wood, *Radicalism*, 84–85: "Access to government therefore often came quickly and easily to those who had the necessary social credentials."

17 **Robert Carter's uncles** Landon Carter served in the House of Burgesses from 1748 to 1764; Charles Carter, from 1747 to 1764; Robert Wormeley Carter, from 1775 to 1776; Charles Carter, the son of Robert Carter's uncle Charles, from 1758 to 1775. Rowland, "Carters," 254, 252, 279.

17 **"When there are so many"** *Armitage's Impartial List of the Ladies of Pleasure of Williamsburg, with a Preface by a Celebrated Wit*, reprint ed. (Williamsburg, Va., 1775; reprint ed., n.d.), v.

17 **"there is not a publick"** "Journal of a French Traveler in the Colonies, 1765," *American Historical Review* 26 (July 1921), 743.

17 **"Burn me"** Landon Carter, 9 Nov. 1771, 2:640. This is only one of many references. See also: 12 Feb. 1774, 2:795; 13 Mar. 1776, 2:1000; 14 Apr. 1772, 2:669.

17 **In addition to dice** For a brief description of the lottery involving William Byrd III, see *The Correspondences of the Three William Byrds of Westover, Virginia, 1684–1776*, ed. Marion Tinling (Charlottesville, Va., 1977), 611.

17 **"They are all professed gamesters"** "French Traveler," 742–43.

18 **In turn, the same taverns** Thad W. Tate, *The Negro in Eighteenth-Century Williamsburg* (Williamsburg, Va., 1965), 48, 53.

18 **In this manner, the ruling class** Isaac, *Transformation*, 49, de-

scribes the "well-known preoccupation with balance as essential to preserving virtue."

18 **"they are haughty"** Andrew Burnaby, *Travels Through the Middle Settlements in North America, In the Years 1759 and 1760*, reprint ed. (Ithaca, N.Y., 1963), 24.

18 **Moreover, they were increasingly well educated** Bowers, 34. Jefferson sometimes called the town "Devilsburg" (Malone, 80).

18 **But their insecurities** This reading of the Virginia gentry in the mid-eighteenth century is general in much of the scholarship of the past three decades. See, for instance, Kenneth A. Lockridge, *On the Sources of Patriarchal Rage: The Commonplace Books of William Byrd and Thomas Jefferson* (New York, 1993), 90–99.

18 **Virginian fortunes depended** Breen, *Tobacco*, xviii. Many authors make reference to the effect of unstable tobacco markets on the pre-Revolutionary gentry, but Breen's volume is unquestionably the most detailed treatment of the subject. See also Woody Holton, *Forced Founders: Indians, Debtors, Slaves, and the Making of the American Revolution in Virginia* (Chapel Hill, N.C., 1999).

18 **They were commodity rich** Isaac, *Transformation*, 22–23, 27–29. T. H. Breen, "Horses and Gentlemen: The Cultural Significance of Gambling Among the Gentry of Virginia," *William and Mary Quarterly*, 3rd series, 34 (Apr. 1977), 240–41. Wood, *Radicalism*, 117: "Many of the planters were living on the edge of bankruptcy."

18 **George Washington, in order** Douglas S. Freeman, *George Washington: A Biography* (New York, 1948), 2: 320–21.

18–19 **Almost exclusively, the Virginia gentry . . . in the counties.** Morton, 231. Isaac, *Transformation*, 60–65, discusses seating and entrance/exit patterns, as well as the relationship between sermon content and gentry politics. On 120–21, he discusses the "highly secular" "tone" of the Virginia gentry's religiosity. Sydnor discusses the power of the vestries, 83–84. For a description of colonial fixations on rank (and not class) and how they manifested themselves in common rituals such as church seating, see Gordon S. Wood, *Radicalism*, 21–24.

19 **"negative image"** Isaac, *Transformation*, 163–64. See also Lewis, 173.

19 **"clearer proof"** William Fristoe, *Concise History of the Ketocton Baptist Association* (Staunton, 1808), 151, quoted in James David

Essig, "A Very Wintry Season: Virginia Baptists and Slavery, 1785–1797," *Virginia Magazine of History and Biography* 88 (Apr. 1980), 174. Selby, *Revolution,* 34, discusses the Anglican viewpoint, which claimed essentially the same relationship between disenfranchisement and dissenting church membership. Isaac, *Transformation,* 153. "French Traveler," 743.

19 **"the Colonists are"** James Otis, *Rights of the British Colonies Asserted and Proved* (Boston, 1764), 29. Gary B. Nash, *Race and Revolution* (Lanham, Md., 1990), 7.

19 **"Slavery is in violation"** See Nash, 97. Arthur Lee, "Address on Slavery," Rind's *Virginia Gazette,* 19 Mar. 1767, reprinted in Nash, 91–96.

19 **In Williamsburg, however** Tate, 28.

19 **"Negro cooks"** Quoted in ibid., 37.

19 **They played violins** Isaac, *Transformation,* 85–86, discusses black musicians at white gatherings.

20 **"shaves, dresses hair"** Quoted in Tate, 35–36.

20 **Underneath their breeches** Ibid., 55–56.

20 **"This is so common"** "The Journal of Ebenezer Hazard in Virginia, 1777," ed. Fred Shelley, *Virginia Magazine of History and Biography* 62 (Oct. 1954), 410. Tate, 55.

20 **"Caesar"** William Wirt, *Life of Patrick Henry* (Philadelphia, 1818), 65. The French traveler provides a slightly different account, which is repeated in Henry Mayer's excellent recent biography of Patrick Henry. In this account, Henry more straightforwardly argues that America will soon produce its own Cromwell, hears cries of treason, and offers a "silky apology" when he becomes aware that he has gone too far. Henry Mayer, *A Son of Thunder: Patrick Henry and the American Republic* (New York, 1991), 85–87. "French Traveler," 745. Jefferson's validation of Wirt's version is quoted in "French Traveler," 728, and Wirt, 65: "I well remember the cry of treason, the pause of Mr. Henry at the name of George III, and the presence of mind with which he closed his sentence, and baffled the charge vociferated."

20 **three black men** For a description of the gallows that day, see "French Traveler," 745.

20 **"kissed the a—"** "Diary of Colonel Landon Carter," *William and Mary Quarterly,* 1st series, 16 (1908), 259, quoted in Sydnor, 48.

20 **In general, the sons of Virginia patriarchs married**   When
William Byrd secretly married a woman from Philadelphia, his
mother was stunned: "I was so surprised as to cry out Good God is
my Son Married & never acquainted me with it!" Mrs. Maria Byrd
to William Byrd III, 17 Feb. 1761, "Letters of the Byrd Family," *Virginia Magazine of History and Biography* 38 (1930), 350. See also
Daniel Blake Smith, *Inside the Great House: Planter Family Life in
Eighteenth-Century Chesapeake Society* (Ithaca, N.Y., 1980), 151, on
kinship ties and intermarriage among Virginian families.

20 **Instead, Carter, in early April**   See *Marriages and Deaths from the
Maryland Gazette, 1727–1839,* comp. Robert Barnes (Baltimore,
1976), 28: "CARTER, Mr. Robert, of Westmoreland, in Va., and
Frances, youngest daughter of the Hon. Benjamin Tasker, were
married Tues. last (April 2), by Rev. Mr. Malcolm (April 4, 1754)."
Carter cites the same date in his journals.

20–21 **Frances's dowry . . . ten thousand pounds.**   Morton, 39, 57, 167–68.
Carter bought this one-fifth share for 6,150 pounds sterling in
1769. Ronald L. Lewis, *Coal, Iron, and Slaves: Industrial Slavery in
Maryland and Virginia, 1715–1865* (Westport, Conn., 1979), 12: the
Baltimore Iron Works was one of "two of the largest industrial en-
terprises in colonial America." See also 22–23.

21 **As well, the marriage . . . thirteen straight times.**   Morton, 37, 38.
It was Charles Carroll who called Dulany "the best lawyer on this
Continent." R. H. Spencer, "The Honorable Daniel Dulany,
1722–97," *Maryland Historical Society Magazine* 13 (June 1918). Subsequently, he would turn tory, and lose much of his reputation. See
also Gordon S. Wood, *The American Revolution: A History* (New
York, 2001), 40, 50. *A Biographical Dictionary of the Maryland Legislature, 1635–1789,* ed. Edward C. Papenfuse (Baltimore, 1985),
2:799.

21 **They bore children**   RCIII provides a list of his children, their
birthdates and, in some cases, their deaths; in vol. 16, DU. He also
provides a list of grandchildren. Morton, 220. Frances Tasker accepted many of the gender distinctions of her time, in ways that
would give her power and cost her dearly. She gave birth to seventeen children, and saw many of them die, and the pulse of preg-
nancy and recovery wore her down, depressed her, and in all
likelihood shortened her life: she died at the age of forty-nine.

Carter made lists of his children periodically in his papers. Seventeen children, it should be noted, was a large number; but the mortality rates were consistent with those of other families. Daniel Blake Smith, *Inside the Great House: Planter Family Life in Eighteenth-Century Chesapeake Society* (Ithaca, N.Y., 1980), 26, 35, 176, 260. For a discussion of the effect of frequent pregnancies on the mothers, see Smith, 76–79, 158–59.

21 **Carter enmeshed himself** Morton, 127–28.

21 **"I have experienced"** Quoted in Rowland, "Robert Carter," 122.

22 **In 1758, Carter** The councillors, in his grandfather's time, had been the most powerful men in Virginia, possessing special access to the royal offices that controlled land grants. Isaac, *Transformation*, 136. Wood calls the councillors "the colonial counterparts to the English House of Lords" (*Radicalism*, 121). Bernard Bailyn, *The Ideological Origins of the American Revolution*, rev. ed. (Cambridge, Mass., 1992), 275, calls them "the group closest to a privileged order."

22 **"Send it by the first"** Rowland, "Robert Carter," 119–20.

22 **At first, he approached** *Legislative Journals of the Council of Colonial Virginia*, ed. H. R. McIlwaine, 2nd ed. (Richmond, 1979), vol. 3. See records for the year 1759.

22 **By 1760, however** RCIII, 24 Sep. 1776, vol. 13, DU.

22 **He purchased a house** M. Kent Brinkley and Gordon W. Chappell, *The Gardens of Colonial Williamsburg* (Williamsburg, Va.), 42.

22 **He acquired silver** These purchases are well summarized in Rowland, "Robert Carter," 118, 124–28. Isaac, *Transformation*, 118: "There was a direct connection between status and sufficient wealth to support a great household."

22 **He remodeled . . . husband and wife.** Mark R. Wenger, interview and tour with the author, Robert Carter House, Colonial Williamsburg, 5 June 2003.

22 **"Dind" and "supped"** George Washington, 6 Nov. 1769, 5 May 1769, *The Diaries of George Washington*, ed. Donald Jackson (Charlottesville, Va., 1976–78), 2:193; 2:148.

22 **He bought lottery . . . missed their steps.** Rowland, "Robert Carter," 123. RCIII to Thomas Bladen, 5 June 1761, CWF: "At present I can't command one thing qualified for the turf." Fithian, 24–25, describes horse racing in the Carter circle. Breen, "Horses

and Gentlemen," 251, makes a list of prominent Virginian families who left ample evidence of their horse-racing and gambling interests: Carter is not among them. Fithian, 33–34: "I observe in the course of the lessons, that Mr Christian is punctual, and rigid in his discipline, so strict indeed that he struck two of the young Misses for a fault in the course of their performance, even in the presence of the Mother of one of them!"

22 **"sack if worn"** Quoted in Rowland, "Robert Carter," 124, 126. Jan Lewis writes (6) of "a conscious, perhaps desperate attempt on the part of (Virginia's) settlers to make it conform to an imported image." Wood notes that Jefferson was also fixated on British fashions (*Radicalism*, 203).

22 **Frances Carter** Rowland, "Robert Carter," 118. See also Brown, *Good Wives*, 272: "Fancy clothing constituted one of the most personal expressions of gentility." Isaac, *Transformation*, 43–44.

23 **Attending a palace** Rowland, "Robert Carter," 130. This comparison is based upon the estimated value of slave cabins at Nomony that Carter himself compiled in the 1780s (Barden, 31), and is more useful as a dramatic comparison than a hard one, given that two decades separate the valuation of the cabins and the purchase of the dress. Since the value of a pound did not decline during this period, however, any fluctuations in its value would likely make this comparison more extreme, not less.

23 **"harmonicas"** RCIII to John M. Jordan, 23 May 1764, CWF. Fithian, 30.

23 **He purchased books** Rowland, "Robert Carter," 125.

23 **He began to read . . . in full.** Bowers, 20. Malone, 76.

23 **Fauquier quickly adopted** Morton, 49.

23 **As well, Carter befriended** Page, 147.

23 **"heard more good sense"** Thomas Jefferson to L. H. Girardin, 15 Jan. 1815, quoted in Eleanor Davidson Berman, *Thomas Jefferson Among the Arts: An Essay in Early American Esthetics* (New York, 1947), 174.

23 **"White, Red, or Black"** Quoted in Gordon S. Wood, *The American Revolution: A History* (New York, 2001), 102.

23 **"derived great advantages"** Page, 146–47. Sydnor, 13, notes that every biography of Jefferson emphasizes the early mentorship Jefferson received from these same men during the same time period.

23 **"sold part"** Quoted in Rowland, "Robert Carter," 132. Barden, 95.

23 **"Mary Anna"** RCIII to Scott, Pringle, Cheap, and Company, 29 Apr. 1767, CWF.

24 **"discovered the cruel"** Page, 147.

24 **he was among** Morton, 53. "The Proceedings of the Virginia Committee of Correspondence, 1764," *Virginia Magazine of History and Biography* 9 (1902): 353–58.

24 **But his membership** James LaVerne Anderson, "The Virginia Councillors and the American Revolution: The Demise of an Aristocratic Clique," *Virginia Magazine of History and Biography* 82 (Jan. 1974), 66–70. Morton, 52. Bailyn, 275–78, describes the rise of anti-Council sentiment in the decade before the Revolution.

24 **"As Duty and Affection"** McIlwaine, 1361.

24–25 **In trying to understand . . . the same set of republican ideals.** Edmund S. Morgan, 373. Bernard Bailyn asks a similar question (23): "From whom, from what, were the ideas and attitudes derived?" See also 24, 28, 34. See 30–31 regarding legal literature. Bailyn cites Montesquieu as the most often quoted philosopher in the Revolutionary literature (345).

25 **"very much in a Republican way of Thinking"** Robert Dinwiddie to Earl of Halifax, 12 Mar. 1754, in *Official Records of Robert Dinwiddie*, intro. R. A. Brock (Richmond, Va., 1883), 1:100. Edmund S. Morgan, 373–75.

25 **"Will a complaining"** RCIII to Samuel Athawes, 17 Feb. 1764, CWF.

26 **In 1764, for instance, Carter voted** Rowland, "Robert Carter," 122. This dispute lasted throughout the decade. Isaac, *Transformation*, 143–53, describes the emphasis among gentry and the Council upon imposing impoverishment among the clergy, and in particular he focuses upon Landon Carter's leading role. In this context, then, Robert Carter was directly voting against his uncle's political leadership. See also Holton, 39–43, who stresses the role of debt and tensions between merchants and planters as the source of the violence. See also Bailyn, 252–54.

26 **"The contrariety of opinion"** RCIII to Thomas Bladen, 28 July 1766, CWF. This incident became well known. The actions on the part of the three Councillors have been interpreted as an effort to

protect their class, and their kin: Criswell was landed gentry, and was related to John Robinson, who was Speaker of the House of Burgesses. In this context, it seems clear that Carter refused to protect "order" when justice suggested otherwise. Rowland, "Robert Carter," 129. Wood, *Radicalism,* 178.

26 **"an honest Man"** George Mason to RCIII, 12 Mar. 1776, in *The Papers of George Mason,* ed. Robert A. Rutland (Chapel Hill, N.C., 1970), 1:264.

26 **"beneficence to the poor"** Meade, 1:341–48. Other versions of this story also circulate, but Meade's is particularly detailed. See, for instance, Andrew Price, *Selim the Algerine* (Marlinton, W.Va., 1924). Price does not mention Carter.

27 **"religious villains" and "horrid hellish rogues"** Landon Carter, 13 July 1776, 2:1057.

27 **"I have not forgotten"** RCIII to Thomas Bladen, 9 Mar. 1768, CWF.

27 **"Inquisitiveness to know"** RCIII to Benjamin Tasker, 19 May 1767, CWF.

27 **"Col: Carter hath"** RCIII to Benjamin Tasker, 13 June 1764, CWF.

27 **King Carter too** RCI to Thomas Evans, 23 Feb. 1720/21, in *Letters,* 83.

28 **"numerous + painful"** RCIII to Benjamin Tasker, 30 May 1767, CWF. RCIII to Thomas Bladen, 9 Mar. 1768, CWF.

28 **a man who measured** Malone, 77.

28 **"my infecting Carcass"** Francis Fauquier, in *York County Records, Wills and Inventories* 21, 397, LV.

28 **"His burial was not pompous"** RCIII to Jeffrey Amherst, 9 Mar. 1768, CWF.

28 **"single stone"** Fauquier, 402. Morton, 49–50.

29 **"liberty to choose"** Fauquier, 400.

29 **"an enemy of his country"** Henry Wiencek, *An Imperfect God: George Washington, His Slaves, and the Creation of America* (New York, 2003), 160.

29 **"sincerely loved"** RCIII to Thomas Johnson, 19 Nov. 1768, CWF.

29 **"That Estate should not"** RCIII to Anne Ogle, 6 Aug. 1768, CWF.

29 **"Facts do evince"** RCIII to Anne Ogle, 24 Dec. 1768, CWF.

29 **"I fear that"** RCIII to Anne Ogle, 18 Jan. 1769, CWF.

30 **"I have lately reviewed"** RCIII to Anne Ogle, 1 Feb. 1769, CWF.

30 **"If these Endeavours"** RCIII to Daniel Dulany, 17 Apr. 1769, CWF.

30 **Eighteen years later** Benjamin Lowndes to RCIII, 3 Sep. 1787, WM.

30 **"Lotts"** Daniel Dulany to RCIII, 18 Dec. 1768, MHS.

30 **"Mrs. Carter and I"** RCIII to Daniel Dulany, June 1769, quoted in Rowland, "Robert Carter," 133–34.

31 **One must look elsewhere** Jan Lewis, *The Pursuit of Happiness: Family and Values in Jefferson's Virginia* (New York, 1983), 141, writes that "planters accepted the fact that slavery was part of their money-making venture. Why else did so many of them choose selling a slave as the quickest way to raise cash?"

31 **Instead, he pursued ideals . . . the same role.** Wiencek, 178–88. As Wiencek notes, no major biography of Washington mentions this.

31 **"not exceeding"** George Washington to Daniel Jenifer Adams, 20 July 1772, *The Papers of George Washington, Colonial Series*, ed. W. W. Abbot (Charlottesville, 1983–95), 9:70. See also Wiencek, 120–22.

31 **When men such as Washington and Jefferson** See Wood, *Radicalism*, 190.

32 **And Carter was used to watching** Some of this emerges in Zwelling's essay, which is an acute psychological portrayal of Carter. Zwelling speaks of Carter as being "alternately active and passive, intrusive and withholding" (631), and explores the idea that Carter was affected by the early death of his father, perhaps possessing "vague feelings of responsibility" (630), perhaps falling into a pattern wherein he might be "reenacting an awesome event from his childhood, this time playing the role of parent" (627).

Chapter II

33 **"Is he as grave"** Fithian, 205.

33 **Christmas Day 1773** The details of this Christmas can be found in Fithian, 39–41.

33 **cannonball** Landon Carter, 2 Apr. 1776, 2:1009.

33 **Henry Lee** Fithian, 14, 240.

33 **"step a Minuet"** Ibid., 33–34.

33 **He had allowed** Ibid., 239.

34 **"Poor Boys!"** Ibid., 4.

34 **When he learned** Ibid., 6–7.

34 **Immediately, he began . . . personally.** Ibid., 9, 13, 14, 15, 46. William R. Smith tells Fithian, "I wish ten millions and she were mine, I should be a happy creature" (15).

34 **He could follow the Potomac** Fithian does this more than once. See Ibid., 41, 90.

34 **Fithian gave him** Ibid., 54. Two pistareens "pass here for half a crown." Barden writes that the tip was worth "4d" (191).

34 **"over-grown"** Ibid., 26.

34 **Fithian's hours** Ibid., 31. He describes his hours as slightly different at other points in his journals.

34 **"never pass over"** Ibid., 26.

35 **But he never said** Ibid., 178.

35 **his valentine** Ibid., 65, 230–33.

35 **"small-sword"** Ibid., 161.

35 **And despite the new austerity . . . Fithian thought.** Fithian argued that a link exists between the balls and the "Virginia fevers." For a description of one of the balls, see ibid., 153–56. For "dance or die," see ibid., 177.

35 **"by far the most Humane"** Ibid., 38.

35 **"To get a secret"** Ibid., 38–39.

36 **"grown old"** Ibid., 40.

36 **"For unto us"** Ibid., 40.

37 **That was how Virginians mourned** See Lewis, 68–71. As Lewis notes, there is no way to tell if men such as Jefferson and Carter mourned in private ways that were not recorded in their correspondence and papers. Likewise, there existed rhetorical tropes to suggest that, as Lewis writes, "children are in some measure interchangeable, 'little Angels' every one" (74, 96). Robert and Frances Carter, losing several children, could compensate by bearing more.

37 **"3 dozen sortable hair Combs"** RCIII to James Gildart, "Merchant in Liverpool," 28 Jan. 1772, vol. 1, DU.

37 **he told Peyton Randolph** RCIII to Peyton Randolph, 23 Jan. 1773, vol. 1, DU.

37 **"a new system"** RCIII, 24 Sep. 1776, vol. 13, DU.

38 **But he implied** Zwelling, 618. Bailyn, 117–18: "There was a détente of sorts created by the repeal of the Townshend Duties, the withdrawal of troops from Boston, and the failure of other provocative measures to be taken" that "ended abruptly . . . in the fall and winter of 1773."

38 **"useful Education"** Fithian, 65.

38 **The European tobacco . . . any given year.** Breen, *Tobacco*, 128.

38 **"the planters were a species"** "Additional Queries, with Jefferson's Answers," Thomas Jefferson, *The Papers of Thomas Jefferson*, ed. Julian P. Boyd (Princeton, 1950–), vol. 10, 27. Bruce A. Ragsdale, *A Planter's Republic: The Search for Economic Independence in Revolutionary Virginia* (Madison, Wis., 1996), 23–29. See Wood, *Radicalism*, 179, for a description of the "significance" of this metaphor. See also Bailyn, 232–37, for a discussion of the idea of "slavery" in Revolutionary-era discourse. Bailyn writes, "Slavery as a political concept had specific meaning which a later generation would lose" (233), and suggests that the specific fact of African-American slavery gradually imposed itself on this meaning, forcing many founders to come to terms with the contradiction between their rhetoric and their slaveholding practices.

38 **While his peers compiled** RCIII to John Hyndman, 15 June 1772, vol. 1, DU. See also Morton, 129, 190. RCIII also told his agents that "I have gold + Silver money." RCIII to Clement Brooke, 22 Apr. 1771, MHS.

38 **"the clearest fortune"** Fithian, 26. Susan Kwilecki, "Through the Needle's Eye: Religion in the Lives of Wealthy Colonial Americans" (Ph.D. diss., Stanford University, 1982), 13–14. Alice Hanson Jones, *Wealth of a Nation to Be* (New York, 1980) 10, 57–58, 170–71, 326–27.

39 **"the Benevolent, the Generous"** John Dixon to RCIII, 3 July 1772, WM.

39 **He lent money** For Jefferson, see Morton, 201, and chapter 3 of this book. For others, see Kwilecki, 69.

39 **"Rattle-Snake"** John Dixon to RCIII, 3 July 1772, WM. Carter sued John Dixon to dun several hundred pounds from Dixon's destitute and recently widowed sister-in-law. See also Morton, 202.

39 **In the face of Townshend Act taxes . . . composed of Virginians.** Ragsdale, 77–78.

39 **"Infuse that Spirit"** Quoted in John E. Selby, *Dunmore* (Williamsburg, Va., 1977), 13.

39 **He grew angry . . . permission to meet.** This journal is dated 28 Feb. 1772, and can be found in CFP, sect. 32.

40 **"Plan of Life"** RCIII to John Tazewell, 9 Jan. 1773, vol. 1, DU: "My Plan of Life," he wrote, "is to aid and assi[s]t God's Creatures, not to distress <u>moderate</u> Men or Women."

40 **"greatly retards"** *Journals of the House of Burgesses of Virginia, 1770–1772,* ed. John Pendleton Kennedy (Richmond, Va., 1906), 283–84, quoted in Ragsdale, 121. Davis, 65: "1774 North America's disavowal of the slave trade was a defiance of British authority."

40 **In February . . . doing wrong.** *Journals of the House of Burgesses of Virginia, 1773–1776, Including the Records of the Committee of Correspondence,* ed. John Pendleton Kennedy (Richmond, Va., 1905), 307, 308, 314. Hening, 8:522–23. The law is here called "An Act for amending the acts concerning the trials and outlawries of slaves."

41 **Second, the debate on the slave bill** Morton, 51.

41 **"scourged"** RCIII, 9 Mar. 1777, vol. 14, DU.

41 **Nomony Hall** Thomas Tileston Waterman, *The Mansions of Virginia: 1706–1776* (Chapel Hill, N.C., 1946), 136–44. Fithian, 61, 72–73, 80–82, 134, 145, 203.

42 **"The Great Man"** William North to Benjamin Walker, 9 Mar. 1784, Historical Society of Pennsylvania, quoted in Fritz Hirschfeld, *George Washington and Slavery: A Documentary Portrayal* (Columbia, Mo., 1997), 69.

42 **He practiced** Fithian, 30. Carter also had an organ he left in Williamsburg.

42 **"uncultivated"** Ibid., 92.

43 **Mostly, however, conversations . . . when they were fresh.** Ibid., 39, 110, 132, 194.

43 **"Such amazing property"** Ibid., 161.

43 **When thunderstorms** Ibid., 150.

43 **"copy Mr. Carter"** Ibid., 165.

43 **He measured** Carter ordered "12 best glass tubes to make Thermometers & Barometers," 28 Mar. 1774, vol. 1, DU. Fithian, 191, 196.

43 **He invented** Fithian, 74.

43 **Sometimes, he sounded like he was anyone** Ibid., 85.

43 **Sometimes, he sounded like he was traveling** Ibid., 117.

43 **"discreet, and sensible"** Ibid., 22.

44 **Smallpox was sweeping** Elizabeth A. Fenn, *Pox Americana: The Great Smallpox Epidemic of 1775–82* (New York, 2001) 41–42.

44 **Two daughters** Fithian, 202.

44 **And since the early symptoms** Fenn, 16.

44 **"use it for a Chest"** Fithian, 61.

44 **He bragged . . . "Dissolution."** Ibid., 182.

44 **"This hot weather"** Ibid., 132.

44 **"tedious to endure"** Ibid., 32.

44 **"Souls of Women"** Ibid., 83.

44 **"Ann Tasker Carter"** Ibid., 61. Zwelling, 621, uses this event to discuss "naming patterns" that "could blur the distinctiveness and individuality of the various family members."

45 **"a Subject for"** Fithian, 182.

45 **"Last year"** Ibid., 44–45.

45 *"Now I must die"* Ibid., 194.

45 **Unlike debt** See Lewis, 19: "Here again we see the mode common to Virginians: Vice, crime and violence are endemic, expected. One will keep his own house in order and try to isolate himself from anyone or anything troublesome. The mode is restraint and avoidance."

45 **Throughout the summers** Fithian, 146, 152.

45–46 **"eruptive fever" . . . "with a Fever!"** Ibid., 137–38.

46 **In December 1773** Benjamin Woods Labaree, *The Boston Tea Party* (New York, 1964), 126–45, esp. 141.

46 **Gathering in the Apollo Room . . . Virginia and England.** Selby, *Revolution,* 9. "Association of Members of the Late House of Burgesses," 27 May 1774, *The Papers of Thomas Jefferson,* Boyd, 1:107. See Ragsdale, 174–81, 203–4.

46 **"trade"** Fithian, 75. See also Wood, *Radicalism,* 37, where he quotes John Locke as saying, "Trade is wholly inconsistent with a gentleman's calling." As Wood argues, this precept was more romance than reality, and disappeared altogether during the cultural changes surrounding the American Revolution. The idea that someone who was not closely involved in trade was best suited for public service was a slower casualty of the Revolution (Wood, *Radicalism,* 107). Carter made this transition when he chose to

enter "trade," but his aristocratic leanings prevented a comfortable transition.

47 **"I purpose to manufacture"** RCIII to David Patterson, 24 July 1773, vol. 1, DU. Morton, 145, 179–80.

47 **Carter had switched** Morton shows Carter diversifying into grain production as early as 1760, and exporting large amounts of wheat and Indian corn by 1767. Morton, 144–45, 151. Mullin, 126, links Washington and Carter together in this regard. Selby, *Revolution*, 32. By 1769, wheat harvests in Virginia were growing rapidly. Wiencek, 91.

47 **Unlike other Virginia** Morton 167, 199.

47 **He was amazed** RCIII to John Hough, 18 June 1772, vol. 2, DU.

47 **"What is the Current"** RCIII to Clement Brooke, 9 Nov. 1773, vol. 2, DU.

47 **"there has been a fraud"** RCIII to Robert Prentis, 24 July 1773, vol. 1, DU.

48 **In March 1773** RCIII to William Taylor, 1 Mar. 1773, vol. 1, DU.

48 **"You know that every work"** RCIII to Andrew Reid, 22 Nov. 1773, vol. 1, DU.

48 **"I do not Recollect"** RCIII to John Hough, 20 June 1774, vol. 2, DU.

48 **"I must have wheat"** RCIII to Robert Prentis, 22 Aug. 1772, vol. 1, DU.

48 **"I have bought large"** RCIII to Christopher Lowndes, 20 Nov. 1773, vol. 1, DU.

48 **"I have Bread"** RCIII to Captain G. Dobbie, 10 May 1774, vol. 1, DU.

48 **"The very best"** RCIII to William Dennis, 20 May 1774, vol. 2, DU. Debt relationships were "pervasive" in colonial America, according to Wood, *Radicalism*, 64. As Wood suggests, debt sometimes guided the relationship between patron and client, but there were many men who were both debtor and lender. Similarly, patrons who understood how they guided the lives of debtors also understood the risk under which they placed themselves by becoming debtors (Wood, *Radicalism*, 69).

48 **"If you insist"** RCIII to Williamson Ball, 9 Feb. 1773, vol. 1, DU.

48 **"Parallelogram[s]"** RCIII to John Dixon, 9 Dec. 1774, vol. 2, DU.

In this regard, Carter reproduced in miniature a national political debate about paper money. By the summer of 1775, the Continental Congress authorized a national paper currency. See Pauline Maier, *American Scripture: Making the Declaration of Independence* (New York, 1998), 14.

48 **He did not stop** RCIII to James Gildart, 10 Sep. 1773, vol. 1, DU.

49 **"I have been constrained"** RCIII to Lord Fairfax, 12 Sep. 1774, vol. 2, DU.

49 **"That Sett"** RCIII to Robert Prentis, 29 Oct. 1774, vol. 2, DU.

49 **"The Crop of Wheat"** RCIII to William Taylor, 15 July 1774, vol. 2, DU.

49 **"I had rather be"** RCIII to Rowland and Hunt, 21 July 1774, vol. 2, DU.

49 **He did not raise rents** Leniency toward tenants was a holdover of "aristocratic paternalism." As Wood notes (*Radicalism*, 55–56), Carter allowed some of his tenants to fall behind ten years in their rent. "In the years after mid-century," according to Wood, this spirit dissipated (*Radicalism*, 114).

49 **"for bear"** RCIII to William Carr, 27 Jan. 1774, vol. 1, DU.

49 **When his overseers** RCIII to William Taylor, 14 Dec. 1773, vol. 1, DU.

50 **When a tenant asked** RCIII to John Orr, 29 Sep. 1773, vol. 1, DU. RCIII to George Lewis, 24 July 1780, vol. 3, DU.

50 **"pleased with taciturnity"** Fithian, 37.

50 **"I read all"** RCIII to John Hyndman, 7 May 1775, vol. 2, DU. Many Americans were fixated with buying newspapers to keep track of political and military developments (Maier, 82).

50 **When the Continental Congress** RCIII to John Dixon, 9 Dec. 1774, vol. 2, DU. Ragsdale, 218.

50 **"by this . . . I conclude"** Fithian, 111. As Wood writes (*Radicalism*, 175–76), many Americans saw the rift between "patriots" and "courtiers," courtiers describing those men who benefited from connections and a closed society. A great many loyalists, in fact, came from the upper reaches of society and were accustomed to certain artificial advantages maintained by the crown's influence.

50 **Others came** Fithian, 111, 138.

50 **He needn't have worried** See, for instance, ibid., 59, 196, 198.

50 **"dependance on Great Britain"** Thomas Jefferson to John Randolph, *Papers of Thomas Jefferson,* Boyd, 1:242. Maier, 21.

50 **"to persevere"** RCIII to William Taylor, 12 Aug. 1774, vol. 2, DU.

51 **"I hope and expect"** RCIII to William Mathis, 14 Nov. 1774, vol. 2, DU.

51 **And once the Continental** Ragsdale, 237.

51 **"What's this"** Fithian, 195–96. Fithian, 110: "They are now too patriotic to drink tea." See Wood, *Radicalism,* 92: "Success of any sort in eighteenth-century Anglo-American society put a premium on certain traits of character—on circumspection, caution, and calculation; on the control and suppression of one's real feelings."

51 **Like many slaves** See Jennifer Olsen Kelley and J. Lawrence Angel, "The Workers of Catoctin Furnace," *Maryland Archeology* (1983).

51 **This was work best done** Wiencek, 96, 114.

52 **And all each one** Barbara J. Heath, *Hidden Lives: The Archaeology of Slave Life at Thomas Jefferson's Poplar Forest* (Charlottesville, Va., 1999), 21–26, esp. 25. Wiencek, 117–18.

52 **"well instructed"** Fithian, 34. Barden, 159.

52 **There were four more slaves** Fithian, 31.

52 **There were two butchers** Barden, 161.

52 **There was Tom Henry** Ibid., 615.

52 **"a good breast of milk"** RCIII to Richard Dozier, 25 Nov. 1778, vol. 3, DU.

52 **Many performed more** Barden, 637.

52 **Nelson, who kept** RCIII to Robert Prentis, 5 Dec. 1774, vol. 2, DU. Fithian, 78.

53 **"500 pounds"** Fithian, 132.

53 **Up in Baltimore** Ronald L. Lewis, *Coal, Iron, and Slaves: Industrial Slavery in Maryland and Virginia, 1715–1865* (Westport, Conn., 1979), 20, 25, 150, 185, 193. Kelley and Angel, 2.

53 **"Brutus"** RCIII, vol. 13, DU.

53 **"overwork"** Fithian, 184.

53 **"Servant Thomas"** RCIII, 1774, vol. 13, DU. Barden, 184.

53 **A supplicant slave** Fithian, 129. The slave was telling Carter that his overseer did not provide the promised allocation of Indian corn.

54 **Natt Single** Barden, 136–37.

54 **One slave father** Fithian, 182–83.

54 **"too hot"** Ibid., 140, 152. Fithian called Gumby both "Dadda" and "Daddy."

54 **Most slaves needed . . . that particular night.** Heath, 60. Hirschfeld, 44.

54 **In all likelihood, they ate alone . . . Emancipation Proclamation.** Booker T. Washington, "Up from Slavery," in *The Booker T. Washington Papers*, ed. Louis R. Harlan (Urbana, Ill., 1972–89), 1:217.

54 **"long room"** Fithian, 141.

54 **Carter offered to bet** Ibid., 66.

55 **Probably, though, it wasn't pride** Ibid., 83.

55 **The rite was simple . . . without smudging.** Sarah Withrow, e-mail communication with the author, 5 July 2004.

56 **The best months** Fithian, 44.

56 **Like most planters** Ibid., 119, 221–29. John Randolph Barden, "The Carter Family Library: A Survey of Extant Volumes from the Libraries of Councillor Robert Carter of Nomony Hall and his Descendants," presented to VHS, 1992. See also Barden, "Reflections of a Singular Mind: The Library of Robert Carter of Nomony Hall," *Virginia Magazine of History and Biography* 96 (Jan. 1988).

56 **He had a set** RCIII to John James Maund, 10 Dec. 1792, vol. 9, DU.

57 **"uneasiness"** Fithian, 181.

57 **When she felt pain** Ibid., 207.

57 **"incessant, bright"** Ibid., 127, 142, 146, 150.

57 **"Ben child"** Ibid., 144.

57 **"without *rest* or *pleasure*"** Ibid., 183.

57 **"I love to see her"** Ibid., 132.

57 **"Temper, Oconomy"** Ibid., 207.

57 **Fanny might** Ibid., 150.

57 **Priscilla would ignore** Ibid., 65–67.

58 **"some mischievous person"** Ibid., 128.

58 **"retired from the World"** Ibid., 135.

58 **"young likely"** Ibid., 86.

58 **Carter, who forbade** Ibid., 61–62.

58–59 **On the night of September 5, 1774, . . . house at night.** Ibid., 184–85.

59 **Within several days** Ibid., 185, 188–89.

59 **"play the fiddle"** Lucia Stanton, *Slavery at Monticello* (Thomas Jefferson Memorial Foundation, 1996), 39.

59 **"Man"** Fithian, 88.

59 **Sally, with whom Ben** Ibid., 134.

59 **That same week** Ibid., 187, 191–92.

60 **Robert Bladen Carter** Ibid., 127–28, 135.

60 **He cut school** Ibid., 149, 190.

60 **He slandered** Ibid., 116.

60 **He beat his sisters** Ibid., 48, 110.

60 **He disappeared** Landon Carter, 3 June 1773, 2:753: "A Son of the Councellor's came to see his uncle Landon; I made him wellcom and gave his cousins a holiday to entertain him. His name is Robert, a lean spare boy, but . . . a lively one. It seems he was left at large."

60 **The story stuck** Fithian, 37–38.

60 **"pleased with the Society"** Ibid., 48.

60 **"particular Taste"** Ibid., 70.

60 **When a visitor** Ibid., 177.

60 **"Negro Fellow"** Ibid., 70.

60–61 **Perhaps most amazing, however, was his affinity . . . "Angelic Train."** Ibid., 72–73. The poem is titled "On Being Brought from Africa to America," and the quotation here is reproduced from Fithian's journal.

61 **When he heard that** Ibid., 177.

61 **"horsing"** Ibid., 50, 64, 116, 121. Carter also "flogg'd" his son, for "not having given seasonable Notice" (ibid., 156).

61 **And the other Carter children** Ibid., 48, 142. Child rearing, during this period, was undergoing a revolution as well. Examples of intense corporal punishment were plentiful among prewar gentry, but the model for Robert and Frances Carter's child rearing was more likely to be John Locke's *Some Thoughts Concerning Education*, which preached environmentalism and example, and dissuaded parents from inflicting physical punishment on their children whenever possible. The Carters appear to have leaned toward the enlightened model, although these instances of physical punishment still took place. See Wood, *Radicalism*, 49–50.

61 **The rate of population** Barden, 96–97.

62 **They were listed by family** Ibid., 110–12.

62 **"Negro Argy"** RCIII to George Newman, 29 Dec. 1789, vol. 9, DU.

62 **While his neighbors** Barden, 201.

62 **Jefferson all but . . . extra work.** Stanton, *Monticello*, 27, 28. Thomas Jefferson, *Jefferson's Memorandum Books*, eds. James A. Bear, Jr., and Lucia C. Stanton (Princeton, N.J., 1997), 2:1265, 1328, 1416.

62 **Washington, "work . . . 'till it is dark."** George Washington, *Diaries*, 1:232–34. George Washington to William Pierce, 30 Mar. 1794, *Writings of George Washington*, ed. John Fitzpatrick (Washington, D.C., 1931–44), 33:309. George Washington to James McHenry, 29 May 1797, *The Papers of George Washington, Retirement Series*, ed. Dorothy Twohig (Charlottesville, Va., 1998), 1:160. George Washington to John Fairfax, 1 Jan. 1789, *The Papers of George Washington, Presidential Series*, ed. Dorothy Twohig (Charlottesville, Va., 1987), 1:223. Wiencek, 93, 95, 111. See also Hirschfeld, 31.

62 **"Estimate on the actual"** *The Garden and Farm Books of Thomas Jefferson*, ed. Robert C. Baron (Golden, Colo., 1987), 367. Stanton, *Monticello*, 23.

63 **"the secret & pleasant"** William Fitzhugh, *William Fitzhugh and His Chesapeake World, 1676–1701: The Fitzhugh Letters and Other Documents*, ed. Richard Beale Davis (Chapel Hill, N.C., 1963), 314. See Kathleen M. Brown, *Good Wives*, 265. Barden, 153.

63 **"every day I discover"** Landon Carter, 9 May 1772, 2:678.

63 **"long enough remembered"** Ibid., 22 Apr. 1772, 2:672–73.

63 **"correct but seldom"** Charles Carroll to Charles Carroll, 1 Feb. 1808, MHS, quoted in Kwilecki, 64.

63 **"chastise(ment)," and spoke of unsold slaves as "refuse"** Henry Laurens, *The Papers of Henry Laurens*, ed. Philip M. Hamer (Columbia, S.C., 1968–). See Laurens to Arnold, Albert, and Alexander Nesbitt, 7 Aug. 1764, 4:360: "The Negroes are of an ordinary sort only one remove from refuse." See also Laurens to Abraham Schad, 23 Aug. 1765, 4:665: "Also the Runaway Castillio, chastise him to deter him & others from coming to me again. . . . I have just discover'd that my Negroes have made a very great mistake in sending that poor wretch May instead of Castillio, but now I send this Chap by a Negro of mine who I hope will deliver him safe be-

fore tomorrow night. He says you are too hard upon him, tho his back does not shew any thing like it. Don't fail to give him his full deserts."

63 **"these outlying Negroes"** RCIII to George Newman, 15 July 1788, vol. 8, DU.

63 **"ride to a certain Stump"** Fithian, 165. See Mullin, 70–71. In this excellent passage, Mullin describes how Carter, whom he calls "this surprising man," "executed the patriarchal role almost perfectly."

63 **And such indifference** Stanton, *Monticello,* 29. Fithian, 192: Carter "is not pleased" with a sermon preached "against the practise of abusing slaves."

Chapter III

65 **"RC—& his servant"** RCIII, 15 Mar. 1778, vol. 12, DU.

65 **When the sheriff . . . to anyone who would listen.** Richard Dozier, "Richard Dozier's Historical Notes 1771–1818," ed. John S. Moore, *Virginia Baptist Register* (1989), 1391, 1432. Lewis Peyton Little, *Imprisoned Preachers and Religious Liberty in Virginia* (Lynchburg, Va., 1938), 450–51. James B. Taylor, *Virginia Baptist Ministers,* series 1 (New York, 1859), 140–42.

66 **Like the other Baptist preachers** Wesley M. Gewehr, *The Great Awakening in Virginia, 1740–1790,* reprint ed. (Gloucester, Mass., 1965), 107. Differences between the Regular and Separate Baptists during this time period are defined differently from author to author. Gewehr writes, "The Regular Baptists were orthodox Calvinists, while the Separates tended strongly towards Arminianism, or the doctrine of free grace" (109). Gewehr also notes that there may have been a difference in matters of dress and behavior (109). See also Thomas E. Buckley, *Church and State in Revolutionary Virginia, 1776–1787* (Charlottesville, Va., 1977), 13–14. Charles F. James, *Documentary History of the Struggle for Religious Liberty in Virginia,* reprint ed. (New York, 1971), 179, emphasizes that Regular Baptists sought permission to preach from civil authorities and Separate Baptists did not. See also Bailyn, 249. John Leland, "The Virginia Chronicle," in *The Writings of the Late Elder John Leland,* ed. L. F. Greene (New York, 1845), 105. Morgan Edwards, *Materi-*

als Toward a History of the Baptists in the Province of Virginia (1772), 127. The original of this last document is housed at Furman University.

66 **Unlike the ministers . . . and the enslaved.** See Gewehr, 110–11. He describes "short, contracted verses," and quotes W. T. Thom, *The Struggle for Religious Freedom in Virginia: The Baptists* (Baltimore, 1900), 17, regarding " 'jerks', excessive trembling, falling, rolling on the ground, crying and 'barking' like dogs." See Daniel Fristoe, quoted in Edwards. Contemporary descriptions of Separate revivals commonly describe such phenomena, and modern historians do not seem to dispute them. Gewehr, 139, 143–44, discusses the grammatical tics of the preachers. Gewehr, 114, describes the holy whine: "a rising and falling of the tone to relieve the strain" of "open air preaching."

66 **Even among this group . . . rebuke.** Robert Baylor Semple, *History of the Rise and Progress of the Baptists in Virginia*, rev. ed. G. W. Beale (Richmond, Va., 1894), 473. Taylor, 145–48.

66 **King Carter's Christ Church** Isaac, *Transformation*, 288, 421.

66 **"strolled"** James David Essig, "A Very Wintry Season: Virginia Baptists and Slavery, 1785–1797," *Virginia Magazine of History and Biography* 88 (Apr. 1980), 172–73. William Lumpkin, "Col. Robert Carter, a Baptist," *Virginia Baptist Register* 8 (1969), 345.

66 **When Henry Self . . . given blood.** RCIII, 9 Aug. 1778, vol. 12, DU. Dozier, 1395. The sixteenth article of the Declaration of Rights of the Virginia Constitution was added on a motion from James Madison. It stated that "all men are equally entitled to the free exercise of religion, according to the dictates of conscience." Gewehr, 203. There are many discussions of Madison's role in composing that article. See Selby, *Revolution*, 109. See also Selby for a discussion of the larger significance of the Virginia Declaration of Rights, which was largely composed by George Mason (*Revolution*, 101–4).

Within two years, a "Henry Self" appears in the minutes of the Morattico BC. On 4 Nov. 1780, he is excommunicated for drunkenness and swearing (*Morattico BC Minutes, 1788–1844*, LV).

67 **"Home rejoicing"** RCIII, 6 Sept. 1778, vol. 12, DU. RCIII, "1777–June," vol. 17, DU. Dozier, 1395. Carter and Dozier provide different estimates of how many individuals were present. Moncure

Conway, "The Recantation of Colonel Carter of Virginia," *Open Court* (1889–90), 1838–39. Conway's article reproduces excerpts from Carter Papers belonging to "Mr. W. R. Benjamin of New York."

67 **In turn, Carter became** RCIII to William Parrot, 20 Nov. 1780, vol. 3, DU. *Morattico BC Minutes*, 15 Sept. 1783, LV. See also RCIII, rent roll, 1791–93, LC, which describes Lunsford "in Possession" of several hundred acres of Robert Carter's land. Lumpkin, 349.

67 **"Many of them only"** Samuel Davies, *Letters from the Rev. Samuel Davies, Showing the State of Religion in Virginia, Particularly Among the Negroes*, 2nd ed. (London, 1757), 30, quoted in Sobel, 181. For a brief discussion of Davies, see Bailyn, 251. Selby notes that Patrick Henry's oratorical style was based on Davies's (*Revolution*, 33).

67 **"political Contrivance"** RCIII to Thomas Everard, 1 June 1778, vol. 3, DU. RCIII to Thomas Jefferson, 27 July 1778, vol. 3, DU.

67 **He would identify** It is widely regarded that most of the important political figures in America's founding were either Deists or, as Wood writes, "lukewarm churchgoers and scornful of religious emotion and enthusiasm" (*American Revolution*, 129). See also Wood, *Radicalism*, 158, 330, for descriptions of Deism and the founders.

68 **God, Carter believed** See Wood, *Radicalism*, 104–5, for a discussion of "disinterestedness."

68 **Parson Smith** Washington attended church apparently as a matter of social form. Wood, *Radicalism*, 198.

68 **"Before Service giving"** Fithian, 167.

68 **By contrast, the services** Gewehr, 135, discusses how men such as Madison became "champions of the Baptists."

68 **"very orthodox"** James Madison to William Bradford, 24 Jan. 1774. *The Writings of James Madison*, ed. Gaillard Hunt (New York, 1900), vol. 1, 21.

68 **"Did I hear"** Little, 107. Little cites this speech from William Henry Foote, *Sketches of Virginia*, 317, and *The Baptist Memorial and Monthly Record*, May 1845. But he doubts its authenticity. Little, 106–26. He does affirm, however, that Henry defended the jailed ministers, and that Henry likely gave an "eloquent speech in their behalf" (Little, 121–22).

69 **"although a majority"** *Works of Thomas Jefferson,* Ford, 1:63. It should be noted that among the "zealous churchmen" whom Jefferson considered political opponents in this conflict, he counted Robert Carter Nicholas, one of Robert Carter III's cousins. As with Landon Carter, Robert Carter's religious dissent would likely have perturbed this close family member.

69 **Reasonable gentlemen** Garnett Ryland, *The Baptists of Virginia, 1699–1926* (Richmond, Va., 1955), 78–79. Little, 130–31.

69 **In the late 1760s** Essig, 175.

69 **Roughs waited** Little, 391, 404, 461.

69 **At times, the persecutions** Ibid., 66. Ryland, 31. Gewehr, 115. Thom, 17.

69 **A minister named** Ryland, 115. Little, 473.

69 **"my Palace in Culpeper"** James Ireland, quoted in Little, 161–66.

69 **"praying that they may be treated"** *Journals of the House of Burgesses, 1770–1772,* Kennedy, 12, 22, and 24 Feb. and 14 Mar. 1772.

69 **"such incredible and extravagant"** James Madison to William Bradford, 1 Apr. 1774. *Writings of James Madison,* Hunt, 1:22.

69–70 **Acts of Toleration . . . if not law.** *Virginia Gazette,* 26 Mar. 1772, reprinted, with auxiliary matter, in Edwards, 107–9. Ryland, 93. Bailyn, 258. Isaac describes it as a "crisis of self-confidence" that prevented the House from acting on the bill, and does not mention Dunmore's intervention. Rhys Isaac, "Evangelical Revolt: The Nature of the Baptists' Challenge to the Traditional Order in Virginia, 1765 to 1775," *William and Mary Quarterly,* 3rd series, 31 (July 1974), 367. Charles F. James, 180.

70 **By 1776, he had even resigned** He eased his way out, providing no straight answer, telling "the gentlemen of the vestry" on 24 Oct. 1775 that he could not attend a church meeting because business compelled him to stay in Williamsburg, slowly settling his accounts with the parish over the next year, then telling the clerk on 5 Oct. 1776, "I do hereby resign my place," but providing neither excuse nor formal renunciation. RCIII to Cople Parish Vestry, 23 Oct. 1775, vol. 3, DU. RCIII to Reubin Jordan, 5 Oct. 1776, vol. 3, DU.

70 **Despite new laws** Sylvia R. Frey, *Water from the Rock: Black Resistance in a Revolutionary Age* (Princeton, N.J., 1991), 54.

70 **"struck out at the power"** Wood, *Radicalism,* 183. Wood also notes

that "no person living off royal patronage was too insignificant to be challenged" (214).

70 **"Our new Traders"** RCIII to John Hyndman and Company, 18 Apr. 1777, vol. 3, DU. Gold and silver specie were the most trusted currency. See Wood, *Radicalism,* 65.

71 **When Dunmore shut** Holton, 29. Ragsdale, 201–2.

71 **And when Dunmore seized** Virginians did not discover that Dunmore's seizure of gunpowder occurred so close to Lexington and Concord until later, of course, and they were then concerned about the confluence of events. Selby, *Revolution,* 21.

71 **George Washington, who** Ibid., 18, 49.

71 **Patrick Henry, whom** Ibid., 5.

71 **Militias formed** Sometimes burgesses wore hunting shirts and carried tomahawks, in sympathy. Ibid., 42. See 45–49 for a description of how disorderly these armed volunteers could be.

71 **No one knew how** The idea that the founding fathers were threatened, as well as empowered, by Revolutionary fervor during this period, is broadly argued. John Adams, for instance, was concerned that the evolving governmental forms might not be "so quiet as I could wish" (quoted in Maier, 36). See also Holton; Wood, *Radicalism.*

71 **Mason, for instance** Selby, *Revolution,* 50.

71 **"the World"** Robert Beverley to William Fitzhugh, 20 July 1775, in Robert M. Calhoon, ed., " 'A Sorrowful Spectator of These Tumultuous Times': Robert Beverley Describes the Coming of the Revolution," *Virginia Magazine of History and Biography* 73 (1965), 54.

71 **William Byrd III** *Three William Byrds of Westover,* ed. Tinling, 613.

71 **"meanest creatures"** William Hicks, quoted in Bailyn, 277.

71 **"the good people of Virginia"** See RCIII, vol. 3, DU. This broadside appears to be Virginia Council, 1775, "To All the Good People of Virginia," Williamsburg, and can also be found in Early American Imprints, series I.

72 **"murmur[ed], saying that"** RCIII to John Pinkney, 18 July 1775, vol. 3, DU.

72 **"Your orders"** RCIII to Captain Richard Parker, 10 Sep. 1775, vol. 3, DU.

72 **"loyalty"** *Executive Journals of the Council of Colonial Virginia,* ed.

Benjamin Hillman, reprint ed. (Richmond, Va., 1966), 17 June 1774, 6:578.

72 **"manager"** See *Executive Journals of the Council of Colonial Virginia,* Hillman, May or June 1775, 6:584. See also *Journal of the House of Burgesses, 1772–1776,* Kennedy, 239.

72 **That same month, he tried to divert RCIII,** "An Address made by him in the Virginia Assembly . . . ," NYPL. The third edition of Thomas Paine's *Common Sense* briefly disintegrates—from a structural standpoint—into similar calculations, designed to argue that the new United States could easily afford to construct a navy to defend itself. Paine, 102–7.

72 **At the same time, Carter clearly felt** For a discussion of apocalyptic thought during this period, see Ruth H. Bloch, *Visionary Republic: Millennial Themes in American Thought, 1756–1800* (New York, 1985), 53–73.

73 **Small events that took** RCIII, 10 Feb. 1776, vol. 13, DU. Landon Carter, 13 Feb. 1776, 2:980.

73 **"Memorable Rain" . . . "Mighty Casm."** RCIII to Joseph Cross, 9 Jan. 1776, vol. 3, DU. See also RCIII to Mrs. ___ Corbin, 27 Sep. 1775, vol. 3, DU.

73 **Left unmentioned** Selby, *Revolution,* 58.

73 **sacking of Norfolk** Selby notes that Norfolk, which had displayed loyalist sympathies in the early skirmishes of the war in Virginia, was actually destroyed more by American than by British forces, but that public consensus that the British were solely responsible shifted quickly into place, and has not been displaced (*Revolution,* 82–84).

73 **"Pamphlet styled"** These are culled from contents notes at the beginning of RCIII, vol. 13, DU.

73 **In November 1774** RCIII, daybook, LC, cited in Barden, 191. See also RCIII to Joseph Dozier, 27 Jan. 1777, vol. 3, DU.

73 **He began to build** RCIII, 10 Sep. 1776, vol. 13, DU. Barden, 137.

73 **"flower Casks"** RCIII, 29 June 1774, vol. 13, DU. RCIII, 10 Sept. 1776, vol. 13, DU. Morton, 175.

74 **"the Best"** RCIII to Yewell Atwell, 19 Sep. 1778, vol. 3, DU. See also RCIII to John Turberville, 11 Apr. 1778, vol. 3, DU. RCIII to Lord Thomas Fairfax, 15 May 1776, vol. 3, DU.

74 **"overseers of 4 tithables"** RCIII to John Augustine Washington, 23 Nov. 1775, vol. 3, DU.

74 **"Social commerce"** RCIII to F. L. Lee, 23 Aug. 1775, vol. 3, DU. Copy of letter, Hugh Hamilton to Robert Ritchie, 22 Aug. 1775, vol. 3, DU. See also RCIII to John Hyndman and Company, 1 July 1783, vol. 5, DU.

74 **"Olive oil"** RCIII, vol. 13, DU.

74 **"our Situation, here"** RCIII to Mrs. Nelson, 25 Oct. 1775, vol. 3, DU.

74 **"Furniture & Liquor"** RCIII to "Mr. Rose," 22 Apr. 1776, and RCIII to "Col. D. Diggs," 22 Apr. 1776, vol. 3, DU.

74 **His mail** RCIII to Christopher Lowndes, 22 Sep. 1776, vol. 3, DU.

74 **"to work an eternal separation"** Quoted in Benjamin Quarles, "Lord Dunmore as Liberator," *William and Mary Quarterly,* 3rd series, 15 (Oct. 1958), 495. Edward Rutledge to Ralph Izard, 8 Dec. 1775, *Correspondence of Mr. Ralph Izard* (New York, 1844), 1:165.

74 **Virginians loyal** Holton, 158, writes that Dunmore's act "pushed" Carter "from the loyalist to the patriot camp."

74 **"the most formidable enemy"** Quarles, 495. John Hancock to George Washington, 2 Dec. 1775, *Letters of Members of the Continental Congress,* ed. Edmund C. Burnett (Washington, D.C., 1921–36), 1:267. George Washington to Richard Henry Lee, 26 Dec. 1776, in Richard Henry Lee, *Memoir of the Life of Richard Henry Lee* (Philadelphia, 1825), 2:9, quoted in Quarles, 495.

75 **On September 25** RCIII, vol. 13, DU: "Wife delivered of a daughter 17th day of sepr 1775—was named Judith Carter . . . My daughter Judith died 25th of Sepr 1775." RCIII to James Brooks, 25 Sep. 1775, vol. 3, DU.

75 **As George III** RCIII to Dr. Jones, 28 Feb. 1778, vol. 3, DU. RCIII to H. D. Gough, 12 Oct. 1778, vol. 3, DU. RCIII to William Mitchell, 15 May 1776, vol. 3, DU: "My Son Benjamin is in a declining State." See Maier, 13–14, 26–27, for a brief summary of British military incursions during the fall of 1775, and for descriptions of actions by the Continental Congress during this time.

75 **"Kings they had none"** RCIII, 1776, vol. 13, DU. See Bailyn, 127, for an example of a pamphlet that delineates the link for many colonists between America and ancient Israel. See also Paine, 73.

Like other Americans, Carter thought the author was Benjamin Franklin.

75 **Shortly after, on February 1, 1776** RCIII, 1 Feb. 1776, vol. 13, DU. See Leland, "Virginia Chronicle" in *Writings,* 105: Baptist haircuts were "like Cromwell's round-headed chaplains."

75 **Most strikingly, he renamed** Zwelling, 622.

75 **But such open tribute** Herbert Leventhal, *In the Shadow of the Enlightenment: Occultism and Renaissance Science in Eighteenth-Century America* (New York, 1976), 13–65. See esp. 39, 50, 56–57. Wood, *Radicalism,* 282, explores the idea that many gentry found the traditional role of "gentleman" constraining during this period, and voluntarily sought to detach themselves. Even by these standards, Carter was iconoclastic.

76 **"the consent of his master"** RCIII to Captain Richard Barnet, 3 Mar. 1776, vol. 3, DU.

76 **Then he spent April** RCIII to Major General William Lee, 22 Apr. 1776, vol. 3, DU.

76 **"The whole amount"** RCIII to Lord Thomas Fairfax, 15 May 1776, vol. 3, DU.

76 **"this very late Inclination"** RCIII to Richard Lee, 14 June 1776, vol. 3, DU. Carter may have written "County," not "Country."

76–77 **Instead, he traveled . . . from *him*.** RCIII, daybook, 13 July 1776, vol. 13, DU.

77 **one, Richard Henry Lee** Richard Henry Lee to Patrick Henry, 20 Aug. 1776, in *The Letters of Richard Henry Lee,* ed. James Curtis Ballagh (New York, 1911), vol. 1.

77 **"Sample of hair"** RCIII to Richard Lee, 26 Aug. 1776, vol. 3, DU. There were three Richard Lees with whom Carter may have been in contact during this period, and this letter does not clearly identify which one was its recipient. The nature of the errand, however, as well as the "esq." that follows the addressee's name, argues for the young man, however, not the older, titled ones. Carter called Richard Henry Lee, for instance, "Colonel" in previous correspondence (R. H. Lee, it might be added, was already in transit to Philadelphia, as the letter to Patrick Henry indicates).

77 **In October of that same year . . . dependent on me.** RCIII to Robert Mitchell, 24 Oct. 1776, vol. 3, DU: "Take current money in lieu thereof." RCIII to Thomas Jefferson, acknowledging receipt

of debt, 27 July 1778, vol. 3, DU. RCIII, citations for Thomas Jefferson, 15 Oct. 1771, 1 Nov. 1773, ledger, LC.

77 **As yet, Virginia was barely touched** Fenn, chapter 2. See esp. 55–62.

78 **"Speckled t[r]oops"** RCIII to George Wythe, 2 June 1776, vol. 3, DU.

78 **"Negro Martha" . . . gums and rosins.** RCIII to Joseph Lane, 26 Nov. 1776, vol. 3, DU. See contents notes at beginning of RCIII, vol. 13, DU.

78 **"Negroe John"** RCIII to Henry Franks, 26 Nov. 1776, vol. 3, DU. Fenn, 32–34.

78 **British forces had chased** Maier, 153.

78 **"Water frose"** RCIII, 18 and 21 Jan. 1777, vol. 14, DU.

78–79 **At the end of the month** RCIII, vol. 16, DU.

79 **"Wife and others"** RCIII, 3 Apr. 1777, vol. 15, DU.

79 **"Letter writers" . . . "distroyed."** RCIII to John Hyndman and Company, 18 Apr. 1777, vol. 3, DU. The loyalist is "Mr Patrick Ballantine . . . sentenced to depart from hence, into whose hands this Letter is put."

79 **His letter, however** "Letter miscarried," Carter wrote in a postscript, ibid.

79 **By May, sudden frosts** RCIII, 5 Apr. and 1 May 1777, vol. 14, DU.

79 **He found a celebrated doctor** Lumpkin, 343.

79 **"took the Disorder"** RCIII, 8 May 1777, vol. 14, DU.

79 **"a full & complete Inventory"** RCIII, 16 May 1777, vol. 14, DU.

79 **In the afternoon . . . Peggy.** "1777-June," vol. 17, DU. Robert Mitchell to Clement Brooke, 22 May 1777, vol. 3, DU. Mitchell wrote that Carter and his family departed from Maryland on May 21.

80 **If the two weeks . . . face and arms.** Fenn, 32–36.

80 **"a Fever Heat"** Conway, "Recantation," 1838.

80 **a "most gracious Illumination"** RCIII, 6 Sep. 1778, vol. 15, DU. RCIII, "1777-June," vol. 17, DU. For other details, see ibid., 1838–39.

80 **"Many, many of the human race"** RCIII to George Carter, 4 Dec. 1789, vol. 9, DU.

80 **"a Continuation of Life"** RCIII to Thomas Jones, 29 Dec. 1794, LC.

81 **Carter returned to Nomony** RCIII, daybook, 4 July 1777, vol. 14,

DU. See also RCIII to Richard Lemmon, 9 Jan. 1783, vol. 3, DU. RCIII to Giles Higson, 5 July 1777, vol. 3, DU.

81 **"fundamental Christian doctrine"** Conway, "Recantation," 1838.

81 **"mud Walls"** RCIII to John Ballantine, 7 July 1777, vol. 3, DU: "Robert Mitchell says that you have a Negro, who understands building mud Walls."

81 **"My Signature stands"** Carter also approved when Parson Smith provided a sermon authorizing the use of religion in political oaths. RCIII, 29 July 1777, vol. 15, DU. See also 9 Nov 1777. Supporters of the Revolution called themselves Whigs, adopting the name of the British dissenting party that was associated with Republican principles (Wood, *American Revolution*, 58). Carter's excitement about the oath was a national phenomenon (Wood, *Radicalism*, 215).

81 **Now he feared** Lewis, 51, writes that "the evangelicals' notion of a forbidding, grief-stricken world would seem increasingly plausible" to gentry who "could no longer run it [the world] and dictate to its other inhabitants." This model fits Carter, who had other reasons to see the world as grief-stricken, although the relatively early date of Carter's conversion and the extremity of his choice of sect still suggest a visionary quality not shared by other declining patriarchs. See Zwelling, 624: "As a solitary religious pilgrim who felt besieged, assaulted and forsaken, the role of martyr may well have affirmed his sense of self."

82 **"Jesus, about 30"** RCIII, 6 July 1777, vol. 12, DU. Conway, "Recantation," 1838.

82 **"I . . . doubted"** RCIII, 12 July 1777, vol. 12, DU.

82 **"the females have"** RCIII to David Rice, 15 Jan. 1779, vol. 3, DU.

82 **"At present Robin"** RCIII to James Madison, 16 Feb. 1778, vol. 3, DU.

82 **"does not recommend"** RCIII, 6 Aug. 1777, vol. 14, DU.

82 **"I am informed"** RCIII to Andrew Read, 19 Aug. 1777, vol. 3, DU. This is probably Andrew "Reid," whose fish dam Carter had once found so "hurtful."

83 **"I do presume"** RCIII to John Augustine Washington, 10 Nov. 1777, vol. 3, DU.

83 **"1 copy of a Companion"** RCIII to Dixon and Hunter, 3 Oct. 1777, vol. 3, DU.

83 "a Great Light" RCIII, 19 Dec. 1777, vol. 14, DU.

83 "the Horns of the Moon" RCIII, 25 June 1778, vol. 15, DU.

83 "Dead Bodies, naturally" RCIII, 6 July 1777, vol. 12, DU.

83 "An Evening Prayer" RCIII, loose papers, DU.

84 He read like an addict RCIII to Mrs. Byrd, 19 Nov. 1777, vol. 3, DU.

84 "Roman Catholicks, adopt" RCIII, 10 July 1778, vol. 15, DU.

84 "to teach People" RCIII, vol. 12, DU.

84 The bakery he had built Fithian, 68, 75.

84 Perhaps most significant, however, the Baltimore Works On 7 Dec. 1780, he composed a letter that would have begun the organization of his own munitions plant: "The above letter was entered here by mistake for no such Letter was sent," he added.

85 What iron remained . . . ton of bar iron. Morton, 170.

85 As of 1776 Wood, *Radicalism*, 316–17. Breen, *Tobacco*, xviii–xix.

85 "A Dollar passes" RCIII, 4 Nov. 1777, vol. 13, DU.

86 "Balance is to be" RCIII, 30 Dec. 1777, vol. 14, DU.

86 Even patriots often made Selby, *Revolution*, 150.

86 "absent" RCIII, 25 May 1776, vol. 13, DU.

86 "delinquent" RCIII, 9 Dec. 1777, vol. 14, DU.

86 On December 3 . . . concurring. RCIII, 3 Dec. 1777, vol. 14, DU.

86 On December 9 . . . "my Senses." RCIII, 9 Dec. 1777, vol. 14, DU.

87 "How shall we" RCIII, 13 Jan. 1778, vol. 14, DU.

87 "a Bright Sun" RCIII, 4 Mar. 1778, vol. 14, DU.

87 "Comune with your own" RCIII, 15 Mar. 1778, vol. 14, DU.

87 "He spoke to the Negroes" RCIII, 23 Apr. 1778, vol. 15, DU.

87 "Ye must be born again" RCIII, 3 May 1778, vol. 15, DU.

87 Two days later, he mounted RCIII, 5 May 1778, vol. 15, DU.

87 "Whites & Blacks" RCIII, 16 and 17 May 1778, vol. 15, DU.

87 "Such a heavenly confusion" Leland, "Virginia Chronicle," in *Writings*, 114–15: "It is nothing strange to see a great part of the congregation fall prostrate upon the floor or ground; many of whom entirely loose the use of their limbs for a season . . . at associations, and great meetings, I have seen numbers of ministers and exhorters, improving their gifts at the same time."

88 By May 24 RCIII, 24 May 1778, vol. 15, DU. This list of sermons and meetings is largely culled from RCIII, religious notes, vol. 12, DU. See also RCIII to Joseph Everitt, 22 Oct. 1785, vol. 6, DU.

88 On June 18 RCIII, 18 June 1778, vol. 15, DU.

88 "RC—& his servant Negro Sam" RCIII, 15 Mar. 1778, vol. 12, DU. Carter's ability and willingness to socialize with social inferiors was a mark of prewar gentry, who were so secure in their position that their rank was not threatened by such gestures. During the Revolution, however, where rank became vastly less secure, such gestures became more threatening to gentry. Interestingly, this instance provides another example of how Carter utilized the conservative ethos of the prewar gentleman to devise a role that actually exceeded the radicalism of men participating more fully in the Revolution (Wood, *Radicalism*, 42).

88 **extraordinary events** Semple, 57: "It was not unusual to have a large proportion of a congregation prostrate on the floor; and, in some instances, they have lost the use of their limbs. No distinct articulation could be heard unless from those immediately by. Screams, cries, groans, songs, shouts, and hosannas, notes of grief and notes of joy, all heard at the same time, made a heavenly confusion, a sort of indescribable concert."

89 **"a pretty general Acquaintance"** RCIII to Henry Goff, 14 Apr. 1778, vol. 3, DU.

89 **He continued to attend** RCIII, 16 July 1778, vol. 15, DU.

89 **On June 29** RCIII, 29 June 1778, vol. 15, DU.

89 **"My soul is beclouded"** RCIII, vol. 15, DU. See Zwelling, 623.

89 **"O that I knew"** RCIII, 8 July 1778, vol. 15, DU.

89 **"Sarah Stanhope"** RCIII, 19 Dec. 1777, vol. 14, DU.

90 **But his willful innocence** The idea that gentry suddenly "discovered" their social inferiors is something to which Wood alludes (*Radicalism*, 224). Interestingly, he uses Landon Carter as his example, and portrays him as possessing vastly less control and vastly more confusion about the discovery. To put it another way, Carter's transition took place in a comparative absence of insecurity, unlike that of other planters.

90 **"it does not appear fit"** . . . **"at your house shortly."** RCIII to Thomas Jefferson, 27 July 1778, vol. 3, DU.

90 **"I fear, many good natured Deists"** RCIII, 16 Aug. 1778, vol. 15, DU.

91 **"My heart, how dreadful hard"** Isaac Watts is cited by Bailyn (40–41) as one of several "early eighteenth-century freethinking Whigs" who was well recognized by the colonists on matters of "church and education," alongside Francis Hutcheson and Philip

Doddridge, both of whom appear in Carter's library. John Randolph Barden, " 'Innocent and Necessary': Music and Dancing in the Life of Robert Carter of Nomony Hall, 1728–1804" (M.A. thesis, William and Mary, 1983), 58. He cites Isaac Watts, *Hymns and Spiritual Songs in Three Books* (Glasgow, 1786), 213, 245.

91   **"was carried upon a Bed"** . . . **"this Night."** RCIII, 21 Apr. 1778, vol. 15, DU.

91   **"Sarah landry Maid"** RCIII, 22 Apr. 1778, vol. 15, DU.

91   **"Negro Sarah Landy Maid Weeped"** RCIII, 23 Apr. 1778, vol. 15, DU.

91   **"Negro Tom"** RCIII, 23 Apr. 1778, vol. 15, DU.

91   **"Negro Lucy"** RCIII, 16 Aug. 1778, vol. 15, DU.

91   **"If ye then be risen"** Lumpkin, 348.

91   **"O that I may have a saving"** RCIII, 30 Aug. 1778, vol. 15, DU.

92   **Eleazer Clay, probably** Gewehr describes Clay as "one of the few men of some wealth and influence who joined the Baptists when they were still a despised sect" (124). Clay preached in Chesterfield County in the early 1770s. As Gewehr notes, he was never arrested, although local officials employed a vagrancy law to arrest other Baptists (124–25). Little describes a "cow-hiding" threat made to Clay, 215–16.

92   **"he hoped & expected that the Civil Power"** RCIII, 9 Aug. 1778, vol. 15, DU. See also 15 Aug. 1778, for an account of the second attack. See also Zwelling, 624, for a brief discussion of these ideas about the timing of Carter's conversion.

92   **"Sarah Howey"** . . . **"preciousness of time"** RCIII, 30 Aug. 1778, vol. 15, DU.

92   **Time now precious** RCIII, 6 Sep. 1778, vol. 15, DU.

93   **If Carter had joined a Methodist** Gewehr, 158. The Methodists were also growing in number during this period, making them, in other ways as well, a compelling match for Carter. See also 164–65: "In contrast to the doctrines of predestination and the final perseverance of all saints, as held by the Presbyterians and many of the Baptists, the Methodists believed in Arminianism, or the universal redemption of all true believers."

93   **The Presbyterian ministers** Gewehr, 106, 113.

93   **There were Quaker meetings** See Davis, 203. As Davis also notes (207), the Quaker community claimed few black members, even

though their antislavery positions were both firmer and more consistent than those preached by other dissenting sects—a likely, partial explanation for why Carter did not join them himself.

93 **"such place as the circumstances"** Thomas Jefferson, *Notes on the State of Virginia,* ed. William Peden (New York, 1982), 137–38. There are many descriptions of this draft legislation available: see Nash, 11. See also John T. Noonan, Jr., *Persons and Masks of the Law: Cardozo, Holmes, Jefferson, and Wythe as Makers of the Masks,* rev. ed. (Berkeley, Calif., 2002), 47–53. As Noonan observes, "No text of an emancipation bill survives" (53).

93 **"Black Member to be dealt"** *Tussekiah BC Minutes,* 26 Aug. 1786, quoted in Robert G. Gardner, "Virginia Baptists and Slavery, 1759–1790, Part II," *Virginia Baptist Register* 25 (1986), 1267.

93 **They were the religion** Gewehr, 150. The difference was the intensity of the Baptists' perceived marginality, not the fact of it: they were regarded by many as "outlandish" and "deformed," and "hardly any of them looked like other people." Gewehr, 253. Semple, 116. See Selby, *Revolution,* 33.

93 **By 1778, they were also the only** Carter, who would never acquire a fiery tongue, reservedly called persecution "arbitrary Procedure." RCIII, 9 Aug. 1778, vol. 15, DU. See Bailyn, 261, for a brief discussion of how "despised" the Separates were. There are contradictory indications about whether Lunsford's church was Regular or Separate, but the degree of persecution, the accounts of interracial activities, and some of the doctrinal rules at Morattico suggest strongly that they were perceived as a Separate meeting. Kwilecki, 148: "The Baptists Carter joined in 1778 were probably Separates."

Chapter IV

97 **"It unanswerably follows"** Paine, 78.

97 **"Real heart religion"** Dozier, 1404–5.

98 **The February 27, 1783, business meeting of the Morattico Baptist Church** 27 Feb. 1783, *Morattico BC Minutes,* Robert Carter Papers, VBHS. All of the details in this section regarding the church meeting can be found in this source, including the information on the church subscription. The minutes do not indicate whether the meeting took place at Lunsford's Meeting House or the Kil-

marnock site (upon which can now be found both the modern
Morattico Baptist Church and the grave site of Lewis Lunsford)
or a third site, although the minutes themselves make reference to
the two sites of worship. In all likelihood, however, the meeting
took place at Lunsford's: Dozier's diary shows a large amount of
church activity in the vicinity during that period, and Carter's
presence, as well, implies that the meeting took place at the site
nearer Nomony. Also, some confusion exists about Lunsford's
Meeting House. Moore (1437) states that Lunsford's "was in
Northumberland, and was the meeting place for the Yeocomico
Baptist Church," described later in this chapter. He also cites
Dozier as the source for claiming that the Meeting House "burned
in December, 1798," but Dozier actually wrote that "C's m.h."
"burnt down" (1427). In all likelihood, the Meeting House received
a new title in the 1790s: "Lunsford's meeting ho. Called sometimes
Carter's meeting ho.," Dozier wrote in 1797 (1425). Morton, however, places Lunsford's at Aries, which was in Westmoreland, not
Northumberland. He also writes that the Meeting House was also
known as the "Factory" (237), citing Dozier, and "the G. W. Beale
MSS" at VBHS as source. But Dozier's notes refer both to an
"Aries" and "Lunsford's Meeting House," often on the same page,
implying that Lunsford's Meeting House was not, in fact, the Factory. Dozier also referred to a "Morattico Meeting House," which
could be Kilmarnock (1417), and sometimes he simply wrote
"Meeting House." "Aries," however, might denote an outdoor service, as in "hr. by sun at night at Aries" (1398). Lastly, it should be
noted that Carter himself referred to Aries, the Factory, and the
Spinnery to denote religious meetings on his Aries plantation.

98 **"easy"** RCIII to Richard Caddeen and Son, 14 June 1785, vol. 6,
DU: "a Coat . . . To be full & Easy across the breast & Shoulders . . . Waist small . . . Sleeves large and Easy."

98 **"one hand"** RCIII to Samuel Jones, 24 Nov. 1790, vol. 9, DU.

99 **He could reflect** Dozier, 1399.

99 **He could also recall** Lewis Lunsford to RCIII, 18 Sep. 1780,
VBHS.

99 **In the century prior** Law required that every man and woman attend services. See Lewis, 43.

99 "**the severest contests**" *Works of Thomas Jefferson,* Ford, 1:62. For a description of this engagement, see Gewehr, 200–6. See Buckley, 8–27, for another description of the conflict over religious liberty in Virginia in 1776.

99 **no sect had fought harder** Buckley, 176. Gewehr, 200: "We have plenty of evidence that the dissenters fought the Revolution for more than independence from England." Bailyn, less sympathetic, describes the ideas among the dissenting religions in the pre-Revolution period as "unstable compounds of narrow denominationalism and broad libertarianism" (257). See also Bailyn, 259–60, for a discussion of the alliance between "sectarian particularism and political idealism," which he also characterizes as "unstable."

101 "**An Act to Authorize**" Hening, vol. 11, 39–40.

102 "**Within a month**" John Rippon, *The Baptist Annual Register for 1790, 1791, 1792, and Part of 1793* (1793), 107. Lumpkin, 349. "Declaration of Faith and Practice," *Morattico BC Minutes,* 1778–1844, LV.

102 "**engross much of the time**" Charles F. James, 91. He describes the Cople Parish petition as "essentially the same as the addresses from Mecklenburg and Lunenburg." Mecklenburg is here quoted (87). Gewehr, 261: "One can scarcely realize the far reaching upheaval involved in this transition, which made even the aristocratic Northern Neck willing to listen to the gospel, although expounded by black men."

102–3 "**That God would give me**" . . . "no abiding place." RCIII, religious writings, LC. See also "Sacrifices, Altars, Tithes," CFP. This form of essay writing and note-taking was common among students in the mid- and late eighteenth century. See Maier, 104: "Young men were taught to copy and often memorize compelling passages from their readings for future use." Bernard Bailyn observes that Revolutionary pamphlets were "almost submerged in annotation" (23). See also Bailyn, 27.

103 "**experience[s] of grace**" RCIII to John Toler, 20 Nov. 1778, vol. 3, DU.

103 **He provided the funds** RCIII, vol. 17, DU.

103 **On one day in 1778** RCIII, 15 Mar. 1778, vol. 15, DU.

103 "**Black sister Betty Bell**" 19 July 1788, RCIII, clerk, *Morattico BC Minutes,* VBHS.

103 **"inquiries"** See ibid. The Baptists, like the Methodists, punished through excommunication a variety of social deviations: "swearing, quarreling, superfluity in dress and apparel, intemperance of all sorts, 'playing or dancing wanton tunes,' horse racing 'as it is commonly carried on,' the use of cards and dice." Gewehr, 260, quoting the minister and writer David Thomas.

103 **He signed off** See *Morattico BC Minutes*, 1778–1844, LV, for: 27 Feb. 1783; 30 May 1781; 17 Jan. 1783; 11 Feb. 1780; 8 Oct. 1780; 6 July 1782; 26 Mar. 1784, LV.

103 **He even attended meetings** 30 May 1781, *Morattico BC Minutes*, 1778–1844, LV.

104 **"I do in behalf of"** RCIII to George Wythe, 19 Jan. 1779, vol. 3, DU. He also debated with him whether or not American law students should be taught Greek or Jewish history. RCIII to George Wythe, 11 Feb. 1784, vol. 5, DU. As more gentlemen turned toward evangelical religion, these renunciations of Deism multiplied in number. Lewis, 52.

104 **"darling Amusement"** Fithian, 48.

104 **"I believe it would not"** RCIII to Francis Christian, 23 June 1779, vol. 3, DU.

104 **He threw open** Lumpkin, 344–45. Dozier also makes numerous references to services at Nomony Hall.

104 **By day, his factory** RCIII, 21 Apr. 1778; 31 May 1778; 18 June 1778, et al., vol. 12, DU.

104 **"I wish he would lay aside"** RCIII to David Rice, 15 Jan. 1779, vol. 3, DU.

104 **In May 1779 . . . nothing for a month and more.** RCIII to Mrs. Turberville, 27 Sep. 1786, vol. 7, DU. RCIII, vol. 16, DU. Barden, 245.

104–5 **Responding to the debilitating . . . tobacco certificates.** Carter cites these taxes under the heading "General Assembly January 1778" in RCIII, vol. 14, DU. For brief discussions of Virginia taxes during this period, see Selby, *Revolution*, 152, 178, 233; Barden, 292–93.

105 **"Previous to that tax"** RCIII to William Carr, 11 Jan. 1785, vol. 7, DU.

105 **"If the yearly payments"** RCIII to Abraham Vaughan, 19 Oct. 1785, vol. 7, DU.

105 **"heavy public claim"** RCIII to Clement Brooke, 12 July 1779, vol. 3, DU. RCIII to Daniel Dulany, 10 July 1779, vol. 3, DU.

105 **"the Notion of Profits"** RCIII to R. H. Lee, 5 Oct. 1781, vol. 4, DU.

105 **slaves as legal tender** McColley, 25. Ballagh, 69.

106 **"This Resolution"** RCIII to Clement Brooke, 17 Feb. 1779, vol. 3, DU.

106 **"considerable loss"** RCIII to John Sutton, 19 Oct. 1782, vol. 5, DU.

106 **"Doctor Todd"** RCIII to Doctor Todd, 30 Aug. 1777, vol. 3, DU. RCIII to Thomas Everard, 3 Nov. 1777, vol. 3, DU.

106 **"the present time"** RCIII to John Sutton, 14 Apr. 1781, vol. 3, DU. See also RCIII to David Boyd, 26 Oct. 1780, vol. 3, DU, and RCIII to John Sutton, 29 Apr. 1779, vol. 3, DU: "The late Judgment of divine Providence in destroying all the fruit of trees in these parts is little thought of by the People, for they continue to be very careless concerning divine things."

106 **He hired John Sutton** RCIII to John Pound, 27 Oct. 1778, vol. 3, DU.

106 **"God & Literature"** RCIII to Henry Toler, 5 Nov. 1779, vol. 3, DU. RCIII to Henry Toler, 3 Jan. 1782, vol. 3, DU.

106 **Even Lunsford received lists** See RCIII to Lunsford, 20 Jan. 1781, vol. 3, DU. Wood notes that the way that colonial lenders constructed their ledger sheets—a page for each debtor—implied how strongly debt relationships were also personal relationships. These book accounts could be incredibly detailed, and long-standing (Wood, *Radicalism*, 67, 68). Carter's debt ledgers were detailed, and he did indicate, later in life, that he could recall them from memory with great precision. See chapter 5. See also Kwilecki, 157.

106 **"you may never expect"** RCIII to Thomas Dudley, 21 Nov. 1780, vol. 4, DU.

107 **"I am apprehensive"** RCIII to Lawrence Washington, 2 Feb. 1780, vol. 3, DU.

107 **"Ticket marked Clear"** RCIII, 12 Feb. 1778, vol. 14, DU.

107 **"forbiding Hostilities"** RCIII to James Madison, 16 Feb. 1778, vol. 3, DU.

107 **"I do forbid you"** RCIII to Thomas Olive, 8 May 1781, vol. 4, DU.

107 **"provide themselves plantations"** RCIII to Original Young, 28 Dec. 1781, vol. 4, DU. RCIII to James Hunter, 29 Nov. 1780, vol. 4, DU: "I Shall want in the Course of next year, 1781, about

twenty five thousand Pounds to discharge publick taxes—Pray advise me what you will allow for Pig-iron deliverable at the Baltimore Furnace in Maryland."

107 **On September 18** Lewis Lunsford to RCIII, 18 Sep. 1780, VBHS.

107 **On December 30** Selby, *Revolution*, 220–25.

108 **"few men in the field"** Lafayette to Thomas Nelson, 26 Aug. 1781. *Lafayette in Virginia, Unpublished Letters,* ed. Gilbert Chinard (Baltimore, 1928), 52.

108 **"dictator"** Selby, *Revolution*, 284–85.

108 **On January 12 . . . two hundred pounds.** RCIII to Richard Parker, "Attorney," 13 Jan. 1781, vol. 4, DU. RCIII to Fleet Cox, 13 Jan. 1781, vol. 4, DU.

108 **Then, in the first week** RCIII to John Sutton, 14 Apr. 1781, vol. 4, DU. Barden, 249.

108 **"put themselves under"** RCIII to "the Comanding Officers . . . at the towns of Portsmouth, York, & Gloucester, or other places in the State of Virginia," 30 Oct. 1781, vol. 4, DU. See also RCIII to William Preston, 16 Apr. 1782, vol. 4, DU, and RCIII to Nathan Morgan, 16 Apr. 1782, vol. 4, DU. In the first letter, Carter reported the number of slaves that have escaped at thirty-two; in later letters, he reported thirty-three. Morton, 56.

108 **"horned cattle"** RCIII to Mr. South, 11 June 1781, vol. 4, DU.

109 **"Bearer Negro Tom"** RCIII to Thomas Olive, 30 Apr. 1781, vol. 4, DU. RCIII to Richard Sanford, 7 May 1781, vol. 4, DU.

109 **"Joan" and "Patty"** RCIII to Thomas Olive, 24 July 1781, vol. 4, DU. RCIII to James Clarke, 28 July 1781, vol. 4, DU.

109 **The House of Delegates immediately began** Selby, *Revolution*, 315–17.

109 **"Our people still retain"** Joseph Jones to James Madison, 8 June 1783, in *Letters of Joseph Jones of Virginia, 1777–1787,* ed. Worthington Chauncey Ford (New York, 1971), 114.

109 **"the public claims"** RCIII to John Sutton, 19 Oct. 1782, vol. 5, DU.

109 **He longed for the recovery** RCIII to "the Comanding Officers . . . ," 30 Oct. 1781, vol. 4, DU.

110 **"Government disappointed me"** RCIII to Clement Brooke, 11 Dec. 1781, vol. 4, DU. Selby, *Revolution*, 315–17.

110 **"I nither give nor Sell"** RCIII to Samuel Jones, 24 Nov. 1790,

vol. 9, DU. See also Morton, 102, 106, 111. Clearly, there were events that led Carter to sell slaves, despite his testimony otherwise. See, for instance, RCIII to William Hazard, 3 Jan. 1783: "I will Sell, but not hire Negro Tom." Likewise, at times he declined to "buy or sell" slaves to defer humanitarian cases when other slaveholders wanted him to purchase slaves to protect them. At the same time, however, Carter bought and sold slaves very rarely, much more rarely than most slaveholders, even progressive ones.

110 **"I stamped Tiffany"** . . . **"Velvet Corks."** RCIII to Hurst, 1 Sep. 1785, vol. 7, DU. RCIII to Travis Jones, 4 May 1786, vol. 7, DU.

110 **"possession & profits"** RCIII to John Hyndman and Company, 4 Mar. 1785, vol. 6, DU. RCIII to Ben Branum, 4 Sep. 1780, vol. 4, DU.

110 **Carter, who had spurned** RCIII to Thomas Jones, 7 Dec. 1781, vol. 4, DU. RCIII to John Peck, 6 Dec. 1784, vol. 6, DU.

110 **Thirty-three had left** RCIII to "the Comanding Officers . . . ," 30 Oct. 1781, vol. 4, DU.

110 **Some few may have remained** Barden, 251. Frey, 172–205, discusses in detail the relocation of slaves and free blacks after the Revolutionary War.

111 **"Several of my own"** George Washington, *Writings of George Washington,* ed. Fitzpatrick, 26:370. Wiencek, 256.

111 **But when Carter received word** RCIII to William Preston, 16 Apr. 1782, vol. 4, DU. RCIII to Nathan Morgan, 16 Apr. 1782, vol. 4, DU. RCIII to Garland Moore, 30 Oct. 1781, vol. 4, DU. RCIII to William Musgrove, 8 Apr. 1782, vol. 4, DU.

111 **Nomony had industrialized** Barden, 144.

111 **"Care + Management"** RCIII, 1 Jan. 1782, CFP, sect 28. Sobel, 49.

111 **Slave craftsmen** Barden, 147.

111 **A slave named Jack Smith** RCIII, LC, in ibid., 152.

111 **Meanwhile, the slave population** Morton, 100–10.

111 **"men of gallantry"** RCIII to Clement Brooke, 7 Jan. 1783, vol. 5, DU.

111 **Tom Henry** William Dawson to RCIII, 21 July 1788, CFP, sect. 22.

111 **Sam Harrison** Fithian, 54.

111 **Sukey, who in 1774** Barden, 173, 619.

112 **"fits"** RCIII to Bennett Neal, 15 Sep. 1781, vol. 4, DU.

112 **He was not remotely** Nor the only American. See J. Franklin

Jameson, *The American Revolution Considered as a Social Movement,* intro. Frederick B. Tolles, reprint ed. (Princeton, 1967), 5.

112 **"the last stage"** *The Federalist,* 15, in Alexander Hamilton, *Writings,* ed. Joanne Freeman (New York, 2001), 19.

112 **"Our trade was never more"** James Madison to James Monroe, 21 June 1785, *Papers of James Madison,* eds. William T. Hutchinson and William M. F. Rachal (Chicago, 1962–), vol. 8, 307. Ragsdale, 258–65.

112 **"Times are Verry dull"** Richard Lemmon to RCIII, 2 June 1785, MHS.

112 **"Gold & Silver"** RCIII to John Turner, 5 Nov. 1781, vol. 4, DU.

112 **"cover"** RCIII, 23 Mar. 1783, LC.

112 **"Abuses"** George Mason to RCIII, 27 Oct. 1781, *Papers of George Mason,* Rutland, 2:700.

112 **"I am more defective"** RCIII to John Chinn, 25 May 1799, LC.

112 **"excuses"** RCIII to John Sutton, 27 Dec. 1783, vol. 5, DU.

112 **When he neglected** RCIII to John Sutton, RCIII to James Harrison, 23 Apr. 1783, vol. 5, DU. RCIII to William Carr, 26 Feb. 1784, vol. 5, DU.

112 **Other Virginia families** RCIII to Philip Lee, 20 Mar. 1785, vol. 6, DU. See also RCIII to Richard Lemmon, 7 Dec. 1783, vol. 5, DU.

113 **With great deference** See, for instance, RCIII to George Mason, 1 Aug. 1791, vol. 9, DU. Henry did, however, subsequently serve on Carter's behalf.

113 **By February 1783** There are numerous references to Robert Bladen Carter's mismanagement of Billingsgate in his father's correspondence. See, for instance, RCIII to Doctors Andrus and Hazillett, 11 June 1782, vol. 5, DU: "As soon as I return to Virginia I shall mention to my son Robt Bladen Carter, the great impropriety & Evil of his late Conduct—and I shall use my endeavours with him to satisfy your Claim against him—" See also Richard Lemmon, 11 July 1782, vol. 5, DU: "I have Spoken to my Son Robt Bladen Carter of the Tobo Debt due from him to Docor Andrus and Hazillett—I fear he is not provided either with Tobacco or Country to produce to Satisfy that Claim—or any other against him.

"R. B. Carter has Spoken to me concerning the Balance due from him to you—his enemies, (whom he calls his friends) have in-

fluenced him to think and talk very absurdly on your Demand. . . . I have obtained a Lot of R B C's debts lately according to
his own account—which are very considerable—he has for a long
time been in possession of a plantation, Negroes and Stocks part of
that proportion of Estate I intend for his Use—which plantation is
the Subject for his Creditors to apply too—his Brothers and Sisters
would have just cause for complaining if their father was to apply
any part of their proportion of his Estate to satisfy RBC's Debts."

113 **When Bob sold her sister** RCIII, 10 June 1784, vol. 16, DU. Barden, 310–11.

113 **By June, it became clear** Carter transcribed "A list of Claims of the
Creditors of Mr Robt Bladen Carter" in Jan. 1785, vol. 6, DU.

113 **On July 4, 1783** RCIII to Thomas Beale, 4 July 1783, vol. 5, DU. For
the auction, see RCIII, 1 and 2 Dec. 1784, vol. 6, DU. RCIII to Je-
remiah Bailey, 15 Apr. 1784, vol. 5, DU. Advertisement for the auction can be found in May 1784, vol. 5, DU. RCIII to William
Hammond, 24 Jan. 1785, vol. 6, DU, acknowledges that "Negroes
&ca" were auctioned to satisfy RBC's debts, and raised "162,800 lb
Crop Tobacco and L 215"16"6 cash" toward that end.

113 **"Mrs. Baylor"** RCIII to Mann Page, 27 Oct. 1787, vol. 8, DU.

114 **"3 pair of Worsted Stockings"** RCIII to Richard Parker, 10 Feb.
1786, vol. 6, DU. RCIII to Walker Muse, 4 Oct. 1787, vol. 8, DU.
RCIII to Murphy, 11 Oct. 1787, vol. 8, DU. "Genteel youth after the
Revolution were characterized by idleness and instability," according to Lewis (120). See also Lewis, 126. Lewis emphasizes a para-
digm shift during the Revolution that implies greater stability
among Virginia gentry youth prior to the war. See also Zwelling,
626.

114 **When two sold Billingsgate slaves . . . his own black servants.**
RCIII to Stephens Thomson Mason, 9 Mar. 1785, vol. 6, DU.
Stephens Thomson Mason to RCIII, 14 Jan. 1785, NYPL. RCIII
to Stephens Thomson Mason, 21 Mar. 1785, vol. 6, DU. Carter told
"Will" to procure new shoes: RCIII to George Newman, 19 Mar.
1785, vol. 6, DU. Carter spelled it "Stephens Tomson Mason."
Carter regarded "Tolbot," whose name was often written different
ways within the body of one letter, as a difficult slave. See RCIII to
John Sutton, 2 Mar. 1780, vol. 3, DU: "Some time ago Mr Gordon
delivered to Negro Tolbot a broad ax expecting that he was to work

with out Carpenters here, but neither Tobert or his Wife have appeared Since—it is thought that they are gone up to Leoplantation—this late Conduct of Tolberts is uniform with his former behaviour, what ever your own mind may Suggest in this affair, act accordingly."

114 **"That State has been productive"** RCIII to Thomas Jones, 16 Sep. 1796, MHS.

114 **By 1785, he was established** Lumpkin, 353. Frey, 251.

115 **"we are mostly Illiterate"** William Bledsoe to RCIII, 19 May 1790, VBHS.

115 **"waited on Colonel Carter"** Francis Asbury, *The Journal and Letters of Francis Asbury*, ed. Elmer T. Clark (London, 1958), 1: 495, 615–16.

115 **"neglect or forsake the service"** See Edwards, 107–9.

115 **"It affords very pleasing feelings in me"** RCIII to John Sutton, 16 July 1781, vol. 3, DU.

115–16 **"I Never Refuse"**. . . . **"what Condition it will."** Samuel Straughan to RCIII, 27 Sep. 1786, CFP, sect. 22.

116 **"Ralph"** RCIII, LC, quoted in Barden, 187.

116 **"Dennis"** RCIII to Newyear Branson, 18 Apr. 1785, vol. 6, DU.

116 **"Charles"** RCIII to John Turberville, 22 Apr. 1785, vol. 6, DU. RCIII to Job Carter, 3 May 1785, vol. 6, DU. RCIII to Clement Brooke, 19 May 1785, vol. 6, DU.

116 **"Old Abraham"** Edmond Newman to George Newman, June 1788, CFP, sect. 72.

116 **"Negro Jerry of Forest plantation"** RCIII to Samuel Straughan, 6 July 1787, vol. 7, DU.

116 **"Negro Michael"** RCIII to Bennett Neal, 15 Sep. 1781, vol. 4, DU.

116 **"Black Billy"** Barden 153, 657–58.

117 **He scolded** RCIII to George Newman, 20 June 1785, vol. 6, DU.

117 **"Negro Joe"** RCIII to John Sutton, 24 Feb. 1781, vol. 4, DU.

117 **"Presley informs"** RCIII to George House, 1 July 1788, vol. 8, DU.

117 **"It is no uncustomary thing"** RCIII to Alexander Campbell, 16 Sep. 1788, vol. 8, DU.

117 **And over and over, he interceded** RCIII to Andrew Read, 19 Aug. 1777, vol. 3, DU. RCIII to John Turberville, 4 May 1776, vol. 3, DU. RCIII to John Simpson, 15 Apr. 1785, vol. 6, DU.

117 **Jefferson's estimate** Quoted in Nash, 60.

117 **John Laurens of South Carolina** Wiencek, 218, 222–27, 232–33. Davis, 79–80.

117 **states such as Pennsylvania enacted** See Arthur Zilversmit, *The First Emancipation: The Abolition of Slavery in the North* (Chicago, 1967).

117 **"grieved at having slaves"** Marquis de Chastellux, *Travels in North America, in the Years 1780, 1781, and 1782,* ed. and trans. Howard C. Rice, Jr. (Chapel Hill, N.C., 1963), 2:439.

117 **And from the moment** They were also interested in rewarding slaves loyal to the Revolution. But not that interested: see Wiencek, 248.

118 **By 1785, petitions** Nash, 14.

118 **"Self Examination"** In his daybook for 1778, Carter described one event where Rice preached to "about 75 White people," with "Self Examination insisted on—" RCIII, 15 July 1778, vol. 15, DU. See Berlin, *Slaves Without Masters,* 24–25. Rice described in Davis, 201.

118 **In 1783, Jefferson . . . after 1800.** Jefferson, *Notes on the State of Virginia,* 214. Nash, 11. Ballagh, 132. Morton, 256.

118 **Washington and Henry** For instance, Davis, 196–97. McColley, 159.

118 **Having banned . . . "shall be free."** Hening, 9:471–72; 12:182.

118 **Subsequent bills** Ibid., 12: 345; 13: 200. See also Christopher Doyle, "Judge St. George Tucker and the Case of Tom v. Roberts," *Virginia Magazine of History and Biography* 106 (Autumn 1998), 428.

118 **"this Permission to buy"** Reprinted in Fredrika Teute Schmidt and Barbara Ripel Wilhelm, "Early Proslavery Petitions in Virginia," *William and Mary Quarterly,* 3rd series, 30 (Jan. 1973), 138–40.

119 **"motion was made to throw it"** Ibid., 135. James Madison to George Washington, 11 Nov. 1785, *Papers of James Madison,* eds. Hutchinson and Rachal, vol. 8. *Writings of James Madison,* ed. Hunt, 2:192.

119 **"men of virtue enough"** Thomas Jefferson to Jean Nicolas Demeunier, 26 June 1786, *Papers of Thomas Jefferson,* ed. Boyd, 10:63.

119 **"We, however, came off with whole bones"** Asbury, 1:488–89.

119 **"Petition of sundry persons"** RCIII, 8 and 10 Nov. 1785, vol. 16, DU.

119 **"a Subject that our Legislature"** RCIII to Samuel Jones, 24 Nov. 1790, vol. 9, DU.

119 **He ordered a copy** RCIII to James Hayes, 18 Nov. 1785, vol. 7, DU. RCIII to Thomas Parker, 2 Dec. 1785, vol. 7, DU.

119 **"Judgements will follow us"** RCIII to Samuel Jones, 24 Nov. 1790, vol. 9, DU.

119 **In so doing, however, he also created** Morton, 96.

119–120 **"a good deal beaten and bruised"** RCIII to Newyear Branson, 13 Feb. 1790, vol. 9, DU.

120 **When Thomas Olive . . . "power of Correction from him."** RCIII to "the Trustees In behalf of the Creditors of Robert Bladen Carter," 9 Sep. 1784, vol. 6, DU.

120 **But Carter did not fire Olive . . . he did not fire him.** RCIII, daybook, 15 Nov. 1784, vol. 16, DU.

120 **Carter was still practicing** See Davis, 47: "Evangelical religion also gave a new thrust to the ancient desire to Christianize human bondage by imbuing both master and servant with a spirit of charity and forbearance."

121 **"unfeeling bloodsuckers"** Quoted in Mayer, 406.

121 **"the Profits arising"** RCIII to Henry Tazewell, 19 May 1785, vol. 6, DU.

121 **On any given plantation . . . a larger concern.** Stanton, *Monticello*, 13.

121 **"being well satisfyed"** RCIII to Newyear Branson, 30 Mar. 1787, vol. 7, DU.

121 **"irregular Conduct"** RCIII to William Carr, 12 July 1785, vol. 6, DU.

121–22 **Within a year . . . Aquarius.** Correspondence describing the removal of slaves can be found in RCIII to Samuel Straughan and James Harrison, 4 Apr. 1787, vol. 7, DU. RCIII to Vincent Branson, 4 Apr. 1787, vol. 7, DU. RCIII to George Newman, 2 Dec. 1785, vol. 7, DU. RCIII to John Caddeen, 25 Jan. 1786, vol. 7, DU. RCIII to George Newman, 3 Sep. 1787, vol. 7, DU. RCIII to George Newman, 23 Oct. 1787, vol. 8, DU. Carter's correspondence provides evidence that he began to plan these removals early in the decade. See RCIII to John Hackley, 26 Aug. 1782, vol. 5, DU: "My intention is to Settle Negroes on that tract and I do purpose to have two quarters, thereon imediately." See also RCIII to John Sutton, 19 Oct. 1782, vol. 5, DU. RCIII to John Sutton, 7 Nov. 1783, vol. 5, DU. Barden, 316–24, provides a thorough overview.

122 "parcel of Earthern Bowls" RCIII to Henry Hill, 18 May 1785, vol. 6, DU.

122 He sent letters RCIII to Robert and Richard Lemmon, 7 Aug. 1787, vol. 7, DU.

122 He began selling assets Morton, 172.

122 He relinquished control Ibid., 76.

122 "a Garden for each Tenement" RCIII to "Sir," 18 Dec. 1790, vol. 9, DU. See also Kwilecki, 79.

122 "hereditary slavery to be contrary" *Minutes of the Baptist General Committee . . . May 1791* (Richmond, 1791), 5, quoted in Essig, 181. Semple, 303–4. Gewehr, 240.

122 In church after church This comparison can be made utilizing the research in Gardner, 1259–64.

122 "free male members" 10 Mar. 1787, *Morattico BC Minutes,* 1778–1844, LV.

123 "Disappointment" Dozier, 1408. More precisely, he writes: "Disappt. Mr. Carter exhorted . . . Disappt, that is, no preacher came."

123 "There is much stupidity" RCIII, 4 Nov. 1778, vol. 15, DU.

123 "Because we cannot dive" Henry Toler to RCIII, 4 Sep. 1779, CFP, sect. 22.

123 "the Company of each" Henry Toler, diary, VBHS, quoted in Morton, 244.

123 "Where is it written?" RCIII, religious writings, LC.

123 "from a Pilgrim not satisfied" RCIII to Lewis Lunsford, 16 Dec. 1789, vol. 9, DU.

124 "a coalition of Monarchy men" Quoted in Mayer, 379.

124 "Monarchy, or a corrupt" Quoted in ibid., 378.

124 "What right had they to say" Quoted in ibid., 402, 405.

124 "I have lived long enough" *The Complete Anti-Federalist,* ed. Herbert J. Storing (Chicago, 1981), 5:212.

124 "Neighbours" RCIII to Walter Jones, 12 Dec. 1788, vol. 8, DU. Carter wrote: "I am well pleased to find that my Neighbours and Countrymen stand aloof and have marked all Antifederalists, for I apprehend that it would be necessary to Support the constitution inch by inch." See also RCIII to SF Carter, 30 Jan. 1789, vol. 8, DU, where he complimented Richard Bland Lee for "the part he took with the Feoderalists." Mayer, 379.

124 **"soul of Virginia"** Storing, 5:235.

124 **"I can foresee no evil"** George Washington to James McHenry, 22 Aug. 1785, in *The Papers of George Washington, Confederation Series,* eds. W. W. Abbot and Dorothy Twohig (Charlottesville, Va., 1992–), 3:198.

124 **In private, men such as Washington** Wiencek, 267.

124 **"ashamed"** *Records of the Federal Convention of 1787,* ed. Max Farrand (New Haven, Conn., 1911), 1:511, quoted in Nash, 14.

125 **George Wythe eventually** Noonan, 33, 61. Michael Brown, one of the freed slaves, was also poisoned. See Julian P. Boyd, "The Murder of George Wythe," *William and Mary Quarterly,* 3rd series, 12.4 (Oct. 1955), 530–31, for a description of Wythe's estate.

125 **"make the Adults among them"** David Humphrey, *David Humphrey's "Life of General Washington" with George Washington's "Remarks,"* ed. Rosemarie Zagarri (Athens, Ga., 1991), 78.

125 **"ultimately on an easier footing"** Thomas Jefferson to Nicholas Lewis, 29 July 1787, *Papers of Thomas Jefferson,* ed. Boyd, 11:640. Thomas Jefferson to Edward Bancroft, 26 Jan. 1789, *Papers of Thomas Jefferson,* ed. Boyd, 14:492. Stanton, 35.

125 **"tolerating Slavery"** RCIII to John Rippon, 27 Aug. 1788, vol. 8, DU.

125 **"Cash or Tobacco"** RCIII, public notice, 1 Mar. 1785, vol. 6, DU. See also RCIII to John Peck, 1 Sep. 1785, vol. 6, DU.

125 **"it has and ever will be"** RB Carter to RCIII, 9 June 1786, CFP, sect. 22.

126 **"the Whites & black[s]"** RCIII to George Newman, 23 Oct. 1787, vol. 8, DU. Sobel, 163.

126 **"launch"** RCIII to George Newman, 28 Dec. 1786, vol. 7, DU. William Fitzhugh to Oliver Luke, 15 Aug. 1690, Fitzhugh, 279.

126 **"till each of them arrive"** RCIII to James Manning, 9 Feb. 1786, vol. 7, DU. Carter's "pre-emptive solution" receives a brief but astute discussion in Duncan J. MacLeod, *Slavery, Race, and the American Revolution* (New York, 1974), 138.

126 **"Girls are not"** RCIII to Benjamin Dawson, 14 Apr. 1792, vol. 9, DU.

126 **"one thousand Pounds"** A well-mannered insult, as well, to the suitor himself, Richard Bland Lee. RCIII to Richard Bland Lee, 2 Dec. 1789, vol. 9, DU.

126 **"Literature he detests"** RCIII to James Manning, 9 Feb. 1786, vol. 7, DU. Carter wrote "his turn to dissipation."

126 **"be entered immediately"** RCIII to James Manning, 16 Aug. 1787, vol. 7, DU.

127 **Carter instead found a place** RCIII to Samuel Jones, 27 Aug. 1790, vol. 9, DU. Carter wrote, "It so turns out that John is not to Live at Mr Bowen's—but that you had Consented to take the Youth into your family, and to instruct him in Such Subjects, as you may Judge most advantageous—A Circumstance, I consider most favorable."

127 **"I cannot consent"** RCIII to James Manning, 24 Sep. 1787, vol. 8, DU.

127 **"a Separation of my two Sons"** Ibid. J.T. did visit Nomony on 20 Nov. 1790: he "got to this place," RCIII grudgingly wrote to Samuel Jones, 24 Nov. 1790, vol. 9, DU.

127 **"I cannot think of exposing"** RCIII to William Dawson, 6 Feb. 1788, vol. 8, DU.

127 **"as proper temperature"** RCIII to James Manning, 18 June 1789, vol. 8, DU.

128 **"no letter from you"** RCIII to Frances Carter, 14 Aug. 1787, vol. 7, DU.

128 **"29 yd black bombazeen"** RCIII to Travis Jones, 6 Nov. 1787, vol. 8, DU.

128 **"Old companion"** RCIII to Henry Toler, 1 Nov. 1787, vol. 8, DU. Carter wrote "Toller." RCIII to Thomas Jones, 3 Nov. 1787, vol. 8, DU.

128 **"private"** RCIII to Henry Toler, 1 Nov. 1787, vol. 8, DU.

128 **"The Example and Custom"** RCIII to Robert Rogers, 7 Dec. 1787, vol. 8, DU.

128 **"a majority shall determine"** 29 Sep. 1788, *Yeocomico BC Covenant,* VBHS. Among other covenant rules, RCIII proposed that "women do not speak in the Churches," and cited Corinthians 14:34–35.

129 **"union and fellowship"** 14 Mar. 1789, RCIII, clerk, *Yeocomico BC Minutes,* VBHS. Dozier, 1437.

129 **"interesting and important"** RCIII, public announcement, 27 Nov. 1787, vol. 8, DU.

129 **"Classes"** RCIII to "Dear fellow Citizens," 6 Feb. 1788, vol. 8, DU.

RCIII to Joseph Pierce, 6 Feb. 1788, vol. 8, DU. RCIII to James Bland, 5 Dec. 1787, vol. 8, DU.

129 **"Mr Moyse"** RCIII, 25 Jan. 1788, LC. See esp. Barden, "Innocent and Necessary," 70. Kwilecki, 161. Morton, 245. Barden and Morton spell it "Myse." Carter later spells it Moyce in RCIII, 20 May 1791, vol. 16, DU: "Mr Moyce of Philadelphia put the Sumary View of the heavenly Doctrine of the New Jerusalem Church by E, Swedenborg into R C's hands."

129 **"a late trying season"** RCIII to George Newman, 28 Jan. 1788, vol. 8, DU.

129 **"a very little Sleep"** RCIII to Henry Toler, 13 Oct. 1789, vol. 9, DU.

130 **"Take 2 qts rye bran"** "A Receipt for a Consumption," included within RCIII to Newyear Branson, 21 Jan. 1788, vol. 8, DU. His impatience with doctors also appears to have grown at this time. See RCIII to Timothy Harrington, 14 Mar. 1792, vol. 9, DU: "Your Patients would have done just as well without that Attention shewn by the frequent Visits."

130 **"Agues, which were"** RCIII to George Prestman, 7 Oct. 1789, vol. 9, DU.

130 **"We have been alarmed"** Lewis Lunsford to RCIII, 11 Dec. 1789, CFP, sect. 8.

130 **"this American world"** Alexander Hamilton to Gouverneur Morris, 29 Feb. 1802, in *The Papers of Alexander Hamilton*, ed. Harold C. Syrett (New York, 1961–), 25:544. Wood, *Radicalism*, 367.

130 **"deny[ing] myself,"** RCIII to Robert Rogers, 7 Dec. 1787, vol. 8, DU.

130 **"whomever of your acquaintances"** RCIII to Sarah Fairfax Carter, 7 Apr. 1789, vol. 8, DU.

130 **"the latest petition"** RCIII to John Rippon, 27 Aug. 1788, vol. 8, DU. For a discussion of Jefferson, see Davis, 172–74.

130 **"the present deficiency"** RCIII to John Leland, 9 Apr. 1788, vol. 8, DU.

131 **"Negro Jesse"** . . . **"ready money dealer."** RCIII to Solomon Nash, 15 Dec. 1789, vol. 9, DU.

131 **"Robert Carter requests"** RCIII, advertisement, 23 July 1789, vol. 9, DU.

131 **"Disappointments in our first"** RCIII to Thomas Jones, 28 Sep. 1794, LC.

132 **"Once a man get wrong"** Semple, 178. Lumpkin writes that Carter's "search was betrayed by faulty exegetical and hermeneutical presuppositions" (354). Kwilecki, 161, 168.

132 **"a religious life, exclusively pursued"** William James, *The Varieties of Religious Experience,* intro. Reinhold Niebuhr (New York, 1997), 24.

132 **Just as Carter left** Gewehr, 116, 258. Zwelling, 628: "Formerly a member of the colonial elite, Carter, in a more egalitarian society, preferred the fringe."

132 **"I have never seen anything more like"** Minton Thrift, *Memoirs of Jesse Lee,* 97, quoted in Gewehr, 172. See Gewehr, 106, for description of size of Baptist Church in Virginia during this period. See also Leland, "Virginia Chronicle," in *Writings,* 116–17; Thom, 39–42, Rippon, 100.

132 **"odd tones"** Gewehr, 200. Buckley, 171. Semple, 39, 59.

132 **"no more be popular"** Leland, "Virginia Chronicle," in *Writings,* 123.

132 **"by a large majority"** *Minutes of the Baptist General Committee . . . 1793* (Richmond, Va., 1793), 4, quoted in Essig, 182.

132 **Within a decade, church records** Both Morattico and Nomony Baptist churches swelled during this period (Gewehr, 175). See W. Harrison Daniel, "Virginia Baptists and the Negro in the Early Republic," *Virginia Magazine of History and Biography* 80 (1972), 60. Berlin, *Slaves Without Masters,* 83–84.

133 **"universal restoration"** RCIII to John Sutton, 16 July 1781, vol. 3, DU. See also Morton, 249–50.

133 **"A true believer may finally fall"** RCIII, religious writings, LC.

133 **"Man is somewhat more"** RCIII to James Manning, 4 Dec. 1789, vol. 9, DU.

133 **But the achievement of Robert Carter's decade** See Winthrop D. Jordan, *White Over Black: American Attitudes Toward the Negro, 1550–1812* (Chapel Hill, N.C., 1968), 296: "What the emphasis on man as a political being did do during the Revolutionary era was to channel the religious ideal of equality toward reconsideration of the Negro's external legal status. . . . Clergymen stopped preaching up the necessity of converting Negroes and began preaching the sinfulness of enslaving them."

134 **"We Seem to be detached"** RCIII to John Peck, 1 Sep. 1785, vol. 6, DU.

134 **"Upon examination"** RCIII to Asa Hunt, 26 Dec. 1787, vol. 8, DU. The same quote appears in Lewis Lunsford, 5 Oct. 1787, VBHS.

134 **"We believe that Christ's Church"** RCIII, daybook, 1 Sep. 1785, vol. 16, DU.

134 **"the Regulation of social Life"** RCIII, daybook, 20 Sep. 1778, vol. 15, DU.

134 **"I delight in real Believers"** RCIII to James Benn, 26 Jan. 1793, vol. 10, DU.

135 **"universality of redemption"** RCIII to John Rippon, 8 May 1790, vol. 9, DU. This argument for the link between radical egalitarian political and evangelical Protestant religious thought during the period can also be found in Jameson, 100.

Chapter V

136 **"A man has almost as good"** Anonymous to RCIII, 5 Aug. 1796, LC. See Morton, 267, Barden, 368–69. On the letter can be found: "nameless—but it is thought written by Reverend Thruston."

136 **"great big pulpit"** Eddie Carey, quoted in Lawrence Latane, "Gift of Freedom: Tale Handed Down," *Richmond Times-Dispatch,* 21 July 1991. See also MacLeod, 81.

137 **He was accompanied . . . one trusted agent.** RCIII to James Manning, 4 Dec. 1789, vol. 9, DU. RCIII to John Tasker Carter, 4 Dec. 1789, vol. 9, DU. RCIII to Richard Bland Lee, 2 Dec. 1789, vol. 9, DU. RCIII to Richard Bland Lee, 24 Dec. 1790, vol. 9, DU.

137–38 **He was surrounded . . . no longer governed.** Morton, 103. See Barden, 322–23.

138 **His oldest son, Robert Bladen** RCIII to John Tasker Carter, 4 Dec. 1789, vol. 9, DU.

138 **Even Dunmore** Morton, 201. However, see RCIII to Thomas Williams, 9 Dec. 1802, LC, and RCIII to Thomas Swann, 30 Dec. 1802, LC, where Carter speaks of an unpaid debt approximating 1,000 pounds.

138 **Since the passage** Carter himself noted Virginia census figures in an LC daybook entry for 17 Sep. 1791: "All other Free Persons . . . Indians, Mullatoes + free Blacks . . . 12,866." Berlin, *Slaves Without Masters,* 46, 48.

138 **Virginians could also reflect** Ballagh, 24–25. Morton, 262.

138 **"Plan for Liberating"** Ferdinando Fairfax, "Plan for Liberating the Negroes Within the United States," *American Museum,* Dec. 1790, reprinted in Nash, 146–50.

138 **"I apprehend that an Act"** RCIII to John Waller, 22 July 1789, NYHS.

139 **"Whoever brings forward"** Thomas Pleasants, Jr. to James Madison, 10 July 1791, *The Papers of James Madison,* Hutchinson and Rachal, 14:91. Joseph J. Ellis, *Founding Brothers: The Revolutionary Generation* (New York, 2001), 81–119, provides an insightful study of this debate.

139 **"Queres"** These "Queres" can be found between the letter entries for 17 Dec. and 21 Dec. 1790, RCIII, vol. 9, DU.

139 **"constitution"** 29 Sep. 1788, *Yeocomico BC Covenant,* VBHS.

140 **"I like a little rebellion"** Thomas Jefferson to Abigail Adams, 11 Feb. 1787. *The Papers of Thomas Jefferson,* Boyd, 11:174.

140 **"terror"** Charles-Edmond Genet, quoted in O'Brien, 288. See O'Brien, 280–89, for an overview of the response to the Haitian Revolution in America. See also Berlin, *Slaves Without Masters,* 40.

140 **"Democratic societies"** O'Brien, 210–18.

140 **"Citizen Robert Carter"** RCIII to John James Maund, 28 Feb. 1795, LC. See also RCIII to J. T. Carter, 21 May 1794, LC; Benjamin Dawson to RCIII, 12 July 1794, LC. Unlike many of his peers who chose the same appellation, infatuated by developments in Paris, Carter began to call himself "Citizen" only in 1794 after news of Robespierre and the Reign of Terror had circulated across America, after the Haitian Revolution and the Whiskey Rebellion had transformed events in Europe into exemplars of revolution gone too far.

140 **"Friend to Man I Am"** See, for instance, RCIII to Francis Bailey, Feb. 1791, vol. 9, DU.

140 **Swedenborg was an aristocrat** See George F. Dole and Robert H. Kirven, *Scientist Explores Spirit: A Compact Biography of Emanuel Swedenborg with Key Concepts of Swedenborg's Theology* (New York, 1992), 4, 14, 15, 16, 18, 27.

141 **"shivering"** Emanuel Swedenborg, *Swedenborg's Journal of Dreams, 1743–1744,* intro. Wilson Van Dusen, 2nd ed. (Bryn Athyn, Pa., 1989), 36.

141 **"In the end it was given me"** Ibid., 58.

141 **From this new faith . . . when they lived.** Emanuel Swedenborg, *Heaven and Its Wonders from Things Heard and Seen,* trans. J. C. Ager (New York, 1964), 23, 258, 343, 354.

141 **"deranged balance"** Ralph Waldo Emerson, *Representative Men,* ed. Pamela Schirmeister (New York, 1995), 81.

141 **"heavens and hells"** Ibid., 91.

141 **"all country parsons"** Ibid., 97.

141 **"mystical and Hebraic"** Ibid., 82.

141 **"fine secret"** Ibid., 72.

141 **"The number 'twelve' "** Emanuel Swedenborg, *The Apocalypse Revealed, Wherein Are Disclosed the Arcana There Foretold Which Have Hitherto Remained Concealed,* trans. John Whitehead (New York, 1968), 1:305.

142 **"Saw that a boy"** Swedenborg, *Dreams,* 87.

142 **Not only did he believe** Emanuel Swedenborg, *A Compendium of the Theological Writings of Emanuel Swedenborg,* ed. Samuel W. Warren (New York, 1974), 732, 736.

142 **"The coming of the Lord"** Emanuel Swedenborg, *The True Christian Religion Containing the Universal Theology of the New Church* (New York, 1909), 761, 763.

142 **He wrote Francis Bailey** RCIII to Francis Bailey, 24 Jan. 1791, Vol. 9, DU.

142 **"attentive readers"** RCIII to Francis Bailey, 29 Nov. 1791, quoted in Blackmer, 394.

142 **"frequently announced"** RCIII to Dr. Samuel Jones and George Carter, 29 Oct. 1792, vol. 10, DU.

142 **"in an elegant manner"** Samuel and John Adams to RCIII, 22 Mar. 1792, quoted in Blackmer, 401.

142 **"by an Olive-tree"** RCIII, "Dreams," vol. 16, DU.

142 **"Ten or Tenths"** RCIII to Nicholas Carroll, 21 July 1798, LC.

143 **"We find that the Lord"** RCIII, "Dreams," vol. 16, DU.

143 **"The second Advent"** RCIII to Thomas Jones and George Carter, 29 Oct. 1792, vol. 10, DU.

143 **"critical period"** Herbert J. Storing, *What the Anti-Federalists Were For* (Chicago, 1981), 25–26.

143 **"In the year 1810"** RCIII, wastebook, 1794–95, LC. For an overview of millennialism during the American 1790s, see Bloch, 119–231.

144 "The Instances you mention" Thomas Jones to RCIII, 2 Sep. 1791, LC.

144–45 In his first paragraph . . . Carter himself had designated. See vol. 11, DU, for Carter's private copy of the Deed of Gift. All quotes cited here can be found in this copy. Capitalization, abbreviation, and word choice vary slightly in the copy on record at the Northumberland County Courthouse.

145 Only one loose journal entry See "July 1791," loose papers, DU.

145 "This day Mr William Spearman" RCIII, 5 Sep. 1791, daybook, LC.

145 "Negroe Jerry" RCIII to Charles Jones, 6 Sep. 1791, vol. 9, DU.

145 For three months . . . Baltimore. RCIII to Opie Lindsey, 10 Sep. 1791, vol. 9, DU. RCIII to George Prestman, undated but late 1791, vol. 9, DU. RCIII to William Dawson, 19 Sep. 1792, vol. 9, DU.

145 But he did not mention RCIII to Thomas Edwards, 26 Dec. 1791, vol. 9, DU. Carter did append a note across a page of his journal for December 1791 and January 1792, describing how much he paid to record the Deed of Gift.

146 "We are informed that" *Virginia Gazette,* 28 Sep. 1791.

146–47 Beginning on December 26, 1791 . . . he conceded. RCIII to Thomas Edwards, 26 Dec. 1791, 30 Jan. 1792, 31 Jan. 1792, vol. 9, DU; RCIII to John James Maund, 6 Jan. 1792, vol. 9, DU; Thomas Edwards to RCIII, Jan. 1792, LC, described above.

147 "bargain for themselves" RCIII, 1 Feb. 1792, LC.

147 "residency of Slaves" Ibid. RCIII to John James Maund, 10 Feb. 1792, vol. 9, DU.

147 "Prince also Agrees" RCIII, 13 Feb. 1792, daybook, LC. RCIII, "Proposals to Prince & others," 13 Feb. 1792, CFP, sect. 41.

147 Finally, on February 28, 1792 . . . freed men and women. *Westmoreland County Deeds and Wills* 18, 213–14, LV. *Westmoreland County Orders,* 1790–95, 151, LV.

148 "Abram" RCIII to John Peck, 6 Mar. 1792, vol. 9, DU.

148 "to those whom it may concern" George Newman, 26 Apr. 1792, vol. 9, DU.

148 "in writing" RCIII to John Peck, 6 Mar. 1792, vol. 9, DU.

148 "common Stock" RCIII to Christopher Collins, 13 Mar. 1792, vol. 9, DU. RCIII also wrote George Newman the same day with a similar letter.

148 "two Lads" RCIII to Littlebury Apperson, 30 Apr. 1792, vol. 9, DU. Carter here spelled it "Littleberry."

148 **In a variation of an old scheme** RCIII, "To every Person whom it may concern," 30 Apr. 1792, vol. 9, DU.

149 **the "second channel"** RCIII to George Newman, 30 Apr. 1792, vol. 9, DU.

149 "your negroes" Littlebury Apperson to RCIII, 4 May 1792, CFP, sect. 22.

149 **When May 29 arrived . . . ten more.** RCIII, 29 May 1792, daybook, LC. RCIII, daybook, 28 July 1792, LC. RCIII, 4 Aug. 1792, daybook, LC. *Westmoreland County Orders, 1790–95,* 160, LV. *Westmoreland County Deeds and Wills* 18, 213–14, 239, 244, LV.

149 **"Samson Robinson agrees"** RCIII, daybook, 31 May 1792, LC.

149 **"free Man"** John James Maund to RCIII, 10 Jan. 1792, loose papers, DU.

149 **"I am very much inclined"** RCIII to John Latham, 22 Dec. 1792, vol. 10, DU.

150 **"Jack" and "Dick"** RCIII to Robert Newman, 22 Dec. 1792, vol. 10, DU.

150 **"every Expence arising"** RCIII, Deed of Gift, 11:17, DU.

150 **By the early months of 1793** *Westmoreland County Deeds and Wills* 18, 291, 292, LV. RCIII to John James Maund, 29 Jan. 1793, vol. 10, DU. Barden, 357.

150 **"Bett"** RCIII to George Prestman, Jan. 1793, vol. 10, DU.

150 **Gloucester Billy** RCIII, daybook, 1790–92, LC, in Barden, 362.

150 **"prefers to mould Bricks"** RCIII to Spencer Ball, 23 Apr. 1796, LC.

151 **"I cannot consistantly furnish Means"** RCIII to Mary Lane, 19 Feb. 1793, vol. 10, DU.

151 **"It is not expected that the Diminution"** RCIII to Thomas Stowers, 3 May 1793, vol. 10, DU.

151 **"present wish is to accommodate"** RCIII to Christopher Collins, 7 Oct. 1791, vol. 9, DU.

151 **"dispossess" a "Mr. Holcomb"** RCIII to George Newman, 27 Aug. 1792, vol. 9, DU.

151 **"positive Grant"** Christopher Collins to RCIII, 21 Dec. 1792, CFP, sect. 22. RCIII to Christopher Collins, 21 Dec. 1792, vol. 10, DU: "What have you done?" Carter asked Collins. Collins was

disturbed with Carter's willingness to "venture this . . . to accommodate 8 People."

151 **"Negro Sarah"** RCIII to Benjamin Dawson, 22 July 1794, LC. RCIII to Benjamin Dawson, 22 Apr. 1793, vol. 10, DU. See Barden, 364–65.

151 **By 1797, entire plantations** Spencer Ball to RCIII, 26 May 1797, quoted in Barden, 365.

151–52 **"Slaves are thought"** RCIII to William Thornton, 24 Sep. 1792, vol. 9, DU.

152 **"S. Capitol Street"** RCIII to David Burnes, 22 Jan. 1793, vol. 10, DU. Carter spelled the name "Burns."

152 **"five contiguous lots"** RCIII to David Burnes, 11 Mar. 1793, LC.

152 **When Burnes told him** David Burnes to RCIII, 27 Mar. 1793, LC. RCIII to David Burnes, 9 Apr. 1793, LC.

152 **Five hundred pounds** In preparation for the October 1791 public sale of lands in the District of Columbia, 40-by-100-foot lots were created. See Bob Arnebeck, *Through a Fiery Trial: Building Washington 1790–1800* (New York, 1991), 67. In all likelihood, Burnes, who was deep in debt, was offering Carter the lowest price he could: the commissioners of the city project, in the winter of 1793, stipulated that they would allow private sales of lots provided that the prices were no less than fifty pounds per lot, and one hundred pounds per lot on an "open square" (Arnebeck, 150). And Carter was not remotely the only wealthy man who was lukewarm toward the idea of investing in the lots: sales were not rapid during this time. See Arnebeck, 70, 119, 134, 139.

152 **"It is a long time"** George Carter to RCIII, 8 May 1793, CFP, sect. 22.

152 **"Library"** RCIII to Benjamin Dawson, 22 Apr. 1793, vol. 10, DU. See also this note: "The following Statement is not made from real Documents now before us, but partly on supposition, R. Carter having left all his Books and papers at his former residence the 8th day of May 1793," RCIII, 1793, rent book, 1793–97, LC. See also RCIII to Spencer Ball, 24 Dec. 1800, LC.

152 **He traveled light** RCIII, 6 May 1793, vol. 10, DU. RCIII, 28 May 1793, vol. 10, DU. Benjamin Dawson to RCIII, 7 Aug. 1793, CFP, sect. 22.

153 "an inventory of the furniture" RCIII to Benjamin Dawson, 22 Apr. 1793, vol. 10, DU. RCIII to JT Carter, 26 Apr. 1793, vol. 10, DU.

153 "united states" Blackmer, 398. RCIII to Christian Kramer, 5 Mar. 1792, quoted in Blackmer, 399.

153 **The journey started pleasantly . . . nine days before.** Described by RCIII in 10, 12, and 15 May 1793, vol. 18, DU.

153 "I died" RCIII, 16 May 1793, vol. 18, DU. See also Zwelling, 627.

153 **On May 19, four days** RCIII, 19 May 1793, vol. 18, DU.

153 **Three days later, he purchased** RCIII, 11 May 1793, vol. 18, DU. Kwilecki, 85.

154 **He ordered a "Pent house"** RCIII, 11 July 1795, 19 June 1795, vol. 18, DU. "1795" may be read "1793."

154 **He built** RCIII, 11 July 1795, 12 July 1795, vol. 18, DU. "1795" may read "1793."

154 **He ordered ducks** Benjamin Dawson to RCIII, 7 Aug. 1793, CFP, sect. 22. RCIII, 12 June 1793, vol. 18, DU. 13 and 20 Aug. 1793, vol. 18, DU.

154 "enter'd . . . with a street Commissioner" RCIII to Benjamin Dawson, 2 July 1793, vol. 10, DU.

154 "spoke at both places" RCIII, 16 June 1793, vol. 18, DU.

154 "Mr Welfrahrt" RCIII, 26 May 1793, vol. 18, DU.

154 "Meeting held at R C's House" RCIII, 28 July 1793, vol. 18, DU. RCIII, 24 July 1793, vol. 18, DU.

154 "tarred and feathered" RCIII, 1, 2, and 3 May 1794, wastebook, LC. During this same period, Carter describes himself attending worship, and visiting family friends with his three daughters—so it seems unlikely that he was the victim.

155 "several impediments" RCIII to Hugh Quinlan, 18 Mar. 1798, LC.

155 **Six months later** Dozier, 1426.

155 "the vast majority" . . . "seem anxious to have them." See the opening note to this chapter.

156 "public Acts" RCIII to Mary Lane, 19 Feb. 1792, vol. 9, DU.

156 **"The names of master & slave"** See "A Circular letter of Valediction on leaving Virginia by John Leland" in RCIII, Apr. 1791, vol. 16, DU.

156 "Not exercised with comfort" Dozier, 1417.

157 **"His Zeal in the Cause"** Spencer Ball to RCIII, 26 May 1797, quoted in Barden, 374.

157 **But Dawson got the "library"** RCIII to Spencer Ball, 24 Dec. 1800, LC.

157 **"execute Leases of Lots"** Benjamin Dawson to RCIII, 17 Sep. 1793, CFP, sect. 22. RCIII to Benjamin Dawson, 27 Nov. 1793, vol. 18, DU.

157 **By the beginning of 1794 . . . almost apologetically.** Benjamin Dawson to RCIII, 4 Apr. 1794, LC. RCIII to Benjamin Dawson, 21 Apr. 1794, LC. RCIII, 15 Mar. 1794, wastebook, LC. Benjamin Dawson to RCIII, 6 May 1794, LC.

157 **"tenements"** RCIII to Benjamin Dawson, 22 July 1794, LC.

158 **"List of the Negroes"** Benjamin Dawson to RCIII, 15 Aug. 1794, LC.

158 **"this business requires expedition"** RCIII to Benjamin Dawson, 7 Sep. 1795, LC.

158 **Dawson, plainly excited** Benjamin Dawson to RCIII, 26 Oct. 1795, LC.

158 **"The Extravagance of this Man"** John James Maund to RCIII, 6 Oct. 1795, LC.

158 **"There is a manifest alteration"** Benjamin Dawson to RCIII, 25 Feb. 1796, CFP, sect. 22.

158 **"large white House"** John James Maund to RCIII, 4 Mar. 1794, LC.

158 **"I have no prospect"** RCIII to Spencer Ball, 23 Apr. 1796, LC.

159 **On August 16, 1796** RCIII to Benjamin Dawson, 16 Aug. 1796, LC. See also RCIII to Robert Mitchell, 18 Nov. 1803, LC. RCIII to Spencer Ball, 11 Aug. 1795, LC. In RCIII to Robert Mitchell, RCIII refers to a box, not two hats. Carter made an exception for J.T. and George, whom he allowed to pay him "absolute Fee" for their properties. The date August 16 is also questionable, although Carter cites it in his letter to Mitchell. There is also some indication that Carter held some land for himself. RCIII to John Wickham, 26 July 1796, LC. RCIII to John Chinn, 25 May 1799, LC, confirms the one-hundred-dollar rent payments.

159 **"true & lawful"** "Power of Attorney," RCIII to Benjamin Dawson, 24 Nov. 1796, LC. *Westmoreland County Orders, 1797–99,* 4, LV.

159 **"distribution of your Negroes"** Spencer Ball to RCIII, 26 May 1797, quoted in Barden 374.

159 **"countenance"** RCIII to JT Carter, 14 Apr. 1796, LC. Carter wrote that "General Lee countenances your present Courtship; and you ask my opinion + approbation." He then told J.T. that "you are of full age," and offered neither approval nor disapproval.

159 **"read and considered"** Benjamin Dawson to RCIII, 26 July 1797, CFP, sect. 22.

159 **"in Consideration of the sum of one dollar"** RCIII to Benjamin Dawson, 16 Aug. 1797, LC. In the Westmoreland County records, the Deed of Trust is dated 20 Nov. 1797. *Westmoreland County Deeds and Orders* 19, 356, LV.

160 **"struck" him "several times"** Benjamin Dawson to RCIII, 6 Nov. 1797, CFP, sect. 22.

160 **Deed of Trust** *Westmoreland County Deeds and Orders* 19, 356–57, LV.

160 **"marks"** Certificate of Freedom, Mary Coleman, 9 Jan. 1824; Certificate of Freedom, Ann Grigg, 13 Apr. 1826; Certificate of Freedom, Anne Gaskins, 3 June 1826, all in *Frederick County Free Negro and Slave Records,* LV.

160 **"eloped"** See, for instance, RCIII to Spencer Ball, 14 Aug. 1794, LC.

160 **"disposed"** See, for instance, chapter 2 or RCIII to Thomas Swann, 24 Oct. 1801, LC.

160 **"certified"** Berlin, *Slaves Without Masters,* 93–95, provides an overview of the "inadequacy of the freedom-paper system" (93).

161 **Sally Brutus; Anthony Harris** Barden, 400. *Frederick County Order Book* 30, 48–49:118, 271, 277, LV. *Frederick County Minutes, 1801–5,* 290–91, LV.

161 **Benjamin Taylor** Notley Maddox to RCIII, 9 Sep. 1800, MHS.

161 **Tom Richardson** RCIII to Samuel Jay, 9 Jan. 1803, LC.

161 **Boatswain Bailey** Emancipated as Boatswain Dailey: *Westmoreland County Deeds and Wills,* 21, 62–63, LV. Barden, 401. *Frederick County Minutes, 1809–13,* 258; *Frederick County Superior Court Order Book, 1809–14,* 170, LV.

161 **Patty and Richard Johnston** Mordecai Miller to RCIII, 7 Dec. 1803, CFP, sect. 22. Berlin, *Slaves Without Masters,* 99–101, discusses the crime of "manstealing" during this period.

161 **He wrote letters confirming** Notley Maddox to RCIII, 9 Sep. 1800, MHS. RCIII to Samuel Jay, 9 Jan. 1803, LC.

161 **He wrote several letters** RCIII to Randolph B. Latimer, 11 Aug. 1801, LC. RCIII to James Madison, 12 Aug. 1801, LC.

161 **"Doctor McHenry"** RCIII to "Doctor McHenry," 13 Sep. 1800, LC. RCIII, 18 Jan. 1803, LC.

161 **"Full Freedom"** RCIII to James Clarke, 18 Jan. 1803, LC.

161 **"More"** RCIII to Peregrine Nowland, "Tavern-Keeper," 29 July 1803, LC. RCIII to John Rindell, 20 Aug. 1803, LC.

161 **And when Patty Johnston** RCIII to Mordecai Miller, 7 Dec. 1803, LC.

162 **"Let it be remembered"** RCIII to Samuel Jay, 9 Jan. 1803, LC.

162 **"a matter," "a capital evil," "a great Disappointment"** RCIII to John Wickham, 16 Mar. 1800, LC. RCIII to Philip Dawe, 31 July 1800, LC. RCIII to JT Carter, 12 Mar. 1801, LC.

162 **"hold[ing] . . . all"** RCIII to JT Carter, 12 Mar. 1801, LC.

162 **On February 5, 1801** RCIII to George Carter, 5 Feb. 1801, LC.

162 **"If you do not come forward"** RCIII to Benjamin Dawson, 7 Sep. 1801, LC.

163 **"to ask, demand, sue for"** RCIII to Thomas Swann, 24 Oct. 1801, LC.

163 **"dispose of certain Negroes"** RCIII to Thomas Swann, 24 Oct. 1801, LC.

163 **"The Dead remain"** RCIII to Lady Harriet Essex, 22 July 1793, vol. 18, DU.

163 **"May our internal"** RCIII to Benjamin Dawson, 9 Aug. 1798, LC.

163 **"The government of a family"** RCIII to Elizabeth Whiting, 28 Oct. 1797, LC.

163 **"I do acknowledge"** RCIII to H. L. Maund, 3 Mar. 1803, LC.

163 **"real Christians"** RCIII to Robert Carter Maund, 26 Nov. 1803, LC.

163 **"violent Convulsive fits"** John James Maund to RCIII, 17 Mar. 1798, LC.

163 **Lunsford, while still the pastor** Semple, 473–74.

164 **Even Maund** According to Thomas Brown, an early governor of Florida, Maund haunted the upstairs rooms of the tavern for years after his death, clothed in his dressing robe. See Brown, "Tom Brown's Memoirs," 77–82, 115–16.

164 **"hearers encreasing"** RCIII, 18 Aug. 1793, vol. 18, DU.

164 **He made the usual** RCIII, 8 June 1793, vol. 18, DU.

164 **"R C—read sermon"** RCIII, 3 Oct. 1793, 3 Nov. 1793, vol. 18, DU.

164 **"Crouded Congregation"** RCIII, 17 Oct. 1793, 1 Dec. 1793, vol. 18, DU.

164 **"This Morning R C performed"** RCIII, 8 Dec. 1793, vol. 18, DU.

164 **"very slow here."** Henry Didier to RCIII, 10 Feb. 1793, quoted in Blackmer, 415. See Kwilecki, 172.

165 **But now he was the only one** RCIII, 9 Feb. 1794, LC. "No meeting there," Carter wrote.

165 **"animal magnetism"** RCIII to Col. Arthur Campbell, 9 Feb. 1798, in "Councillor Carter's Comments on the Baltimore Society of 1797," *New-Church Messenger* (1892), 139. Blackmer, 416. Bloch, 168.

165 **"a passenger"** RCIII to Robert Berkeley, 10 Feb. 1804, LC.

165 **"RC paid; RC received"** RCIII, 7 Nov. 1795, wastebook, LC.

165 **He fell back upon** RCIII, 19 Oct. 1794, LC. RCIII, 26 Apr. 1795, wastebook, LC.

165 **"nothing could please my taste"** SF Carter to RCIII, 22 Sep. 1794; LC. RCIII to Spencer Ball, 2 Oct. 1794, LC. RCIII to SF Carter, 29 Sep. 1794, LC.

165 **He brought his cook** RCIII, 3 Dec. 1793, vol. 18, DU: "Negro Sarah Johnson—to 6 Dollars & 67 Cents wages from 31st July 1793 to 1st Day December following 4 Months at 1 Dollar & 66 Cents per Month." Barden suggests that Sarah Johnson is probably the same Sarah whose quaking and weeping in religious fervor had moved Carter in 1778 (624–25).

165 **"old wall"** See RCIII, 17 Mar. 1794, LC.

166 **"Congress of Jews"** See RCIII, 1 May 1794, wastebook, LC.

166 **"Prophetic Conjectures"** RCIII, 29 May 1794, wastebook, 1794–95, LC. See Bloch, 172, for a discussion of this same pamphlet.

166 **"read Some Remarks"** RCIII, 15 June 1794, wastebook 1794–95, LC.

166 **"citizens"** RCIII, 1 May 1794, LC. Zwelling, 629: "He became increasingly millenarian and apocalyptic in outlook, examining his own private quests in light of large-scale contemporary trends and occurrences."

166 **"there appears to be great Darkness"** Benjamin Dawson to RCIII, 2 June 1794, LC.

166 **"Attend!"** RCIII to SF Carter, 12 May 1795, LC.

167 **"After becoming an independent Nation"** RCIII to John Chinn, 4 May 1798, LC.

167 **"manifest neglect"** RCIII to Philip Dawe, 3 July 1800, LC.

167 **"each of them"** RCIII to Benjamin Dawson, 29 Mar. 1797, MHS. See Sobel, 50. Sobel writes that Carter recommended apprenticeships for freed slaves, but that is not entirely accurate: he recommended apprenticeships *until* slaves were freed.

167 **When Robert Carter died** George Carter to Robert Berkeley, 30 Mar. 1804, LC. G.C. wrote that his father "died very suddenly on the night of the 10th."

167 **He kept his promise** Robert Carter III's will can be found in the Baltimore County Registry of Wills, 1802–5, Book 7, Folio 264, Maryland State Archives.

167 **In a letter written the same day** George Carter to Augustine Washington, 30 Mar. 1804, LC. The family friend described here is Robert Berkeley, who would shortly marry one of Robert Carter's daughters.

168 **In the county of Frederick alone . . . passed away.** *Frederick County Deed Book* 26, 236, 246, LV. *Frederick County Deed Book* 27, 134, 420, LV. *Frederick County Deed Book* 28, 17, 330, LV.

168 **"protect"** Robert Mitchell to George Carter, 25 Apr. 1804, quoted in Barden, 381.

168 **"take immediate possession"** George Carter to John Wickham, 22 July 1813, George Carter, letter book, VHS.

168–69 **On April 3, 1805 . . . held illegally in bondage.** *Frederick County Superior Court Order Book,* 1804–12, 142–48, LV. *Frederick County Order Book* 36, 262–63, LV. William W. Hening and William Mumford, *Reports of Cases Argued and Determined in the Supreme Court of Appeals of Virginia* (Philadelphia, 1808–11), 2:134, 138.

169 **"The Federal Court"** George Carter to John Wickham, 22 Nov. 1812, George Carter letterbook, VHS.

169 **"a Deed without a Name"** George Carter to John Wickham, 20 Feb. 1815, George Carter, letterbook, VHS.

169 **"Moin"** Benjamin Dawson to George Carter, 18 Jan. 1813, CFP, sect. 52.

169 **"being the daughter of woman"** Certificate of Freedom for Nancy Dickson, 12 Aug. 1826, *Frederick County Free Negro and Slave Records,* LV.

169 **"Agents"** Certificate of Freedom for Sarah Brutus, 22 Apr. 1835, *Frederick County Free Negro and Slave Records*, LV.

169 **"Henry Allen"** Certificate of Freedom for Henry Allen, 6 Oct. 1835, *Frederick County Free Negro and Slave Records*, LV.

169 **Even George Carter** See listings for "Prince Jones," "Sarah Jones," and "Peggy Newman" in Barden, 496–97, from *Loudon County Records of Free Negroes, 1778–1838*, 40, 59–60, LV.

169 **Finally, the Deed of Gift** Certificate of Freedom for Elias Reed, 5 Oct. 1852; Certificate of Freedom for Emily Banks, 5 Apr. 1852, both in *Frederick County Free Negro and Slave Records*, LV.

170 **"the past is nothing"** RCIII to SF Carter, 12 May 1795, LC.

170 **"Citizens of my Standing"** RCIII to Thomas Jones, 13 Oct. 1798, LC.

170–71 **"My prayers"** RCIII to John James Maund, 21 Aug. 1794, LC. This letter is not addressed, but it responds to a letter Maund sent Carter shortly before.

171 **"seemed greatly pleas'd"** John James Maund to RCIII, 27 Oct. 1794, LC. Maund wrote that he "read that part of your letter which regards Politics to the President."

171 **"powerful" motive** George Washington to Tobias Lear, 6 May 1794, *Writings of George Washington*, Fitzpatrick, 33:358. Wiencek, 273. Mary V. Thompson, "And Procure for Themselves a Few Amenities: The Private Life of George Washington's Slaves," *Virginia Cavalcade* 48.4 (Autumn 1999).

171 **To execute that will, he chose** Bushrod Washington arranged the meeting between George Washington and Maund. See Bushrod Washington to George Washington, 27 Apr. 1794, Washington Papers, uncollected letters: "I take the liberty of writing by Mr Maund who is going to Philadelphia, and of introducing him to you." Washington's problems with his relatives, and his correspondence with Lear, are described in Wiencek, 273, 297–98, 338–43. For Bushrod Washington's business relationship with Carter, see, for instance, "A list of Papers put into the hand of Mr. Bushrod Washington," between 16 and 17 Sep. 1789, vol. 9, DU.

171 **"perfectly Just, + Correct"** George Carter to Thomas Bowerbank, 20 Feb. 1813, George Carter, letterbook, VHS.

171 **"be sanctified"** Dozier, 1426.

171 **"a family *all* the members of which"** Thomas Jefferson to Elizabeth Carter, 1 Oct. 1790, in *Papers of Thomas Jefferson,* Boyd, 17:551.

172 **"If Five hundred Dollars"** RCIII to JT Carter, 19 May 1800. Carter's late papers are filled with records of substantial loans: see, for instance, 23 Feb. 1802, 3 May 1802, 28 July 1802, LC. An account book from the period is archived at MHS. See also Kwilecki, 111.

172 **Even with Dawson's graft** Morton, 78.

172 **"Cape Francois"** RCIII, 11 July 1793, vol. 18, DU.

172 **"engaged to lend"** RCIII to Elias Ellicott ("Comissioner"), 18 Mar. 1801, LC.

172 **"We have been informed"** Commissioners of the District of Columbia to RCIII, 3 June 1796. Washington Papers, uncollected letters.

172 **"elegant"** David Carroll to RCIII, 8 Apr. 1799, LC. Arnebeck, 531, shows how lots in this area were available later in 1799. Carter was not the only wealthy man actively courted by the proprietors and commissioners of the project. See Arnebeck, 158–60, 177–78.

172 **New Jerusalem** Robert Morris, quoted in Arnebeck, 183. Also see 68.

Conclusion

174 **"All the value which attaches"** Ralph Waldo Emerson, "The Poet," *Essays and Lectures,* ed. Joel Porte (New York, 1983), 462–63.

174 **Martha Washington** Wiencek, 358. John P. Riley, "Written with My Own Hand: George Washington's Last Will and Testament," *Virginia Cavalcade* 48 (Autumn 1999), 168–77.

174 **Edward Coles** William W. Freehling, *The Reintegration of American History: Slavery and the Civil War* (New York, 1994), 16. Schwarz, 75–78. Davis, 181–82.

176 **"during their Lives"** Carter, in fact, was adamant on this point. See RCIII to Benjamin Dawson, 22 July 1794, LC.

176 **There were freed slaves** Christopher Collins to RCIII, 21 Dec. 1792, CFP, sect. 22.

176 **From 1792 to 1804, however** *Frederick County Deed Book* 26, 236, 246. *Frederick County Deed Book* 27, 134, 420. *Frederick County Deed Book* 28, 17, 330. *Westmoreland County Deeds and Wills* 18, 213–14, 239, 244, 291. *Westmoreland County Deeds and Wills* 21, 62–63. "List

of Persons, To Whom Certificates of Emancipation Have Been Delivered, Manumitted by Robert Carter," 1795, *Westmoreland County Papers*. "List of 24 Negroes, To Whom Certificates of Emancipation Were Delivered by Robert Carter," January 1796, *Westmoreland County Papers*. "List of Negroes, To Whom Certificates of Emancipation Were Delivered by Robert Carter," January 1797, *Westmoreland County Papers*. All records can be found in LV. *Westmoreland County Papers* are still boxed and unprocessed: see boxes 82 and 83.

Barden writes that "280 manumissions have been confirmed through extant court records," and writes also that "all the evidence suggests that every man or woman who was alive at the time they were scheduled to be freed received a certificate of emancipation." He also writes that "the actual number of people freed from the Nomony Hall estate is likely to have been closer to five hundred or even six hundred" (386). Barden includes a stunning, thorough census of all Nomony slaves that describes whether or not, and how, their emancipations are recorded (505–693). He also includes lists of freed slaves that were listed without plantation affiliation but whose names roughly match ones on Carter's list (501–3).

176 **No County records survive** Tom Richardson, for instance, who was jailed in 1803, and for whom Carter certified his freedom; Oliver Robinson, who was renting land in 1797. No record exists for 1798, as well. Barden, 611, 613.

176 **"according to their own Will + Pleasure"** See George Carter to John Wickham, 22 July 1813, George Carter, letter book, VHS. When Carter sued Dawson, he was particularly concerned that the minister was keeping, or not collecting, the payments for the hire of the remaining slaves, payments that Carter regarded as "valuable." Berlin, *Slaves Without Masters*, 32: "The very nature of the process makes it impossible to determine how many masters freed their slaves by merely setting them out on their own."

176 **"They intended to pass"** Anne Maund to George Carter, 1 July 1808, Tench Tilghman Papers, MHS, quoted in Barden, 407–8, and Morton, 269.

177 **Many more escaped to freedom** Barden, 620–21. This lineage was described for me in an April 14, 2002, telephone conversation with

Henry Robert Burke, an Ohio historian and descendant of Baptist Billy Burke. See americanodyssey.net/burkegen.html

177 **None of Robert Carter's freed slaves** Stanton, 11.

177 **Some made their way to the North** Burke.

177 **There are no censuses for hearts and minds . . . crypt of the church.** Rebecca Aleene Ebert, "A Window on the Valley: A Study of the Free Black Community of Winchester and Frederick County, Virginia, 1785–1860" (M.A. thesis, University of Maryland, 1986), 22, 27, 28, 29, 31, 32, 38.

177–78 **Anecdotal histories of the Northern Neck** Frank Delano, interview with the author, Warsaw, Va., June 2000. Inez Selden Johnson, "Black History," in *Westmoreland County Virginia, 1653–1983*, ed. Walter Biscoe Norris, Jr. (Montross, Va., 1983), 525.

178 **Where Robert Carter's Deed of Gift** Jordan, 374: "In retrospect, the pity of antislavery's failure was that in the decade after the Revolution, success against slavery itself seemed almost within reach. If the Negro had been freed in the late eighteenth century rather than in 1863, if only in Virginia, he would have suffered far less degradation, . . . he would have undergone a shorter period of association with a radically debased status. The protracted battle for abolition in the nineteenth century generated by reaction defenses of slavery which deliberately subverted his equality. . . . A general emancipation after the Revolution would have been more than an improvised weapon in a fratricidal war. It would have come as a glorious triumph, the capstone of the Revolution; guilt could easily have been foisted onto the British and the whole nation stirred with pride." See also Barden, 12, and 423, for a further irony: "On July 21, 1861, seventy years after the start of the Nomony Hall emancipation plan, two armies met in Prince William County, Virginia, on land that had once formed a portion of Robert Carter's Bull Run Tract. The First Battle of Bull Run marked the onset of horrendous conflict between the armies of the United States and the Confederate States of America."

178 **Nomini Hall is not open** This tour of the Nomini cemetery was provided by Dalton W. Mallory, 7 July 1998. Frank Delano writes that the location of Carter's remains "isn't known," though they are located within the family cemetery: see Delano, "A Man of Con-

science," *Fredericksburg Free Lance–Star,* 3 Mar. 2001. A full description of the renovations to Nomini Hall can be found in Jan
Ohrmundt, "New Life for Nomini Hall: Old House Glows
Again," *Westmoreland News,* 3 Apr. 2002. The family history cited
here provided in Morton, 206, and in conversation with the current Nomini owner, Thomas Lee Arnest, 7 July 1998. Directions
provided by Frank Delano, e-mail communication with the author, 26 Feb. 2001. Nomini Hall is a residence, of course, not a museum; therefore, details provided here represent a snapshot circa
2004. For instance, the sign, the wooden gate, and the flowers were
not on-site during my first visit, in 1998. Similarly, the first time I
visited, the roads were unnamed, but now the road that winds
alongside the fence is called "Nomini Hall Road," and the drive-
way that leads to the Nomini house has been named after Fithian.
Lastly, the family has erected a stone in the cemetery that lists the
deceased buried there: Robert Carter's name is engraved on this
stone, as of this writing, facing away from the likely position of his
grave.

179 **An archaeology professor** Kathryn Murray Turano, "Nomini Hall
Dig May Be 'Dadda' Gumby's House," *Westmoreland News,*
12 Nov. 1998. Turano, "Probing the Past at Nomini," *Westmoreland
News,* 9 Apr. 1998.

180 **In fact, it is plausible . . . "alarming mischiefs."** *The Statutes
At Large of Virginia, from October Session 1792, to December Session
1806, . . .* ed. Samuel Shepherd, reprint ed. (New York, 1970), 1:238,
239. Ballagh, 127.

180 **"newspapers of the time"** McColley, 119.

180 **"it was then circulated"** Warner Mifflin, "The Defense of Warner
Mifflin," in *The Life and Ancestry of Warner Mifflin,* comp. Hilda
Justice (Philadelphia, 1905), 85.

181 **As Conor Cruise O'Brien** Conor Cruise O'Brien, *The Long Affair: Thomas Jefferson and the French Revolution, 1785–1800*
(Chicago, 1996), 284. Davis, 72, 179–80.

181 **"absorb"** Philip D. Morgan, 273.

181 **"fixed more securely"** McColley, 2. Davis, 122.

181 **"Virginia's republicans"** Edmund S. Morgan, 385.

182 **"zeal to abolish slavery"** John Taylor, *Construction Construed, and
Constitutions Vindicated,* reprint ed. (Union, N.J., 1998), 292. John

Chester Miller, *The Wolf by the Ears: Thomas Jefferson and Slavery*, rev. ed. (Charlottesville, Va., 1991), 261.

182 **"tendency to create disquiet"** *Annals of the 6th Congress, 2nd Session*, 231, quoted in McColley, 121.

182 **"a day dream"** Quoted in Merrill D. Peterson, *The Jefferson Image in the American Mind* (New York, 1960), 49.

182 **"sufficient"** Quoted in ibid., 49.

183 **"New Englanders had marched south"** Joanne Pope Melish, *Disowning Slavery: Gradual Emancipation and "Race" in New England, 1780–1860* (Ithaca, N.Y., 1998), xiii. George Washington Parke Custis, "Liberty and Slavery," *Religious Intelligencer* 10 (1825), 30, quoted in Melish, 215.

183 **At the very least, Robert Carter . . . to the masters.** Ballagh, 144. Davis, 89.

183 **Instead, emancipation would become an event** Davis, 72: "Many historians have understandably been captivated by the romantic notion of slaves liberating themselves by force of arms."

184 **Virginian leaders such as Madison and Jefferson had political reasons** Especially Jefferson and Madison. James H. Hutson, *Religion and the Founding of the American Republic* (Washington, 1998), 78, 83–84.

184 **"It is said that *Mr. Robert Carter*"** Rippon, 220.

184 **"unstable disposition"** Semple, 178.

184 **In turn, the histories of the Swedenborgian New Church** Marguerite Beck Block, *The New Church in the New World: A Study of Swedenborgianism in America*, intro. Robert H. Kirven, reprint ed. (New York, 1984), 82–86. Block writes: "However disillusioned Carter may have become with the New Church, he remained a staunch abolitionist to the end" (86).

185 **"enlightened Republicanism"** Wood, *Radicalism*, 27: "Despite the best efforts of enlightened elites to spread orthodox Christianity and reason, many ordinary people still believed in an occult world of spirits and demons and still relied on a wide variety of magical practices." See Wood, *American Revolution*, 132. The importance of the pamphlet literature lies at the crux of Bailyn, *The Ideological Origins of the American Revolution*.

185 **"basic principles"** Maier, 135.

185 **his love of newspapers** Jameson, 58.

185   **Robert Carter Nicholas** Selby, *Revolution*, 107.

185   **Benjamin Rush of Pennsylvania** Wood, *Radicalism*, 282, 366. Nash, 31–33.

186   **And if one looks at their journals** Lewis, 82–83. Michael Mullin, "British Caribbean and North American Slaves in an Era of War and Revolution, 1775–1807," in *The Southern Experience in the American Revolution*, eds. Jeffrey J. Crow and Larry Tise (Chapel Hill, N.C., 1978), 248: "The dynamic personalism that infuses the rich plantation records of such tobacco patriarchs as Landon and Robert "Councillor" Carter and George Washington is nowhere evident in comparable records for rice plantations." See also Morton, 160.

186   **Men such as Washington, Jefferson, Lee** Kwilecki, 73: "The dramatic rhetoric of self-sacrifice for the sake of liberty or republicanism, typical of Washington and Hancock, is absent from [Carter's] writings."

186   **"hired out"** Morton, 107.

187   **In part, this division is specific** See Jameson. Charles A. Beard, *An Economic Interpretation of the Constitution of the United States*, intro. Forrest McDonald, rev. ed. (New York, 1986). See Tolles, x–xi.

188   **In contrasting economic activity with political activity** A similar calculus can be found in Jameson, 27. This distinction has most vividly affected the reception of Beard's volume, which its own author described as "more severely criticized, and so little read" of any "book on the Constitution" (xliv). See McDonald in the same volume for a description of that reception (xviii–xxiii). As McDonald notes, the book was initially excoriated as an effort to tear down the reputations of the authors of the Constitution by arguing that they acted out of economic self-interest, a claim Beard denies (lii). Interestingly, Jameson's work endured no similar excoriation, in part because of a distinction that exists, more or less, to this day, in works such as those of Gordon Wood and Woody Holton, between arguing that the founders were influenced *socially* as opposed to *economically*. The former claim, somehow, carries less anti-canonical weight than the latter. See McDonald (xxxiii–xxxiv), and on the confusion between acting

out of economic self-interest and acting in recognition of economic factors (xiii).

188 **"Was it essentially profitable"** Mark M. Smith, *Debating Slavery: Economy and Society in the Antebellum American South* (New York, 1998), 12.

188 **Similarly, recent scholars** David Brion Davis, for instance, has described the need to "move beyond a simple dichotomy of 'economic motives' and 'humanitarian ideals'" (85). Those few scholarly efforts to analyze Carter's Deed of Gift rapidly converge on this problem. Berlin, in *Slaves Without Masters,* suavely writes that "Carter's interest in the future of his slaves went beyond humanitarian concern. . . . Carter minimized the economic dislocations of large-scale emancipation," and "foresaw no drop in either production or profits" (59). Allan Kulikoff writes that Carter tried to turn "his ex-slaves into a dependent peasantry" and that he "succeeded for a few years" (433). Allan Kulikoff, *The Development of Southern Cultures in the Chesapeake, 1680–1800* (Chapel Hill, N.C., 1986), 433. Berlin's argument, certainly, both dovetails with Carter's stated desire in the Deed of Gift to provide as little inconvenience as possible to his neighbors and is supported by the evidence of Carter's management of his finances at the time: Carter unquestionably believed that the Deed of Gift could be executed with comparatively little financial sacrifice. I believe that Carter saw the Deed of Gift—as an economic system—in the context of indentured-servant or apprentice contracts, wherein the servant was obliged to work for an appointed term and then received freedom. After emancipation, Carter's freed slaves would then become hired workers, with vestiges of contractual dependency. In this manner, Carter's Deed of Gift looked backward to the system of white indentured servitude that helped settle Virginia during the time of his grandfather and great-grandfather, and looked ahead to the sharecropping and crop-lien systems of the late nineteenth century. Carter's comparative lack of interest in providing "reparations"—education, deeds of land—but his extraordinary interest in refusing to relocate his freed slaves, and in providing rentals and whatever other forms of support that ensured the Deed of Gift was executed, are facts that argue that Carter saw free

blacks much the way he saw his white tenants and hires, whether
or not those tenants and hires did the same.

189 **the fortune he left to his children** Kwilecki, 88: Carter "more or
less maintained the fortune he inherited, without substantial gains
or losses."

189 **"All significant moral change"** Davis, 17.

189 **"if manumission rates"** Philip D. Morgan, 270.

189 **not one single emancipated slave** Barden, 354.

190 **"requires expedition"** RCIII to Benjamin Dawson, 7 Sep. 1795,
LC.

191 **"We should not expect his disengagement"** Andrew Burstein, *The
Inner Jefferson: Portrait of a Grieving Optimist* (Charlottesville, Va.,
1995), 290–91.

191 **"ought to be effected"** Richard Brookhiser, *Founding Father: Rediscovering George Washington* (New York, 1996), 180.

191 **"Had there been a practicable way"** Douglas Southall Freeman,
Washington, abr. Richard Harwell (New York, 1968), 741.

191 **"the most humane yet practical"** Richard Norton Smith, *Patriarch: George Washington and the New American Nation* (New York,
1993), 346.

191 **"no workable answer"** Joseph J. Ellis, *American Sphinx: The Character of Thomas Jefferson* (New York, 1997), 173.

192 **"the Virginia statesman"** McColley, 116.

192 **"had not the spirit"** Quoted in Burstein, 279. See, for instance,
James Madison to Robert Pleasants, 30 Oct. 1791, in *The Papers of
James Madison,* Hutchinson and Rachal, 14:91: Madison tells
Pleasants, an antislavery advocate, "Those from whom I derive my
public station are known by me to be greatly interested in that
species of property." He then speaks against antislavery petitions,
warning Pleasants, "It may be worth your own consideration
whether it might not produce successful attempts to withdraw the
privilege now allowed to individuals, of giving freedom to slaves."
Madison's statement perfectly blurs rationalization, threat, and
political acuity. One could argue that Madison simply understood
that the petitions and Deeds of Gift would not solve the problem
and would entrench slavery, but that he was at a loss to conceive
another solution.

A brief but passionate statement concerning Carter in this context can be found in Paul Finkelman, *Slavery and the Founders: Race and Liberty in the Age of Jefferson*, 2nd ed. (New York, 2001), 187: "Malone and Wilson ignore the examples of thousands of other southerners—led by George Washington, Robert 'Councillor' Carter, and John Laurens—who voluntarily freed their slaves during the nation's first few decades. Was Washington impractical? Was Carter unkind? Clearly not." Finkelman here refers to Dumas Malone and Douglas L. Wilson, who reiterated in the twentieth century arguments familiar to the eighteenth century. Finkelman's sentence (one of three in his volume referring to the Deed of Gift) is remarkable: to my knowledge, no other historian has created a pantheon, however small, that places Robert Carter alongside a more famous founder. See also 170–96, generally, for a discussion of "presentism" and the reputation of Jefferson.

192 **"slaveholders strenuously resisted"** Ira Berlin, *Many Thousands Gone*, 23.

192 **"the great Virginia liberals"** McColley, 186.

192 **"No other New World slavocracy"** Freehling, 183.

193 **"the paradox is American"** Edmund S. Morgan, 5.

193 **"My own experience"** Ellis, 7.

193 **"Thomas Jefferson," Julian Bond writes** Julian Bond, preface, Stanton, 7.

194 **But we ought to consider** See John Hope Franklin, "The Moral Legacy of the Founding Fathers," in *Race and History: Selected Essays, 1938–1988* (Baton Rouge, La., 1989), 161: "Racial segregation, discrimination, and degradation are no unanticipated accidents in this nation's history. They stem logically and directly from the legacy that the founding fathers bestowed upon contemporary America. The denial of equality in the year of independence led directly to the denial of inequality in the era of the bicentennial of independence. The so-called compromises in the Constitution of 1787 led directly to the arguments in our own time that we can compromise equality with impunity and somehow use the Constitution as an instrument to preserve privilege and to foster inequality. It has thus become easy to invoke the spirit of the founding fathers whenever we seek ideological support for the social, political, and economic inequities that have become part of the American way."

Index

ANDREW LEVY was born in Mount Holly, New Jersey, in 1962, and raised in suburban New Jersey. After graduating from Brown University in 1984 with degrees in mathematics and English, he worked as a telecommunications analyst on Wall Street for a brief period before receiving an M.A. in creative writing from Johns Hopkins in 1986 and a Ph.D. in literature from the University of Pennsylvania in 1991. Levy has published *The Culture and Commerce of the American Short Story*, widely reviewed in scholarly venues as "work of major importance," co-authored *Creating Fiction: A Writer's Companion*, and co-edited *Postmodern American Fiction*, an innovative anthology that has been adopted in over one hundred colleges and universities and was the focus of reviews and feature articles in *The New York Times*, *The Atlantic*, *Chronicle of Higher Education*, *Spin*, and elsewhere.

Levy has also written for the *Chicago Tribune* and *The Philadelphia Inquirer* and has won awards for his teaching. He has published widely on American literature and culture in scholarly venues, including articles on Benjamin Franklin, Frederick Douglass, Edith Wharton, and Edgar Allan Poe. He lives in Indianapolis with his wife, Siobhán, and son, Aedan.

ABOUT
THE TYPE

This book was set in Caslon, a typeface first designed in 1722 by William Caslon. Its widespread use by most English printers in the early eighteenth century soon supplanted the Dutch typefaces that had formerly prevailed. The roman is considered a "workhorse" typeface due to its pleasant, open appearance, while the italic is exceedingly decorative.